MAKING THINGS BETTER

TIMELESS LESSONS FROM STEVE JOBS ON FIXING WHAT'S BROKEN

BEN KLAIBER

FRAMEWISE PRESS

How to Read This Book

This book is meant to be used, not consumed.

You don't need to read it front to back. You don't need to agree with every chapter. And you don't need to finish it in one pass.

Start with the problem you're facing right now. Find the chapter that speaks to it. Read that. Apply it. Then come back when conditions change.

Some chapters will feel immediately relevant. Others won't. That's expected. Systems fail in patterns, and those patterns reveal themselves at different moments.

This is a working book. Return to it as your context shifts, as new constraints appear, and as old assumptions stop holding up.

Read what you need. Skip what you don't. Come back when it matters.

That's how it's designed to work.

✿ Formatted with Vellum

PREFACE

In May 1998, Steve Jobs told Business Week: "This is not a one-man show. What's reinvigorating this company is two things: One, there's a lot of really talented people in this company who listened to the world tell them they were losers for a couple of years, and some of them were on the verge of starting to believe it themselves. But they're not losers. What they didn't have was a good set of coaches, a good plan, a good senior management team. But they have that now."

Steve understood what most people miss: breakthrough doesn't come from heroic individuals. It comes from fixing the systems that produce results.

Making Things Better isn't another biography of Steve Jobs. It's a field guide for anyone trying to fix what's broken in their organization, their work, or their world.

For twenty years, I've helped organizations identify what's actually broken versus what people say is broken, cut through the noise of inherited assumptions, and build the clarity and coherence that enables real improvement. The patterns that made Steve Jobs and Apple exceptional aren't about charisma, genius, or reality distortion fields.

They're about learnable methods: forensic problem-solving, strategic arrangement, and relentless focus on serving people rather than satisfying checklists.

This book extracts those methods from Steve's documented history and translates them into frameworks you can apply regardless of your context, scale, or industry.

You'll learn to:

- **Recognize when "impossible" is actually just "we've never tried".**
- **Decode competitive attacks as strategic intelligence instead of noise.**
- **Distinguish between fixing weaknesses and abandoning strengths.**

- **Create coherence that produces breakthrough results from what you already have.**
- **Maintain conviction about what serves people when critics demand you compromise.**

Leaders facing real challenges, not academics studying theory. Whether you're running a Fortune 500 division or a five-person team, launching products or fixing processes, fighting for resources or attention to what's broken, you'll find patterns that apply.

This resonates with CEOs rebuilding companies, entrepreneurs launching something new, consultants cutting through organizational fog, educators transforming how students learn, and anyone who's thought "there has to be a better way" and then faced resistance from people defending how it's always been done.

What Makes This Different:

Steve Jobs was fired from Apple in 1985, spent eleven years in the wilderness, and returned in 1997 to find the company ninety days from bankruptcy. Within a decade, he'd transformed it into the most valuable company in the world. But the transformation didn't come from Steve being Steve. It came from fixing what was broken: the strategy, the products, the culture, the alignment between what Apple said and what Apple did.

These pages contain the consistently overlooked, misunderstood, or misrepresented patterns that made that transformation possible.

Not the mythology of the "reality distortion field" or the cult of genius, but the actual methods: how to see what's broken clearly, how to interrogate inherited assumptions until they confess they're not actually constraints, how to build systems that produce coherent results, how to maintain focus on serving people when everyone's telling you to serve conventions.

You won't find hagiography here. You'll find frameworks, diagnostics, and actionable guidance drawn from documented history and tested in consulting work across industries. You'll find the lessons that matter. The ones that travel across contexts and help you fix what's actually broken in your world.

Steve's story provides the case studies. Your work provides the application.

Now let's fix what's broken and make things better.

ACKNOWLEDGMENTS

Writing a book is never a solitary act, even when you're the one staring at the blank page. This book exists because people believed in it, and in me, when both needed believing in.

Shari & John, Ahlia & Jonathan, Jackie, Ronn, Rohit & Rachel, Emory, Kim, Ashley, Krystal, Alex, Courtney, Gabe, Tammy, Aaron, Jon, Maxx & Maxine, Aunt Becky, Teresa, and SoSo, in no particular order.

If this book helps you fix what's broken in your world, their fingerprints are all over that success.

CHAPTER 1

THE LESSONS THAT WOULDN'T LET GO

Years ago, I wrote a book about Steve Jobs. I'd spent years studying everything he'd built, said, and believed. I dissected product launches, combed through interviews, analyzed the way Apple thought about design. I was convinced I understood what made him different and what made Apple different.

I was wrong. Not completely, but enough that it matters.

I understood the *what*. I didn't yet understand the *so what*.

Here's what changed:

I spent the last two decades in the trenches with real companies including startups burning cash on tools that don't talk to each other, mid-market firms drowning in their own data, enterprises where good people quit because bad systems made their jobs impossible.

I've seen brilliant teams crippled by fractured CRMs. I've watched sales reps waste hours hunting for information that should take seconds.

I've sat in meetings where everyone knew the dashboard was lying, but nobody knew how to fix it.

In every single one of those situations, there was always one lesson or another that I had learned from Steve Jobs that wasn't just relevant, it was what lit the path to the solution.

Those lessons stood the test of time and they're worth sharing in the here and now. They can make our world better.

One core lesson was this: technology exists to serve people, not the other way around. It sounds obvious. Look around at today's software rot in most everything we use. Clearly, it is not as obvious as it sounds.

Most companies build their systems backwards. They buy software because it's popular, implement tools because a vendor sold them hard, create workflows because "that's how it's always been done." Then they force their people to adapt. They hire smart, capable employees and watch them slowly break under the weight of systems that weren't designed for how humans actually think and work.

That's how we got where we are today.

Steve Jobs never did that. Every product, every interface, every decision started with a simple question: How do people actually want to do this?

Not "How can we make them do this?" Not "What's technically possible?" Not "What does the competition do?"

How do people actually want to do this?

That question and the obsessive commitment to answering it honestly is why the iPhone changed everything. It's why Apple's products feel different. And it's why years into running MMWB, I can tell you with absolute certainty: this principle doesn't just work for consumer electronics. It works for every system in your business.

This book isn't about Steve Jobs. It's about what he taught me that still works.

The companies I work with don't need another visionary. They need someone who can look at their tangled mess of tools, disconnected data, and frustrated employees and say: "Here's what's broken. Here's why it's broken. Here's how we fix it."

That's what this book does.

I'm not going to tell you to "think different" or "stay hungry." I'm going to show you how to take the principles that made Apple revolutionary and apply them to your reality. The one with legacy systems, budget constraints, and people who just need things to work.

Because what I've learned about fixing systems is that the companies that win aren't the ones with the fanciest tools. They're the ones whose tools actually help people do their jobs. Let me show you how to make that happen.

CHAPTER 2
THE PATTERN THAT REPEATS

Before we talk about fixing your systems, we need to talk about why most companies break them in the first place.

I've spent twenty years walking into businesses that look nothing like Apple - manufacturing firms, healthcare startups, mid-market distributors, regional service companies. Different industries. Different scales. Different problems.

But the same pattern, over and over.

They started lean and focused. Then they grew. Success brought complexity. Complexity brought new tools, new processes, new layers. Nobody noticed when the systems stopped serving the people and started requiring them to adapt instead. By the time I arrive, good employees are burning out, critical information lives in someone's head, and the executive team knows something is fundamentally broken but can't quite name what.

This isn't a failure of intelligence or effort.

It's what happens when you lose sight of a simple truth: tools exist to make work easier, not harder.

Steve Jobs understood this in a way most leaders never do. Not because he was a genius, although he was, but because he experienced both sides of it. He built a company from nothing, lost control of it when complexity and politics overwhelmed clarity, spent years in exile learning what actually matters, and came back to prove that focus beats feature lists every single time.

His journey isn't just biography. It's a map of the exact challenges you're facing right now.

The Garage: When Everything Works. Because It Has To.

1976: Apple is incorporated

Steve Jobs and Steve Wozniak started in a garage with no money, no connections, and a radical belief: regular people would pay for computers that just worked, not kits they had to assemble themselves.

They had no choice but to be focused. No budget for features nobody needed. No time for ego. The Apple II succeeded because it did a few things extremely well - it was reliable, expandable, and approachable.

The lesson I see repeated: The best systems in any company are usually built by the people closest to the problem. They're scrappy, purpose-built, and they work because they have to work. No bloat. No politics. Just solutions.

Then success arrives, and everything changes.

The Bloat: When Success Breeds Complexity

1978-1985: Apple grows from startup to corporation

By age 25, Steve was worth over $100 million. Apple hired executives from established companies. They brought "professional management." They added layers, processes, committees. The company that moved fast now moved slow. The culture that said "does this serve the user?" started saying "does this please the board?"

Steve fought it. He lost.

1985: The board removes him from operational authority. He resigns.

This wasn't about competence. It was about what happens when a company forgets why it exists. Apple stopped asking "what do people actually need?" and started asking "what can we sell?"

The lesson I see repeated: Growth doesn't break companies. Losing focus does. Every business I work with has a "Steve Jobs moment" - the point where they realize the tools meant to help them scale are now the main thing slowing them down. The CRM that was supposed to organize leads now requires three people to maintain. The dashboard that promised insights shows data nobody trusts. The automation meant to save time created ten new workarounds.

You didn't fail. You just forgot to ask whether each new tool actually served your people.

The Exile: When You Learn What Actually Matters

1985-1996: Steve in the wilderness

For eleven years, Steve ran two struggling companies. NeXT built powerful computers almost nobody bought. Pixar nearly collapsed multiple times before Toy Story finally hit.

These weren't wasted years. They were essential.

At NeXT, Steve learned that brilliant technology means nothing if people can't use it. At Pixar, he learned that culture and craft matter more than speed. He learned to say no to everything that didn't serve the core mission. He learned that cutting features isn't weakness - it's courage.

The executives I respect most are the ones who've lived through failure. Not because suffering builds character, but because failure forces clarity. Most companies never get that education until it's too late.

The Return: When Focus Becomes Your Competitive Advantage.

1997: Steve returns to Apple as interim CEO

Apple was ninety days from bankruptcy. They had dozens of products. None of them mattered.

Steve's first move wasn't innovation. It was elimination.

He killed 70% of Apple's product line. He refocused the company on four things: a professional desktop, a consumer desktop, a professional laptop, a consumer laptop. That's it.

Wall Street panicked. Employees protested. Steve held firm.

1998: The iMac launches. Apple posts a profit.

Then came the iPod. The iPhone. The iPad. Each one proof that saying no to a thousand ideas lets you say yes to what truly serves people.

Every turnaround I've led starts the same way - with subtraction, not addition. Nine times out of ten, the answer is: too many tools, too many steps, too many systems that don't talk to each other.

Steve proved that fixing broken companies isn't about working harder. It's about removing the friction that makes work harder than it needs to be.

Steve's timeline isn't unique. It's universal.

You start focused. Success brings complexity. Complexity creates friction. Friction burns out your best people. And suddenly you're considering layoffs when what you really need is to fix your systems.

I know this because I've seen it in manufacturing, healthcare, professional services, retail, tech startups, and fifty-year-old family businesses both up close and as a bystander. The industries change. The pattern doesn't.

The companies that win aren't the ones with the most tools. They're the ones whose tools actually help people do their jobs.

That was true when Steve said it in 1997. It's still true now.

The rest of this book is about how to make it true for you.

Not by becoming Apple. By learning what Apple learned: that technology exists to serve people, not the other way around.

Let's start fixing what's broken.

CHAPTER 3

YOU ALREADY KNOW
HOW TO DO THIS

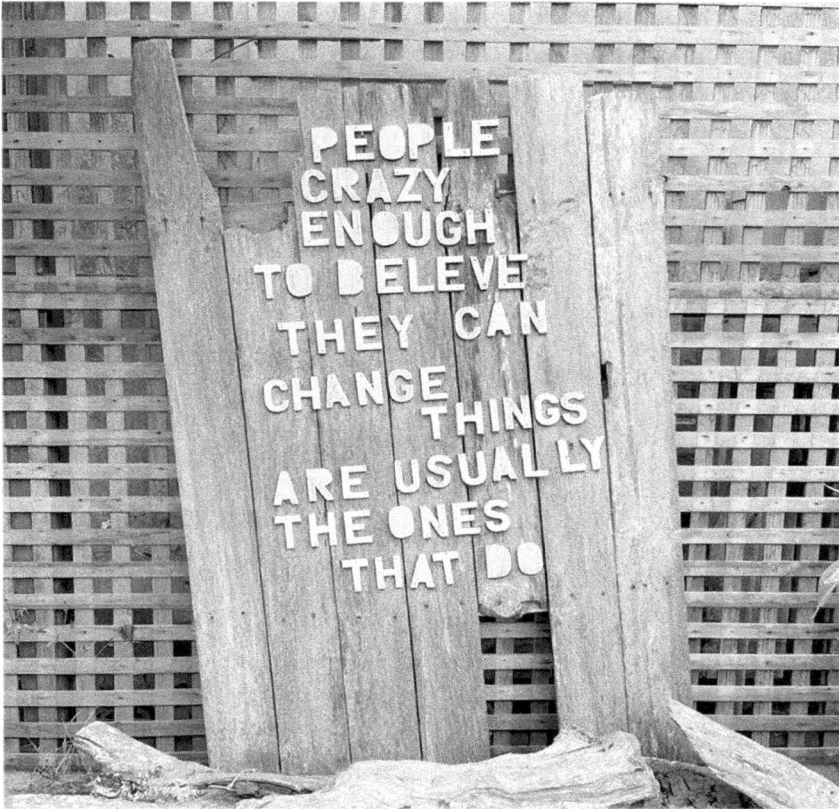

"Everything around you that you call life was made up by people that were no smarter than you." — Steve Jobs

Let that sink in.

Not because Steve Jobs was ordinary - he wasn't. But because the problems he solved are exactly the ones sitting on your desk right now.

How do we build something people actually want to use?

How do we cut through complexity when everyone's screaming for more features?

How do we know what matters and what's just noise?

How do we fix what's broken without starting over?

Steve didn't have special answers to these questions. He just refused to accept bad ones.

You don't need to be Steve Jobs to apply what he learned. You just need to be willing to ask better questions.

You Already Have Permission

When I started MMWB, I thought my job was to study companies like Apple and translate their genius into something mere mortals could use.

Turns out, a big aspect of my job is to help leaders see what they already know but have been talked out of believing: that when a system makes work harder instead of easier, the system is wrong - not the people using it.

You already know your CRM shouldn't require a training manual.

You already know your team shouldn't spend two hours a week reconciling conflicting data that should be cleaned up automatically.

You already know that if your best employee can't find critical information without reaching out to three people, something is fundamentally broken.

You know this.

But somewhere along the way, someone convinced you that complicated equals sophisticated. That if the tool is hard to use, you just need more training. That if good people are struggling, maybe they're not the right people.

Steve Jobs never accepted that logic. Neither should you.

What This Book Actually Does

Most books about Apple fall into one of three traps:

Trap One: The Inspiration Trap They reduce everything to slogans. "Think different!" "Stay hungry!" Great. Now what? How does that help you fix your broken dashboard on Tuesday morning?

Trap Two: The Biography Trap They chronicle every product launch, every boardroom drama, every brilliant quote - but never connect it to the specific problem you're trying to solve right now.

Trap Three: The Worship Trap They treat Steve like a mythical figure whose success can't be understood, only admired from a distance. Which is both inaccurate and useless.

This book avoids all three.

I'm not here to inspire you with Steve's story. I'm here to show you what he figured out about making systems work - and then show you how I've applied those same principles to companies that look nothing like Apple.

Companies where the workflow software creates more work than it saves. Organizations where every decision requires three meetings and two follow-up emails. Teams spending more time reporting on progress than actually making it.

Different industries. Different scales. Same core problems. Same core solutions.

How I Know This Works

My first book about Steve Jobs was based on fifteen years studying every-thing Apple built, said, and believed. I understood the history and facts. I understood the principles.

But I didn't yet understand how hard it is to actually apply them in the real world.

That required repeatedly walking into companies where:

- **Good people were burning out because bad systems made simple tasks impossible.**
- **Leaders knew something was broken but couldn't articulate what.**
- **Every "solution" added another tool that didn't integrate with the last five tools.**
- **The people closest to the problem had already figured out the workaround, but nobody asked them.**

In every single case, the breakthrough came from the same place Steve Jobs started: Stop asking what's technically possible. Start asking what people actually need.

Not "How do we implement this new platform?" but "Why are our people wasting three hours a week on this task?"

Not "What features does the competition have?" but "What's preventing our team from doing their best work?"

Not "How do we do more?" but "What can we stop doing?"

Those questions sound simple. They're not. They require you to ignore vendor pitches, resist the pressure to look sophisticated, and trust that the person doing the work probably knows more about fixing it than the consultant selling you software.

Steve trusted that instinct. It's why Apple's products feel different. And it's why the principles behind them still work - not just for consumer electron-ics, but for every system in your business.

What You'll Find Here

This isn't a Steve Jobs biography. You don't need another one of those. This is a field guide to applying lessons that didn't expire - written by someone who's spent two decades testing them in environments nothing like Apple.

You'll get:

- **Real examples from both worlds - What Apple did, and what I've seen work (or fail) when applied to companies with budgets, politics, and legacy systems**
- **Honest trade-offs - Steve made brilliant calls and terrible ones. I'll show you both, and more importantly, why it matters for your decisions.**
- **Actionable frameworks - Not "be visionary" but "here's how to identify which tool is actually causing the bottleneck."**
- **Plain language - No jargon without translation. If I can't explain it clearly, it's not worth your time.**
- **You won't get:**
- **Hagiography that pretends Steve never made mistakes.**
- **Abstract principles without concrete application.**
- **Advice that requires you to rebuild your entire company before it's useful.**

The World Is Not Finished.

Steve once brought his teenage son Reed to Apple for two days of executive meetings. "You're going to be in the room with the best people in the world making really tough decisions," he told him.

I can't put you in that boardroom. But I can show you what actually happened there - and more importantly, why those decisions worked when so many others failed.

By the end of this book, you'll see Apple not as an unreachable ideal, but as proof that the companies that win are the ones who never stop asking: "Are we making this easier for people, or harder?"

You'll recognize patterns in your own operation. The places where complexity crept in, where tools stopped serving and started demanding, where good people started looking for the exits because bad systems made their jobs unbearable.

And you'll have a framework for fixing it. Not someday. This quarter. Because here's what Steve Jobs proved, and what I've seen validated over and over:

The turnaround doesn't start with cutting people. It starts with cutting friction.

The rest of this book shows you how. Are you ready?

CHAPTER 4

CLEAR MIND. HEALTHY BODY. BEATING HEART

Think different.

Here's to the crazy ones. The misfits. The rebels. The troublemakers. The round pegs in the square holes.

The ones who see things differently. They're not fond of rules. And they have no respect for the status quo. You can quote them, disagree with them, glorify or vilify them.

About the only thing you can't do is ignore them. Because they change things. They invent. They imagine. They heal. They explore. They create. They inspire. They push the human race forward.

How else can you stare at an empty canvas and see a work of art? Or sit in silence and hear a song that's never been written? Or gaze at a red planet and see a laboratory on wheels?

While some see them as the crazy ones, we see genius. Because the people who are crazy enough to think they can change the world, are the ones who do.

Steve Jobs
1955 2011

Photo by Charlie Wollborg

Was Steve Jobs a one-of-a-kind genius, or was he something more useful: a guide?

Because if he was a genius, his story is inspiration. If he was a guide, his story is a map.

In my work helping companies fix what's broken, here's what I've learned:

Genius is overrated. Pattern recognition is everything.

Steve Jobs didn't invent brilliant solutions out of thin air. He identified what was broken, understood why it was broken, and applied three principles consistently until the system worked again. The same three principles work whether you're rescuing Apple from bankruptcy or fixing a mid-market company's fractured CRM.

Let me show you what I mean.

The Pattern That Saved Apple (And Can Save You)

In 1997, Apple was ninety days from bankruptcy. They had dozens of products, fragmented teams, and a culture that had forgotten what it stood for.

When Steve returned, he didn't start with innovation. He started with diagnosis.

He saw a company that had lost three essential things:

- **A clear mind - Nobody knew what mattered anymore.**
- **A healthy body - Operations were chaotic, wasteful, broken.**
- **A beating heart - People had stopped believing their work mattered.**

Fix those three things, and everything else becomes possible. Ignore them, and no amount of talent or funding will save you.

I see this exact pattern in every struggling company I work with. The specifics change. The structure doesn't.

The Mind: Clarity, Not Compromise

When Steve returned as CEO, his first move wasn't a new product. It was elimination.

He killed 70% of Apple's product line. He walked into meetings and asked one question over and over: "What is this for? Who is this for?"

If the answer wasn't crystal clear, it was cut.

This wasn't ruthlessness. It was coherence. Because when a company loses clarity, every decision becomes a negotiation. Every meeting becomes friction. Every project takes twice as long as it should because nobody's sure what they're actually trying to accomplish.

Here's the pattern in practice:

I've walked into organizations with multiple project management tools, redundant and conflicting customer databases, and overlapping systems that nobody can quite explain.

When I ask "Which data is accurate?", the honest answer is often: "We're not sure, but we're afraid to find out." That's not a technology problem. That's a clarity problem.

The breakthrough comes when we stop asking "What tools do we have?" and start asking "What does our team actually need to accomplish?"

Once you have that answer - truly have it, not the vendor pitch version - the path forward becomes clear.

The pattern repeats: eliminate the redundant systems, focus on what serves the actual work, train people properly on what remains. When you do this, productivity improves and stress drops because people can finally focus on their jobs instead of managing tools.

The lesson: Clarity isn't declared in a mission statement. It's designed into every workflow, every tool, every decision. If your people can't trust the system, it's not serving them - it's misdirecting them.

The Body: Operations as Compassion

Steve's second move was bringing in Tim Cook to rebuild Apple's supply chain.

This wasn't about cost cutting. It was about creating capacity. Cook rebuilt operations so efficiently that Apple could refresh entire product lines worldwide in under a week. No clearance sales. No devalued inventory sitting on shelves. Margins improved. Innovation accelerated.

The company could take creative risks because the foundation held.

Most people think operations is boring. Steve understood it as compassionate. Because when your systems work, your people can focus on the work that actually matters.

Here's the pattern in practice:

I've seen multiple companies where talented people spend more time fighting sales systems and having to be tech ninjas to complete a task than they can spend actually getting their work done.

The problem isn't the people. It's that the systems were often built for the convenience of developers and often on specs written by people with little to no understanding of the workflow involved, not for the humans who have to use them every day.

Sure, not everyone can afford dedicated UX/UI people. But my experience is the real problem is a disdain for the expertise of teams considered 'lower ranking front line people'.

What do I mean? Look, if the person who spends their days untangling subscription nightmares isn't in the room when you're building the new subscription system, don't act surprised when it ships without the basic functions that would have prevented months of chaos and lost revenue. You built it for the system you imagined, not the reality your customers actually live in.

The knowledge you needed was already in-house, but you need a facilitator who ensures the right voices get heard when building these tools.

The fix isn't buying more software. It's stepping back and asking: "Where are people wasting time? Where does the system force workarounds?" Then rebuilding workflows around how the work actually gets done.

When you remove that friction everything changes. Not because people work harder, but because the obstacles that were exhausting them disappear.

The lesson: Your systems should make work easier, not harder. If your best people are spending half their day fighting tools instead of doing their jobs, you don't have a people problem.

You have a systems problem.

The Heart: Fragile Ideas, Fierce Protection

Steve's third move was the hardest to quantify but maybe the most important: he restored people's belief that their work mattered.

When he returned to Apple, Jony Ive was walking out the door with his resignation letter. Steve stopped him. Not with money or titles. With attention.

He listened. He asked questions. He promised that design would no longer be overruled by committee consensus.

Years later, at Steve's memorial, Ive said this: "Steve understood better than almost anyone that powerful ideas begin as fragile, barely formed thoughts that could be so easily missed or compromised."

That's not sentiment. That's strategy.

Because when people believe their work matters - not just as output, but as meaningful contribution - they do things no spreadsheet can predict. They solve problems you didn't know existed. They catch mistakes before they become disasters.

They stay when things get hard.

Here's the pattern in practice:

I've watched organizations where the people closest to the work see problems daily but have stopped mentioning them because nothing changes. Meanwhile, leadership wonders why engagement keeps dropping and momentum stalls.

The knowledge is already there. The solutions often already exist in the minds of the people doing the work. But when your systems and culture don't create space for those insights to surface, or worse, when they actively discourage them, you lose access to your most valuable problem-solvers.

When you change that dynamic and create systems that actually encourage and act on frontline insights the transformation is immediate.

People don't just share one idea. They share dozens. Because they finally believe someone will listen.

The lesson: Your best solutions are probably already known by the people doing the work. But if your systems ignore them, punish them for speaking up, or reward consensus over competence, those solutions will walk out the door.

How This Shows Up in Your World

- **Apple's turnaround wasn't magic. It was method:**
- **Get clear on what actually matters (and cut everything else).**
- **Build systems that make the right work easier (not just possible).**
- **Protect the people who know how to make things better (and remove the obstacles in their way).**

This pattern applies across contexts that look nothing like Apple: distributors with legacy systems, startups drowning in compliance tools, services firms where founders bottleneck everything, manufacturers losing people to competitors who pay less but waste less time. Different industries. Different problems. Same three principles.

Mind, body, heart.

Clarity, operations, belief.

Cut the noise. Remove the friction. Trust your people.

Steve proved this works at the highest level. I've proven it works everywhere else.

The question isn't whether it can work for you. The question is: are you willing to be honest about what's broken?

Because here's the uncomfortable truth: most companies know exactly what's wrong. They just haven't given themselves permission to fix it.

You have that permission. Let's get started.

Metal Detectors, Not Magic

In September 1995, while Apple was floundering, Steve Jobs told Fortune magazine: "You know, I've got a plan that could rescue Apple. I can't say any more than that it's the perfect product and the perfect strategy for Apple. But nobody there will listen to me."

Notice what he did not say.

He did not say "I have a vision."

He did not say "I see the future."

He said "I have a plan."

A plan is not magic. It is logic, sequence, and trade-off. It is knowing where the landmines are and how to avoid them.

Yet many still insist Steve's success was supernatural. Some kind of fluke of genius, impossible to replicate. This belief does more than mislead. It disempowers.

It turns leaders into spectators, waiting for a messiah instead of sharpening their own tools.

The truth is simpler and far more useful: Steve did not predict the future. He designed it. And he left a trail of evidence so clear, it's like he handed us the map.

The Minefield Test

Imagine a field where people keep stepping on landmines. Explosions happen daily. Everyone agrees: "Stay out. It's too dangerous."

Then one person walks across, calmly and repeatedly, for years.

At first, people call him lucky. But after a decade, they should ask: How?

That's Apple's story in digital music. Before iTunes, the field was littered with failed players, broken stores, and angry consumers. Illegal downloads offered unlimited songs, no limits on burning or sharing - better than any record store on the planet.

Everyone else saw an impossible problem: how do you compete with free?

Steve saw something different. He saw the landmines everyone else kept hitting:

Variable pricing that punished loyal fans. Buy one hit song for 99 cents, another for $1.99. Albums priced higher than their individual tracks combined. Customers felt manipulated.

DRM that treated buyers like thieves. Buy a song, but you can't play it on this device. Or that one. Or burn it to CD more than twice. Paying customers got a worse experience than pirates.

Subscription models that felt like renting, not owning. Pay forever or lose everything. Stop the subscription and your entire library disappears.

Steve's solution wasn't magical. It was surgical:

Any song. Ninety-nine cents. You own it. No restrictions.

He knew what people actually wanted: not to steal, but to own music easily, affordably, and without shame. As he later told Time Magazine: "In essence, we would make a deal with people. If they would pay a fair price, we would give them a better product, and they would stop being pirates."

And he kept that deal sacred. When record labels pushed to raise prices, Steve refused: "If we go back and raise prices now, we will be violating that implicit deal. And they would never buy anything from iTunes again. Users would say, 'I knew it all along that the music companies were gonna screw me, and now they're screwing me.'"

That wasn't idealism. It was integrity as strategy.

When Everyone Else Hit the Mines

Meanwhile, Microsoft launched the Zune with everything the music industry demanded:

Songs you thought you owned, but could only play with an active subscription.

Wi-Fi sharing that took so long "the girl's gotten up and left."

Albums that withheld hit songs to force CD sales.

No burning. No real ownership. Just friction.

Steve's verdict was devastatingly human: "You're much better off taking one of your earbuds out and putting it in her ear. Then you're connected with about two feet of headphone cable."

The Zune wasn't killed by Apple. It was killed by ignoring how people actually live.

The Real Tool: Vigilance, Not Vision

Steve did not wave a wand. He used a metal detector.

He listened - "so intently," as Jony Ive said.

He questioned - "Is this good enough?"

He protected fragile ideas from committee logic.

He said no, not to be difficult, but to preserve focus.

And when engineers said "We can't do that. It's impossible," he did not retreat. He said: "No, no, we're doing this. Because I'm the CEO, and I think it can be done."

That moment - overriding objections with one decision - wasn't arrogance. It was accountability.

Because someone has to decide. Someone has to say: This is the path. Follow me.

What This Looks Like When You Apply It

I see this pattern constantly in my work. A leader will ask: "What's the best CRM?" or "Which collaboration tool should we use?"

But those aren't the real questions. The real questions are:

"What's broken in our current process that makes this feel impossible?", and "What's causing the friction?"

"What decisions are being made in shadow systems because the official tools don't serve the people doing the work?" Where are the spreadsheets, email chains, and hallway conversations happening because your "official system" is unusable?

"What standards have we abandoned that turned 'make it excellent' into 'ship something and clean up the mess later'?" When did you stop asking "is this good enough?" and start accepting "it's done"?

Steve didn't save Apple by following a playbook. He saved it by reclaiming a standard and letting that standard guide every trade-off.

You Don't Need Magic. You Need a Metal Detector.

Here's what that actually means in practice:

Listen to what people are actually doing, not what they say they're doing. Watch how your team works around the system. Those workarounds are your landmines.

Question whether "industry standard" is actually serving anyone. Just because everyone else does it that way doesn't mean it's right. The Zune followed industry demands. iTunes followed human needs.

Protect the solutions that work, even when they're unpopular.

When Steve refused to raise iTunes prices, the music industry was furious. He held the line because he knew raising prices would break the deal with customers. What deal are you tempted to break for short-term gains.

Say no to preserve yes. Every "maybe" dilutes your focus. Every "let's try both approaches" splits your energy. Steve killed 70% of Apple's products not because they were bad, but because they distracted from what mattered.

Take accountability for the decision. Someone has to decide. If you're the leader, that someone is you. Not the committee. Not consensus. You.

The Map Is Already There

Steve didn't have supernatural insight. He had discipline.

He looked at a field everyone else called "impossible" and asked: "Where are the landmines? How did everyone else step on them? How do I walk a different path?"

Then he walked that path with absolute commitment. No compromises. No hedging. No "let's try it both ways and see what happens."

That's not magic. That's method.

And it works whether you're launching a digital music store or fixing a broken workflow in Toledo, Ohio.

The question isn't whether you can see the future. The question is: Are you willing to use the metal detector?

Are you willing to look honestly at where people are struggling? To question what everyone else accepts? To hold a standard even when it's inconvenient?

Because the landmines are already visible. You just have to be willing to look.

The rest of this book shows you how to look - and more importantly, what to do once you see them.

THERE IS NO 'TEN POINT PLAN' for Success

The Romanian philosopher Emile M. Cioran once wrote: "We define only out of despair. We must have a formula to give a facade to the void."

That line cuts deep, especially in business.

We crave formulas because uncertainty is exhausting.

We want checklists because leadership is hard.

We beg for a ten-point plan because rebuilding trust, coherence, and momentum feels like trying to assemble a bicycle mid-ride.

But Steve Jobs never offered one. Not because he was secretive. Because he knew that you cannot evaluate your way into greatness.

Innovation is not a spreadsheet. It is not a process you install like software. It is the outcome of total commitment - where mind, body, and heart are firing in alignment.

And Apple's return was not the work of a lone genius. It was the reawakening of a system Steve treated as a living organism. Not a machine to be optimized, but a culture to be healed.

The Standard, Not the Metric

In 1996, shortly after returning, Steve was asked: "How long will it take to turn Apple around?"

He paused. Then said simply: "We aren't going to turn Apple around. We're just going to make the best computers in the world."

That statement was audacious - almost delusional - for a company weeks from bankruptcy. As writer Del Miller later observed, it hung over the Macintosh world "like some wistful hallucination that wouldn't go away, and over the months, it began to take on a new form, that of a new reality."

Notice what Steve did not say:

"We'll cut costs by twenty percent."

"We'll launch three new products in twelve months."

"We'll increase market share to fifteen percent."

He named a standard, not a metric. A purpose, not a pivot. And it worked. Not because it was clever marketing, but because it was true. It came from an artistic vision. A moral stance. A refusal to accept that "good enough" was the best a company could offer.

This was Steve putting a dent in the universe not with force, but with fidelity.

Why Formulas Fail (And Principles Don't)

Here's what I've learned over twenty years:

Principles are portable. Formulas are not.

A formula says: "Do steps 1 through 10 and you'll get result X."

A principle says: "If you honor this truth consistently, you'll know what to do when the situation changes."

Steve didn't copy Apple's past. He studied why things worked (or failed), then tailored those insights to the reality in front of him.

That's the difference between following a playbook and understanding the game.

What This Looks Like in Practice

When I walk into a company, leaders almost always ask some version of: "Just tell us what to do. Give us the steps."

I understand why. They're exhausted. They've tried three different initiatives. None of them stuck.

They want certainty.

But the companies that turn around aren't the ones who follow my checklist. They're the ones who internalize the principle behind it. Let me show you what I mean.

The formula says: "Implement a CRM to track customer interactions."

The principle says: "Make it easier for your people to serve customers well."

Those sound similar. They're not.

The formula leads to: buying software, mandating adoption, tracking compliance, wondering why engagement drops.

The principle leads to: watching how your team actually works, identifying where information gets lost, building (or configuring) something that removes friction instead of adding it.

Same goal. Completely different outcome.

The formula says: "Hold weekly status meetings to improve communication."

The principle says: "Create the conditions where people can do their best work."

The formula gives you a calendar invite. The principle makes you ask: "Is this meeting helping or performing?" "Are we solving problems or just reporting them?" "Would everyone here rather have this hour back?"

The formula says: "Streamline your product line to 20% fewer SKUs."

The principle says: "Say no to anything that dilutes focus on what truly matters."

The formula is math. The principle is judgment. One you can delegate to a spreadsheet. The other requires you to know what you stand for.

The Metal Detector Revisited

Remember the man walking safely across the minefield?

He's not lucky. He's equipped with a metal detector, respect for the signal, and the discipline to step only where it's safe.

He doesn't have a map that says "step here, then here, then here." The mines didn't come with a diagram.

He has a tool that reveals what's hidden. And the discipline to trust what it shows him.

That's what principles do. They don't tell you the exact path. They help you see the danger clearly enough to choose your own path.

What Steve Actually Did (That You Can Do Too)

Steve didn't save Apple with a formula. He did it with relentless commitment to a few core principles:

Make things people actually want to use. Not "make things technically impressive." Not "make things the market research says we should make." Make things that serve human needs so well that using them feels effortless.

Say no to protect yes. Every mediocre project you say yes to dilutes the excellent one you should be building. Every feature you add because someone asked for it makes the core experience worse for everyone.

Trust the people closest to the problem. The best solutions rarely come from the executive suite. They come from the designer who sees the interface fail, the support person who hears the same complaint fifty times, the developer who knows where the code is fragile.

Hold the standard when everyone wants you to compromise. When the music industry demanded variable pricing, Steve said no. When retailers wanted cheaper products with worse margins, Steve said no. When engineers said "we can't," Steve said "we must."

These aren't steps. They're commitments.

You can't put them in a project plan. You have to live them every day until they become your instinct.

The Questions That Matter.

When I work with companies, the turnaround never comes from following my ten-point plan (I don't have one).

It comes when the leader finally asks the right questions:

Not "What should we do?" but "What standard are we committed to?"

Not "How do we compete?" but "What do we stand for?"

Because once you know your standard - once you really know it, the way

Steve knew "make the best computers in the world" - the decisions become clearer.

Not easier. Clearer.

You'll still face hard choices. You'll still have to say no to things other people want. You'll still have moments where you're not sure it's working.

But you'll know whether you're walking toward your standard or away from it. And that clarity, that fidelity to what matters, is what transforms companies.

Not a checklist. A commitment.

The Hallucination That Became Reality

Steve's declaration that, "we're just going to make the best computers in the world", sounded delusional in 1996.

By 1998, it was starting to feel possible.

By 2001, it was undeniable.

By 2011, when Steve died, Apple wasn't just making the best computers. They'd redefined what a computer could be.

That didn't happen because Steve had a better formula than everyone else.

It happened because he had a clearer standard. And he never, ever compromised it.

Your Turn

You don't need my ten-point plan.

You need to know what you stand for. What your standard is. What you refuse to compromise on even when it would be easier, cheaper, or more popular to give in.

Once you have that - truly have it, not as a mission statement on the wall but as a filter for every decision - you'll know what to do.

Not because someone gave you the formula. Because the principle showed you the path.

The rest of this book is about how to find that principle, hold that standard, and apply it to the messy reality of your actual business. Not Apple's business. Yours. Let's keep going.

Arithmetic

Lemony Snicket once wrote: "I suppose I'll have to add the force of gravity to my list of enemies."

It's a line that lands with weary humor. The kind you feel when the world insists something is impossible, while you're already doing it.

Take Apple. For decades, critics have sounded the alarm: In big trouble. Losing its cool. Doomed.

The New Yorker's James Surowiecki once tallied four hundred eighty words of such forecasts, then - almost as an afterthought - admitted there might be less reason for panic than meets the eye.

His closing line? "Apple has always been the proverbial bumblebee: it shouldn't be able to fly, but it does."

Except, that isn't true. The bumblebee myth is a 1930s cocktail party error.

The story goes that a tipsy aerodynamics expert, asked about insect flight, scribbled a few equations and concluded bees lacked the lift to fly. A biologist, delighted to humble the "hard sciences," spread the tale far and wide. The next morning, sober, the expert realized his mistake.

He had modeled bees like airplanes - with fixed wings, steady airflow.

But bees don't fly like planes. They fly like helicopters, using rapidly rotating wings, dynamic vortices, unsteady lift.

Bees should fly. Their design is not flawed. It's different. So is Apple's.

What looks like defiance in their choices - simplicity over specs, focus over features, coherence over compromise - is not magical. It's arithmetic.

Let's do the math.

The Hidden Costs Nobody Measures

When a product requires ten workarounds to function, the cost is not just time. It's trust.

When a workflow forces people to become translators between systems, the output is not efficiency. It's exhaustion.

When leadership measures activity instead of impact, the result is not growth. It's noise.

When systems don't talk to each other, what adds up is lost revenue.

I've worked with teams across industries - logistics, education, manufacturing, software - and I've seen the same patterns emerge again and again. Not because people are careless, but because systems evolve faster than understanding. And the cost of that gap shows up in quiet, compounding losses.

When the Math Breaks Down

Here's a pattern I see constantly: A company invests heavily in a new platform. Adoption is low. Leadership blames the team.

But looking closer, the truth is simpler and more painful:

The new system demands seventeen clicks to find all the information needed to properly serve a customer on the phone. The old system took three.

The interface is missing basics - no tracking visibility, no efficient way to handle common requests, no way to process refunds or promotions cleanly. The holes are so big you could fly a jumbo jet through them.

The math is clear: Friction has come to outweigh function because nobody thought coherently about the actual process.

This isn't a technology problem. It's an understanding problem.

The Supplement Company: A Case Study in Broken Math

Now consider what happened at one supplement company I worked with. This is a story that reveals how easily good intentions can backfire when systems lack coherence.

First came the cart add-on. Marketing launched a "special deal" offer at checkout: after the initial purchase, customers were presented with an extra item at a discounted price. In theory, a smart upsell. In reality, a failure of basic coherence.

No one asked: What if the "deal" is the exact same item the customer just bought? No one bothered to look at the interface on a smartphone to see how impossible it was to close the box without accepting the deal for a second purchase - instantly, with no confirmation.

So customers who purchased a six-month supply were, moments later, sometimes offered a smart upsell, but also sometimes offered that same six-month supply at a lower price.

Confused, they assumed it was a correction - a better rate on their original order.

They accepted. Then they saw their $150 order become $300.

Outrage followed. Calls flooded in. Refunds were demanded. It was at that point a coin toss. Sometimes they got through to a person in time to catch the order while it was within customer support's reach, but more often than not, the next part of the call would involve delivering the bad news of this setup:

The order? Impossible to stop since it was in the warehouse system, which was no-man's land to the support team. Calls going overly long as customers demanded explanations and felt scammed by the refusal to stop the order.

The process? Wait for it to ship to the customer - 3-10 business days. Then get a label for return. Finally, send it back and wait another 3-10 business days for that to arrive at the warehouse.

Sounds fun as a customer, right?

Best part? The customer's refund? Held up until the return. There are a lot of customers out there who can't spare an extra $150+ for another four weeks.

What we did was convince the company to empower its customer support team to communicate directly with the warehouse. Now agents could - in real time - stop those duplicate orders before they shipped.

Result? Customer relief. No wasted product. No

pointless double shipping. Shorter call times.

A win across all sections. Except for one thing.

Blindly, leadership kept logging every canceled order as a lost sale. Metrics tanked. Morale dipped. Trust eroded.

No one asked the obvious question: Where does that customer go next?

Eventually, we did. When we tracked the data, we found that in most cases, the same customer placed the correct order within forty-eight hours.

Same person. Same intent. No true lost sale. Just a broken interface and metrics that punished honesty through misrepresentation.

But that was only half the story.

The Subscription Tailspin

There was another even deeper wound coming from the subscription model itself. The "set it and forget it" promise that so many industries rely on: software, supplements, wellness kits, even industrial supplies.

Convenience is the pitch. The reality? A quite costly yet quiet erosion of trust unless you have the safeguards in place.

Here's how it played out:

A customer signs up for a six-month supply, shipped twice a year, that can sometimes cost up to $350 or more.

They move. Change jobs. Forget to update their address. Life happens.

Despite emails, alerts, and renewal notices, they only notice when the charge hits their card - which many times is after the order is already in the warehouse, being packed for an address they left six months ago.

What happens next is painful for everyone:

1. The company issues a full refund.
2. $350 of product is lost.
3. Shipping and labor are wasted.
4. The customer feels misled.

5. The support team feels powerless.

Multiply this across tens of thousands of accounts and the losses compound daily. This is not noise. It is a silent hemorrhage.

Crucially, even after the company gave customer support the power to cancel orders pre-shipment in the process we just covered, no one tracked the value of what was being saved.

So when KPIs showed "rising cancellations," leadership assumed performance was declining, not realizing those cancellations were preventing far greater losses.

To clear things up, we built a simple tracking system that linked canceled orders to their destination status and clearly identified recoverable vs. unrecoverable orders being caught and stopped before heading into the abyss.

The insight was immediate: The customer support team was not costing money. They were saving it - by hundreds of dollars a day. Turns out that catching and saving even 8-10 orders of $130-300 each day can add up to some real money. Who knew?

Why These Failures Persist

So why do these problems happen even in well-intentioned organizations?

Because tools are too often built before the process is understood. They emerge not as solutions, but as assumptions dressed in code.

Because KPIs, when measured in isolation, become distorting lenses. A rising cancellation rate looks like failure, until you see those cancellations prevented six-figure losses.

Because the most valuable sensors in any system - frontline teams, support agents, warehouse staff - are kept in silos. They're denied visibility and punished for acting on what they know to be true.

This isn't negligence. It's myopia. The belief that automation equals intelligence. That more data equals better decisions. That efficiency means doing more of the same, only faster.

But real efficiency isn't speed. It's alignment.

The Arithmetic of Dignity

Steve Jobs did not beat gravity. He understood lift.

Bees don't defy physics. They work with different physics than airplanes do.

Apple doesn't ignore market realities. They measure different things than their competitors do.

When everyone else was measuring specs, Apple measured "Does this feel right?"

When everyone else was counting features, Apple counted "Does this actually work the way humans think?"

When everyone else was optimizing for cost, Apple optimized for coherence. The result looked like magic. It was arithmetic.

At MMWB, we call this the arithmetic of dignity.

It means designing systems that work with human fallibility instead of punishing it.

People forget. They move. They misread prompts. They assume good intent.

A great system doesn't punish that. It anticipates it and builds in grace and treats the user with dignity.

The Numbers That Actually Matter

Here's what I've learned: The companies that thrive aren't the ones with the most sophisticated tools. They're the ones whose tools actually support the work people are trying to do.

They measure:

- How much time their people spend on work vs. Workarounds.
- Whether their systems create trust or erode it.
- What problems their frontline teams see that executives don't.
- Where processes fail and why.

They don't ask "How do we automate this?" They ask "Should we be doing this at all?"

They don't measure "How many calls did we handle?" They measure "How many problems did we actually solve?"

They don't celebrate "We processed 10,000 transactions!" They ask "How many of those transactions went smoothly for the customer?"

Different arithmetic. Different results.

What This Means for You

You don't need to defy logic to thrive. You need to correct the formula.

Stop measuring activity. Start measuring impact.

Stop building tools first. Start understanding the work first.

Stop siloing your best problem-solvers. Start listening to what they already know.

The numbers always add up when you're counting the right things.

Steve proved it at Apple. I've seen it work in logistics, healthcare, manufacturing, and professional services.

The arithmetic of dignity isn't a luxury. It's how the math actually works when you stop ignoring half the equation.

Are you ready to do the real math?

CHAPTER 5
'MERE MARKETING' MYTHS

Photo by Raneko

Steve Jobs was not merely a marketer. He was a systems thinker. A translator of complexity into clarity. And a designer of coherence across technology, humanity, and time.

Calling him just a marketer is like calling a conductor a ticket seller. It confuses the surface with the source.

Steve excelled at vision, integration, elevation, and communication. Not spin. Not hype. The work of making meaning out of noise.

His co-founder Steve Wozniak put it plainly when asked: "Was Steve more a marketing guy or a technology guy?"

Woz didn't hedge. He said, "He was a good mix. He understood technology and knew which people to listen to. He wasn't quite an engineer, but he was close to it."

That closeness mattered. Because Steve didn't sell products. He sold understanding.

The Lost Interview: A Man Unfiltered

For years, most people knew Steve only through polished keynotes. The black turtleneck, the applause, the reveal.

Then came Steve Jobs: The Lost Interview. A full-length conversation filmed in the 1990s, buried in a reporter's garage for two decades.

No product launch. No script. Just Steve, speaking from his heart about computing, creativity, and what it means to build something that lasts.

What emerges is not a showman, but a philosopher of tools.

He speaks of how great products begin not with focus groups, but with taste. The ability to recognize quality, even when it has no market data yet.

He describes leadership not as command, but as curating the conditions where brilliance can emerge and protecting it from compromise.

This was Steve unmediated. And it changes everything.

Aspen 1983: A Vision Twenty Years Ahead

In 2013, another artifact surfaced: Steve's talk at the 1983 International Design Conference in Aspen.

The audience? Designers and thinkers, many born before computers existed. Think about that part.

Steve stood before them and said:

"We're going to put an incredibly great computer in a book that you can carry around with you, that you can learn how to use in twenty minutes."

A computer book. Wireless. Networked. Portable.

This was 1983. The Macintosh had not yet shipped. The internet was a military experiment. Mobile phones were bricks.

Yet Steve described email on the go, software bought over phone lines with credit cards, and the end of physical software stores as obvious next steps.

He was not predicting the future. He was designing the path to it. And he was asking their help.

When the iPad arrived in 2010 - thin, intuitive, wireless, instant - it was not a surprise. It was a promise kept.

Here's what people miss when they dismiss Steve as "just marketing":

Marketing is about convincing people they want what you made.

What Steve did was understand what people needed before they could articulate it.

That's not persuasion. That's insight.

Market research told Apple customers wanted more features, more options, more controls. Steve knew they wanted relief.

The App Store succeeded not because surveys demanded it, but because Steve remembered the frustration of floppy disks, shrink wrap, and version conflicts. He built the antidote: a curated store meant to ensure quality, not just quantity.

That's not marketing. It's empathy made operational.

Two truths rise from this:

First: Your past experiences - the ones you think are irrelevant, forgotten, or too niche - are not waste. They are latent fuel.

Steve's calligraphy class at Reed, his time at Atari, his trips to India - none seemed practical at the time. All shaped the Mac, the iPod, and the App Store.

The typography that made the Mac beautiful? Calligraphy class.

The simplicity that made the iPod work? Zen practice in India.

The understanding that technology should feel like play? Atari.

Second: Passion is not noise in the data. It is the signal.

When everyone else was counting features, Steve was asking: "Does this spark joy or create frustration?"

When everyone else was chasing market share, Steve was asking: "Will people love this?" When everyone else was optimizing cost, Steve was asking: "Is this worthy of our time?"

Different questions. Different outcomes.

Why This Matters for You

Here's what I've seen working with a variety of companies:

They invest heavily in external messaging while their internal systems quietly corrode trust.

They run customer surveys, yet ignore the daily friction their own employees endure - the duplicate data entry, the contradictory tools, the workarounds that become permanent.

They celebrate "innovation" while punishing the very behaviors that make it possible: curiosity, candor, time to reflect. The disconnect is staggering.

A company will spend six figures on a rebrand while their customer service team still can't see order history without switching between three systems.

They'll launch a "customer first" initiative while their own processes make it nearly impossible for frontline staff to actually help customers.

They'll talk about "empowering people" while their tools require seventeen clicks to complete basic tasks. That's not a marketing problem. That's a coherence problem.

What Steve Actually Taught Us

Steve's genius was not in selling. It was in seeing - deeply, persistently, humanly. He understood that:

You can't market your way out of a bad product. Fix the product first. Then tell people about it.

The best marketing is the product itself. When something works beautifully, people tell their friends. When it's frustrating, no ad campaign will save you.

Internal coherence creates external credibility. If your team doesn't believe in what you're building, customers won't either.

Passion beats research. Data tells you what happened. Passion tells you what's possible.

The Most Powerful Thing You Can Build

The most powerful thing any leader can do is what Steve did:

Look past the metrics. Ask what the system is actually rewarding and have the courage to align it with the mission.

Because coherence is not packaging. It is architecture and the most powerful thing you can build is not a product. It is trust.

Trust that the tool will work.

Trust that the system supports you.

Trust that the company means what it says.

That's not something you market. That's something you earn - one coherent decision at a time.

Where This Shows Up in Your World

When I work with companies, the breakthrough rarely comes from better messaging. It comes from finally aligning what they say with what they do. Teams that claim "quality is non-negotiable" but celebrate hitting deadlines regardless of what ships. Leaders who preach "collaboration" but structure every decision around a single approval bottleneck. A professional services company that brands itself as "innovative" while punishing employees who question outdated processes.

The gap between message and reality isn't a marketing failure. It's a systems failure. And you can't spin your way out of it.

Steve didn't win because he was a better marketer than Microsoft or Dell. He won because he built systems - products, processes, culture - that actually delivered on the promise.

When he said "it just works," it actually worked (mostly).

When he said "we care about the details," the details were immaculate.

When he said "this will change everything," it did.

That's not marketing. That's integrity. And integrity, it turns out, is the best marketing strategy there is.

The question isn't: How do we message this better?

The question is: How do we make this actually work the way we say it does? Answer that, and the marketing takes care of itself.

"One way to remember who you are is to remember who your heroes are."
— Steve Jobs

Steve did not emerge fully formed. He was assembled, piece by piece, by the people he admired.

Not celebrities. Not influencers. Builders. Outliers. Those who refused to accept the world as it was.

And their influence shows up everywhere: in the back of the Macintosh case (polished, though no one would see it), in the refusal to ship a product that "almost works," in the belief that technology should serve humanity, not the other way around.

The Artists: Risking Failure to Stay True

Bob Dylan was more than a soundtrack to Steve's youth. He was a compass.

As Steve told Fortune in November 1998: "One of my role models is Bob Dylan. As I grew up, I learned the lyrics to all his songs and watched him never stand still. If you look at artists, if they get really good, it always occurs to them at some point that they can do this one thing for the rest of their lives, and they can be really successful to the outside world, but not really be successful to themselves. That's the moment an artist really decides who he or she is. If they keep on risking failure, they're still artists. Dylan and Picasso were always risking failure."

Risking failure. Not avoiding it. Choosing it to stay honest.

Ansel Adams shaped Steve's visual language. For years, Adams's stark, luminous photographs were the only art in his home and later, in the NeXT offices. Adams once said: "There is nothing worse than a sharp image of a fuzzy concept." Steve lived that. Clarity of purpose mattered more than polish.

The Builders: Visionaries Who Were Cast Out

Edwin Land, founder of Polaroid, was a kindred spirit and a warning.

Like Steve, Land dropped out of college. Like Steve, he stood at the inter-section of art and science. And like Steve, he was fired from his own company. Not for repeated failure, but for one bold misstep: Polavision, an instant movie system that lost to videotape.

"All he did was blow a lousy few million, and they took his company away from him," Steve said.

Land's response? He sued Eastman Kodak for copying Polaroid's instant film and after fourteen years, won $925 million - then the largest patent settlement in history.

He wasn't angry about competition. He was angry about laziness. "I expected more of Eastman," he said.

Steve felt the same about Android. Not because it competed, but because it copied, without the courage to invent.

Years later, reflecting on Land's exile, Steve said: "Dr. Land, one of those brilliant troublemakers, was asked to leave his own company, which is one of the dumbest things I've ever heard of. So Land, at seventy-five, went off to spend the remainder of his life doing pure science, trying to crack the code of color vision. The man is a national treasure. I don't understand why people like that can't be held up as models: This is the most incredible thing to be. Not an astronaut, not a football player, but this!"

The Mentors: Who Saw Him When No One Else Did

At twelve, Steve called Bill Hewlett, the co-founder of Hewlett-Packard, at his home number - listed in the phone book.

He needed parts for a school project. Hewlett answered. Listened. Sent the parts. And offered Steve a summer job in the factory. That moment - of a child reaching out, and a titan responding with generosity - never left him.

Years later, when twelve-year-old Allen Paltrow emailed Steve with a photo of an Apple logo shaved into his hair, Steve arranged for him to attend the opening of the Fifth Avenue Apple Store. When he arrived, the entire staff gave the boy a standing ovation.

Steve wasn't repaying a debt. He was passing on a belief: You are allowed to reach. And someone might just answer.

Hewlett and Packard became his north star. As Steve told Access Magazine in 1984: "Hewlett-Packard has a revolutionary attitude toward people, a belief that people should be treated fairly, that the differentiation between labor and management should go away. And they built a company, and they lived that philosophy for thirty-five or forty years, and that's why they're heroes."

When Steve was forced out of Apple, he went to them first. Not to complain, but to apologize. "For screwing up so badly."

The Outliers: Who Hired Him When No One Would

Nolan Bushnell, the founder of Atari, hired Steve in 1974. Steve was nineteen. Unkempt. Often unbathed. Deep in his hippie phase.

As Bushnell later wrote in Finding The Next Steve Jobs: "Very few companies would hire Steve, even today. Why? Because he was an outlier. To most potential employers, he'd seem like a jerk in bad clothing."

But Bushnell saw past the surface. He saw curiosity. Disruption. The refusal to accept "how it's done."

He let Steve work nights to avoid offending colleagues. He held keg parties with live bands. He turned the lobby into a jungle arcade. He asked interviewees: "What is a mole?" and "Why do tracks run counter-clockwise?" - questions Steve later borrowed.

Bushnell's culture wasn't chaos. It was intentional design of a system that rewarded creativity, not compliance.

Apple, Steve said, was an Ellis Island company. One built by "extremely bright individual contributors who were troublemakers at other companies."

Sound familiar?

The Architect of Home: Eichler and the Back of the Cabinet

Steve grew up in a Joseph Eichler home - affordable, modern, with radiant heated floors and floor-to-ceiling glass.

"Eichler did a great thing," Steve told Walter Isaacson. "His houses were smart and cheap and good. They brought clean design and simple taste to lower-income people... I love it when you can bring really great design and simple capability to something that doesn't cost much. It was the original vision for Apple."

But the deepest lesson came from his father, Paul.

While building a fence, Steve asked why they used fine wood on the back since no one would see it. Paul replied: "Because you'll know it's there."

That wasn't about perfectionism. It was about integrity.

Later, when the housing market crashed, Paul returned to being a mechanic. Young Steve, asked in fourth grade what he didn't understand about the universe, answered: "I don't understand why my dad is so broke."

Yet he was proud - because his father refused to "suck up" or become "slick" to sell.

His college fund? Built from $50 junkers, fixed in the garage, sold for $250 "and not telling the IRS."

Paul may not have been Steve's biological father. But he gave him something rarer: a standard.

The Heretics: When Sales Runs the Show

Steve had heroes. And he had heretics.

The heretics were not competitors. They were those who confused motion with progress. People who hid behind market research while abandoning vision.

"Product people are the core of a successful company," he said. "Handing the reins to sales guys was the biggest sign of a company being dead inside."

IBM's CEO? "A smart, eloquent, fantastic salesperson... who didn't know anything about the product."

Xerox? Run by "the sales guys."

Microsoft under Steve Ballmer? "When the sales guys run the company, the product guys don't matter so much and a lot of them just turn off."

In Steve's eyes, humanity was the differentiator. He saw engineers and artists as kindred spirits. Both driven by self-expression, both obsessed with how things ought to be.

As he told Isaacson: "In the seventies, computers became a way for people to express their creativity. Great artists like Leonardo Da Vinci and Michelangelo were also great at science. Michelangelo knew a lot about how to quarry stone, not just how to be a sculptor."

That was the thread tying it all together: The best work lives at the inter-section where craft meets care, where systems serve people, where the back of the cabinet is finished - not for show, but because you know it's there.

This isn't just biography. It's a blueprint for how you build your own standard.

Who are your heroes? Not the people you admire from a distance, but the ones who shaped how you think about work, quality, integrity?

Every leader I work with has them, though most rarely articulate it. The teacher who refused to accept mediocre work. The first boss who showed them what real standards look like. The competitor who pushed them to be better.

Those people aren't footnotes. They're your operating system.

And who are your heretics? The examples of what you refuse to become?

The company that chose profit over people and paid for it later. The leader who sacrificed long-term excellence for short-term wins. The organization that let process kill creativity.

Knowing your heretics is as important as knowing your heroes. Because they show you where the guardrails are - the lines you won't cross even when it would be easier or more profitable to do so.

The Back of the Cabinet

Here's what I see in companies that have lost their way: They've forgotten why the back of the cabinet matters.

They ship products that "mostly work." They implement systems that "get the job done" even though everyone knows they're clunky. They tolerate processes that waste people's time because "that's just how it is."

Not because they're lazy or incompetent. Because they've lost touch with their standard.

No one is asking: "Would our heroes accept this?"

No one is saying: "We'll know it's there, even if customers don't."

The result is drift. Slow erosion of what made them great in the first place.

The turnaround starts when someone remembers.

When a leader says: "This isn't who we are. This isn't the standard we hold."

When a team decides: "We're going to finish the back of the cabinet, even though no one will see it."

When an organization chooses integrity over convenience.

That's not nostalgia. That's navigation. Using your heroes as a compass to find your way back to what matters.

Here's the questions I ask leaders when they're stuck:

"If your hero walked into this room right now and saw what you're building, what would they say?"

Not "would they be impressed?" - but "would they recognize their influence in your work?"

Would Bill Hewlett see the same respect for people he showed you?

Would your mentor recognize the standards they taught you?

Would the person who took a chance on you when no one else would see that same courage to bet on outliers?

If the answer is no, you know what needs to change.

If the answer is yes, you know you're on the right path.

The Legacy You're Building

Steve didn't just learn from his heroes. He became one - for a generation of builders who came after him.

Not because he was perfect. He wasn't. But because he held a standard and never let go of it, even when it would have been easier to compromise.

You're doing the same thing, whether you realize it or not.

The people who work with you are watching. They're learning what matters by what you tolerate and what you reject. They're building their own standard based on yours.

Twenty years from now, someone will remember the choice you made today - to finish the back of the cabinet or to ship it half-done. To hold the line on quality or to let it slide "just this once."

That's not pressure. That's opportunity.

You get to be someone's hero. Someone's proof that integrity still matters. Someone's example of what's possible when you refuse to settle.

The question is: What standard are you passing on?

And when they remember who you are by remembering who your heroes were, what will they see?

Heroes & Heretics

"One way to remember who you are is to remember who your heroes are."
— Steve Jobs

STEVE DID NOT EMERGE FULLY FORMED. He was assembled, piece by piece, by the people he admired.

Not celebrities. Not influencers. Builders. Outliers. Those who refused to accept the world as it was.

And their influence shows up everywhere: in the back of the Macintosh case (polished, though no one would see it), in the refusal to ship a product that "almost works," in the belief that technology should serve humanity, not the other way around.

The Artists: Risking Failure to Stay True

Bob Dylan was more than a soundtrack to Steve's youth. He was a compass.

As Steve told Fortune in November 1998: "One of my role models is Bob Dylan. As I grew up, I learned the lyrics to all his songs and watched him never stand still. If you look at artists, if they get really good, it always occurs to them at some point that they can do this one thing for the rest of their lives, and they can be really successful to the outside world, but not really be successful to themselves. That's the moment an artist really decides who he or she is. If they keep on risking failure, they're still artists. Dylan and Picasso were always risking failure."

Risking failure. Not avoiding it. Choosing it to stay honest.

Ansel Adams shaped Steve's visual language. For years, Adams's stark, luminous photographs were the only art in his home and later, in the NeXT offices. Adams once said: "There is nothing worse than a sharp image of a fuzzy concept." Steve lived that. Clarity of purpose mattered more than polish.

The Builders: Visionaries Who Were Cast Out

Edwin Land, founder of Polaroid, was a kindred spirit and a warning.

Like Steve, Land dropped out of college. Like Steve, he stood at the intersection of art and science. And like Steve, he was fired from his own company. Not for repeated failure, but for one bold misstep: Polavision, an instant movie system that lost to videotape.

"All he did was blow a lousy few million, and they took his company away from him," Steve said.

Land's response? He sued Eastman Kodak for copying Polaroid's instant film and after fourteen years, won $925 million - then the largest patent settlement in history.

He wasn't angry about competition. He was angry about laziness. "I expected more of Eastman," he said.

Steve felt the same about Android. Not because it competed, but because it copied, without the courage to invent.

Years later, reflecting on Land's exile, Steve said: "Dr. Land, one of those brilliant troublemakers, was asked to leave his own company, which is one of the dumbest things I've ever heard of. So Land, at seventy-five, went off to spend the remainder of his life doing pure science, trying to crack the code of color vision. The man is a national treasure. I don't understand why people like that can't be held up as models: This is the most incredible thing to be. Not an astronaut, not a football player, but this!"

The Mentors: Who Saw Him When No One Else Did

At twelve, Steve called Bill Hewlett, the co-founder of Hewlett-Packard, at his home number - listed in the phone book.

He needed parts for a school project. Hewlett answered. Listened. Sent the parts. And offered Steve a summer job in the factory. That moment - of a child reaching out, and a titan responding with generosity - never left him.

Years later, when twelve-year-old Allen Paltrow emailed Steve with a photo of an Apple logo shaved into his hair, Steve arranged for him to attend the opening of the Fifth Avenue Apple Store. When he arrived, the entire staff gave the boy a standing ovation.

Steve wasn't repaying a debt. He was passing on a belief: You are allowed to reach. And someone might just answer.

Hewlett and Packard became his north star. As Steve told Access Magazine in 1984: "Hewlett-Packard has a revolutionary attitude toward people, a belief that people should be treated fairly, that the differentiation between labor and management should go away. And they built a company, and they lived that philosophy for thirty-five or forty years, and that's why they're heroes."

When Steve was forced out of Apple, he went to them first. Not to complain, but to apologize. "For screwing up so badly."

The Outliers: Who Hired Him When No One Would

Nolan Bushnell, the founder of Atari, hired Steve in 1974. Steve was nineteen. Unkempt. Often unbathed. Deep in his hippie phase.

As Bushnell later wrote in Finding The Next Steve Jobs: "Very few companies would hire Steve, even today. Why? Because he was an outlier. To most potential employers, he'd seem like a jerk in bad clothing."

But Bushnell saw past the surface. He saw curiosity. Disruption. The refusal to accept "how it's done."

He let Steve work nights to avoid offending colleagues. He held keg parties with live bands. He turned the lobby into a jungle arcade. He asked interviewees: "What is a mole?" and "Why do tracks run counter-clockwise?" - questions Steve later borrowed.

Bushnell's culture wasn't chaos. It was intentional design of a system that rewarded creativity, not compliance.

Apple, Steve said, was an Ellis Island company. One built by "extremely bright individual contributors who were troublemakers at other companies."

Sound familiar?

The Architect of Home: Eichler and the Back of the Cabinet

Steve grew up in a Joseph Eichler home - affordable, modern, with radiant heated floors and floor-to-ceiling glass.

"Eichler did a great thing," Steve told Walter Isaacson. "His houses were smart and cheap and good. They brought clean design and simple taste to lower-income people... I love it when you can bring really great design and simple capability to something that doesn't cost much. It was the original vision for Apple."

But the deepest lesson came from his father, Paul.

While building a fence, Steve asked why they used fine wood on the back since no one would see it. Paul replied: "Because you'll know it's there."

That wasn't about perfectionism. It was about integrity.

Later, when the housing market crashed, Paul returned to being a mechanic. Young Steve, asked in fourth grade what he didn't understand about the universe, answered: "I don't understand why my dad is so broke."

Yet he was proud - because his father refused to "suck up" or become "slick" to sell.

His college fund? Built from $50 junkers, fixed in the garage, sold for $250 "and not telling the IRS."

Paul may not have been Steve's biological father. But he gave him something rarer: a standard.

The Heretics: When Sales Runs the Show

Steve had heroes. And he had heretics.

The heretics were not competitors. They were those who confused motion with progress. People who hid behind market research while abandoning vision.

"Product people are the core of a successful company," he said. "Handing the reins to sales guys was the biggest sign of a company being dead inside."

IBM's CEO? "A smart, eloquent, fantastic salesperson... who didn't know anything about the product."

Xerox? Run by "the sales guys."

Microsoft under Steve Ballmer? "When the sales guys run the company, the product guys don't matter so much and a lot of them just turn off."

In Steve's eyes, humanity was the differentiator. He saw engineers and artists as kindred spirits. Both driven by self-expression, both obsessed with how things ought to be.

As he told Isaacson: "In the seventies, computers became a way for people to express their creativity. Great artists like Leonardo Da Vinci and Michelangelo were also great at science. Michelangelo knew a lot about how to quarry stone, not just how to be a sculptor."

That was the thread tying it all together: The best work lives at the intersection where craft meets care, where systems serve people, where the back of the cabinet is finished - not for show, but because you know it's there.

This isn't just biography. It's a blueprint for how you build your own standard.

Who are your heroes? Not the people you admire from a distance, but the ones who shaped how you think about work, quality, integrity?

Every leader I work with has them, though most rarely articulate it. The teacher who refused to accept mediocre work. The first boss who showed them what real standards look like. The competitor who pushed them to be better.

Those people aren't footnotes. They're your operating system.

And who are your heretics? The examples of what you refuse to become?

The company that chose profit over people and paid for it later. The leader who sacrificed long-term excellence for short-term wins. The organization that let process kill creativity.

Knowing your heretics is as important as knowing your heroes. Because they show you where the guardrails are - the lines you won't cross even when it would be easier or more profitable to do so.

The Back of the Cabinet

Here's what I see in companies that have lost their way: They've forgotten why the back of the cabinet matters.

They ship products that "mostly work." They implement systems that "get the job done" even though everyone knows they're clunky. They tolerate processes that waste people's time because "that's just how it is."

Not because they're lazy or incompetent. Because they've lost touch with their standard.

No one is asking: "Would our heroes accept this?"

No one is saying: "We'll know it's there, even if customers don't."

The result is drift. Slow erosion of what made them great in the first place.

The turnaround starts when someone remembers.

When a leader says: "This isn't who we are. This isn't the standard we hold."

When a team decides: "We're going to finish the back of the cabinet, even though no one will see it."

When an organization chooses integrity over convenience.

That's not nostalgia. That's navigation. Using your heroes as a compass to find your way back to what matters.

Here's the questions I ask leaders when they're stuck:

"If your hero walked into this room right now and saw what you're building, what would they say?"

Not "would they be impressed?" - but "would they recognize their influence in your work?"

Would Bill Hewlett see the same respect for people he showed you?

Would your mentor recognize the standards they taught you?

Would the person who took a chance on you when no one else would see that same courage to bet on outliers?

If the answer is no, you know what needs to change.

If the answer is yes, you know you're on the right path.

The Legacy You're Building

Steve didn't just learn from his heroes. He became one - for a generation of builders who came after him.

Not because he was perfect. He wasn't. But because he held a standard and never let go of it, even when it would have been easier to compromise.

You're doing the same thing, whether you realize it or not.

The people who work with you are watching. They're learning what matters by what you tolerate and what you reject. They're building their own standard based on yours.

Twenty years from now, someone will remember the choice you made today - to finish the back of the cabinet or to ship it half-done. To hold the line on quality or to let it slide "just this once."

That's not pressure. That's opportunity.

You get to be someone's hero. Someone's proof that integrity still matters. Someone's example of what's possible when you refuse to settle.

The question is: What standard are you passing on?

And when they remember who you are by remembering who your heroes were, what will they see?

Artistically Driven

"Why not go out on a limb? That's where the fruit is." — Mark Twain

Steve Jobs did not build products for markets. He built them for people. Especially the ones no market research could see.

His secret was not engineering alone. It was that he harnessed the mind of a businessman to the heart of a poet.

That duality let him see what others dismissed as impossible. Not because the tech wasn't ready, but because the human need was too quiet, too complex, too inconvenient for conventional logic.

The Device That Disappeared

Take the iPad.

Before its launch, the industry was unanimous: tablets were dead. Unwieldy. Underpowered. A proven failure.

The crowd's approved formula was fixed: shrink a laptop, add a touch-screen, call it mobile.

The priority? Word processing. Coding. Spreadsheets.

The interface? A keyboard. A mouse. A single pointing device translating clicks into commands.

Hours after the keynote, "iPad a disappointment" trended online.

Blogger Paul Thurrott called it "a high-priced unnecessary trinket." Months later, he wrote: "Anyone who believes this thing is a game changer is a tool."

They missed the point entirely.

Because the iPad was not a computer with a screen. It was a screen that became whatever the human needed.

A piano where fingers dance across keys that respond like ivory.

A pond where you simply tilt the device, and water sloshes; fish dart toward your touch.

A canvas that lets charcoal smudge under your fingertip and blend virtual paint in real time.

This is not feature creep. It is embodiment. The device disappears. The person remains.

And that requires more than engineering. It requires the soul of an artist.

The Proof Is in the Lives Changed

Virginia Campbell was ninety-nine. An avid reader for decades, glaucoma had reduced her world to a magnifying loupe - painstaking, exhausting, isolating.

She had never used a computer. Had no desire to learn its complicated ways. Then came the iPad.

A slide of her finger. A tap on a book. Text enlarged - bright, crisp, effortless on the eyes. Reading was joy again.

She began writing poetry. Her daughter Ginny said: "It's changed her life. The thing that's so neat is there's nothing between you and the screen."

Campbell composed this tribute:

To this technology ninny it's clear In my compromised hundredth year, That to read and to write Are again within sight Of this Apple iPad pioneer.

This was not convenience. It was restoration. And she was not alone.

Autism Speaks estimates that twenty-five percent of people with autism are nonverbal. For them, the world is not silent - it is trapped. The iPad changed that.

With apps built around imagery not language, nonverbal children found voice.

GPS identifies location. The screen shows matching icons: a fridge for hunger, a bed for tired, a book for story time.

A tap communicates need. A swipe joins classmates in the Pledge of Allegiance.

They are not "using a device." They are participating in the world. That is not a trinket. It is a lifeline.

The Real Question

So how deep did Steve's artistic priorities run? Bone deep.

The Mac was not built to compete with PCs. It was built so a poet could write without wrestling a command line.

The iPod was not about storage capacity. It was about "a thousand songs in your pocket" - a phrase that lands in the heart, not the spec sheet.

The iPhone was not a phone with email. It was the first device that knew when you tilted it, that responded to movement, pressure, intent.

Steve did not predict the future. He designed for the human condition in all its fragility, creativity, and longing.

What This Means for the Work You Do

Here's what I've learned from years of watching systems succeed or fail:

The most transformative tools are not those that do more. They are those that get out of the way.

They trust the user. They honor the body. They assume intelligence, not require training.

This principle applies whether you're building consumer electronics or business systems.

The question isn't, 'What features can we add?' It's, 'What's standing between the person and their work?'

When I walk into a company, I see this disconnect constantly:

Systems built for the spreadsheet, not the human.

Tools designed to track activity, not enable accomplishment.

Processes that assume compliance, not creativity.

The result? People adapt. They find workarounds. They build shadow systems. They spend half their energy fighting the tools meant to help them.

And leadership wonders why productivity is flat despite investing millions in "digital transformation."

The iPad Principle Applied to Business Systems

Let me show you what the iPad principle looks like when applied to business tools:

Bad system thinking: "We need a dashboard that shows all our KPIs in one place."

iPad thinking: "What decision is this person trying to make, and what's the simplest way to surface only the information they need for that decision?"

The first approach gives you seventeen charts, eighty-three data points, and analysis paralysis.

The second approach gives you clarity.

Bad system thinking: "We need a form that captures every possible data point about a customer."

iPad thinking: "What does the person serving this customer actually need to know right now?"

One approach gives you a seventeen-field form and ten minutes of friction. The other gives you three fields and a conversation.

Bad system thinking: "We need everyone to follow the same process in the CRM."

iPad thinking: "How do different roles actually work, and how can the system adapt to them instead of forcing them to adapt to it?"

One leads to rigid workflows and frustrated users. The other leads to tools that fade into the background while real work happens.

Where the Fruit Actually Is

The critics were wrong about the iPad because they measured the wrong things.

They counted processing power, ports, and multitasking windows. Steve counted joy, restoration, and participation.

They asked, "Can it run Excel?" Steve asked, "Can it help a ninety-nine-year-old read again?"

Different questions lead to different outcomes.

Businesses repeat the same mistake. We track features shipped, tickets closed, and adoption rates, when we should be measuring time saved, frustration removed, and problems actually solved.

The real question is not, "Does it do everything?"

It's "Does it get out of the way of the work?"

The Artist's Standard

Steve's artistic drive wasn't about aesthetics - though Apple products are beautiful.

It was about this: Does this serve the human or serve the system?

Every time he had to choose, he chose the human.

Even when it meant:

- Saying no to features everyone else was adding.
- Making products more expensive to manufacture.
- Losing short-term market share to maintain long-term integrity.
- Being called a disappointment by people who couldn't see what he saw.

That's not stubbornness. That's standard.

And it's the same standard that separates companies that transform from companies that just optimize.

Going Out on the Limb

The fruit is on the limb. Always has been.

The safe choice is the trunk - solid, proven, supported by decades of "this is how it's done."

The limb is where you ask: "What if we designed this for the human first and the system second?"

Most companies won't go there. It's uncomfortable. It requires you to challenge assumptions. It means you might be wrong.

But that's where Virginia Campbell gets to read again.

That's where nonverbal children get to participate.

That's where your employee stops fighting the system and starts doing the work they were hired to do.

The limb is where the transformation happens.

Not in the next feature release. Not in the next platform upgrade. But in the moment when you finally ask: "What if we got out of the way?"

Here's what I ask teams when they're drowning in complexity: "If you could start over, knowing everything you know now, what would you eliminate?"

Not add. Eliminate.

What forms would you delete? What steps would you skip? What data would you stop collecting? What approvals would you remove?

The answers are always immediate. Because everyone already knows what's in the way.

The hard part isn't identifying it. The hard part is having the courage to remove it.

That's the artistic drive Steve had. The willingness to subtract, to simplify, to trust that less - when it's the right less - becomes more.

ou have your own version of the iPad waiting to be built. Not a consumer product, but a system that could transform how your people work.

It's the process everyone tolerates but nobody loves.

It's the tool that requires seventeen clicks when it should take three.

It's the workflow that assumes compliance instead of trusting competence.

You know what it is. You've known for a while.

The question is this: Are you willing to step out on the limb?

To design for the human, even when the system resists?

To eliminate features instead of adding them?

To trust that the tool should disappear so the person can remain?

That's where the fruit is and where the poets wait. And that's where the work that actually matters begins.

Let Passion Inspire Your Products

"When I say artist, I mean the one who is building things." — Jackson Pollock

Steve Jobs did not enter the MP3 player market because it was big. He entered it because it was broken - and because he loved music too much to leave it that way.

In 2001, the market for portable digital music players was tiny. Clunky. Fragmented. Most held a dozen songs. None felt human.

To Steve, that wasn't a barrier. It was an invitation.

He trusted his gut - and his decades of listening - to build something the world didn't know it needed.

The result? "What's on your iPod?" became a social ritual.

As Steven Levy wrote in The Perfect Thing: "Simply handing over your iPod to a friend, your blind date, or the total stranger sitting next to you on the plane opens you up like a book."

It was not a device. It was a confession.

Presidential candidates. Celebrities. New hires. Travel companions. All found themselves revealing more than playlists. They revealed selves. Because music, as Steve knew, is identity made audible.

When biographer Walter Isaacson asked to see Steve's "ten thousand songs in his pocket," he found a sonic autobiography:

Six volumes of Dylan's Bootleg Series. Fifteen Dylan studio albums. The Beatles. The Rolling Stones. Joan Baez. Aretha Franklin. B.B. King. Buddy Holly. Then: Coldplay. Alicia Keys. Dido. Moby. And woven through it all: Bach. Yo-Yo Ma.

This was not a library. It was a life etched in waveform.

Steve could hear the difference between Glenn Gould's 1955 and 1981 recordings of the Goldberg Variations and explain it like a theologian describing grace: "The first is an exuberant, young, brilliant piece, played so fast it's a revelation. The later one is so much more spare and stark. You sense a very deep soul who's been through a lot in life. It's deeper and wiser."

When asked which he'd save in a fire, the Beatles or the Stones, he did not hesitate: "I would grab the Beatles. The hard one would be between the Stones and Dylan. Somebody else could have duplicated the Stones. No one could have been Dylan or the Beatles."

After his liver transplant, his first outing was to Sun Records - the birthplace of rock and roll. Later, when a friend gifted him an original 1950s Jerry Lee Lewis 45 record with "To Steve, from Jerry Lee" scrawled on the sleeve, Steve called it "the coolest thing ever."

This was not fandom. It was recognition. He saw in artists what he sought in engineers: the courage to be irreplaceable.

The Real Work: Bridging the Divide

To Steve, the gap between art and technology wasn't just a problem - it was THE problem.

As he told CNN Tech in 2011:

"One of the things I learned at Pixar is the technology industries and the content industries do not understand each other. In Silicon Valley, most people think the creative process is a bunch of guys in their early thirties sitting on a couch, drinking beer, and thinking of jokes. People in Hollywood think technology is something you just write a check for and buy. These are like ships passing in the night."

His answer was Apple's core belief. One he repeated, almost like a prayer:

"It's in Apple's DNA that technology alone is not enough. That it's technology married with liberal arts, married with the humanities, that yields us the result that makes our hearts sing."

This was not marketing. It was architecture.

He believed creativity was not a department. It was a responsibility shared by coders, designers, supply chain managers, and support staff alike.

As he told Playboy in 1985: "Your thoughts construct patterns like scaffolding in your mind. You are really etching chemical patterns. In most cases, people get stuck in those patterns, just like grooves in a record, and they never get out of them."

His mission? Help people break the groove.

Not by adding features. By removing friction. By honoring the user's time, attention, and dignity.

"What drove me?" Steve once reflected. "I think most creative people want to express appreciation for being able to take advantage of the work that's been done by others before us. I didn't invent the language or mathematics I use. I make little of my own food, none of my own clothes. Everything I do depends on other members of our species and the shoulders that we stand on. And a lot of us want to contribute something back... to add something to that flow. That's what has driven me."

That is the opposite of ego. It is stewardship.

What Passion Actually Looks Like in Practice

Here's what people miss about Steve's passion for music: It wasn't hobby. It was research.

He understood music as a universal human need - not entertainment, but expression, identity, connection. He knew what it felt like to build a perfect playlist, to discover a new artist, to share a song that captures exactly what you're feeling.

And he knew the existing MP3 players disrespected all of that.

Clunky interfaces that required a manual. Capacity so limited you had to choose which parts of your identity to bring with you.Sync processes so complicated they felt like punishment.

The market research said: "The market is too small. Don't bother."

His passion said: "This is broken. People deserve better." He was right. They were wrong.

In my years working with teams who build systems - not just software, but workflows, cultures, daily rhythms - I've seen how often passion is mistaken for noise.

Leaders are told: "Focus on the data. Cut the sentiment. Optimize for scale."

But Steve's legacy shows the truth: The most scalable systems are the ones built with deep care. The most resilient products are the ones that refuse to treat people as edge cases.

When I walk into companies, I look for two things:

First: What does leadership actually care about?

Not what they say in the mission statement. What keeps them up at night? What frustrates them about how things work? What would they fix if nothing else mattered?

That's where the passion is. And that's where the real opportunity lives.

Second: Where is that passion being ignored in the actual systems?

The CEO who talks about "empowering people' but whose approval process requires six signatures for a $500 purchase.

The founder who cares deeply about customer experience but whose support team can't access the information they need to actually help people.

The leader who values innovation but whose systems punish anyone who tries something new.

The gap between what you care about and what your systems actually support - that's where companies break down.

The Question Steve Asked (That You Should Too)

Apple was drowning when Steve returned. Red ink. Shrinking market share. A product line no one believed in.

He did not start with a SWOT analysis. He started with a question: "What do people long for, and what are we making harder?"

The answer was music. Expression. Dignity.

Your answer will be different. But the question works everywhere: What do your people long for in their work? And what are your systems making harder?

Maybe it's:

- **Sales teams who long to focus on relationships but spend half their day updating the CRM.**

- **Support staff who long to solve problems but are measured on call time instead of resolution.**
- **Managers who long to develop their teams but are drowning in administrative tasks.**
- **Employees who long to do excellent work but are stuck in processes designed for compliance, not quality.**

You don't need to love Dylan to apply Steve's lesson. You only need to care enough about your people to ask: What groove have they been stuck in? And what would it take - not to fix them, but to free them?

When Data Contradicts Passion

Here's where most leaders stumble: The data says one thing. Their gut says another.

Steve faced this constantly. Market research said tablets were dead. His gut said people wanted them, just not the way they'd been built before.

Analysts said the iPod's price point was too high. His gut said people would pay for something that actually worked beautifully.

Consultants said Apple needed more product lines. His gut said they needed fewer, better ones.

Every time, he trusted passion over data - not because data doesn't matter, but because data tells you what happened, not what's possible.

Passion tells you what could be.

That doesn't mean ignore the numbers. It means don't let the numbers kill what you know to be true about human needs.

The Stewardship Standard

Steve's reflection about standing on shoulders and contributing back - that's the key.

He didn't build the iPod to dominate a market. He built it to contribute something meaningful to the flow of human creativity and connection.

That changes how you make decisions:

Market domination thinking: "How do we capture the most users?"

Stewardship thinking: "How do we serve people so well they can't imagine going back?"

Market domination thinking: "What features do competitors have that we need?"

Stewardship thinking: "What can we remove so the essential experience shines through?"

Market domination thinking: "How do we lock people into our ecosystem?"

Stewardship thinking: "How do we make something so useful and respectful that people choose to stay?"

Different motivations. Different outcomes.

What Are You Building For?

Here's the uncomfortable question: Are you building systems because that's what you're supposed to do? Or because you genuinely care about making work better for the people using them?

Are you implementing tools because a vendor sold you on them? Or because you've experienced the pain your team is feeling and refuse to accept it?

Are you optimizing processes because efficiency looks good on a dashboard? Or because you believe your people's time and dignity matter? The answer shows in the results.

Systems built from obligation feel like obligation, while systems built from passion feel like possibility.

The Artist's Responsibility

"When I say artist, I mean the one who is building things.", Steve Said.

You're building things. Maybe not consumer electronics, but systems, processes, ways of working that shape how hundreds or thousands of people spend their days.

That makes you an artist, whether you think of yourself that way or not. And the artist's responsibility is the same one Steve felt:

To care enough about the work that you refuse to ship something that disrespects the people who'll use it.

To trust your passion even when the data says you're wrong.

To honor the shoulders you stand on by contributing something worthy back to the flow.

The best products and the best systems are not built for markets, but for people by artists. The ones who are building things. The ones who care too much to leave them broken. Are you one of them?

CHAPTER 6

THE STORM
BEFORE THE CALM

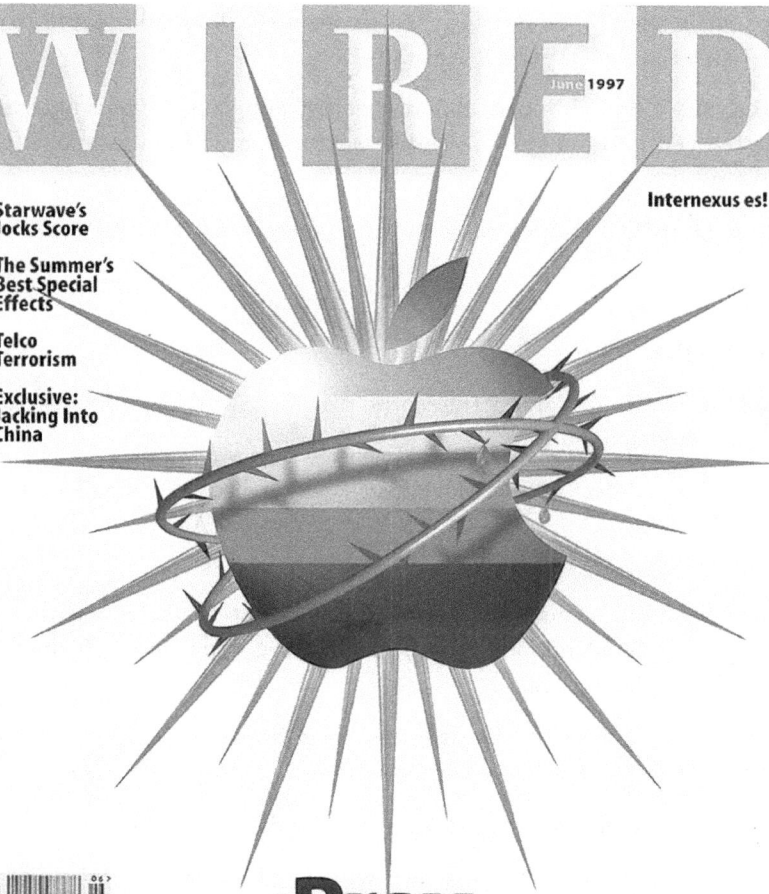

Wired magazine 'Pray Apple 1997' front cover

"Apple's situation was outright ugly. But through ugly situations come beautiful opportunities." — Rob Siltanen, on the Think Different campaign

To understand the magnitude of Apple's return, you must first feel the depth of its fall.

How close was Apple to collapse in 1996?

Steve put it plainly, years later: "We were ninety days from going bankrupt." That is not metaphor. It is arithmetic.

Market share had dropped to four percent and kept falling. Quarterly losses carved into the stock price like acid. Hope was not fading. It was drowning.

To grasp how this happened, we must go back to 1985 - the moment the storm began.

The Exile

CEO John Sculley declared: "There is no place for Steve Jobs at Apple, now, or at any time in the future."

Steve - the architect of the Macintosh - was exiled to a small building across the street. One office. No duties. No voice. And with him gone, Apple's compass broke.

Sculley believed a computer's only rightful place in the home was for work. So Apple abandoned music, gaming, art, education - all the very realms where people live.

On the surface, it looked like success. Stock prices rose. Sales doubled. Profits tripled.

But the growth had a source Sculley missed: artists and designers.

They were not drawn to PCs, which were rigid, text-based, inconsistent. They flocked to the Mac because it was visual, intuitive, and expressive. It was an electronic canvas. And Steve had designed it that way.

PCs used fixed typewriter fonts. The Mac offered typography as emotion.

PCs demanded obscure keyboard commands. The Mac used a mouse - pointing, clicking, understanding.

PC apps reinvented menus with every release. The Mac had consistency, which meant users could learn one application and use that knowledge to navigate almost any new application based on that pattern of operation.

But without Steve, Apple could not scale that vision. It kept selling the Apple IIe unchanged for ten years. Ten years of control by what many would have argued should have been ideal: software engineers controlling the product and marketing people just pushing it out to sales as if it were a can of cola.

In 1992, its best home computer was the six-year-old Apple IIGS, barely updated. The Macintosh saw only incremental upgrades with no break-throughs.

Worst of all, Sculley licensed Apple's interface patents to Microsoft.

That decision birthed Windows 95 - a poor imitation of the cosmetics of this new GUI thinking, but where all the key elements of consistency, flexibility, and empowerment for the user were completely lacking. It was nothing more than a PC wearing Mac's skin.

Sculley was not a leader. He was a steward watching the ship take on water. Not exactly the kind of thinking that rallies the troops, wouldn't you agree?

The Spiral

He resigned in 1993. The board cycled through CEOs like spare parts: Spindler. Then Amelio. Three leaders in a decade. No strategy. Only survival.

Spindler flooded the market with discounted Macs and lost sixty-nine million dollars in a single year. Over one billion dollars in unsold inventory sat in warehouses, soon to be written off.

The PowerBook 5300 shipped with batteries that burst into flame. A full recall followed. Reputation bled.

Desperate, Apple tried to sell itself to Phillips, Kodak, AT&T, IBM, Toshiba, Compaq, Sony. No one wanted it.

Sun Microsystems offered eight dollars a share - substantially below market value. Only board member Gil Amelio objected. The board, seeing no better option, made him CEO.

Amelio took the helm in February 1996. His metaphor? "Apple is a ship loaded with treasure, but there's a hole in the ship. My job is to get everyone to row in the same direction."

When a reporter asked, "What about the hole?", he had no answer.

His plan failed on all fronts:

Sears as a retail outlet? No traction.

Licensing the Mac OS and Newton? Confusion.

Building a next-generation OS? Collapse.

The in-house OS, Copland, imploded. The backup plan with IBM failed. Apple was forced to shop for an operating system - a public humiliation.

People fled. Fifteen hundred laid off. Two thousand resigned. Workforce shrank from seventeen thousand six hundred to thirteen thousand four hundred in one year.

In 1996, CalPERS - the California Public Employees Retirement System - named Apple the worst-run company in America.

That year, Apple lost eight hundred sixteen million dollars. Under Amelio, the total reached one point six billion.

The company was not just broken. It was erased.

Wired magazine's suggested soundtrack? Ain't Too Proud To Beg.

Meanwhile, in the Wilderness

Steve's NeXT was barely breathing.

Bound by Apple's post-departure contract, NeXT could not sell to homes or schools. Their only legal market was corporations and universities.

Its machines were brilliant. Ahead of their time. But the market was not ready - nor allowed to see them.

By 1993, four of five co-founders had left. So had the head of sales. The marketing chief. NeXT abandoned hardware. Shut factories. Laid off most staff.

Their OS - NeXTStep - was a life raft. But would it float?

Then came the call. Apple needed a new operating system and was looking to buy one.

Steve had already tried. Apple said no. But a NeXT engineer went around the official channels, called Apple's engineers directly, and offered to show them what they were missing. This time, someone listened.

In February 1996, Apple bought NeXT for four hundred million dollars. Steve came with the deal. Interestingly enough, considering the later revisionism about him being disliked, his return to Apple was insisted upon by NeXT's engineers, who knew the OS could not thrive without him.

The press called it the one hundred forty million dollar apology.

Steve returned as a consultant with no title and no authority. Amelio's plan was transparent: use Steve as a prop for the market, let him advise while ensuring he couldn't actually change anything. A human scarecrow to signal "we're listening to the visionary" while keeping him safely contained.

But Steve saw the same old patterns: committee thinking, incrementalism, fear. He would not repeat 1985. So he told the board the truth in terms they couldn't misunderstand—either he led fully and accountably, or he left.

Amelio was out after five hundred days. In 1997, the board named Steve interim CEO. Three letters—iCEO—that would change everything.

The storm had not passed. But the ark was back in the hands of its builder.And this time, he knew where the shore was.

What This Story Actually Teaches

This isn't just dramatic business history. It's a pattern that repeats in companies of every size. Vision gets replaced by management when leaders start treating innovation companies like commodity businesses.

Short-term wins mask long-term erosion as stock prices rise while foundations crumble. Core customers get taken for granted because they keep buying, so nobody asks why. Innovation stops and incrementalism takes over, selling the same product unchanged for years. Desperate moves compound the damage through licensing deals, fire-sale pricing, and failed acquisitions. Leadership churn accelerates the spiral with three CEOs in a decade, each bringing a different plan that contradicts the last.

When the ship is sinking, talent jumps first.

I've walked into companies at every stage of this spiral. Sometimes early, when the warning signs are just appearing. Sometimes late, when everyone knows it's broken but nobody can articulate how to fix it. But when the most trusted individuals on the team leave Friday meetings and make 'strategic exits' that day, everyone know's the situation has become critical.

Sound familiar?

The symptoms look different depending on the industry:

A logistics company that optimized costs so aggressively they lost the customers who valued reliability over price.

A software company that added so many approval layers to prevent mistakes they made shipping anything on time impossible.

A professional services firm that grew so fast they promoted people into management without teaching them how to lead, then wondered why culture collapsed.

Different circumstances. Same pattern.

The Turnaround Blueprint Hidden in This Story

Here's what most people miss about Apple's near-death experience: The turnaround didn't start when Steve became CEO.

It started when he was allowed to tell the truth.

As a consultant with no authority, Steve could see clearly what everyone else had rationalized:

The product line was incoherent. The strategy was survival, not vision. The culture rewarded politics over excellence. The best people were leaving because they'd stopped believing.

Amelio wanted Steve as a mascot. Steve insisted on accountability. That's the moment everything changed.

Because you can't fix what you won't name. And most companies in decline have convinced themselves that acknowledging the depth of the problem would make it worse.

It doesn't. It makes turnaround possible.

The Questions This Raises for You

If you're reading this and feeling uncomfortable recognition, here are the questions worth asking:

Are you managing growth or managing decline? Growth feels like momentum. Decline feels like treading water while insisting you're swimming.

Who are your core customers, and are you still serving them? Apple forgot the artists and designers who made the Mac essential. Who did you forget?

When did incrementalism replace innovation? If your answer to every challenge is "do what we did last year, but 10% better," you're not innovating. You're stalling.

How many "plans" have you tried in the past five years? If the answer is more than two, you don't have a strategy problem. You have a commitment problem.

Are your best people still engaged, or are they quietly looking? Talent doesn't leave because of one bad quarter. They leave when they stop believing the direction will change.

Who's allowed to tell the truth? If everyone in leadership is saying "we just need to execute better," nobody's addressing the real problem.

The Moment of Choice

Apple in 1996 had a choice: keep pretending the plan would work, or admit they were ninety days from bankruptcy and needed a completely different approach.

They chose truth. And truth, painful as it was, created the opening for real change.

Your version of this choice might look different:

Admitting the new system rollout failed and starting over, instead of forcing adoption.

Acknowledging that the acquisition didn't create the synergies everyone promised.

Recognizing that the strategy that got you here won't get you there.

Accepting that the leadership team needs different skills than it currently has.

The storm doesn't pass because you ignore it. It passes when you finally face it.

Why This Chapter Matters

The rest of this book is about what Steve did after becoming CEO - how he rebuilt Apple from near-bankruptcy to the most valuable company on Earth.

But none of that was possible until Apple admitted how close to the edge they were.

The storm before the calm isn't just backstory. It's the prerequisite for transformation.

You can't turn around what you won't admit is broken. And you can't rebuild what you're still pretending works.

The ark was back in the hands of its builder. But first, everyone had to admit: the ark was sinking.

Are you ready to admit what's sinking? Because that's where the real work begins.

CHAPTER 7
THE TURNAROUND

d is powerful, polished and carefully conceived."

d Pogue, The New York Times

opard, Apple's operating system widens its lead
ically and technologically."

aig, USA Today

Photo by Tom Coates

When Steve walked onstage at Macworld in January 1998, he had one job: report the facts.

Two words summed it up: Total turnaround.

He stunned the world with the Microsoft deal. That alone could have been a disaster if not perfectly handled. The crowd's reaction to Bill Gates appearing onscreen was one of those epic moments where you could hear the air leave the room. This was not a surrender, but a strategic realignment. Microsoft would buy a small amount of non-voting stock and, crucially, commit to producing Office for Mac for five more years. Steve just secured one of the most vital pieces of software on the Mac. Without it, the Mac would be a pariah of the office world.

Two months later, Michael Dell told a tech symposium: "If I ran Apple, I'd shut it down and give the money back to shareholders."

Well, I guess when you haven't got the vision or the guts to lead this kind of revival, that is where your logic leads you. Steve was a different kind of leader.

Steve neither shut down, nor surrendered. He rebuilt.

The numbers told the story:

Apple's online store traffic jumped from one million hits per day in 1996 to ten million in 1997.

Market value rose from one point eight billion dollars in mid-1997 to four billion a year later.

The iMac sold nearly eight hundred thousand units in its first five months.

For the first time since 1995, Apple was profitable - earning three hundred nine million dollars in 1998.

But skeptics did not vanish. They evolved.

The Apple Hierarchy of Skepticism

Steve mapped their doubts like terrain, publicly naming it the Apple Hierarchy of Skepticism - inspired by Maslow's model.

There were three levels. And you could not skip ahead.

Level One: Survival

The question was blunt: Will you last ninety days? Steve answered by acting fast and visibly.

He replaced the board. Rebuilt the management team. Ended the war with Microsoft - not by conceding, but by securing a vital lifeline: Office for Mac.

Confidence returned. Survival was no longer in doubt.

Level Two: Stable Business

Now the question shifted: Can you sustain? Apple delivered forty-five million dollars profit in the first quarter under the new team. Fifty-five million the next.

New hires. A redesigned online store. The Think Different campaign.

Now this broke many people's minds at the time for not focusing on specs and not even showing the products! This was not advertising - it was reclamation of Apple's place in the universe.

A beacon of the human values that Apple was once the shining lighthouse for. He re-lit that beacon, knowing he was calling his people back home. And return they did.

Heads tilted, conversations across the nation about "Think different? Isn't it differently?" as the grammar battles raged. But one thing was certain: that wordplay combined with a loud rejection of conformity, of being silent in the face of oppression, and of defying rejection for ideas that would change the world put a jet engine behind Apple's comeback.

Momentum built not in spikes, but in a steady climb.

Level Three: Product Strategy

Only after stability could vision return. Steve cut the product line from fifteen offerings to four, ignoring the practice of chasing every possible customer while pleasing none fully. It was simple to him because he knew the customer he wanted to thrill, and he understood the ones he could never truly satisfy.

Then came the iMac. Colorful, all-in-one, for the home. Not for work. For living.

And this enabled a whole campaign built around their primary product advantage: making tech that took complex steps and turned them into something as simple as connecting a microwave.

Campaigns showed time-trial side-by-sides of unboxing, assembling, and getting a computer on the internet.

It was laughable to see a plain-as-day comparison of the two options for consumers:

PC: multiple assembly steps for the computer, multiple steps for OS setup, then even more for configuring the internet.

The iMac? You opened the box, plugged it into the wall and an internet cable, hit the power switch, and started browsing.

It was a brutal and effective demonstration that everything promised in

"Think Different" was real, tangible, and available at the Best Buy down the street today.

The iMac became the single best-selling PC ever created. When you understand its genesis, is there any wonder why?

The rains were receding.

What This Teaches About Real Turnarounds

Most turnaround stories get sanitized. They focus on the hero CEO, the brilliant strategy, the triumphant comeback. Steve's turnaround was messier and more instructive than that.

Here's what actually happened:

He didn't start with vision. He started with survival - literally making sure Apple would exist in ninety days.

He didn't try to do everything at once. He explicitly sequenced the work: survive, then stabilize, then strategy.

He didn't avoid hard choices to maintain consensus. He replaced the board, rebuilt leadership, cut 70% of products.

He didn't pretend complexity was sophistication. He made computers so simple a child could use them.

He didn't hide the turnaround behind closed doors. He named the skepticism publicly and addressed each level systematically.

This is the opposite of what most struggling companies do.

The Pattern You Need to Recognize

When companies face crisis, they typically make these mistakes:

Mistake 1: Trying to skip levels

They want to jump straight to "innovative product strategy" when they haven't solved "will we survive the quarter?" You can't strategize your way out of a cash flow crisis. You have to stop the bleeding first.

Mistake 2: Pursuing stability through addition

They think: "We need more products, more markets, more revenue streams." Steve did the opposite: fewer products, clearer focus, deeper excellence.

Mistake 3: Hiding the severity from themselves

Leadership knows it's bad, but they keep the full truth from the board, the team, sometimes even from each other. Steve publicly named where Apple was in the hierarchy. No pretense. No spin.

Mistake 4: Optimizing for consensus

They make decisions that keep everyone comfortable instead of decisions that work. Steve replaced people who couldn't execute. He cut products people loved. He made hard choices and stood by them.

Mistake 5: Confusing activity with progress

They launch initiatives, form committees, create task forces - all motion, no direction. Steve had clarity: survive, stabilize, then strategy. Every action mapped to one of those three.

How This Applies to Your Situation

You might not be ninety days from bankruptcy. But the hierarchy of skepticism applies at every scale.

When you're implementing a new system:

Level One: Will it actually work? (Survival) Level Two: Can we sustain adoption? (Stability) Level Three: How do we optimize and scale? (Strategy)

When you're rebuilding a broken process:

Level One: Can we stop the immediate damage? (Survival) Level Two: Can we maintain the fix without constant intervention? (Stability) Level Three: How do we make this excellent, not just functional? (Strategy)

When you're turning around a struggling department:

Level One: Do we have the right people in place? (Survival) Level Two: Are they aligned and productive? (Stability) Level Three: How do we scale what's working? (Strategy)

The mistake is trying to solve Level Three problems when you haven't addressed Level One.

The Microsoft Deal: Making Peace With Reality

The most controversial move Steve made was partnering with Microsoft - Apple's sworn enemy.

The crowd at Macworld was stunned. Some were angry. How could he?

But Steve understood something critical: ideological purity doesn't matter if you're dead.

Apple needed Office. Without it, businesses wouldn't touch Macs. Without business customers, Apple couldn't survive.

So he made the deal. Not because he liked Microsoft, but because survival required it.

This is the hardest lesson for leaders in crisis: Sometimes the right move contradicts everything you've stood for. Sometimes you have to partner with your rival, cut your favorite product, abandon your original vision.

Not because you were wrong. Because circumstances changed.

The question isn't "Does this feel right?" The question is "Does this keep us alive long enough to fight another day?"

The iMac: Simplicity as Strategy

When the iMac launched, critics called it a toy. No floppy drive? No expansion slots? Just pretty colors?

They missed the point entirely.

The iMac wasn't for power users. It was for everyone else - the people who found computers intimidating, who didn't want to learn DOS commands, who just wanted to check email and browse the web.

The side-by-side comparison demolished the competition:

PC setup: 45 minutes of assembly, configuration, troubleshooting. iMac setup: Plug in two cables. Press power. You're online.

That's not marketing. That's understanding what actually matters to most people.

And here's what I see companies miss constantly: they optimize for the power users and ignore everyone else.

The CRM is built for the sales ops team who loves data, not the rep who just needs to log a call.

The project management tool is designed for the PM who wants Gantt charts, not the team member who just needs to know what they're working on today.

The dashboard shows every possible metric because someone might need it, instead of the three numbers that actually drive decisions.

The iMac principle: Design for the person who has the least patience for complexity.

If it works for them, it'll work for everyone. If you only design for power users, you've lost 80% of your audience.

What "Think Different" Actually Meant

The Think Different campaign didn't show products. It showed people: Einstein, MLK, Gandhi, Picasso.

People who changed the world by refusing to accept it as it was.

This confused everyone. Where are the specs? The features? The comparisons?

But Steve understood: Apple wasn't selling computers. They were selling permission to be different.

Permission to care about design. Permission to reject complexity. Permission to believe technology should serve humanity, not the other way around.

That's not a product strategy. That's an identity.

And when you give people permission to see themselves differently, they'll pay a premium for the tools that let them live that identity.

The Question for Your Turnaround

If you're in any version of turnaround - a struggling project, a broken system, a declining department - here's the question that matters:

What level of the hierarchy are you actually at?

Not where you want to be. Not where you were last year. Where you actually are right now.

If you're at Level One (survival), stop planning your Level Three strategy. Focus on: Do we have the right people? Are we addressing the critical issues? Can we stabilize this before it collapses completely?

If you're at Level Two (stability), don't chase shiny new initiatives. Focus on: Can we sustain what's working? Are we building momentum or just treading water? Do we have the foundation for the next level?

Only when you've genuinely stabilized can you focus on Level Three - the strategy, the optimization, the scaling.

Skip levels and you fail.

Name the level honestly and you can move forward.

Steve didn't save Apple with genius alone. He saved it by seeing clearly where they were, what they needed at that level, and refusing to pretend they were somewhere else.

Can you do the same?

The rains are receding. But first, you have to acknowledge the flood.

Mountains Are Not Climbed in a Day

By 1999, Apple's stock had risen from thirteen dollars to one hundred eighteen. A tenfold increase. Market value reached twenty billion.

In 2000, Business Week named Steve one of the Top Twenty-Five Managers of the Year. Fortune, which once called him a snake oil salesman, put him on the cover with the headline "Stevie Wonder."

Yet the climb was not smooth.

2001 brought Apple's first unprofitable quarter since Steve's return. The year ended with a twenty-five million dollar net loss, down from seven hundred eighty-six million the year before.

Why? Brilliant moves like the new OS, first retail stores, and education gains were offset by missteps.

The G4 Cube, heavily promoted, failed to resonate. DVD-ROM drives, chosen over CD-RW, left users unable to burn CDs - a critical oversight.

Setbacks are not failures. They are data.

In 2002, Apple returned to profit: sixty-five million. Sixty-nine million in 2003. But the work was far from done. Profit margins were just 0.4%, well below the industry average of 2%.

Apple remained ninth in PCs, behind Dell, HP, IBM, even Acer and Legend.

Microsoft earned two point six billion dollars in one quarter - nearly fifteen times Apple's entire software revenue. In that span, Microsoft made more profit than Apple had in the previous fourteen years.

To most, Apple's rise still seemed impossible.

To Steve, it was inevitable - because he was not chasing market share. He was rebuilding coherence.

Here's what people miss when they tell Apple's comeback story:

The turnaround took years. Not months.

From near-bankruptcy in 1997 to stable profitability took five years. From stable profitability to dominance took another decade. Progress was not linear.

Stock up tenfold, then an unprofitable quarter. Breakthrough products alongside complete flops. Magazine covers followed by margin pressure.

The critics never stopped.

Even after the turnaround was undeniable, Apple was still ninth in PC sales. Microsoft was still making fifteen times their revenue. The "Apple is doomed" narrative persisted.

Steve never measured success the way everyone else did.

Market share? Ninth place. Revenue? A fraction of Microsoft's. Margins? Below industry average.

Yet he kept building - because he knew something others didn't.

The Difference Between Recovery and Transformation

Most turnarounds aim for recovery: get back to where you were, stop the bleeding, return to profitability.

Steve aimed for transformation: become something entirely different from what you were.

Recovery asks: "How do we survive?"

Transformation asks: "What do we want to become?"

That's why the setbacks didn't derail him.

The G4 Cube failed. So what? It taught them what people didn't want. The DVD-ROM decision was wrong. So what? They learned and moved on.

He wasn't trying to execute a perfect plan. He was trying to build a company capable of sustained excellence - which means capable of learning from failure.

Here's what I see in companies trying to turn around:

Year One: Enthusiasm

New leadership, new strategy, new energy. Everyone's excited. Quick wins happen. Momentum builds.

Year Two: Resistance

The easy fixes are done. Now comes the hard work. Some initiatives fail. People get tired. Skeptics resurface.

Year Three: The Valley

This is where most turnarounds die. Progress has slowed. Results are mixed. Leadership loses confidence or the board loses patience. They abandon the strategy and start over.

But this is exactly when the real transformation begins.

Because transformation isn't about the first wave of changes. It's about building the systems, culture, and capabilities that sustain change over time.

Apple in 2001 - unprofitable quarter, failed Cube, margin pressure - was in The Valley.

Most boards would have panicked. Most CEOs would have pivoted.

Steve kept building.

What "Rebuilding Coherence" Actually Means

Steve said he wasn't chasing market share - he was rebuilding coherence.

What does that mean in practice?

Coherence means: Every part of the system supports every other part.

The product line is clear and focused. The retail experience reinforces the brand. The operating system enables the hardware. The marketing reflects the actual experience. The support feels like part of the product.

Nothing contradicts. Nothing creates friction. It all flows. A logistics company that optimized costs so aggressively they lost the customers who valued reliability over price. A software company that added so many approval layers to prevent mistakes they made shipping anything on time impossible.

That takes years to build.

You can't coherence-sprint your way there. You have to make hundreds of aligned decisions over thousands of days.

Product decisions. Hiring decisions. Process decisions. Partnership decisions. Investment decisions.

Each one either moves you toward coherence or away from it.

The Pattern I See in Companies That Fail at This

They give up in The Valley.

Year One goes great. Year Two shows promise. Year Three gets hard, and they lose faith.

Not because the strategy was wrong, but because they expected transformation to be faster, smoother, more linear than it actually is.

They expected climbing a mountain to feel like walking uphill.

It doesn't. It feels like:

Taking three steps forward and one step back. Reaching what you thought was the summit and realizing there's another ridge beyond it. Weather that forces you to wait. Equipment that fails. Routes that don't work. Setbacks that feel like failures until you realize they're teaching you something essential.

The companies that make it are the ones who expected this - who built their timeline around "years, not quarters" and their culture around "learn and adapt" instead of "execute perfectly."

The Metrics That Mislead

In 2003, Apple was ninth in PC sales with margins below the industry average. By those metrics, they were losing.

But Steve was measuring different things:

- Are we building products people love?
- Is our brand becoming stronger?
- Are we creating the capabilities for future breakthroughs?
- Is our culture protecting excellence?

Those aren't quarterly metrics. They're trajectory metrics. And trajectory matters more than position when you're climbing a mountain.

This is where most companies get lost. They measure what's easy to measure: sales, margins, market share, efficiency.

They ignore what's hard to measure: trust, capability, coherence, learning.

Then they wonder why hitting their numbers doesn't translate to transformation.

What Matters in Year Three

If you're in any version of transformation - fixing systems, rebuilding culture, turning around performance - here's what matters more than results in Year Three:

Are you learning faster than you're failing?

The G4 Cube failed. But they learned what customers didn't value, which made the iPod and iPhone better.

Are you building capability, not just outcomes?

Apple's retail stores didn't just generate revenue. They built the capability to control customer experience - which became critical for iPhone launches.

Are your people still engaged, or are they exhausted?

Transformation is a marathon. If your team is burning out by Year Three, you won't make it to Year Five.

Are you holding the standard, even when it's hard?

Steve could have cut corners to hit margin targets. He didn't. He kept the standard, even when Wall Street complained.

Are you measuring trajectory or just position?

Position: ninth in PC sales. Trajectory: building the foundation for iPod, iPhone, iPad. Which matters more?

The Uncomfortable Truth

Most transformations fail not because the strategy was wrong, but because leadership ran out of patience.

The board wanted results faster. The CEO needed a win to keep their job. The team was tired of fighting.

So they declared victory early ("we're back to profitability!") or they pivoted to something easier or they brought in new leadership who promised a faster path. And the transformation died in Year Three, just when it was about to become real.

Steve had something most leaders don't: time. Not unlimited time or infinite patience, but enough time to let the strategy compound. Enough time to learn from the G4 Cube's failure, to build retail stores everyone said wouldn't work, to develop an OS that would eventually run the iPhone. Enough time for coherence to emerge from what initially looked like disconnected bets.

What This Means for You

If you're trying to transform anything - a company, a department, a system - here's what you need to accept:

Year One will feel great. Quick wins, visible progress, momentum.

Year Two will feel productive. Real work happening, systems changing, people adapting.

Year Three will feel hard. Progress slows. Some things fail. Doubt creeps in.

This is normal. This is not a sign you should quit.

This is the valley between base camp and summit. This is where amateur climbers turn back and experienced ones keep going.

The question isn't whether you'll hit The Valley. The question is: what will you do when you do?

Will you keep building coherence, even when the metrics don't show it yet?

Will you keep the standard, even when cutting corners would be easier?

Will you trust the trajectory, even when position looks discouraging?

Mountains are not climbed in a day. But they are climbed - one step at a time, through setbacks and storms, by people who refuse to measure success by how far they've come and instead focus on whether they're still moving toward the summit.

In 2003, Apple was ninth in PC sales with razor-thin margins.

By 2011, they were the most valuable company on Earth.

The difference wasn't luck. It was coherence, compounding over time. The climb wasn't smooth. But it was relentless.

Are you willing to be relentless? Even in The Valley?

That's where transformation actually happens.

Eighteen Years Later: The Dent in the Universe

Fast forward. Apple's revenue: forty-six point three billion dollars. That was more than double Microsoft's.

Net income: thirteen point zero six billion - also nearly double Microsoft's six point six two billion.

One product (the iPhone) generated twenty-four point four two billion in a single quarter. That was more than all of Microsoft's product lines combined.

CFO Peter Oppenheimer announced: "We're pleased to have generated over forty-one billion in net income and over fifty billion in operating cash flow in fiscal 2012."

Apple ranked sixth on the Fortune 500. Ahead of J.P. Morgan, Bank of America, Ford, GM, AT&T, Verizon, Hewlett-Packard, and Fannie Mae. Only ExxonMobil earned more profit.

This was not magic. It was method applied relentlessly, across eighteen years.

The Math of Transformation

Let's be clear about what eighteen years means:

From 1997 to 2012: 72 quarters. 216 months. Roughly 4,680 days. That's over 112,000 hours.

Every single one of those hours was a choice:

Do we cut corners or hold the standard?

Do we chase the trend or trust our vision?

Do we please the critics or serve the customer?

Do we add complexity or fight for simplicity?

Eighteen years of choosing coherence over convenience. That's not a slogan. That's the actual work.

What People Get Wrong About the Numbers

When people see Apple's 2012 results, they think: "The iPhone was a home run."

They're not wrong. But they're missing the structure beneath the home run. The iPhone didn't succeed because Steve had one brilliant idea in 2007. It succeeded because from 1997 to 2001 he rebuilt the foundation by killing incoherent products, establishing the principle of designing for humans not specs, and proving Apple could deliver on promises.

From 2001 to 2007 he built the capabilities that made the iPhone possible. iTunes taught them digital distribution, iPod taught them mobile hardware, retail stores taught them customer experience. Each success created capacity for the next, building muscle memory for integration and execution at scale.

In 2007 he launched the iPhone—not as a miracle, but as the natural next step built on everything they'd learned. It was possible only because the foundation held.

The breakthrough product was the outcome of structural excellence.

That's the part nobody copies. They see the iPhone and try to build their own. They skip the eighteen years of groundwork.

It doesn't work.

The Real Lesson

People point to the iMac, the iPod, the iPhone and call them breakthroughs. They were.

But the deeper breakthrough was structural: Answer the skeptics before they speak.

Steve didn't wait for critics to say "Apple can't sustain this." He built sustainability into every decision. He didn't argue with doubt. He obsoleted it with results.

Do not announce vision until stability is proven.

He could have talked about the iPhone in 2002. He didn't. He waited until the iPod was a massive success, until retail stores were profitable, until the foundation could support the weight of that vision.

Never let a misstep define the mission. Let it refine it.

The G4 Cube failed. The first Apple TV underwhelmed. MobileMe was a disaster. None of it derailed the mission. Each taught them something that made the next thing better.

What This Looks Like in Practice

In my years working with teams rebuilding systems - not just products, but workflows, cultures, daily rhythms - I've seen how often leaders mistake speed for progress.

They want the transformation in months, not years. They want the breakthrough without the groundwork, the vision announcement before they've built the capability to deliver it. It doesn't work.

Here's what does: In years one and two, you build stability by fixing what's broken, establishing standards, and proving you can execute consistently. Don't overpromise—underdeliver, then exceed. In years three through five, you build capability by developing your people, refining your processes, learning from every initiative, and stacking small wins into the foundation for bigger ones.

By years six through ten, you can build momentum. Now you can take bigger risks because your vision has credibility. Now the breakthrough becomes possible because you built the structure to support it. In years eleven through eighteen, you compound the gains as each success enables the next, capabilities multiply, culture reinforces itself, and excellence becomes normal rather than exceptional.

Most companies quit in Year Three.

They're in The Valley. Results are mixed. Critics are loud. Leadership loses faith.

Apple in Year Three (2000) was making progress but still ninth in PC sales with razor-thin margins. If they'd quit then, there's no iPhone. No $46 billion in revenue. No dent in the universe.

Steve didn't rush. He sequenced. That's the lesson most leaders miss. They try to do everything at once— fix the culture, launch new products, enter new markets, transform operations, rebrand, and restructure all simultaneously. It fails because organizations can't absorb that much change at once without collapsing into chaos. Not because any individual goal is wrong, but because they're trying to climb five mountains simultaneously.

Steve climbed one mountain at a time. From 1997 to 1998, he focused solely on survival—stopping the bleeding, rebuilding leadership, securing the Microsoft deal, and proving Apple wouldn't die.

From 1998 to 2001, he stabilized by proving Apple could still innovate with the iMac, control experience through retail stores, and build platforms with OS X. From 2001 to 2007, he built new capabilities as iTunes proved digital distribution, iPod proved mobile excellence, and each success funded the next.

From 2007 to 2011, he transformed the industry as the iPhone redefined mobile, the iPad created a new category, and the App Store became a platform. Each stage enabled the next. Skip one and the whole sequence fails.

What $46 Billion Actually Represents

Apple's 2012 revenue wasn't just money, it was proof. Proof that simplicity beats feature lists, that designing for humans beats designing for specs, that saying no beats saying yes, that long-term excellence beats short-term wins, that coherence beats complexity, and that standards beat compromise.

Every principle Steve stood for, validated at massive scale.

But here's what people miss: those principles were true in 1997 when Apple was ninety days from bankruptcy.

They didn't become true when Apple became successful. They were true all along. The eighteen years proved they were right. They didn't make them right.

The Method, Not the Magic

This wasn't magic. It was method applied relentlessly over eighteen years. And by method, I mean repeatable principles, consistently enforced: every product decision filtered through whether it served humans or specs, every partnership judged by whether it strengthened coherence or diluted it, and every hire evaluated by a single standard, could this person truly hold it. Every process designed around: "Does this enable excellence or create friction?"

Eighteen years of the same questions, asked honestly, answered with discipline.

That isn't genius. It's craft. The kind that can be practiced, repeated, and refined by anyone willing to do the work. And it's exactly why most won't commit to it, because craft demands patience over quick wins, standards over convenience, learning over defending, and building over announcing.

Where Most Transformations Die

They fail in the gap between vision and capability. A leader can see what's possible, the vision, while the organization lacks the ability to deliver it yet, the capability gap. At that moment, there are only two responses. One is to lower the vision to match current capability, wrapped in language like "let's be realistic," "that's too ambitious," or "we should focus on what we can do now." The result is predictable and permanent mediocrity. The other response is to build capability to meet the vision by clearly stating where the organization is going, identifying what must be learned, and mapping the path forward step by step. That path leads to transformation, even if it takes time. Steve Jobs chose the second response every time. The iPhone existed as a vision years before the capability did. He didn't shrink the vision to fit reality, he expanded reality to meet the vision. Most leaders choose the first response because it's faster, easier, and feels realistic. They're right. It is more realistic. And it's exactly why they'll never put a dent in the universe.

What Beginning Looks Like

The most powerful thing you can do is begin by accepting that the first step is not brilliance, it's clarity. Clarity about where you actually are rather than where you wish you were, what you actually need rather than what would be nice to have, who you actually serve rather than who you aspire to serve, and what you actually stand for rather than what sounds good in a mission statement. That kind of clarity is harder than brilliance. Brilliance is exciting and impressive, clarity is uncomfortable and forces honesty. Brilliance feels like progress, clarity feels like work. But brilliance without clarity is just noise, while clarity, paired with discipline, becomes transformation.

Eighteen Years from Now

Where will your company be in eighteen years?

Not where you hope. Where your current trajectory leads.

If you keep making the same choices, following the same patterns, tolerating the same compromises - where does that path end?

Most leaders can't answer this honestly.

They know intellectually that their current path won't lead to excellence. But they keep walking it anyway because changing paths is hard, uncertain, and takes years to show results.

Steve in 1997 could have kept Apple on its current path. Slightly better Macs. Slightly better margins. Slightly less decline.

He'd still be ninth in PC sales today. Or more likely, bankrupt.

Instead, he chose the eighteen-year path. The one that looked impossible. The one critics called delusional. The one that required holding a standard when everyone else said to compromise.

Eighteen years later: $46 billion in revenue.

Not because he was smarter than everyone else.

Because he was willing to take the long path when everyone else wanted shortcuts.

Your Eighteen Years Starts Now

You don't need to build the next iPhone. What you need is to begin the eighteen-year journey toward your own version of excellence. Not tomorrow. Not next quarter. Now.

Every day presents the same set of choices. Do you cut the corner or hold the standard? Do you announce the vision or quietly build the capability behind it? Do you chase the latest trend or trust the principles you claim to stand on? Do you add complexity or fight relentlessly for simplicity?

Those choices compound. Make the right one today, then make it again tomorrow, and the day after that. Repeat it for 4,680 days. That's how real excellence is built. That's how you put a dent in the universe.Not with magic. With method, applied relentlessly.

The clock starts now.

CHAPTER 8
CREDIBILITY VS INCREDIBILITY

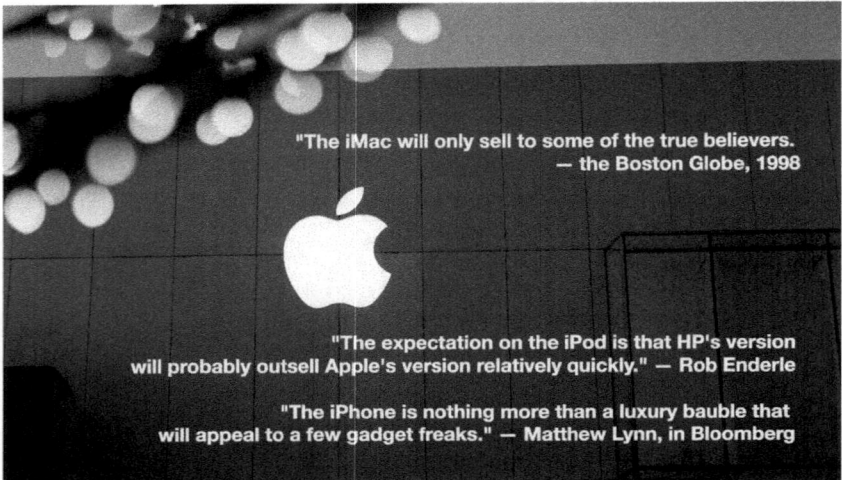

"The iMac will only sell to some of the true believers.
— the Boston Globe, 1998

"The expectation on the iPod is that HP's version will probably outsell Apple's version relatively quickly." — Rob Enderle

"The iPhone is nothing more than a luxury bauble that will appeal to a few gadget freaks." — Matthew Lynn, in Bloomberg

"War is show business. That's why we're here." — Wag the Dog

Apple's comeback teaches many lessons. One of the most vital is this: Do not believe everything the world says about you, especially when it sounds like a script handwritten by your opposition.

For twenty years, the press has repeated the same headline: Apple is doomed.

The details change. The narrative does not.

The Ritual of Doubt

In December 2012, NBC's Rock Center aired Tim Cook's first major interview as CEO. He was met not with curiosity, but with ritual.

Question after question followed the same arc:

Even though you are the most valuable company in the world...

Even though you just broke every sales record in history...

Will Apple survive the year?

It wasn't inquiry. It was incantation, an attempt to summon decline by treating it as inevitable. The implication was clear: that Apple's success had to be punished by gravity, that excellence must eventually collapse under its own weight.

The idea sounds familiar, but it isn't a law of nature. It's a habit, often used to advance an agenda. To believe Apple was destined to return to irrelevance, you'd have to believe Steve Jobs defied physics, that he waved a wand, that coherence itself was magic. It wasn't.

He didn't defy anything. He designed. He sequenced. He protected focus. And the results, trillions in cumulative revenue, billions of lives touched, entire systems reshaped, aren't anomalies. They're evidence.

The Noise and the Signal

Every leader encounters the same pattern. The louder the success, the louder the chorus of "yes, but." Scrutiny grows, skepticism sharpens, and narratives form around the expectation that the rise must be followed by a fall.

The press, in particular, never ignored Apple. It relied on Apple for drama, conflict, and the enduring myth of the fallen titan. Drama fuels attention. But drama is not data, and narrative is not strategy.

Steve Jobs understood this early. When the world declared the Mac dead in 1985, he built NeXT. When critics dismissed the iPod as a toy, he built the iTunes Store. When analysts said the iPhone was too expensive, he removed the keyboard. When pundits called the iPad useless, nonverbal children found their voice.

He didn't argue with the noise. He answered it with work.

How to Spot the Pattern

Over the years, watching how systems rise and fall, certain patterns become impossible to ignore. When credibility is being manufactured rather than honestly questioned, the same moves appear again and again.

They sound reasonable on the surface, but they're designed to undermine confidence without ever engaging the real work.

The False Equivalence

"Yes, sales are up, but morale is down." The statement sounds balanced, even thoughtful, until you notice what's missing. No one asks what actually broke morale. Was it the way success was achieved, or was it the constant external drumbeat insisting the success won't last? The comparison creates doubt without doing any diagnosis.

The Historical Trap

"All empires fall." The line gets invoked as if Apple were Rome, rather than a company capable of learning, adapting, and redesigning itself. It treats history as destiny, ignoring that the entire point of innovation is to create futures that didn't exist before.

The Personality Pivot

"Can anyone replace Steve?" The question assumes culture is a person rather than a system of choices repeated every day. It ignores the reality that principles embedded into design, process, and standards don't vanish when a founder leaves the room.

The Goalpost Shift

When Apple succeeds at one thing, critics immediately demand another. When that next bar is cleared, the criteria quietly move again. The iPhone sells millions, but can they sustain it? They sustain it for years, but what's next? The iPad launches, but it's just a big iPhone. The iPad succeeds, but what about innovation? The target is never meant to be reached.

These aren't genuine questions. They're attacks dressed up as inquiry.

Why This Pattern Exists

Here's what I've learned over time: the narrative of inevitable decline serves almost everyone except the company doing the work.

It serves competitors who need to believe that Apple's success is temporary, because accepting sustained excellence would require them to confront their own shortcomings. It serves media outlets that depend on conflict and tension to drive attention, where the story of a rising company quickly becomes less interesting than the promise of a fall. It serves analysts who must constantly forecast disruption and reversal to justify their role, even when the underlying fundamentals remain strong. And it serves cynics who find comfort in the idea that every winner eventually fails, because it reframes inaction as wisdom.

None of these groups benefit from Apple succeeding over the long term. So a narrative is constructed in which success must be fleeting, gravity must win, and coherence must eventually break. That story only becomes self-fulfilling if leaders internalize it. The moment you stop believing the narrative, it loses its power.

You don't need to be Apple to encounter this pattern.

Every successful initiative triggers the same ritualized doubt.

You implement a new system that actually works, and within weeks the response is, "Yes, but will it scale?" You fix a broken process, and a few months later the question shifts to an entirely different problem. You deliver results ahead of schedule, and within a few quarters the concern becomes whether the pace can be sustained. The success is acknowledged just long enough to be questioned.

The sequence is remarkably consistent. First, the success is denied outright. When denial no longer holds, it's framed as temporary. When it continues, the metrics quietly change. When those metrics improve, attention turns to questioning leadership. And when leadership proves itself, the prediction becomes inevitable decline.

The goal of this pattern isn't to understand what worked or why it worked. It's to undermine confidence in the success itself.

The Two Paths Forward

When you run into manufactured incredibility, there are really only two paths available.

The first is to engage the narrative. You defend yourself, explain why the critics are wrong, counter every argument, and try to prove your legitimacy point by point. This path feels responsible, even rational, but it's exhausting. And more importantly, it doesn't work. The narrative you're fighting isn't grounded in evidence, it's driven by agenda. You can't reason your way out of someone else's motivated reasoning, no matter how airtight your case is.

The second path is to obsolete the narrative entirely. Instead of arguing, you build something so clear, so functional, and so undeniable that the story being told about you no longer matters.

Steve Jobs never defended the iPod in interviews. He sold a hundred million of them. He didn't debate whether the iPhone would succeed. He shipped it and let people decide. He didn't try to persuade critics that the iPad mattered. He watched it quietly reshape entire industries.

Work is the answer. It always has been.

The Questions That Actually Matter

When doubt shows up, whether it comes from outside voices or your own internal hesitation, there are better questions to ask than "How do I respond?" The right questions cut through noise and reveal whether the criticism deserves your attention at all.

Start by asking whether the criticism is grounded in evidence or driven by agenda. Evidence-based criticism points to specific problems and offers a path toward improvement. Agenda-based criticism predicts failure without engaging the work itself. Then ask what the critic actually wants. Some people want to help you succeed. Others need you to fail so they can feel justified in standing still. The difference matters.

Next, look at the standard you're being held to. Real standards are consistent and measurable. Impossible bars move the moment you clear them. Ask yourself whether success would genuinely change this person's mind, or whether new reasons to doubt would immediately appear. If no amount of evidence will ever be enough, stop trying to persuade them. Finally, ask the most important question of all: are you letting the noise set your agenda, or are you setting it yourself?

Apple offers a clear answer to what happens when you choose the latter. For two decades, predictions of Apple's decline have been constant. For those same two decades, the results have been record-breaking. What Apple proved isn't that decline is impossible, no company is immune to it.

What they proved is that coherence, consistently applied, outperforms conventional wisdom. Serving humans beats serving specs. Saying no beats saying yes. Long-term excellence beats short-term wins. And culture isn't a personality trait, it's a system of choices.

Every "yes, but" Apple faced was answered the same way. Not with arguments. With work.

The Real Lesson

Apple didn't survive in spite of the noise. It survived because it refused to let the noise set the agenda. Steve Jobs didn't wait for the world to believe in him. He built something so coherent, so human, and so obvious in hindsight that belief eventually became unavoidable.

You don't need to be Apple to apply this lesson. What matters is understanding the story being written about you and, more importantly, who is writing it. If critics are pointing to real problems that need solving, listen closely. That feedback is useful. But if they're manufacturing doubt to serve their own agenda, ignore it and get back to building. Write the next sentence yourself.

This is what I tell leaders who find themselves facing manufactured incredibility: your job is not to convince critics. Your job is to build something so clear and so well executed that the criticism becomes irrelevant. Not by chasing perfection, but by being precise about what you stand for and relentless about delivering on it.

The noise will never disappear. Success attracts skepticism. Excellence invites doubt. Achievement creates pressure. That isn't a flaw in the system, it's evidence you're doing something that matters. No one bothers attacking what poses no threat. No one spends decades predicting the downfall of irrelevant companies. The fact that Apple's decline has been forecast for years is proof that it's still seen as dangerous.

The day people stop predicting your decline is the day you've actually declined.

What This Means Tomorrow

Doubt will show up tomorrow, and the day after that, and every time progress becomes visible. A critic will question your strategy. A skeptic will predict your failure. A cynic will reframe your success as luck, timing, or something that can't possibly last. This isn't a sign that you're doing something wrong. It's a signal that what you're building matters enough to be noticed.

What matters is the choice that follows. You can spend your energy defending yourself, clarifying intentions, and trying to earn credibility from people who have already decided not to grant it. Or you can put that same energy into building the next thing. One path feels responsible but leads to exhaustion. The other feels quiet, even risky, but compounds.

Chasing credibility rarely works because credibility is almost never awarded through argument. It's granted through repeated exposure to results. Incredibility, on the other hand, is built. It's the byproduct of doing work so clear and so consistent that explanation becomes unnecessary. When something works, truly works, it speaks for itself.

Steve Jobs understood this instinctively. The iPod, the iPhone, and the iPad were not attempts to win debates. They weren't responses to criticism. They were answers delivered through execution. Not "here's why you're wrong about us," but "here's what we built while you were talking." Each product closed an argument without ever acknowledging it.

That is the deeper lesson. Don't defend the work. Do the work. The world doesn't need more explanations, positioning statements, or carefully worded justifications. It needs evidence. And when evidence is delivered consistently, over time, it becomes impossible to ignore. Even for critics. Especially for critics.

Crisis or Circus?

"Can't have a war without an enemy... You could have one, but it would be a very dull war." — Wag the Dog

Despite record revenue. Despite record user satisfaction. Despite products that millions choose, daily, to create, connect, and care for others, the narrative around Apple stays oddly fixed: impending collapse.

Why?

Because crisis is content, and calm is invisible.

News is a business. Its currency is attention. Attention is won through urgency, conflict, and emotional charge. "Everything is working as expected" does not trigger a click. "Something is breaking" does. And when the subject is a company as culturally dominant as Apple, the promise of a crack in the foundation becomes irresistible.

That's the real engine behind the endless "Yes, but..." coverage. Not careful analysis, but a dependable formula: introduce tension, imply betrayal of identity, forecast reversal, then invite the audience to pick a side. It doesn't matter whether the titan is actually falling. The story only needs to feel like the beginning of a fall.

This is not new. In 1897, artist Frederic Remington cabled publisher William Randolph Hearst from Cuba: "There will be no war." Hearst's reply is legend: "You furnish the pictures and I'll furnish the war." The quote endures because it reveals the mechanism. If reality won't provide the drama, drama will be manufactured. The headline becomes the product.

Over a century later, the assignment hasn't changed, it's just been opti-mized. The modern version doesn't require inventing a war. It only requires framing normal cycles as existential threats: a slower quarter becomes "the end," a product that evolves becomes "stagnation," a strategic constraint becomes "failure of imagination." Add a few anony-mous sources, sprinkle in a chart, and you can sell the sensation of decline without proving any decline exists.

Apple is uniquely profitable for this machine because it triggers tribal emotion on both sides. Simply mentioning Apple in a negative frame pulls attention like gravity. Some readers click because they want to witness the downfall. Others click because they're furious at the distortion and can't resist responding. Either way, the outcome is the same: engagement spikes, conflict spreads, and ad revenue flows.

And once a narrative becomes profitable, it becomes self-reinforcing. Outlets learn which angles travel, which phrasing gets repeated, which hot takes become "debates," and which debates become recurring content. The incentive is not truth. The incentive is momentum. The same storyline can be repackaged endlessly because it isn't designed to conclude. It's designed to continue.

That's why "Apple is doomed" never needs to be right. It only needs to be clickable. It needs to create the feeling that something dramatic might happen soon, so you'll check again tomorrow. The business of drama doesn't require collapse. It only requires the suggestion of it, delivered with confidence, repeated until it feels like common sense.

Calm doesn't monetize. Competence doesn't trend. Coherence doesn't scream for attention.

But crisis does. Even when it's borrowed. Even when it's implied. Even when it's manufactured.

The Pattern of Manufactured Crisis

Two million pre-orders in the first twenty-four hours, a record at the time. By any reasonable measure, that should have framed the story. Instead, the dominant headlines called it "boring," "disappointing," and a "letdown." The conclusion was written before the data had a chance to speak.

CBS MoneyWatch published analyst projections estimating six to ten million units sold in the first weekend. When Apple later reported five million units sold in three days, a pace no previous smartphone launch had achieved, the numbers were not contextualized or re-evaluated. They were reframed as failure. The headline read: "Apple Stock Spanked For Low iPhone 5 Sales."

The contradiction was striking. Expectations were selectively elevated, then selectively remembered, and finally used as a cudgel. The same performance that would have been celebrated for any other company became evidence of decline. The narrative didn't bend to the facts. The facts were forced to serve the narrative.

The pattern repeated with the iPad mini in 2013. Erik Sherman, writing for CBS News, cited "anonymous supply chain sources" claiming sales would drop twenty to thirty percent compared to the same quarter the year before. The problem was obvious to anyone paying attention: the iPad mini had not existed the year before. There was no historical baseline to compare against.

No meaningful correction followed in the body of the article. The claim stood unchallenged where most readers would see it. The clarification appeared only in the comments, where inconvenient truths tend to collect after the damage is done. By the time reality surfaced, the impression had already spread.

These weren't isolated mistakes. They were symptoms of a system optimized for sensation over accuracy. Once a storyline is profitable, it becomes self-sustaining. Numbers are interpreted through it, context is stripped away, and contradictions are ignored as long as the framing holds. Accuracy becomes optional. Momentum does the rest.

The Selective Lens

In 2013, Apple captured 53.3 percent of the U.S. smartphone market, up from 35.8 percent the year before. Android's share fell by nearly eleven percent in the same period. The data wasn't obscure. It was public, measurable, and unambiguous. And yet the headlines told a different story: "Android dominates." "iPhone relevance fading."

The numbers existed. The narrative simply chose not to look at them.

This is how selective framing works. Metrics that support the preferred storyline are amplified. Metrics that contradict it are quietly ignored. Market share becomes less interesting than unit variety. Profitability becomes less relevant than shipment volume. Context is swapped until the conclusion feels inevitable, even when the underlying reality points in the opposite direction.

With enough repetition, the selective lens begins to feel like consensus. Readers stop asking what's being measured and start absorbing what's being implied. Over time, the framing hardens into "common knowledge," even as the data continues to disagree.

Looking back nearly thirteen years later, the volume of stories predicting the iPhone's imminent irrelevance feels almost comical. And yet the pattern never stopped. The same language reappeared with the iPhone 15. Then the 16. Then the 17. Each launch framed as the moment gravity would finally assert itself. Each time followed by adoption, satisfaction, and sustained demand.

Think about that.

The Conflicts of Interest

Some distortions transcend incompetence into deliberate intent. In 2013, the BBC published "Apple Brand Less Inspiring, Survey Says," presenting research from Added Value as independent market analysis. What the article failed to mention: Added Value operates as a subsidiary of WPP, and WPP serves as Samsung's global advertising agency—the very company competing most directly with Apple in smartphones and tablets. The conflict of interest wasn't subtle. It was structural.

Only after sustained public outcry did the BBC append a disclaimer. Not prominently. Not in the headline or opening paragraphs where readers form their understanding. Buried at the bottom, added retroactively, formatted to be skipped. The damage had been done. The headline had circulated. The "independent" study had shaped perception. The correction was procedural theater.

This wasn't journalism failing through oversight. This was institutional credibility being rented out to corporate warfare while maintaining the aesthetic of objectivity.

Then there's the financial manipulation—not alleged, not suspected, but documented and explained by those who profit from it. Jim Cramer, speaking to The Street's audience in a video that would later surface publicly, described his methods for exploiting Apple's product cycles with the casual precision of someone explaining a proven recipe.

He seeded false rumors systematically. First, that the iPhone would launch on all carriers—knowing that every major US phone before it had been carrier-exclusive, making the claim implausible but exciting. Then, more specifically, that Verizon would carry it—when Apple had no such deal in place and no public indication one was being negotiated.

When AT&T exclusivity was finally announced, reality contradicting the manufactured speculation, the stock dipped. Traders who'd positioned themselves short made money on the "disappointment." Profits followed confusion. The confusion had been engineered.

Cramer was remarkably explicit about the ethics of this approach: "You can't foment... That's a violation. You can't create yourself an impression that a stock is down. But you do it anyway because the SEC doesn't understand it." The admission is worth parsing. He acknowledges the illegality, describes the action, then explains that enforcement is unlikely because regulators lack the sophistication to recognize the pattern.

Later in the same video: "It's important to get people talking as if something is wrong... Then you call the Wall Street Journal and feed the reporter inaccurate information." Note the mechanism: create the narrative through rumor, then launder it through institutional credibility by feeding it to reporters who trust their sources without verification. The lie becomes news. The news becomes truth. The truth becomes tradeable.

His stated goal? "Beleaguer all the moron longs"—meaning, punish the investors foolish enough to believe in a company's fundamentals rather than trading on manufactured volatility. His method? "Foment an impression that Research In Motion isn't any good... It might cost me fifteen to twenty million to knock RIM down, but it would be fabulous."

This isn't speculation about market manipulation. It's confession, on camera, by a prominent financial media figure. And it reveals the machinery: creating false narratives costs money, but the returns from exploiting the confusion are "fabulous." The ethics are irrelevant. The legality is manageable. The profitability is sufficient.

This happens routinely, and the timing is telling. Apple faces particularly aggressive rumor campaigns during its SEC-mandated quiet periods—the windows before earnings announcements when the company cannot legally respond to false claims. The silence isn't strategic. It's regulatory. And it creates opportunity for those willing to exploit it.

In April 2013, the pattern played out with clockwork precision. Analysts predicted catastrophic iPhone sales drops—specific numbers, grave implications, market-moving claims—one day before Apple's earnings call. The stock declined on the prediction. Positions were taken.

The next day, Apple reported 37.4 million iPhones sold, up from 35.1 million in the same quarter the previous year. Not a catastrophic drop. Growth. The analysts had been precisely, measurably wrong. Yet there were no corrections, no accountability, no consequences. The narrative had served its purpose. The trades had closed. The next rumor cycle was already beginning.

The pattern persists not despite being repeatedly disproven, but because being disproven doesn't matter. The word "beleaguered" appears in headline after headline not because it accurately describes a company that's been profitable for decades, but because it's useful. Because in the attention economy, "man bites dog" generates clicks. "Dog does its job exceptionally well for twenty consecutive years" does not.

The incentives are clear. The mechanisms are documented. The only question is whether you recognize the pattern when you're inside it.

The Real Lesson

This is not about Apple. It is about you.

Every leader who builds something meaningful will face the same chorus: too big to sustain, too bold to last, too human to scale. The playbook is identical—invent a crisis, amplify it as fact, profit from the reaction. The mechanics don't change. Only the names.

So when the noise rises, and it will rise at the moment you can least afford distraction, plant your feet and ask three questions:

Who benefits if I believe this? Follow the money, not the metaphor. Is the critic selling something you don't have? Do they profit from your doubt? Does their business model require you to fail? Skepticism presented as insight often conceals incentives. Find them.

What are people doing, not saying? Look at behavior, not rhetoric. Are users staying or leaving? Are teams engaged or updating résumés? Are creators building on your platform or routing around it? Actions reveal truth. Words create narratives. Choose which to trust accordingly.

Is this data or drama? Data is specific, testable, repeatable. Drama is vague, urgent, and always conveniently timed. "Sales are projected to disappoint" is drama—unfalsifiable, emotionally charged, strategically ambiguous.

"Sales were 37.4 million units, up 6.5% year-over-year" is data—specific, verifiable, discussable. Learn to distinguish them instantly, because those who profit from confusion will always prefer drama to data.

The Fingerprints of Real Crisis

Real crisis has fingerprints. It leaves evidence you can examine, test, and trace to source.

It shows up in specific problems. Not "things are bad" but "revenue dropped 40% in Q3, driven by the loss of two enterprise contracts and delayed renewals from three others." The specificity matters because vagueness protects bad analysis while precision invites scrutiny and enables response.

It appears in measurable impacts. Not "morale is low" but "voluntary turnover increased from 5% to 23% in six months, concentrated in our product and engineering teams, with exit interviews citing unclear direction and repeated priority changes." Numbers don't lie, but they can be ignored. Don't ignore them.

It reveals observable causes. Not "the market is changing" but "three major customers switched to competitors after we missed two consecutive delivery commitments and they lost trust in our roadmap." Root causes exist. Finding them requires honesty about what actually happened rather than what we wish had happened.

And it creates consistent patterns. Not one bad data point you can explain away, but a trend you can trace backward to understand its origins and forward to predict its trajectory. One quarter might be noise. Three quarters is signal. Six quarters is a system problem that's been visible for a year while leadership debated whether it was real.

Circus has lighting too, but it's designed to distract rather than illuminate.

It relies on vague assertions like "experts say" or "sources indicate" or "analysts believe" without naming anyone who can be held accountable for the claim. Anonymous authority isn't authority. It's rhetoric wearing a lab coat. When no one owns the assertion, no one can be wrong, which means the assertion isn't designed to be true, only to be repeated.

It uses selective framing that highlights every negative while burying every positive, creating the impression of trajectory through editorial choice rather than factual analysis. A company that grew revenue 15% but missed analyst expectations by 2% gets framed as "disappointing," while the growth itself becomes a footnote. The frame becomes the story.

It manufactures urgency with demands to "act now" before "crisis looms" and "time runs out," creating pressure to decide before you can think. Urgency prevents analysis. That's its purpose. Real problems persist long enough to be examined. Manufactured problems evaporate under scrutiny, which is why they demand immediate action.

And it shifts narratives constantly while the conclusion of doom, failure, and decline never changes, revealing the agenda behind the analysis. When the story changes but the verdict doesn't, you're not watching analysis adapt to evidence. You're watching theater maintain its theme regardless of facts. The narrative serves the conclusion. The conclusion doesn't follow from evidence.

What Steve Actually Did

Steve did not respond to every critic equally. He had a filter.

Criticism from users with skin in the game got immediate attention. When developers complained about App Store approval processes, Apple iterated. When designers found workflow friction in Final Cut, teams investigated. When customers reported actual problems, resources moved. Not preferences, but problems.

Criticism from competitors and analysts got results as response. When critics said the iPod would fail, he didn't debate market size projections. He sold 100 million units. When analysts predicted the iPhone would flop, he didn't argue about keyboard necessity. He shipped and let adoption speak. The answer wasn't words. It was evidence that accumulated until the question became irrelevant.

Criticism designed to generate attention got silence. The manufactured scandals, the breathless predictions, the concern-trolling disguised as analysis received no oxygen. Steve engaged not because he was above criticism, but because engaging would validate the premise that these deserved engagement.

The distinction matters: respond to problems, ignore theater.

Problems come with specifics: "This workflow takes twelve steps when it should take three." Theater comes with vagaries: "Experts say Apple is losing its way." Problems come from people who've tried to use what you built. Theater comes from people who profit from your doubt. Problems persist whether you acknowledge them or not. Theater evaporates when you stop feeding it attention.

The framework is simple. Does this criticism come from someone who's tried to accomplish something real with what we've built? Respond. Does it come with specific, testable claims we can verify or refute? Investigate. Does it come from someone whose business model requires us to fail? Ignore.

This isn't about being defensive or dismissive. It's about allocating attention to signal rather than noise, because attention is finite and the noise is infinite.

Where This Shows Up in Your World

This pattern isn't limited to public companies under media scrutiny. It shows up inside organizations anytime real change threatens what people have grown comfortable with.

The mechanics shift slightly. External headlines become internal memos. Named critics become "anonymous concerns." Public predictions become whispered campaigns. But the structure remains identical: manufacture ambiguity, amplify through informal channels, create pressure to abandon what's working before results can accumulate.

The same diagnostic applies. Is it specific or vague? Data or feelings? Names or "people are saying"? The answers reveal whether you're facing legitimate resistance worth addressing or theater designed to protect the status quo.

Now let's talk about what happens after you've distinguished signal from noise. Knowing the difference means nothing if you don't act differently based on what you've learned.

Blinded By the 'Night'

"A liar knows that he is a liar, but one who speaks mere portions of truth in order to deceive is a craftsman of destruction." — Criss Jami

Some critics don't misunderstand Apple. They choose to. They extract statements, strip context, impute motive, then present the reconstruction as discovery. This represents performance art masquerading as journalism, executed by professionals who mistake cynicism for sophistication.

They miss premises, not merely conclusions. They overlook the soil, the light, the tending hands while searching for the forest. They see surfaces and declare depths, then critique Apple for the shallowness they themselves projected.

The iPhone keynote demonstrates this pattern perfectly. When Steve unveiled the device in January 2007, skepticism was reasonable. The claims were extraordinary, and extraordinary claims deserve scrutiny. What followed went beyond reasonable skepticism into suspicion manufactured from whole cloth.

The Manufactured Crisis

Computerworld's Mike Elgan published "How Steve Jobs Blew His iPhone Keynote," building his case on one central point: Apple announced the phone six months before shipping it. To Elgan, this proved desperation rather than transparency.

Elgan constructed three theories to explain the early announcement, each more elaborate than the last, each requiring Apple to be playing chess while he called the moves. His first theory claimed Apple rushed the announcement to avoid looking like it copied the LG KE850, a phone announced days earlier. This required ignoring that the iPhone had been in development for years, that it began as the iPad project before pivoting to phones, and that the two devices shared nothing beyond a touchscreen. Saying they were similar because both had touchscreens is like saying every car copies every other car because they all have steering wheels.

His second theory suggested Steve used the launch to distract from an SEC inquiry into stock option backdating, a questionable practice that was common across the industry at the time and had nothing to do with product development timelines. The logic went: Apple faces unrelated legal scrutiny, therefore this product announcement must be a diversion. The connection existed only in the proximity of headlines.

The third theory proposed Apple added the iPhone to the agenda to hide what Elgan called the "weak product," the Apple TV. This required believing that Apple would unveil one of the most significant consumer products in decades as misdirection for a set-top box, like using a symphony to drown out a squeaky door.

When none of these theories gained traction, Elgan settled on a final explanation: "Maybe the motive was good old fashioned FUD—Fear, Uncertainty, and Denial." Except Apple doesn't use FUD.

FUD is what you deploy when you can't compete on merit. It means announcing products you never ship to freeze competitor sales. It means promising features you'll remove before launch to make alternatives look inadequate. It means creating uncertainty about competitors to drive customers back to the familiar.

Microsoft did this routinely in the 1990s, announcing vaporware to kill competitor momentum, then delivering something different years later or not at all. Apple's pattern ran opposite: under-promise and over-deliver, announce only when ready to ship, let the product speak rather than the speculation.

The Actual Explanation

Steve had explained the timing plainly during the keynote itself, though plainness apparently wasn't interesting enough to report accurately. The iPhone required FCC approval, a regulatory process that takes months and makes all submitted materials public record once filed. Leaks were inevitable. Apple faced a choice: control the narrative by announcing before filing, or let the narrative form through leaked FCC documents, partial information, and competitor speculation.

They chose transparency over secrecy, full story over fragmented leaks. They announced what they'd built, explained when it would ship, and let people decide whether to wait for it. This was the opposite of FUD. It was clarity about what existed and when it would be available.

What Elgan demonstrated wasn't unique to him or to Apple coverage. The method repeats across domains: ignore the stated explanation, construct a more cynical alternative, then present the construction as insight that the naive public missed.

The same pattern appeared with Apple TV. Steve called it a "hobby," describing it as an experiment rather than a flagship product. "We haven't fully cracked the code," he said, "but we want to learn." Critics interpreted this honesty as failure, as though admitting uncertainty about an emerging category was weakness rather than intellectual honesty about developmental state. They wanted either bold claims Apple couldn't support or silence until perfection. Candor about exploration wasn't a permissible option in their framework.

This isn't about defending Apple or attacking critics. It's about recognizing a pattern that will target anyone building something meaningful. When you announce early to prevent leaks from controlling your narrative, critics will say you're manufacturing hype. When you acknowledge uncertainty about new territory, they'll call it admission of failure. When you explain timing based on regulatory requirements, they'll invent darker motives because dark motives make better stories.

The method is consistent: reject the simple explanation, construct a complex alternative that assumes bad faith, then declare the complexity evidence of sophistication. Call stated reasons naive. Call invented motives insight. Collect the attention.

You cannot prevent this. You can only recognize it and refuse to let it redirect your attention from work to defense, from building to debating, from results to rhetoric.

The Real Pattern

This isn't about one article or one critic. It's about a method that repeats with such consistency it reveals itself as formula: ignore the stated reason, construct a darker alternative, then declare the construction more plausible than plain truth simply because cynicism sounds smarter than credulity.

The logic is circular but effective: "They say X, but that's what they would say if the real reason were Y. Therefore Y is more likely." The stated explanation gets dismissed as PR. The invented explanation gets elevated to insight. And the invention always skews negative because negativity signals sophistication in a way that taking people at their word does not.

This method dominates because drama sells. Complexity doesn't. Nuance requires patience. Conspiracies require only suspicion.

A leader who says "we're still learning" gets labeled indecisive, as though admitting uncertainty about genuinely uncertain territory were weakness rather than intellectual honesty. The alternative—false confidence masquerading as vision—gets praised as leadership until it collides with reality and produces spectacular failure. But by then the critics have moved on to their next target.

A team that ships late to get it right gets called incompetent, as though the discipline to refuse compromise were the same as inability to execute. Meanwhile, teams that ship on time with half-built features get praised for agility until customers discover the gaps and leave. But the quarterly earnings call celebrating the on-time ship happens before the customer churn shows up in retention data.

A company that refuses to overpromise gets deemed unambitious, as though restraint in claims were evidence of limitation in capability. The alternative—announcing vaporware to manipulate markets and freeze competitor sales—gets called strategic until the promised products never materialize and trust evaporates. But the stock price often moves on the announcement, not the delivery, so the incentive structure rewards the promise more than the performance.

The hidden cost of these perverse incentives throughout business culture. Leaders learn to overpromise because underpromising gets punished as lack of vision. Teams learn to ship incomplete because delay gets punished as incompetence. Companies learn to manufacture certainty because admitting uncertainty gets punished as weakness.

The result: a business environment where bold lies outperform cautious truths, where confidence matters more than competence, where the appearance of momentum matters more than the reality of progress.

And when the lies collapse, when the false confidence meets reality, when the appearance of momentum reveals itself as theater, the same critics who rewarded the behavior then savage the failure. The incentives never correct because the people creating them face no consequences for being wrong.

Coherence cannot be rushed. Trust cannot be faked. Truth spoken plainly rarely fits a headline.

But over time, coherence compounds while chaos cancels itself out. Trust, once established through consistent delivery, survives skepticism that would destroy reputations built on hype. And plain truth, boring though it may be in the moment, accumulates into track records that speak louder than any headline.

The question isn't whether you can avoid the cynical method. You can't—it's too profitable for those deploying it and too embedded in how attention gets allocated. The question is whether you'll let it shape your behavior, whether you'll start overpromising because underpromising gets punished, whether you'll manufacture certainty because admitting uncertainty gets called weakness.

Steve refused. He announced when ready, admitted when uncertain, and let results accumulate until they were undeniable. The critics stayed loud for years. The results eventually drowned them out.

That's the choice: play to the critics and build on sand, or ignore them and build on stone. The first gets you better headlines. The second gets you better outcomes.

The Craftsman of Destruction

In observing teams building systems under public scrutiny, I've learned to identify intellectual saboteurs by a singular tell: they never ask "What problem is this solving?" They ask only "What motive can I assign?"

The distinction is everything. The first question seeks to understand function and context—why this choice over alternatives, what tradeoffs were considered, what constraints shaped the decision. It's diagnostic. It assumes the people building things are attempting to solve actual problems and wants to understand whether the solution fits the problem.

The second question bypasses all of that. It assumes bad faith from the start, then works backward to construct evidence. The solution doesn't matter. The problem doesn't matter. Only the imagined motive matters, because the motive is the story.

This manifests with remarkable consistency across contexts.

A leader articulates difficult tradeoffs with transparent reasoning such as "We chose A over B because our customers prioritize X over Y, and our data shows Z", and critics bypass the logic entirely to speculate about hidden agendas. "They chose A because it benefits their bonus structure" or "because it protects their legacy system" or "because they're afraid of the disruption B would cause." The stated reasoning gets dismissed as cover story. The invented motive gets treated as revelation.

A team postpones a launch to resolve quality concerns like finding issues in testing that could affect reliability at scale and critics reframe prudence as coverup. "They're delaying because the product isn't what they promised" or "because early feedback was negative" or "because they're scrambling to match a competitor's announcement." The quality concerns get ignored. The speculation becomes the story.

A company acknowledges uncertainty about a nascent initiative—"We're exploring this space but haven't found product-market fit yet"—and critics transmute candor into incompetence. "They admitted they don't know what they're doing" or "they revealed they're behind competitors" or "they confessed the initiative is failing." The honesty about exploration gets weaponized as admission of failure.

The method never varies: substitute stated intent with imagined motive, then elevate the fabrication to discovery.

Call it insight. Frame it as seeing what others miss. Present it as courage to speak truth the powerful want hidden. Package it as accountability journalism or tough analysis or refusing to take PR at face value.

Collect the clicks. Build the personal brand. Move to the next target when this one stops generating attention.

The saboteur benefits regardless of accuracy because the incentive structure rewards the accusation, not the truth of it. Being provocative drives engagement. Being right is optional. Being boring is fatal. So the method optimizes for provocation over accuracy, for attention over understanding.

And the damage accumulates not just in the specific target, but in the broader culture. Leaders learn that transparency invites attack. Teams learn that admitting uncertainty gets weaponized. Companies learn that candor about tradeoffs becomes ammunition for critics who profit from suspicion.

So they stop being transparent. They stop admitting uncertainty. They stop being candid about tradeoffs. They learn to speak only in polished PR language that reveals nothing, admits nothing, commits to nothing.

The saboteurs call this victory. "See, they're hiding something!", never admitting they created the behavior they critique. The incentive was always toward opacity. They just accelerated it.

The Three Anchors

When critics construct elaborate theories about hidden motives, when speculation drowns out stated reasoning, when cynicism masquerades as sophistication, return to three anchors that separate signal from theater:

Anchor One: The Stated Intent

Did the leader explain their reasoning? Not just what they decided, but why they decided it, what constraints they faced, what tradeoffs they considered?

Steve did. The iPhone announcement came six months early because FCC requirements meant the design would become public record once filed. Apple faced a choice: control the narrative by announcing before filing, or let the narrative form through leaked regulatory documents, partial specs, and wild speculation. They chose transparency about what they'd built and when it would ship.

That's not manipulation. That's not hype. That's honesty about regulatory constraints and the decision to address them directly rather than hide from inevitable leaks. The stated intent was clear, specific, and testable. Either leaks would have happened or they wouldn't. They would have.

Yet critics ignored this explanation entirely to construct theories about diversion tactics, competitive maneuvering, and manufactured FUD. The stated reason was boring. The invented reasons were interesting. So the invented reasons got published.

Anchor Two: The Pattern of Action

Does this decision align with past behavior? Do they have a track record that supports or contradicts the stated intent?

Apple ships what it promises. The iPhone took six months from announcement to delivery, but it shipped exactly as descr bed, with the features announced, at the price stated. No bait and switch. No vaporware. No features quietly removed or delayed to future versions.

Companies that use FUD announce products they never deliver, promise features they can't build, create uncertainty about competitors with claims they can't support. Apple's pattern runs opposite: announce late, ship what you show, under-promise and over-deliver. This has been consistent for decades.

Yet critics treated the early announcement as evidence of FUD tactics despite Apple having no history of such tactics and a clear pattern of doing the opposite. The absence of supporting evidence didn't weaken the theory. It just made the theory more elaborate: "They're changing their strategy" or "This proves they're desperate."

Anchor Three: The Alternative Cost

What would happen if they didn't make this decision? What would the alternative cost?

If Apple stayed silent until June, several things would have happened with certainty: Leaks would have occurred anyway once FCC filing became public record. Competitors would have had six months to prepare counter-announcements and marketing campaigns. Media would have speculated wildly based on incomplete information, potentially setting expectations Apple couldn't meet or creating cor fusion about what the product actually was.

The early announcement protected the product launch by establishing accurate expectations, protected the team by giving them a clear timeline everyone understood, and protected the truth by ensuring the full story came from Apple rather than fragmentary leaks filtered through speculation.

The alternative was staying silent. That carried higher risk of miscommunication, competitor maneuvering, and market confusion. The decision wasn't perfect. It was better than the alternative. Which is what good decisions usually are.

Yet critics evaluated the announcement against an imaginary perfect scenario where secrecy somehow worked, leaks never happened, and competitors stayed frozen while Apple prepared in silence. That scenario never existed. Comparing the actual decision to an impossible alternative is how you make every decision look wrong.

How This Shows Up in Your World

You don't need to be launching the iPhone to face this pattern. Every honest admission becomes ammunition when critics optimize for cynicism over understanding.

You tell your team: "We're trying a new approach, and we'll learn as we go." You're being honest about exploration. This is genuinely new territory, and discovering the right path requires experimentation.

Critics hear: "They have no plan. They're making it up as they go along. Leadership doesn't know what they're doing."

You explain: "We're delaying the launch to get it right." You're exercising discipline. Shipping broken work creates problems that compound, and taking time now prevents crisis later.

Critics declare: "The project is failing. They're in crisis mode. The delay proves they built the wrong thing and are scrambling to fix it."

You admit: "We don't have all the answers yet, but we're committed to figuring it out." You're being candid about uncertainty—this problem is complex, simple solutions don't exist, and intellectual honesty requires acknowledging what you don't know.

Critics conclude: "Leadership is incompetent. They're lost. They're admitting they don't know what they're doing, which means the initiative will fail."

Notice the pattern: honesty becomes evidence of weakness, complexity becomes proof of confusion, humility becomes admission of failure.

Not because that's what you said. But because that's what fits the narrative critics want to tell. And the narrative they want to tell is always more dramatic than the truth, because drama generates attention and attention generates reward.

The inversion is complete: the very qualities that make for good leadership such as honesty about uncertainty, discipline in execution, and humility about limits, get weaponized as evidence of bad leadership by people who profit from suspicion.

You cannot prevent this inversion. You can only recognize it and refuse to let it change your behavior. Because the alternative of false confidence, premature shipping, and manufactured certainty might generate better headlines, but it produces worse outcomes.

The question isn't whether critics will twist your words. They will. The question is whether you'll stop being honest because honesty gets twisted. Steve didn't. He kept explaining reasoning, kept shipping what he promised, kept being candid about uncertainty.

The critics stayed loud for years. The results eventually made them irrelevant.

The Light Arrives

Steve didn't defeat his critics with rhetoric. He obsoleted them with results.

The theories about LG phones, stock options, and weak products all proven absurdly wrong by a device that redefined mobile computing. The critics weren't seeing darkness. They were closing their eyes and insisting the sun wasn't rising.

Six months after the announcement, the iPhone shipped exactly as promised. No features missing. No specifications changed. No apologies required. The only answer that mattered was the one sitting in customers' hands.

The craftsmen of destruction will always be there, finding dark motives in clear statements, inventing conspiracy where there's only complexity. Your job isn't to convince them. Your job is to build something that makes their theories irrelevant. Not by arguing. By arriving.

But there's another type of critic entirely—one that doesn't even bother with elaborate theories or manufactured suspicion. They simply declare things impossible or inevitable based on nothing more than the confidence in their voice. These are the Know-It-Alls and the Not-at-Alls, and they're about to tell you everything they're certain about despite knowing nothing at all.

Know-It-Alls & Not-At-Alls

"I won't insult your intelligence by suggesting that you really believe what you just said." — William F. Buckley Jr.

In most fields, credibility depends on accuracy. In technology punditry, it often depends on volume. You can be wrong for years, repeatedly and publicly, yet still be quoted as an authority. Your main qualification is familiarity with yesterday. Your task is predicting tomorrow. The work is performance, not analysis, where confidence outweighs correction and narrative trumps data.

When rewriting history doesn't work, the next defense is discrediting those who notice.

The Pattern of Perpetual Wrongness

Consider one of the most cited firms in tech: Gartner. In March 2009, it declared the PC industry would suffer the sharpest unit decline in history. By November, it reversed course. Worldwide PC shipments would grow 2.8 percent. By January 2010, it was forecasting the strongest growth rate in seven years. Three positions. Ten months. Zero accountability.

The pattern continues beyond single predictions. In 2005, Gartner predicted Windows Mobile 5 would dominate the smartphone market, just as BlackBerry held firm and iPhone loomed. Windows Mobile's share kept shrinking. In 2011, the firm forecast Microsoft's WP7 would grow by over 1,790 percent in five years, faster than Android, faster than iPhone, faster than its own prior Windows Mobile prediction. WP7 vanished instead.

Why such swings? Gartner, like many firms, is a participant in the market rather than merely an observer. During Microsoft's antitrust trial, internal memos revealed Microsoft paid Gartner hundreds of thousands of dollars in the late 1990s and lobbied it to praise Windows NT while downplaying rivals. The metric was influence, not accuracy.

Rewriting History in Real Time

When present predictions fail, the industry pivots to rewriting the past. A 2013 Bloomberg headline declared: "Samsung Girds for Life After Apple in Disruption." The subhead read "Goodbye, Old Fruit," claiming Samsung had "zoomed past Apple in the smartphone market that the US company pioneered." Samsung was already selling smartphones before 2007, devices like the BlackJack with small keypads and physical keyboards, just like BlackBerry. When the iPhone launched, pundit John Dvorak scoffed: "It's trending against what people are really liking in phones nowadays."

Apple redefined the market rather than entering an existing one. Yet the narrative was being flipped: Samsung became the disrupter while Apple, the actual pioneer, became the legacy player. This represents intentional revisionism designed to soften the cognitive dissonance of a world that keeps choosing simplicity over specs, coherence over choice. Just because our example is in the past doesn't mean the dynamic is any different in 2025.

When rewriting history doesn't work, the next defense is discrediting those who notice.

The Fanboy Label

When rewriting history doesn't work, the next defense is discrediting those who notice. The "fanboy" label typically gets applied to those who observe accurately and speak truths that dispel fake narratives, rather than to those who cheer blindly. When a source consistently notes Apple's growth because the data shows it, they get dismissed as biased. Meanwhile, those who predicted Microsoft's eternal dominance through Windows Vista's collapse, Zune's failure, and WP7's implosion remain credible, fair, and trusted voices.

An ecosystem built itself around one truth for over a decade: Microsoft is inevitable. Apple was beleaguered. Doomed. Irrelevant. When Google Android entered the conversation, it became the new darling hero-killer of the press for many years. Every day brought another prediction of Apple's imminent collapse in the phone market. Slews of fake stories flooded the air: "Only old people want iPhones." "Next year Apple will leave the phone market."

Apple persisted. Writers, consultants, and analysts had built their livelihoods on predictions that were always right on the money during Steve's absence. But when Steve returned, reality and narrative were clearly at odds. Apple shipped the iMac. The iPod. The iPhone. The iPad. Profits rose. Users stayed. Developers flocked. To many in the tech press, this represented heresy rather than progress. When the emperor has no clothes but everyone has built careers describing his robes, admitting the truth costs more than being wrong.

But this ecosystem of wrongness didn't emerge by accident. It was deliberately cultivated.

The FUD Machine and Its Guardians

This ecosystem of wrongness didn't emerge by accident. It was deliberately cultivated. Microsoft's strategy for decades extended beyond products into FUD: Fear, Uncertainty, Doubt. When a rival shipped something better, Microsoft held a press conference and announced a future product with mockups, lofty specs, and a distant timeline. They made the competition look obsolete before it shipped. Consumers waited. Microsoft rarely delivered. But the cycle repeated because no one wanted to admit the emperor was naked.

A class of commentators emerged to curry favor with Microsoft. Their job was protecting the narrative rather than informing readers. They didn't report what was happening. They explained why the competition couldn't win, facts be damned. A decade of rising iPhone sales? Temporary. Fifty-three percent US market share? Anomaly. A trillion dollar valuation? Bubble. But facts accumulate regardless of how inconvenient they are.

How This Shows Up in Your World

You don't need to be Apple to face know-it-alls with terrible track records. Every organization has them: the consultant who's been wrong about every trend for five years but still gets invited to strategy meetings because they worked at a prestigious firm. The analyst who predicted your competitor would dominate but now explains why their failure was actually inevitable, and why yours is coming next. The industry voice who built their reputation on conventional wisdom and attacks anyone who challenges it with dismissive labels rather than data. The internal skeptic who's opposed every successful initiative but frames their track record as "healthy skepticism" rather than consistent wrongness.

These people succeed for reasons that have nothing to do with being right. Certainty sounds like expertise, even when unfounded, so confidence works in their favor. Repeating the same narrative creates the illusion of stability, making consistency valuable. They know the right people, attend the right conferences, use the right jargon, so their connections matter. Nobody tracks their predictions or points out their patterns, which means they're never held accountable.

The most dangerous aspect is how they benefit from your failure. If you succeed despite their predictions, they look foolish. If you fail, they look prescient. Which outcome do you think they're rooting for?

The Three Questions That Expose Them

When someone offers confident predictions or harsh criticism, three questions cut through the noise.

Start with their track record. Not their title. Not their platform. Not their credentials. Their actual history of predictions. Were they right about the last three major shifts in your industry? Or are they still explaining why their wrong predictions were actually right in spirit?

Then examine what they gain if you believe them. Attention? Access? Consulting fees? A seat at a table that requires loyalty to a fading order? Do they profit from maintaining the status quo you're trying to change?

Finally, look at what behavior contradicts their story. They say your initiative is failing. Are users actually leaving? Are your best people checking out? Are metrics declining? Or are they cherry-picking anecdotes while ignoring the overall trend? Actions reveal truth. Narratives reveal agendas.

The Real Pattern

Here's what I've learned working with companies trying to do something different: the loudest critics are often protecting something. Not truth or customers or quality, but the narrative they've built careers on, the status quo they know how to navigate, the conventional wisdom that makes them sound smart. Your potential success threatens their investment because if you succeed doing what they said was impossible, it exposes that they didn't understand what was possible.

Steve did not ignore critics. He studied their patterns and saw the difference between doubt and dogma. Doubt asks questions: "How will this work?" "What are the risks?" Dogma recites scripts: "This can't work." "History proves it's impossible." Doubt helps you refine ideas and strengthen plans. Dogma defends yesterday against tomorrow.

Steve engaged with doubt and ignored dogma. When engineers raised concerns about iPhone's technical feasibility, he listened, then pushed them to solve the problems. When analysts said tablets were dead, he built the iPad and let it speak. When pundits declared Apple's approach unsustainable, he sustained it for fourteen years.

The most powerful thing you can do is not argue with the script but live the next scene coherently, courageously, and without apology. Truth does not need a megaphone. It only needs time.

The know-it-alls predicted the iMac would fail. It saved Apple. They said the iPod was a toy. It sold 400 million units. They declared the iPhone was too expensive. It redefined mobile. They claimed the iPad was useless. It created a category. They insisted Apple couldn't sustain growth. Apple became the most valuable company on Earth.

Every single prediction was wrong. Yet none of them lost their platforms, credibility, or influence. Because accountability isn't the point. Performance is. They're not paid to be right. They're paid to be confident, quotable, and aligned with whoever holds power.

What This Means for You

When you're doing something difficult—transforming systems, changing culture, building something new—you will face know-it-alls. People with impressive credentials and terrible track records. People who speak with certainty about things they don't understand. People who benefit from your failure more than your success. Your job is not to convince them. Your job is to recognize the pattern and let time be your fact-checker.

CHAPTER 9

RETURNING FROM THE POINT OF NO RETURN

Steve and Bill Gates at 'D5: All Things Digital' conference, 2007 - Joe Ito

Returning from the point of no return isn't luck. It is not magic. It is a learnable discipline built from core practices Steve wielded with precision.

He did not rely on one tactic. He moved fluidly across a spectrum: when others declared finality, he reframed. When systems collapsed, he rebooted. When paths vanished, he redrew the map. When momentum stalled, he recommitted publicly and decisively. The key to Apple's revival was not genius. It was flexibility—the willingness to shift approach without losing sight of purpose.

Almost no one believed recovery was possible. Analysts wrote obituaries. Competitors held victory laps. Even insiders whispered: It's over. But Steve and his team heard a different truth: the point of no return is only final if you stop moving.

Let's break down how they walked back from the brink, not in one leap, but in deliberate steps.

Step One: Cancel the Funeral

The first move when everyone declares you dead? Refuse the narrative. Not with arguments. With action.

When Steve returned in 1997, the prevailing wisdom was that Apple was finished. Sell the parts. Return cash to shareholders. Move on. Michael Dell said it publicly: "Shut it down and give the money back.

Steve's response wasn't a rebuttal. It was a refusal. He didn't say "You're wrong about us." He said "We're going to make the best computers in the world." That statement—audacious to the point of delusion for a company ninety days from bankruptcy—did something critical: it declared Apple still had agency. Not survival as the goal. Excellence as the goal.

That reframe changed everything. Because once you accept the narrative of inevitable decline, you've already lost. Every decision becomes about managing the fall rather than building the climb.

What This Looks Like in Your World

You don't need to be ninety days from bankruptcy to face a funeral narrative. It happens whenever a major initiative fails and leadership starts talking about "lessons learned" instead of next steps. When market share slips and the conversation shifts from "how do we win" to "how do we stabilize." When a competitor launches something better and everyone assumes you're now playing catch-up forever. When key people leave and the whisper network declares the culture is broken.

The funeral narrative has a script: "It's over." "The best we can do is manage decline gracefully." "Let's be realistic about our limitations." "Maybe it's time to pivot to something else."

Canceling the funeral means refusing that script. Not "Let's stabilize" but "Let's build what we should have built all along." Not "Let's be realistic" but "Let's be honest about what's actually possible." Not "Let's manage decline" but "Let's redefine what success looks like." The funeral only happens if you attend.

Step Two: Getting Off the Mat

Refusing the narrative is step one. But you still have to stand up.

When Steve returned, Apple wasn't just failing—it was fractured. Fifteen product lines. No coherent strategy. A board that had cycled through three CEOs in a decade. Getting off the mat meant doing the hard work nobody wanted to do: replacing the board with people who believed, rebuilding the executive team with A-players, cutting 70% of products to restore focus, securing the Microsoft deal everyone hated but Apple needed, making decisions that were right but unpopular.

This is where most turnarounds fail. Leaders refuse the funeral narrative (good), but they try to get up without changing anything fundamental (fatal). They want recovery without restructuring. Growth without pain. Transformation without loss. It doesn't work.

Getting off the mat requires you to acknowledge what's actually broken and fix it—even when fixing it means admitting past decisions were wrong, removing people who can't execute the new direction, cutting things people love because they dilute focus, making choices that look harsh in the moment but create space for excellence.

What This Looks Like in Your World

Getting off the mat means answering honestly: What's actually broken? Not what's inconvenient—what's fundamentally not working? Who needs to be in different roles? Not who you wish could do it—who can actually do it? What needs to be cut? Not trimmed—eliminated entirely? What do we need to secure even if it's uncomfortable? The Microsoft deal was humiliating but necessary.

Most organizations know these answers. They just won't act on them because it would require admitting they were wrong, upset people they like, contradict what they said last quarter, or look like failure before it looks like progress. But you can't get off the mat while carrying the weight of everything that put you there.

Step Three: Choose Your Adventure

Once you're standing, you have to choose a direction. Not a defensive direction ("protect what we have"). An offensive direction ("build what should exist").

Steve didn't choose to make slightly better Macs. He chose to make the best computers in the world. That choice determined everything else: which features to include, which partnerships to pursue, which markets to ignore, which standards to hold. When your goal is "best," you make different choices than when your goal is "good enough."

What This Looks Like in Your World

Choosing your adventure means deciding: Are we trying to survive (do whatever keeps us alive), compete (match what others are doing), or lead (define what others should do)? Most organizations claim they want to lead but make decisions like they're trying to survive.

The test is in the tradeoffs. When something is good enough but not excellent, do you ship it or rebuild it? When a customer asks for a feature that would dilute your focus, do you say yes or no? When a competitor launches something flashy, do you copy it or trust your direction? When hitting the numbers requires cutting corners, do you cut them or miss the numbers?

Your stated adventure is your words. Your actual adventure is your choices. Steve chose "best computers in the world." Then he made every subsequent choice through that filter. That's not vision. That's discipline.

Step Four: Act Accordingly

Step Four: Act Accordingly

Once you've chosen your adventure, the hardest part begins: acting like it's already true.

This is the audacity that separates recovery from collapse. When you're ninety days from bankruptcy, when the press has written you off, when your own people doubt the plan—you have to act as if you've already won.

Not delusion. Not denial. Strategic commitment to the future you're building rather than the present you're escaping.

Steve didn't wait for Apple to become excellent before demanding excellence. He didn't wait for stability before making bold moves. He didn't wait for permission before acting like Apple was already what he intended it to become: the best computer company in the world.

It is easy to convince yourself you've fallen too far. That the hole is too deep, the climb too steep, and the cost too high. So let's look at how Steve handled it—the audacity of acting as if.

What This Looks Like in Your World

The final practice is persistence. Not stubbornness—continuing despite evidence you're wrong—but persistence: continuing despite evidence it's hard.

Apple's turnaround took years. There were profitable quarters and unprofitable ones. Successes and failures. The G4 Cube. The first Apple TV. MobileMe. Steve kept moving. Not because every step succeeded, but because stopping meant accepting the point of no return.

Keeping moving means that when something fails, you learn and adjust rather than abandon the mission. When progress slows, you examine obstacles rather than question the direction. When critics multiply, you check your data rather than your narrative. When you're tired, you find ways to sustain rather than reasons to quit.

The point of no return is only final if you stop. As long as you're moving—learning, adapting, building, trying—you haven't returned to it. You're walking away from it. One step at a time.

Cancel the Funeral

Between January 1995 and 2018, Apple had been declared dead seventy-one times, according to the Apple Death Knell Counter. That's not spin. That's the count, tracked, updated, and undeniable.

But the first funeral was held in the summer of 1997. Apple hadn't even flatlined yet, but the press had already wheeled it into the morgue. They strode right into the emergency room and started the service. One by one, they straightened their ties, adjusted their lapel mics, and took the podium like pallbearers at a state funeral.

The Eulogy Begins

Fortune led the eulogy: "By the time you read this story, the quirky cult company will end its wild ride as an independent enterprise." A Forrester Research analyst stepped up, feigned a catch in his throat, and choked out: "Whether they stand alone, or are acquired, Apple as we know it is cooked. It's so classic. It's so sad."

Microsoft's Chief Technology Officer couldn't hide his glee: "The NeXT purchase is too little, too late. Apple is already dead." A software developer leaned over, whispering fiercely to a quietly colluding Financial Times reporter: "The idea that they're going to go back to the past to hit a big home run is delusional."

The organ player hit the first few notes. The choir stood. The lead vocalist cleared her throat and began to step to the mic. And then Steve stepped in front of her. Asked her, politely, to take a seat. He had heard enough.

The Interruption

He pointed to the truth no one wanted to see: Apple was in the Emergency Room. Not the grave. Injured. Bleeding. But breathing.

"What if Apple didn't exist?" he asked. "Think about it. TIME wouldn't get published next week. Seventy percent of the newspapers in the US wouldn't publish tomorrow morning. Sixty percent of the kids wouldn't have computers. Sixty-four percent of the teachers wouldn't. More than half the websites created on Macs wouldn't exist. So there's something worth saving here."

· · ·

THE CROWD SHIFTED in their chairs. Confused. Disoriented. Wasn't this a funeral? they thought. Where were the words 'beleaguered'? 'Doomed'? 'Dead'?

Steve smiled. He understood. Even he had nearly given up just two months earlier. He'd sold nearly all the Apple stock he'd received in the four hundred twenty-four million dollar NeXT deal. "Yes, I sold the shares," he admitted, a tinge of embarrassment in his voice. "I pretty much had given up hope that the Apple board was going to do anything." He had kept one share and a shred of hope.

Building Common Ground, Then Breaking the Spell

He built common ground. Then he broke the spell. "We've reviewed the road map of new products and axed more than seventy percent of the projects," he said. "Keeping the thirty percent that were gems. Plus, we're adding new ones. A whole new paradigm of looking at computers. The product teams at Apple are very excited. There's so much low-hanging fruit. It's easy to turn around."

Thanks for the flowers, he was saying. But Apple's not kicking the bucket today. Definitely not from a bad case of Influenza.

He laid out the road to recovery: "Apple's been executing very well, but on the wrong things." A second opinion had been sought. Dr. Gil Amelio was no longer the attending physician. The new prescription? A new board. Renewed focus. Core assets could be restored.

He even laughed at the irony: Apple's planned OS update had been code-named 'Requiem,' a musical mass for the dead. No wonder people got the wrong idea!

Then he listed the vitals: more than twenty million active Mac users, thousands of developers, a thriving one point five billion dollar Mac software industry. He was fired up. The crowd was hanging on every word. The doom and gloom? Kicked to the curb.

The Final Word

When someone piped up about Michael Dell's early eulogy that had been major news just weeks before, where he had told media he would "Shut Apple down and return the cash to shareholders," Steve smiled. Three words: "Fuck Michael Dell."

Then the call, direct, final, unapologetic: "If you want to make Apple great again, let's get going. If not? Get the hell out." The funeral was officially canceled. Leave the flowers.

What This Actually Teaches

Steve didn't argue with the narrative. He replaced it. Not with promises. With evidence. Not with vision. With facts.

The company everyone declared dead was publishing 70% of US newspapers, educating 60% of students, creating more than half the websites on the internet, supporting a $1.5 billion software industry, and serving 20 million active users. That's not a corpse. That's a patient.

The difference matters. Because once people accept you're dead, they stop trying to help. They stop investing. They stop believing anything is possible. The funeral narrative is self-fulfilling, but only if you let it proceed.

How This Shows Up in Your World

You don't need to be Apple to face a funeral narrative. It happens whenever a major project fails and leadership starts using past tense: "We were trying to..." instead of "We're working on..." It happens when market position slips and the conversation becomes "How do we manage decline?" instead of "How do we regain ground?" When key people leave and whispers turn to "The culture is broken" instead of "We need to rebuild trust." When a competitor launches something better and everyone assumes "We're now playing catch-up forever" instead of "What's our next move?"

The funeral narrative has stages: shock when something bad happens, resignation where people say "I guess this is over," eulogy where people start talking about what was good "back when," and acceptance where everyone treats it as finished and moves on. Most organizations let this play out. Steve interrupted at stage three.

The Anatomy of Canceling a Funeral

Here's what Steve actually did and what you can do.

First, acknowledge the crisis without accepting the conclusion. Steve didn't say "Everything's fine." He said "We're injured, but we're not dead." That's honest without being defeated. This means saying "Here's the actual problem, and here's why it's solvable" rather than "There's no problem." It means "The plan needs to change, and here's how" rather than "Everything's going according to plan." It means "Here's the evidence we can turn this around" rather than "Just trust me."

Second, replace narrative with facts. Steve listed the vitals: 20 million users, thousands of developers, $1.5 billion software industry. Those aren't spin. They're data. This sounds like "We lost three major clients, but we still have 47 who are growing with us" or "The initiative missed its targets, but we learned X, Y, Z that will make the next one succeed" or "Yes, people are leaving, but retention in our top performers is actually up." Facts interrupt narrative. Use them.

Third, draw a clear line between past and future. Steve replaced the board, cut 70% of projects, changed the roadmap. He didn't say "We'll try harder." He said "We're doing different things." This means "Here are the specific changes we're making" rather than "We're committed to improving." It means "We're going to work differently, here's how" rather than "We're going to work harder." It means "Here's the new timeline and why it's realistic" rather than "Give us more time."

Fourth, make it personal and direct. "If you want to make Apple great again, let's get going. If not? Get the hell out." That's not corporate speak. That's a human being drawing a line. This sounds like "I'm asking you to believe this is possible. If you can't, I understand, but I need people who can" or "This will be hard. If you're not up for hard, now's the time to leave" or "I believe we can do this. I need to know if you believe it too." Authenticity cuts through narrative faster than polish.

The Lesson Is Clear

If you intend to restore yourself or your company to health, start by squashing the perception that you're already dead. Because no amount of strategy works if the world has already buried you.

You can have the perfect plan, but if everyone thinks you're finished, they won't invest in you, partner with you, join you, believe you, or give you time. The funeral narrative kills momentum faster than actual problems do.

When facing your own funeral narrative, ask: Are we actually dead, or are we injured?

If you're actually dead, no customers, no revenue, no team, no path forward, then the funeral might be appropriate. But if you have people who still believe, customers who still value what you do, resources you can redirect, and problems you can actually solve, then you're not dead. You're in the emergency room. And emergency rooms are where recoveries begin.

Steve didn't argue with the critics. He didn't defend Apple's past. He didn't promise miracles. He stated facts. Drew a line. Asked people to choose. Then he got to work. The funeral was canceled. The recovery began. Not because he was eloquent. Because he refused to let narrative replace reality.

Somewhere in your organization (or your competitor's), someone is preparing a eulogy. Maybe it's for a project everyone's given up on. Maybe it's for an initiative that failed. Maybe it's for the company itself.

Before you let them finish, ask: Are we in the emergency room or the morgue? If we're injured, what are the actual vitals? What evidence exists that recovery is possible? What needs to change for that recovery to happen? Who's still willing to do the work?

Then interrupt the funeral. Not with spin, but with facts. Not with promises, but with plans. Not with past tense, but with present action.

And when you send them packing? Tell them to leave the flowers. You'll find a use for them.

You've got work to do.

Stand Up

"Stand up and be counted, or sit your ass in the corner and color." — Lori Goodwin

In 2013, Tim Cook stood onstage at WWDC, pride unmistakable in his voice: "Apple paid ten billion dollars to iOS developers, to date. Five billion of that was in the last year alone. The MacBook is the number one laptop in sales. The number one selling desktop computer in the US is the iMac."

Then the stunner: "The Mac install base doubled in 2012 alone."

After five years of fifteen percent average annual Mac growth, five times the PC industry's three percent average, it's easy to forget how Apple got there.

In 1996, Apple wasn't dead. But it was lying flat on its back. The wind knocked out. Bruised. Barely breathing. Nothing was broken. The bones were intact. All it needed was to stand up.

Two words. Deceptively simple.

The Mechanics of Rising

We think of standing as one motion. A single act. But it's not. It's hundreds of micro decisions. Muscles firing in sequence. Balance recalibrated. Weight shifted. Knees locked. Spine aligned. One misfire and you collapse instead of rise.

Steve understood this instinctively. Recovery is not a leap. It is a cascade, each move small, necessary, timed, essential to the whole. Apple did not get off the mat by cartwheeling. It got up joint by joint, decision by decision.

First: Stop the Fall

Steve's earliest moves weren't about growth. They were about stopping the slide.

The Microsoft deal, misreported as a rescue, was not charity. It was strategy. The day before the announcement, Apple's market cap was two point four six billion dollars. Revenue last quarter: one point seven billion. Cash reserves: one point two billion. Microsoft's one hundred fifty million dollar investment? A drop in the bucket by comparison.

But Steve knew the press would scream: "Microsoft saved Apple!" He let them. Because the new narrative, however distorted, was "Apple was saved." Not "Apple is dying." That mattered more than precision.

Then came Think Different. Not just an ad campaign, but something bordering on a religious revival. Steve wasn't selling to customers. He was reigniting his own people. Reminding engineers, designers, marketers: You built the Mac. You made the impossible feel obvious. That's still in you.

Pride returned. Passion followed. Products improved at breakneck speed.

The iMac, a colorful, all-in-one, impossibly simple machine, sold like hotcakes. The iBook, a game-changing, translucent clamshell, bright as candy, redefined the laptop category and brought wireless internet mainstream. The Power Mac G4, bulletproof glass, workstation power under the hood, proved Apple could still thrill professionals.

Each was a muscle flex. Small. Strong. Coordinated.

Second: Own the Ground

But even great products stumbled at the finish line.

Big box stores were landmines, staffed by Windows loyalists. Trained to steer customers away from Apple even when they walked in wanting a Mac. Eyewitness accounts and online posts at the time told of big box store employees actively taking iMacs out of customers' carts! Can you imagine?

Apple was giving half its retail profit to people actively sabotaging its mission.

Steve saw it. His sales team lived it. He decided to fix it. Not with useless complaints, but with stores. Apple Retail was born.

The reaction? Mockery. (Think about that next time you're standing in an Apple store packed to the gills with people.)

BusinessWeek headlined: "Sorry Steve, here's why the Apple stores won't work." Analysts scoffed: "Dell had stores. Gateway had stores. Sony had stores. What's different?"

They all missed the point entirely.

Dell, Gateway, and Sony all sold Windows PCs. In a Best Buy, no one talked you out of Windows. So a Dell store offered no advantage. But Apple? Its software was the difference. Its ecosystem was the value. Its experience was the product.

In Apple Stores, every demo unit worked. No frozen mice, no crashed apps. The experience was at its best every time. Every employee could explain why the Mac mattered, not just list specs. And they could tailor that to the customer's knowledge needs and how they were going to use the device. Every customer could touch, try, feel the coherence. Nothing sold Apple faster than letting people use Macs without interference.

And when the iPod arrived? The stores were ready. The iPhone? Ready. The iPad? Ready.

These weren't just products. They were invitations to music, to apps, to books. The stores made sure the handshake with the products was warm, certain, and most importantly, human.

Third: Build the Engines

Then came the engines: iTunes Store brought music, movies, dignity for creators. App Store launched the modern gold rush. Practically a new economy, born in a weekend. Ten billion dollars paid to developers. Apple's thirty percent cut was not exploitation, but infrastructure.

Each piece fed the next: better hardware brought more users, more users brought more developers, more developers brought better software, better software brought more hardware sales. No single move saved Apple. The sum did.

What This Actually Teaches

Standing up is terrifying. Not because the act is hard. But because trying is.

You gather yourself. Shift your weight and feel the old bruise flare, forcing you to push past the pain. Will the leg hold this time? You plant your hands. Push. Every tendon alive with the memory of collapse. Will your arms hold or fold?

Many freeze under these circumstances. Convinced the fall was final. Convinced motion is risk and stillness is safety.

Steve gave us another way: Don't leap. Sequence. Don't hope. Build. Don't wait for the world to believe. Move, joint by joint, until you're upright.

You don't need to be Apple to understand the mechanics of standing up. Every turnaround follows the same pattern.

Your Step One: Stop the Fall

Before you can rise, you have to stop sliding. This means securing critical partnerships (even uncomfortable ones), stabilizing cash flow, stopping the talent exodus, changing the narrative from "dying" to "recovering." Not glamorous. Essential.

The Microsoft deal wasn't about the $150 million. It was about changing the story from "Apple is finished" to "Apple has a path forward." Sometimes stopping the fall means accepting help you'd rather not need. Making deals you don't love. Swallowing pride to buy time. Do it anyway.

Your Step Two: Own the Ground

Once you've stopped sliding, you need to control your environment. Apple couldn't fix Best Buy. So they built their own stores.

This means identifying where your value gets lost or sabotaged, taking control of those touchpoints, building direct relationships with customers, creating experiences you can guarantee. Where are you giving control to people who don't share your mission? Maybe it's distribution partners who bundle your product with competitors, implementation consultants who undermine your approach, review sites that misrepresent what you do, or channels where your message gets distorted.

You can't control everything. But you can identify the critical touchpoints and own them.

Your Step Three: Build the Flywheel

Once you control your ground, build systems where success compounds. iTunes made iPods valuable. iPods brought people into stores. Stores introduced them to Macs. Macs led them to iPhones. iPhones led to iPads. Each purchase strengthened the ecosystem.

This means finding ways each win creates capacity for the next, building platforms instead of just products, creating feedback loops where customers bring more customers, investing revenue from today's success into tomorrow's capability. The question isn't "What's the next big thing?" The question is "What systems make each success multiply the next?"

The Sequence That Matters

Here's what most turnarounds get wrong: they try to build the flywheel before stopping the fall. They try to own the ground before they have resources. They try to leap when they should be sequencing.

The order matters. First, stop the fall (stabilize, secure, survive). Second, own the ground (control touchpoints, build direct relationships). Third, build the flywheel (create compounding systems). Skip a step and you collapse. Try to do them simultaneously and you spread resources too thin. Sequence them correctly and each enables the next.

The Real Lesson

Standing up is not a miracle. It is mechanics. And the most powerful thing a leader can do is begin, not with a leap, but with a shift of weight. One muscle. One decision. One breath.

Steve didn't announce "We're going to build the most valuable company on Earth." He said: "We're going to make the best computers in the world." Then he made one decision: Stop the fall (Microsoft deal). Then another: Reignite the team (Think Different). Then another: Ship great products (iMac, iBook, Power Mac). Then another: Own the touchpoint (Apple Stores). Then another: Build the platform (iTunes, App Store).

Each decision small enough to execute. Each essential to what came next.

Your Turn

If you're flat on your back right now, project failed, initiative stalled, momentum gone, here's what matters: Don't try to leap.

Ask instead: What's the next muscle to flex? Not the whole recovery. Just the next small, necessary move. Stop the bleeding? Secure a critical partnership? Change one narrative? Fix one broken process? Take control of one touchpoint?

That's your shift of weight. Not glamorous. Not inspiring. Just necessary.

Do that. Then the next thing. Then the next. Joint by joint. Decision by decision.

That, my friend, is how you rise again. Not with a miracle. With mechanics. One breath at a time.

Stand Up

"Stand up and be counted, or sit your ass in the corner and color." — Lori Goodwin

In 2013, Tim Cook stood onstage at WWDC, pride unmistakable in his voice: "Apple paid ten billion dollars to iOS developers, to date. Five billion of that was in the last year alone. The MacBook is the number one laptop in sales. The number one selling desktop computer in the US is the iMac."

Then the stunner: "The Mac install base doubled in 2012 alone."

After five years of fifteen percent average annual Mac growth, five times the PC industry's three percent average, it's easy to forget how Apple got there.

In 1996, Apple wasn't dead. But it was lying flat on its back. The wind knocked out. Bruised. Barely breathing. Nothing was broken. The bones were intact. All it needed was to stand up.

Two words. Deceptively simple.

The Mechanics of Rising

We think of standing as one motion. A single act. But it's not. It's hundreds of micro decisions. Muscles firing in sequence. Balance recalibrated. Weight shifted. Knees locked. Spine aligned. One misfire and you collapse instead of rise.

Steve understood this instinctively. Recovery is not a leap. It is a cascade, each move small, necessary, timed, essential to the whole. Apple did not get off the mat by cartwheeling. It got up joint by joint, decision by decision.

First: Stop the Fall

Steve's earliest moves weren't about growth. They were about stopping the slide.

The Microsoft deal, misreported as a rescue, was not charity. It was strategy. The day before the announcement, Apple's market cap was two point four six billion dollars. Revenue last quarter: one point seven billion. Cash reserves: one point two billion. Microsoft's one hundred fifty million dollar investment? A drop in the bucket by comparison.

But Steve knew the press would scream: "Microsoft saved Apple!" He let them. Because the new narrative, however distorted, was "Apple was saved." Not "Apple is dying." That mattered more than precision.

Then came Think Different. Not just an ad campaign, but something bordering on a religious revival. Steve wasn't selling to customers. He was reigniting his own people. Reminding engineers, designers, marketers: You built the Mac. You made the impossible feel obvious. That's still in you.

Pride returned. Passion followed. Products improved at breakneck speed.

The iMac, a colorful, all-in-one, impossibly simple machine, sold like hotcakes. The iBook, a game-changing, translucent clamshell, bright as candy, redefined the laptop category and brought wireless internet mainstream. The Power Mac G4, bulletproof glass, workstation power under the hood, proved Apple could still thrill professionals.

Each was a muscle flex. Small. Strong. Coordinated.

Second: Own the Ground

But even great products stumbled at the finish line.

Big box stores were landmines, staffed by Windows loyalists. Trained to steer customers away from Apple even when they walked in wanting a Mac. Eyewitness accounts and online posts at the time told of big box store employees actively taking iMacs out of customers' carts! Can you imagine?

Apple was giving half its retail profit to people actively sabotaging its mission.

Steve saw it. His sales team lived it. He decided to fix it. Not with useless complaints, but with stores. Apple Retail was born.

The reaction? Mockery. (Think about that next time you're standing in an Apple store packed to the gills with people.)

BusinessWeek headlined: "Sorry Steve, here's why the Apple stores won't work." Analysts scoffed: "Dell had stores. Gateway had stores. Sony had stores. What's different?"

They all missed the point entirely.

Dell, Gateway, and Sony all sold Windows PCs. In a Best Buy, no one talked you out of Windows. So a Dell store offered no advantage. But Apple? Its software was the difference. Its ecosystem was the value. Its experience was the product.

In Apple Stores, every demo unit worked. No frozen mice, no crashed apps. The experience was at its best every time. Every employee could explain why the Mac mattered, not just list specs. And they could tailor that to the customer's knowledge needs and how they were going to use the device. Every customer could touch, try, feel the coherence. Nothing sold Apple faster than letting people use Macs without interference.

And when the iPod arrived? The stores were ready. The iPhone? Ready. The iPad? Ready.

These weren't just products. They were invitations to music, to apps, to books. The stores made sure the handshake with the products was warm, certain, and most importantly, human.

Third: Build the Engines

Then came the engines: iTunes Store brought music, movies, dignity for creators. App Store launched the modern gold rush. Practically a new economy, born in a weekend. Ten billion dollars paid to developers. Apple's thirty percent cut was not exploitation, but infrastructure.

Each piece fed the next: better hardware brought more users, more users brought more developers, more developers brought better software, better software brought more hardware sales. No single move saved Apple. The sum did.

What This Actually Teaches

Standing up is terrifying. Not because the act is hard. But because trying is.

You gather yourself. Shift your weight and feel the old bruise flare, forcing you to push past the pain. Will the leg hold this time? You plant your hands. Push. Every tendon alive with the memory of collapse. Will your arms hold or fold?

Many freeze under these circumstances. Convinced the fall was final. Convinced motion is risk and stillness is safety.

Steve gave us another way: Don't leap. Sequence. Don't hope. Build. Don't wait for the world to believe. Move, joint by joint, until you're upright.

You don't need to be Apple to understand the mechanics of standing up. Every turnaround follows the same pattern.

Your Step One: Stop the Fall

Before you can rise, you have to stop sliding. This means securing critical partnerships (even uncomfortable ones), stabilizing cash flow, stopping the talent exodus, changing the narrative from "dying" to "recovering." Not glamorous. Essential.

The Microsoft deal wasn't about the $150 million. It was about changing the story from "Apple is finished" to "Apple has a path forward." Sometimes stopping the fall means accepting help you'd rather not need. Making deals you don't love. Swallowing pride to buy time. Do it anyway.

Your Step Two: Own the Ground

Once you've stopped sliding, you need to control your environment. Apple couldn't fix Best Buy. So they built their own stores.

This means identifying where your value gets lost or sabotaged, taking control of those touchpoints, building direct relationships with customers, creating experiences you can guarantee. Where are you giving control to people who don't share your mission? Maybe it's distribution partners who bundle your product with competitors, implementation consultants who undermine your approach, review sites that misrepresent what you do, or channels where your message gets distorted.

You can't control everything. But you can identify the critical touchpoints and own them.

Your Step Three: Build the Flywheel

Once you control your ground, build systems where success compounds. iTunes made iPods valuable. iPods brought people into stores. Stores introduced them to Macs. Macs led them to iPhones. iPhones led to iPads. Each purchase strengthened the ecosystem.

This means finding ways each win creates capacity for the next, building platforms instead of just products, creating feedback loops where customers bring more customers, investing revenue from today's success into tomorrow's capability. The question isn't "What's the next big thing?" The question is "What systems make each success multiply the next?"

The Sequence That Matters

Here's what most turnarounds get wrong: they try to build the flywheel before stopping the fall. They try to own the ground before they have resources. They try to leap when they should be sequencing.

The order matters. First, stop the fall (stabilize, secure, survive). Second, own the ground (control touchpoints, build direct relationships). Third, build the flywheel (create compounding systems). Skip a step and you collapse. Try to do them simultaneously and you spread resources too thin. Sequence them correctly and each enables the next.

The Real Lesson

Standing up is not a miracle. It is mechanics. And the most powerful thing a leader can do is begin, not with a leap, but with a shift of weight. One muscle. One decision. One breath.

Steve didn't announce "We're going to build the most valuable company on Earth." He said: "We're going to make the best computers in the world." Then he made one decision: Stop the fall (Microsoft deal). Then another: Reignite the team (Think Different). Then another: Ship great products (iMac, iBook, Power Mac). Then another: Own the touchpoint (Apple Stores). Then another: Build the platform (iTunes, App Store).

Each decision small enough to execute. Each essential to what came next.

Your Turn

If you're flat on your back right now, project failed, initiative stalled, momentum gone, here's what matters: Don't try to leap.

Ask instead: What's the next muscle to flex? Not the whole recovery. Just the next small, necessary move. Stop the bleeding? Secure a critical partnership? Change one narrative? Fix one broken process? Take control of one touchpoint?

That's your shift of weight. Not glamorous. Not inspiring. Just necessary.

Do that. Then the next thing. Then the next. Joint by joint. Decision by decision.

That, my friend, is how you rise again. Not with a miracle. With mechanics. One breath at a time.

Choose Your Adventure

"He that is down needs fear no fall." — John Bunyan

Before you can return from the point of no return, you must first decide to return. Not hope. Not wait. Choose.

Steve's comeback was not a straight climb. It was a descent into darkness followed by a staunch refusal to lie down in it. He went from broke college dropout to millionaire before he could rent a car. Then he lost it all, not just his company, but his credibility, his momentum, his peace.

"I'm the only person I know that's lost a quarter of a billion dollars in one year," he later said. "It's very character building."

Let that sink in.

The Descent

By 1990, Steve was facing total ruin. He had poured nearly all of his ninety-seven million dollars into Pixar and NeXT. Both were bleeding. Neither was healing.

Pixar: Bought for ten million cash and another fifty million in debt. Sixty million gone in four years. NeXT: Twelve million invested. Zero profit. Five hundred seventy people on payroll. Sixty million dollars a year in overhead, salaries, servers, rent, vanishing into thin air with little to show for it and little on the horizon.

He could lose everything he had left in under twelve months.

At home, Laurene was pregnant and demanding commitment. He hesitated. She left. Worlds shattered.

Pixar had lost money every year for five years. Steve slashed staff. Thirty of eighty people were now gone. He took back employee stock. No severance. No safety net. Only the core animation team remained, fragile, brilliant, irreplaceable, but tenuous with one foot out the door if another shoe dropped.

Tensions boiled over. Pixar's president, Alvy Ray Smith, stood inches from Steve in a shouting match over a petty dispute and quit on the spot. Years of Steve writing blank checks while Pixar leadership treated him as a trust fund, even relocating their office an hour and a half away to avoid him, had reached breaking point.

The San Francisco Chronicle blamed Steve for the cuts, as if he owed them endless cash, no questions asked.

Brief Light, Then Darkness

He and Laurene reconciled. Married in March 1991. Reed was born that fall, bringing a rare light. Then the ground gave way again.

Ross Perot, NeXT's public investor, pulled out, declaring the company hopeless. Co-founders fled: Susan Barnes. Bud Tribble. Then came the day Steve stood in silence as NeXT's computer factory was liquidated. An interviewer asked: "Does the hardware shutdown mean NeXT is a failure?"

Steve put his head down. "I don't want to do this. I can't do this." He stood and walked out, leaving the journalist stunned. He was broken. Inside and out.

The Betrayal

Mike Slade, hired from Microsoft, quadrupled NeXT sales to one hundred twenty-seven million in a year. It wasn't enough.

Cannon, already one hundred million in the hole, loaned NeXT another thirty million. Then another fifty-five million in credit with conditions that included a management change. Enter Peter Van Cuylenburg, Cannon's man, installed as co-president of NeXT. Co-president turned out to be code for: There's only room for one vision.

Van Cuylenburg drove out Slade, then VP of Sales. Then co-founder and hardware genius Rich Page became the fourth of five to leave. Then came the coup: Van Cuylenburg approached Sun's CEO, Scott McNealy, to buy NeXT and eject Steve.

Van Cuylenburg didn't just oppose Steve. He pretended to stand beside him while sharpening the knife. It wasn't rivalry. It was Et tu, Brute? Betrayal dressed in a business suit.

But McNealy, despite being a competitor, critic, and no friend, made just one call. He called Steve and said: "Backstabbing isn't how I do business."

McNealy had something all too rare in business. Honor. That one decision changed history when you think about everything we're talking about.

Van Cuylenburg resigned. The betrayal had reopened the wounds Sculley had cut so deep in Steve's back. Steve told friends he was ready to hand the keys to Cannon and walk away.

Rock Bottom

In February 1993, NeXT shed three hundred more people. At a meeting, Steve slumped in his chair and said quietly: "Everyone here can leave. Except me." He was thirty-six years old and his world was collapsing.

Then, worse came. In March, Paul Jobs, the father who taught him "You'll know it's there," died of lung cancer.

And the past returned, not as memory, but as violence. Burrell Smith, the troubled genius who built the original Mac's logic board, reappeared. Not with a handshake. With a rock. He smashed the windshield of Steve's Mercedes. Then his windows. Then he threw a cherry bomb against the wall of Steve's home.

Smith, a brilliant, broken, bipolar individual, was off his lithium and had lost his mind. He threatened the housekeeper. He rode his bike blocks to stalk the Jobs family. Police took him in handcuffs. A restraining order followed. But the image would not fade: the man who helped Steve build the impossible on the Mac team, now standing before him shattered, raging, and lost.

Steve kept going, somehow.

The Lifeline

Pixar's only hope was Toy Story, the first fully digital feature. It was clearly a moonshot. A lifeline built purely on grit and hope.

In July 1993, production began. By November, Disney shut it down. Woody was a bully. The story didn't work. Everything was ash.

But Pixar didn't panic. They rewrote and gave Woody heart, leadership, and loyalty in a narrative that tugged at the hearts of executives when they saw the rewrite. Disney approved. Production resumed April 1994.

On November 22, 1995, Toy Story opened. Twenty-nine million dollars in three days. Talk about a Christmas miracle. The IPO followed. Stock opened at twenty-two dollars. Thirty minutes later: forty-nine. By day's end, Steve's net worth was now one point five billion dollars.

Laurene gave birth to a beautiful daughter which they named Erin. Reed now had a sister. Life had returned.

Then came the call. From Apple, out of the blue. An offer of four hundred thirty million dollars for NeXT. They closed the deal and Steve came home.

What This Actually Teaches

This isn't just Steve's biography. It's a map of the choice every leader faces when everything falls apart.

The question isn't: Will bad things happen? The question is: When they do, will you choose to return or to stay down?

Most people think that choice comes in one moment, the dramatic decision to "get back up." It doesn't. The choice comes every single day. Every single hour. Sometimes every single minute. Stay down or push. Give up or try one more thing. Hand in the keys or make one more call. Walk away or show up tomorrow.

Steve made that choice hundreds of times between 1990 and 1996. Not once. Not in a single heroic moment. But in a thousand small, unglamorous decisions to keep moving when stopping would have been easier.

Steve's example offers a powerful tool, not only for motivation, but for breaking paralysis and restoring the inner strength that fear has frozen.

Ask yourself one question: Are you fallen or falling?

Fallen means you've hit rock bottom. Falling means you're still on the way down. The actions are different for each. If you're still falling, stop the descent. Identify what you can control. Make the hard cuts now rather than later. Position yourself to land on your feet. If you're already fallen, acknowledge where you actually are, identify what's still intact, and take the smallest possible step forward.

Most people confuse the two. They think they're fallen when they're still falling, so they try to stand up while still in freefall. Or they think they're still falling when they've already hit bottom, so they brace for impact that already happened instead of pushing up.

Steve knew both states. In 1993, he was fallen. He could have handed in the keys, walked away, let the creditors sort the wreckage. He didn't. Because he understood something most miss: Rock bottom is not the end. It is the only honest place to begin.

You cannot fall further. There is no lower. No more illusions to protect. No reputation left to salvage. As he told Stanford's graduating class in 2005: "Remembering that you are going to die is the best way I know to avoid the trap of thinking you have something to lose. You are already naked. There is no reason not to follow your heart."

That is not philosophy. It is physics. When you're on the way down, you're still protecting something: your reputation, your image, your story about who you are. When you're at the bottom, there's nothing left to protect. That's not a weakness. That's freedom. Freedom to admit what actually failed, cut what isn't working, ask for help you need, try things you wouldn't try if you had something to lose, follow your instincts without committee approval, and make decisions based on what's right instead of what looks good.

Steve in 1993 had nothing left to lose. So he made the hard cuts at Pixar. Let the brilliant people who wouldn't commit leave. Rewrote Toy Story from scratch. Bet everything on one moonshot. He couldn't have made those choices from any higher position. The fall gave him the freedom to build what needed building.

If you're reading this and recognizing yourself in any part of Steve's descent, answer the question honestly: Are you fallen or falling? Not what you want to be true. What is actually true.

Then make the choice. Not hope. Not wait. Choose. Choose to stop the fall if you're falling. Choose to push if you're fallen. Not tomorrow. Today. Right now.

Take the smallest possible step. Not a dramatic gesture. Not a grand proclamation. Just one small action that moves you toward recovery instead of away from it. Make one call. Fix one thing. Cut one loss. Save one relationship. Try one more time.

Steve didn't know in 1993 that Toy Story would work, that Apple would call, that he'd come home. He just knew he wasn't done yet. And that knowledge, that choice, made all the difference.

"He that is down needs fear no fall." When you've already fallen, the fear of falling disappears. That's not defeat. That's the starting point. The only honest place to begin.

So ask one more time: Are you fallen or still falling? If you're still falling, catch yourself. Shift your weight. Prepare to land. And if you're already down? Good. Now you know exactly where you stand.

Push.

Act Accordingly

"I'm a success today because I had a friend who believed in me, and I didn't have the heart to let him down." — Abraham Lincoln

It is easy to convince yourself you've fallen too far. That the hole is too deep, the climb too steep, and the cost too high. So, let's look at how Steve handled it.

The Audacity of Acting as If

He returned to an Apple that had just lost a small fortune. Market share: three percent. Morale: shattered. Reputation: in tatters.

His first mission? Accompany CEO Gil Amelio to Microsoft, hat in hand, to beg Bill Gates not to abandon Office for Mac.

Steve walked in. Shook Gates's hand and said: "Bill, between us, we own one hundred percent of the desktop."

Reality? Microsoft had ninety-seven percent. Apple clung to three, tops. But Steve spoke as if they were equals. Not because he was delusional, but because he saw the future as fixed. He knew, with bone-deep certainty, that one day, they would be.

Less than a decade later, Apple's iPhone business alone would generate more profit than Microsoft's entire operation.

Could that have happened if Steve had waited for proof before acting? If he had asked his team to hope instead of build? No.

The Future Tense

To Steve, Apple was not the battered company in front of him. It was the vessel for something larger: the spirit of creativity. The refusal to accept the world as it is.

He didn't wait for the iMac to ship. He didn't wait for profits to return. He didn't wait for the world to believe. He began with belief and made it contagious.

He reminded engineers: You are not fixing bugs. You are continuing a lineage. Einstein. Robert Kennedy. Amelia Earhart. Jim Henson. Alfred Hitchcock. Muhammad Ali. Brilliant. Vilified. Unstoppable.

Then came Think Different, not a mere tagline, but an unforgettable vow that celebrated those who see things differently, who refuse to accept the status quo, who change the world by being crazy enough to think they can.

Chiat/Day created the ad before seeing the iMac. Before the translucent shell. Before the candy colors. Before the sales records. The product came later and proved the belief. That is the deepest lesson.

The Pattern That Changes Everything

You do not wait for success to act like it's coming. You act as if it is already here, because that action builds the path.

Steve didn't fake confidence. He lived the conclusion and invited others to join him in the future tense.

This is the difference between hoping and acting accordingly. Hoping says: "Maybe this will work out." Acting accordingly says: "This is already working, here's what we do next." Hoping says: "I wish things were different." Acting accordingly says: "Things are different. We're making them different right now."

Hoping is passive. Acting accordingly is generative. It creates the conditions for the outcome you've already decided is inevitable.

What This Looks Like in Practice

When Steve walked into that meeting with Bill Gates, he had every reason to act defeated. Apple was 90 days from bankruptcy. Microsoft dominated the market. Steve was there to beg for help.

Instead, he acted as if they were equals negotiating a partnership between giants. Not because the data supported it. Because the future he was building required it.

That stance, that refusal to accept the current reality as permanent, changed the dynamic of the negotiation. Gates couldn't dismiss him as a supplicant. Steve wasn't asking for charity. He was proposing collaboration between the only two companies that mattered. The confidence wasn't fake. It was future-tense.

How This Shows Up in Your World

You don't need to negotiate with Bill Gates to apply this principle. You face the choice every time circumstances say you should act small.

Your initiative failed. Do you show up to the next meeting apologizing, or do you show up with the next version? Your budget got cut. Do you complain about constraints, or do you present what you can do with what you have? Your competitor launched something better. Do you panic and copy them, or do you double down on what makes you different? Your team is demoralized. Do you commiserate about how hard things are, or do you remind them why the work matters?

The circumstances are real. But your response to them creates the next reality.

The Risk of Waiting for Proof

Most leaders wait for evidence before acting confident. "Once we have a few wins under our belt, then we can be ambitious." "Once the team believes, then we can set bold goals." "Once the market validates us, then we can act like we belong."

This is backwards. The wins come from acting ambitious before you have proof. The team believes because you believe first. The market validates you because you acted like you deserved validation.

Steve didn't wait for the iMac to prove Apple could innovate. He acted like Apple was already the innovation leader, then built products that proved it.

What "Act Accordingly" Actually Means

This isn't about fake it till you make it. That implies deception. This is about: Decide what's true about the future, then act consistent with that truth today.

If you've decided your company will be known for quality, act accordingly.

Don't ship products that are "good enough." Don't tolerate processes that create defects. Don't hire people who can't hold the standard.

If you've decided your team will be high-performing, act accordingly. Don't accept mediocre work with weak excuses. Don't skip difficult conversations. Don't tolerate behaviors that undermine performance.

If you've decided you'll return from this setback, act accordingly. Show up like someone who's coming back, not someone who's beaten. Make decisions that build toward recovery, not manage decline. Invest in the future, not just survive the present.

Your actions either align with the future you've chosen or contradict it. There's no middle ground.

The Contagion of Belief

Steve didn't just believe. He made belief contagious. The Think Different campaign wasn't for customers. It was for Apple employees who'd forgotten what they were capable of.

The message was clear: You're not working at a failing computer company. You're continuing the work of Einstein, Ali, and Hitchcock. You're building tools for people crazy enough to change the world.

That reframe changed everything. Engineers stopped seeing themselves as survivors of a sinking ship. They saw themselves as part of a legacy of revolutionaries.

When you act accordingly, you give others permission to do the same. Your confidence in the outcome becomes their confidence. Your refusal to accept defeat becomes their refusal. Your belief in what's possible expands what they believe is possible.

But it starts with you. You have to act as if the future you've chosen is already real, before anyone else believes it.

The Question That Clarifies Everything

What would you do today if you already knew you would succeed? Not hope. Not wish. Knew.

If you knew, with absolute certainty, that your initiative would work, your company would thrive, your vision would materialize, what would you do differently today? Would you make bolder decisions? Set higher standards? Cut things that don't align? Invest in capabilities you need? Say no to distractions? Hold yourself and others accountable? Move faster? Be clearer about direction?

That's what acting accordingly looks like. Not waiting for permission from circumstances. Not waiting for proof from results. Not waiting for confidence from others. Deciding the outcome, then living consistent with that decision.

The Hard Part

The hard part isn't the decision. It's the gap. The gap between where you are and where you've decided to be.

In that gap, everything will tell you to wait. The data says it's not working yet. The critics say you're delusional. The circumstances say you should be realistic. The fear says you should hedge your bets.

Acting accordingly means ignoring all of that and moving forward anyway. Not recklessly. Not blindly. But deliberately. Making the decisions that align with the future you've chosen, even when the present doesn't support them yet.

That's what Steve did. Ninety days from bankruptcy, talking to Bill Gates like they were equals. No proof. No validation. Just a decision about what was true, and the discipline to act consistent with it.

Your Turn

You have your own version of that Microsoft meeting. Maybe it's a pitch to investors who've already said no. A conversation with a team that's lost faith. A decision about whether to kill the project or double down. A moment where you can act small and safe, or big and uncertain.

In that moment, you have a choice: act according to your current circumstances, or act according to your chosen future. Most people choose circumstances. They let the present define what's possible.

Steve chose future. He decided what was true about where Apple was going, then acted like they were already on the path. Not someday. Today. Not when things got better. While things were still broken. That's the difference.

The Deepest Lesson

You do not wait for success to act like it's coming. You act as if it is already here, because that action builds the path.

So ask yourself: What have I decided is true about my future? Am I acting consistent with that decision? Or am I waiting for circumstances to give me permission?

Then go do what you would do if you already knew you'd succeed. Don't fake it. Don't pretend. Don't deceive. Just act consistent with the future you've chosen. Act accordingly.

That's how you bridge the gap between where you are and where you're going. Not by hoping. By building the path, one decision at a time, all aligned with the conclusion you've already reached.

The product comes later and proves the belief. But the belief has to come first. And the belief has to become action. Today.

CHAPTER 10
WHINING VS. WHY-NING

Steve taught us the difference between dwelling and do-welling. When things go wrong, and they will, the choice is immediate: Do you circle the wound or do you trace its source?

The Two Responses

Whining is fault without function. Blame without inquiry. It asks "Who messed up?" then stops. Whiners are not solving. They are stuck in reverse with the engine running, wheels spinning, going nowhere.

Why-ning is different. It is forensic. Focused. Forward. It asks "Why did this happen?" What conditions allowed it? What assumptions failed? What can we build or remove so it never happens again?

It is not about blame. It is about accuracy. And accuracy requires safety, especially the freedom to admit mistakes, name missteps, and surface hidden pressures without fear of punishment. Because the goal is not to assign guilt. It is to restore motion.

The Moment That Set the Tone

Steve walked onstage at Apple in 1997, exactly twelve years to the day after Sculley exiled him. The air in the room was thick with history. With hurt. With the unspoken questions: Will he gloat? Will he settle scores? What happens now?

Steve stepped to the mic and issued a single command: "Okay, tell me what's wrong with this place!"

No defensiveness. No nostalgia. No "I told you so." Just an open door and an invitation to truth.

His comeback did not begin with a product. It began with a question. Because Steve knew that you cannot rebuild a company on slogans. You rebuild it on understanding. And understanding begins when whining ends and why-ning begins.

Why Whining Kills Momentum

Whining has a pattern. You've seen it. The meeting after a failure: "Sales didn't give us good requirements." "Marketing promised features we couldn't deliver." "Engineering was too slow." "Leadership kept changing priorities."

Everyone has a reason why it's not their fault. Everyone can point to someone else. The meeting ends with no clarity about what actually went wrong, just a reinforced sense that success is impossible with these people.

That's whining. It feels productive, "We're being honest about the problems!" But it's not. Because it doesn't lead anywhere.

Whining asks: "Who can I blame?" Why-ning asks: "What can I learn?" Whining looks backward at fault. Why-ning looks backward at cause, then forward to solution.

The Anatomy of Why-ning

When Steve asked "What's wrong with this place?" he wasn't looking for a list of guilty parties. He was conducting a diagnostic.

Why-ning has a structure. First, describe what actually happened. Not who's to blame. What occurred. "We missed the deadline by six weeks" is a fact. "Engineering screwed up again" is blame.

Second, ask why it happened. Keep asking until you hit root cause. Not surface symptoms. "Why did we miss the deadline?" "Because integration took longer than planned." "Why did integration take longer?" "Because the APIs weren't documented." "Why weren't they documented?" "Because we cut documentation time to hit an earlier milestone." "Why did we do that?" "Because leadership communicated that speed mattered more than completeness."

Now you're at root cause: misaligned priorities, not incompetent engineers.

Third, identify what needs to change. Not "try harder next time." Structural changes that prevent recurrence. "We need to stop cutting documentation from timelines." "We need clearer communication about what 'fast' actually means." "We need to validate our assumptions about integration complexity earlier."

This is why-ning: forensic investigation that leads to actionable changes.

The Six Ditches

When organizations get stuck, they usually fall into one of six ditches. Each requires different why-ning.

Ditch One is roadmaps, where you have the wrong plan but the right people. The symptom: good team, working hard, going nowhere. Whining sounds like: "We're doing everything right, why isn't it working?" Why-ning asks: "Is the plan itself flawed? Are we solving the wrong problem? Did our assumptions about the market change?" The fix: change the roadmap, keep the team.

Ditch Two is the destination, where you're moving fast toward the wrong horizon. The symptom: lots of activity, no meaningful progress. Whining sounds like: "We're moving fast, why doesn't it feel like progress?" Why-ning asks: "Where are we actually trying to go? Is that still the right destination? Are we measuring the right outcomes?" The fix: clarify or change the destination before going faster.

Ditch Three is the driver, present but not leading. The symptom: leadership shows up but nothing gets decided or aligned. Whining sounds like: "Why won't they just tell us what to do?" Why-ning asks: "Is leadership equipped for this challenge? Do they have the skills, authority, or clarity needed? What's preventing them from leading effectively?" The fix: change leadership, add support, or clarify authority.

Ditch Four is sideswipes, where external shocks reveal fragility. The symptom: a competitor launches, a regulation changes, a key person leaves, and everything falls apart. Whining sounds like: "How were we supposed to plan for that?" Why-ning asks: "Why did one external event destabilize us so completely? What fragility did it expose? What do we need to be more resilient?" The fix: build resilience into the system, not just react to shocks.

Ditch Five is traffic jams, where good intentions collide. The symptom: everyone's working hard, but nothing moves. Bottlenecks everywhere. Whining sounds like: "Everyone's too busy to help with my priority." Why-ning asks: "Why are good intentions colliding? What's causing the bottleneck? Do we have conflicting priorities? Insufficient capacity? Poor coordination?" The fix: remove the structural cause of collision, don't blame people for traffic.

Ditch Six is mechanical, where the system is broken. The symptom: processes that create more work than they solve. Tools that hinder more than help. Whining sounds like: "This system is terrible, but we're stuck with it." Why-ning asks: "Why is this system broken? What was it designed to do? What changed? Can we fix it, replace it, or work around it?" The fix: fix the machinery, not the operators.

How to Shift From Whining to Why-ning

Create safety first. You can't why-ne in a culture of punishment. If admitting mistakes leads to consequences, people will hide causes instead of revealing them. Steve's "tell me what's wrong" only worked because people believed he wanted truth, not scapegoats.

Separate person from problem. Say "The integration failed" rather than "You failed at integration." This keeps the focus on the problem, not personal blame.

Ask "why" at least five times. Surface answers rarely reach root cause. Keep digging. "We shipped late" leads to "why?" which leads to "testing found bugs" which leads to "why?" which leads to "requirements changed mid-stream" which leads to "why?" which leads to "customer feedback came too late" which leads to "why?" which leads to "we didn't have a feedback loop." That's your root cause.

Focus on what you can control. Why-ning about market conditions you can't change is just whining with more syllables. Focus on variables you can actually influence.

Make it about systems, not people. When you find root cause, frame solutions as system changes. Say "We need earlier customer feedback loops" rather than "Jim needs to talk to customers more." The first is a system fix. The second is a person fix.

What This Looks Like in Practice

Whining culture means blame is immediate and personal, explanations focus on external factors, same problems recur because causes aren't addressed, people hide mistakes to avoid consequences, and energy goes to defending positions rather than solving problems.

Why-ning culture means investigation is thorough and structural, explanations focus on system dynamics, problems get solved because root causes are addressed, people surface issues early because it's safe, and energy goes to improvement rather than defense.

The difference isn't subtle. It's transformational.

Steve walked into a room full of people who'd watched Apple crumble for twelve years. Any of them could have been blamed. Many of them had made mistakes. He didn't ask "Who broke this?" He asked "What's broken here?"

That single question, and the safety it created, allowed truth to surface. Once truth surfaced, solutions became possible. Because you cannot fix what you won't name. And you cannot name what you're too busy blaming.

The next time something goes wrong, and it will, you have a choice. Will you circle the wound or trace its source? Will you ask "Whose fault is this?" or "Why did this happen?" Will you assign blame or identify cause? Will you punish the person or fix the system?

That choice determines whether you stay stuck or start moving. Whining keeps the engine running while the wheels spin. Why-ning shifts you into gear and gets you back on the road.

Each ditch is recoverable. If you choose why-ning over whining. Because motion is not magic. It is method. And the first step is always the same: Stop spinning. Start asking.

Roadmaps

"A good plan is like a road map: it shows the final destination and usually the best way to get there." — H. Stanley Judd

Steve didn't just recover from failure. He reverse-engineered it. After NeXT. After Pixar's near collapse. After Apple's exile. Repeatedly he sat down and asked: What actually broke?

Not who failed. What failed.

The result was his unwritten manual: Rules of the Road, a set of principles for navigating breakdowns without blame. Some called him a whiner for digging so deep. Others saw the truth: Whining repeats the past. Why-ning rewrites the future.

This is not about fault. It is about fixing. And fixing starts with a single act: accurate diagnosis.

The Five Surgical Questions

Steve used five simple, surgical questions to cut through noise and find the real failure point. Each one names a different kind of ditch and pairs it with the way out.

Question One: Was the destination the problem?

The diagnosis: We built a product no one wanted. Not execution. Not effort. The goal itself was misaligned with human need.

The symptom: The team worked hard, the product shipped on time, the quality was good, and nobody bought it.

The fix: Change your destination. Not your people. Not your process. Your goal was wrong.

This is the hardest diagnosis to accept because it means all the effort was aimed at the wrong target. But it's also the most important because continuing toward a wrong destination just gets you there faster.

What this looks like: You built features customers didn't ask for and won't use. You optimized for metrics that don't drive actual value. You chased a market that doesn't exist or doesn't care. You solved yesterday's problem while the world moved on.

The fix isn't execution. It's redirection.

Question Two: Do you need to replace the driver?

The diagnosis: The board approved every bad decision. Leadership confused motion with progress. Competence without vision is dangerous. Authority without accountability is fatal.

The symptom: Lots of meetings, lots of decisions, lots of activity, but the organization keeps drifting or heading toward the wrong outcomes.

The fix: Replace the one controlling the wheel.

This isn't about blame. It's about fit. Sometimes capable people are in roles that require different capabilities. Sometimes they have authority without accountability. Sometimes they're executing a plan they never believed in.

What this looks like: Decisions get made, then unmade, then remade. Strategy changes every quarter based on last month's results. The team is working hard but leadership can't articulate where they're going. Authority and accountability are misaligned.

The fix isn't motivation. It's different leadership.

Question Three: Did we get sideswiped?

The diagnosis: Our "partner" shared our roadmap and then sold it to a competitor. Loyalty is not assumed. It is tested and verified.

The symptom: An external shock, betrayal, competitive move, regulatory change, key departure, destabilizes everything.

The fix: Choose more trustworthy travel companions.

Not every external shock is preventable. But if one sideswipe collapsed your entire operation, the fragility was already there. The shock just revealed it.

What this looks like: You were dependent on one partner, one vendor, one key person. Your competitive advantage relied on information asymmetry that disappeared. A relationship you assumed was solid turned out to be transactional. You built on ground you didn't actually own.

The fix isn't revenge. It's resilience.

Question Four: Was there a traffic jam?

The diagnosis: Every team is waiting for another team to move first. Nothing flows. Break the logjam with one bold decision, even if it's imperfect.

The symptom: Everyone's working but nothing's moving. Bottlenecks everywhere. Good intentions colliding.

The fix: Restore momentum.

Sometimes the problem isn't the plan, the people, or external factors. It's that everything got clogged. Dependencies stacked up. Priorities collided. The system seized.

What this looks like: "We're waiting on Legal." "We're waiting on Finance." "We're waiting on Engineering." Multiple teams need the same resources. Everyone has top priorities that conflict with everyone else's. Consensus is required but impossible to achieve.

The fix isn't patience. It's a bold decision that breaks the jam.

Question Five: Did the car simply break down?

The diagnosis: Hardware said one thing. Software said another. Marketing promised what engineering couldn't deliver. A system is only as strong as its weakest connection.

The symptom: The plan is right, the people are capable, no external shocks, but the machinery of execution is broken.

The fix: Revisit the mechanics.

This is the most fixable problem because it's structural. Tools don't work. Processes create friction. Information doesn't flow. Teams can't coordinate.

What this looks like: Different departments use incompatible systems. Critical information lives in someone's head or inbox. Processes designed for 50 people now serving 500. Tools create more work than they solve.

The fix isn't willpower. It's better machinery.

How Steve Applied This

When Steve returned to Apple, he didn't start with a product plan. He started with diagnosis.

He asked: Why did the Mac stagnate? Destination problem: "Computers for work" ignored music, art, life, the realms where Apple's customers actually lived. Fix: Redefine the destination. Computers for creativity, not just productivity.

Why did Copland fail? Mechanical problem: Engineers working in silos, no shared vision, systems that couldn't integrate. Fix: Build a new OS (or buy one) that actually worked as a coherent whole.

Why did partners hesitate? Traffic jam: No one believed Apple could ship on time or with quality. Fix: Break the jam with the Microsoft deal, one bold decision that proved Apple could deliver.

He didn't blame the teams. He fixed the system.

Here's how to apply this to your situation.

First, name what actually failed. Not who you're mad at. What broke. "We missed the market window" is an outcome. "Our best people left" is a symptom. "The product shipped but nobody bought it" is a result.

Second, run through the five questions. Destination: Was the goal itself wrong? Driver: Is leadership equipped for this? Sideswipe: Did an external shock reveal hidden fragility? Traffic jam: Are good intentions colliding? Mechanical: Is the system of execution broken?

Third, match the fix to the diagnosis. Don't try to fix a destination problem with better execution. Don't try to fix a mechanical problem by replacing leadership. Don't try to fix a traffic jam by working harder. The diagnosis determines the treatment.

Fourth, act on what you learn. Diagnosis without action is just sophisticated whining. Once you know what broke, fix it. Not tomorrow. Now. Change the destination if that's what broke. Replace the driver if that's what's needed. Build resilience if sideswipes keep destabilizing you. Break the jam if that's what's blocking progress. Fix the machinery if that's where execution fails.

A roadmap is not a wish. It is a commitment to truth, to clarity, to motion. And the first direction is always the same: Stop digging. Start asking.

When you're in a ditch, your instinct is to keep driving, press the gas, spin the wheels, hope you break free. That just digs you deeper. The way out starts with stopping. Assessing. Understanding what actually put you in the ditch. Then you act based on accurate diagnosis, not desperate hope.

If you're stuck right now, initiative stalled, momentum lost, efforts not working, run the diagnostic.

Question One: Is the destination wrong? Are you building something nobody actually wants or needs? Is the goal itself misaligned with reality?

Question Two: Is the driver wrong? Is leadership equipped for this challenge? Do they have the clarity, capability, and authority needed?

Question Three: Did you get sideswiped? Did an external shock reveal fragility? Are you too dependent on one partner, one person, one assumption?

Question Four: Is there a traffic jam? Are good people with good intentions colliding? Is everything waiting on everything else?

Question Five: Is the machinery broken? Are processes, tools, and systems creating friction instead of enabling flow?

Be brutally honest. The right diagnosis leads to the right fix. The wrong diagnosis leads to wasted effort fixing problems you don't have while the real problem gets worse.

Why This Matters

Steve could have blamed Sculley for the exile, the board for bad decisions, Microsoft for competition, the market for not understanding. Instead, he diagnosed: wrong destination (work vs. life), wrong mechanics (silos vs. integration), jammed traffic (no credibility). Then he fixed those things.

That's why Apple recovered. Not because Steve was a genius. Because he was a mechanic. He looked at what broke. He fixed what broke. He moved forward.

No whining. All why-ning. That's the lesson. Not "try harder." Diagnose accurately. Not "blame someone." Fix what's broken. Not "hope it works out." Act based on understanding.

Because a roadmap is only useful if it leads somewhere worth going. And you can't know if it does until you're honest about where you actually are, what actually broke, and what actually needs to change.

Stop digging. Start asking. That's how you get back on the road.

The Destination

"When you've lost sight of your path, listen for the destination in your heart." — Katsura Hoshino

Sometimes the problem is not the journey, but the destination itself. Maybe the product was a mirage. No market. No need. No spark. You can execute perfectly, ship on time, hit budget, please stakeholders, and still fail. Because you were driving toward the wrong horizon.

In 1996, Steve stood before Apple's employees and asked: "What's wrong with this place?"

Silence. Murmurs. Fear.

So he stepped in, not with blame, but with clarity: "It's the products! So what's wrong with the products? The products suck! There's no sex in them anymore."

No euphemism. No corporate speak. Just truth that was all at once sharp, necessary, and liberating.

For Apple, the destination was the problem. They had built a business on a flawed idea, convinced by spreadsheets and calculator thinking that more choice equals better choice. Dozens of models with tiny differences.

Opening the Apple catalog gave you a barrage of names like Performa 6320CD, Power Mac 7300/180, and Workgroup Server 8550. Each with strings of numbers that meant nothing to a teacher, a designer, or a student. Just noise.

Walk into a store at the time, and even if you could find an Apple section, at best you'd see rows of Apple machines that were identical except for a sticker on the side. Same beige shell. Same cluttered ports. Same confusing manuals. Same sinking feeling and thought running through a customer's mind: Which one is for me?

Result? A catalog so vast, no product could stand out. Marketing dollars diluted across fifty SKUs, each getting a whisper of attention. Engineers stretched thin, maintaining legacy code for machines no one remembered building. Sales teams memorizing spec sheets, not stories. The machines themselves told the truth: They were not designed. They were assembled, patchworks of old parts, new compromises, and committee logic.

The Why-ning Process

Steve didn't blame the teams. He had been there. He knew the exhaustion of building in the dark. He didn't name names. Instead, he named the failure: no soul in the product. Then he dug deeper, not to punish, but to understand.

Why so many models? No strategy. Just incrementalism. "Let's add a CD-ROM to the 6200 and call it a 6300."

Why so ugly? Designers had no power. Execs told them only to "decorate" what engineering handed them. A coat of beige paint over a mess.

Why not price competitive? Supply chain was fractured. Buying memory from five vendors, hard drives from three. No volume discounts, no standardization. Paying premium prices for parts everyone else bought cheap.

Why no innovation? Teams were busy keeping old machines alive, not imagining new ones.

He turned over every stone. Not to assign fault. To find leverage. Because a great product isn't built. It's uncovered. Stripped of noise. Clarified by constraint. Made honest by ruthless editing.

When the Destination is Wrong

Here's what most leaders miss: You can't execute your way out of a destination problem. If the goal itself is flawed, perfect execution just gets you to the wrong place faster.

The symptoms of a destination problem: The team works hard but results don't follow. Customers don't want what you're building. Every metric looks good except the ones that matter. Success feels hollow or temporary. You keep optimizing for things nobody cares about.

What this looks like in practice: You're building features your competitors have, not features your customers need. You're chasing market share in a shrinking category. You're optimizing for efficiency when the problem is effectiveness. You're measuring activity when you should be measuring impact. The execution is fine. The destination is wrong.

Apple's destination problem was clear. They were trying to be a computer company that offered maximum choice. The market wanted a computer company that offered clarity and delight.

The mismatch was killing them. More models didn't increase sales. It paralyzed customers and exhausted teams. More features didn't create value. It created confusion and bloat. More options didn't attract buyers. It signaled that Apple itself didn't know what mattered.

Steve's fix wasn't better execution. It was a different destination. From "maximum choice" to "maximum clarity." From "computers for everyone" to "best computers for creative people." From "competitive specs" to "coherent experience."

Once the destination changed, everything else could follow.

Ask these questions to diagnose a destination problem.

Question One: If we succeed completely at what we're trying to do, does it actually matter? Not "will it hit our numbers?" but "will it create meaningful value?" If you build exactly what you're planning, will customers care? Will it change anything that matters?

Question Two: Are we solving a real problem or an assumed problem? Have you validated that the problem you're solving actually exists? Or are you building based on what someone thought customers might need?

Question Three: Is the market moving and we're still aiming at where it was? What was true when you set this destination, is it still true? Has the world shifted while you kept driving toward yesterday's horizon?

Question Four: Are we optimizing for the wrong metric? Sometimes the destination looks right on a dashboard but wrong in reality. You're hitting targets that don't actually drive the outcome you need.

Question Five: If this succeeds, what happens next? Does success create momentum or just check a box? Does it lead somewhere or just end?

If any of these questions reveal misalignment, you have a destination problem.

What Fixing Things Actually Requires

Changing destination is harder than changing execution because it requires admitting the current plan is wrong. Not "needs adjustment," wrong. The goal itself is flawed. This is psychologically difficult, especially if you championed the original direction.

It requires abandoning sunk costs. All the work toward the wrong destination doesn't become right by continuing. You have to let it go.

It requires facing stakeholder resistance. People who bought into the original destination will resist. Especially if they're measured by progress toward it.

It requires rebuilding from a new foundation. You can't just tweak. You have to reconceive what you're actually trying to accomplish.

Steve did all of this. He admitted Apple's product strategy was fundamentally wrong. He abandoned models, projects, and initiatives teams had worked on for years. He faced resistance from executives who'd built careers on the old approach. He rebuilt from scratch, four products instead of fifty. It was painful. It was necessary. It worked.

The Pattern in Your World

You don't need to be Apple to face destination problems. I see this constantly: Companies implementing systems because "everyone else is" without asking if they solve actual problems. Teams building features competitors have without asking if customers want them. Leaders chasing metrics that look good in board meetings but don't drive real outcomes. Organizations optimizing processes that shouldn't exist in the first place.

The pattern is always the same: good people, working hard, executing well, going nowhere, because the destination itself is wrong. The fix is always the same too: Stop optimizing the journey. Question the destination.

How to Change Destination

First, name what's actually wrong. Not "execution needs improvement" but "we're building the wrong thing." Be honest and specific about the misalignment.

Second, understand why the wrong destination was chosen. Not to blame, but to prevent repeating the error. Was it based on old assumptions? Competitive pressure? Internal politics? Misunderstood customer needs?

Third, define the right destination. Not vague ("be better") but specific ("build four excellent products instead of fifty mediocre ones"). What does success actually look like? What value does it create? For whom?

Fourth, make the hard cuts. Kill what doesn't serve the new destination. Even if it's good work. Even if people invested in it. Steve cut 70% of Apple's products. That's the kind of ruthlessness required.

Fifth, align everything to the new destination. Metrics, incentives, processes, communication. Everything has to point the same direction. You can't change destination while keeping the old map.

When the product is the problem, you don't optimize the engine. You change the destination. Only then, with true north restored, can you ask the next question: Who is driving?

Because the best driver in the world can't save you if you're heading toward the wrong horizon.

Steve's brutal honesty, "The products suck," wasn't an attack. It was a diagnosis. The destination was wrong. The goal itself was flawed. Once he named that, he could fix it. Not by working harder. Not by optimizing better. By choosing a different destination and driving toward it with absolute clarity.

If you're stuck, working hard but going nowhere, ask honestly: Is the destination itself wrong?

Not "could we execute better?" but "are we building the right thing?" Not "are we efficient?" but "are we effective?" Not "are we hitting targets?" but "do the targets matter?"

Be ruthlessly honest. Because if the destination is wrong, every step forward is a step in the wrong direction. And the bravest thing you can do isn't work harder. It's stop, reassess, and choose a destination worth reaching. Then drive toward it without compromise.

That's what Steve did. Not because the teams were failing. Because the destination was wrong. Fix that first. Everything else follows.

The Destination

"When you've lost sight of your path, listen for the destination in your heart." — Katsura Hoshino

Sometimes the problem is not the journey, but the destination itself. Maybe the product was a mirage. No market. No need. No spark. You can execute perfectly, ship on time, hit budget, please stakeholders, and still fail. Because you were driving toward the wrong horizon.

In 1996, Steve stood before Apple's employees and asked: "What's wrong with this place?"

Silence. Murmurs. Fear.

So he stepped in, not with blame, but with clarity: "It's the products! So what's wrong with the products? The products suck! There's no sex in them anymore."

No euphemism. No corporate speak. Just truth that was all at once sharp, necessary, and liberating.

For Apple, the destination was the problem. They had built a business on a flawed idea, convinced by spreadsheets and calculator thinking that more choice equals better choice. Dozens of models with tiny differences.

Opening the Apple catalog gave you a barrage of names like Performa 6320CD, Power Mac 7300/180, and Workgroup Server 8550. Each with strings of numbers that meant nothing to a teacher, a designer, or a student. Just noise.

Walk into a store at the time, and even if you could find an Apple section, at best you'd see rows of Apple machines that were identical except for a sticker on the side. Same beige shell. Same cluttered ports. Same confusing manuals. Same sinking feeling and thought running through a customer's mind: Which one is for me?

Result? A catalog so vast, no product could stand out. Marketing dollars diluted across fifty SKUs, each getting a whisper of attention. Engineers stretched thin, maintaining legacy code for machines no one remembered building. Sales teams memorizing spec sheets, not stories. The machines themselves told the truth: They were not designed. They were assembled, patchworks of old parts, new compromises, and committee logic.

The Why-ning Process

Steve didn't blame the teams. He had been there. He knew the exhaustion of building in the dark. He didn't name names. Instead, he named the failure: no soul in the product. Then he dug deeper, not to punish, but to understand.

Why so many models? No strategy. Just incrementalism. "Let's add a CD-ROM to the 6200 and call it a 6300."

Why so ugly? Designers had no power. Execs told them only to "decorate" what engineering handed them. A coat of beige paint over a mess.

Why not price competitive? Supply chain was fractured. Buying memory from five vendors, hard drives from three. No volume discounts, no standardization. Paying premium prices for parts everyone else bought cheap.

Why no innovation? Teams were busy keeping old machines alive, not imagining new ones.

He turned over every stone. Not to assign fault. To find leverage. Because a great product isn't built. It's uncovered. Stripped of noise. Clarified by constraint. Made honest by ruthless editing.

When the Destination is Wrong

Here's what most leaders miss: You can't execute your way out of a destination problem. If the goal itself is flawed, perfect execution just gets you to the wrong place faster.

The symptoms of a destination problem: The team works hard but results don't follow. Customers don't want what you're building. Every metric looks good except the ones that matter. Success feels hollow or temporary. You keep optimizing for things nobody cares about.

What this looks like in practice: You're building features your competitors have, not features your customers need. You're chasing market share in a shrinking category. You're optimizing for efficiency when the problem is effectiveness. You're measuring activity when you should be measuring impact. The execution is fine. The destination is wrong.

Apple's destination problem was clear. They were trying to be a computer company that offered maximum choice. The market wanted a computer company that offered clarity and delight.

The mismatch was killing them. More models didn't increase sales. It paralyzed customers and exhausted teams. More features didn't create value. It created confusion and bloat. More options didn't attract buyers. It signaled that Apple itself didn't know what mattered.

Steve's fix wasn't better execution. It was a different destination. From "maximum choice" to "maximum clarity." From "computers for everyone" to "best computers for creative people." From "competitive specs" to "coherent experience."

Once the destination changed, everything else could follow.

Ask these questions to diagnose a destination problem.

Question One: If we succeed completely at what we're trying to do, does it actually matter? Not "will it hit our numbers?" but "will it create meaningful value?" If you build exactly what you're planning, will customers care? Will it change anything that matters?

Question Two: Are we solving a real problem or an assumed problem? Have you validated that the problem you're solving actually exists? Or are you building based on what someone thought customers might need?

Question Three: Is the market moving and we're still aiming at where it was? What was true when you set this destination, is it still true? Has the world shifted while you kept driving toward yesterday's horizon?

Question Four: Are we optimizing for the wrong metric? Sometimes the destination looks right on a dashboard but wrong in reality. You're hitting targets that don't actually drive the outcome you need.

Question Five: If this succeeds, what happens next? Does success create momentum or just check a box? Does it lead somewhere or just end?

If any of these questions reveal misalignment, you have a destination problem.

What Fixing Things Actually Requires

Changing destination is harder than changing execution because it requires admitting the current plan is wrong. Not "needs adjustment," wrong. The goal itself is flawed. This is psychologically difficult, especially if you championed the original direction.

It requires abandoning sunk costs. All the work toward the wrong destination doesn't become right by continuing. You have to let it go.

It requires facing stakeholder resistance. People who bought into the original destination will resist. Especially if they're measured by progress toward it.

It requires rebuilding from a new foundation. You can't just tweak. You have to reconceive what you're actually trying to accomplish.

Steve did all of this. He admitted Apple's product strategy was fundamentally wrong. He abandoned models, projects, and initiatives teams had worked on for years. He faced resistance from executives who'd built careers on the old approach. He rebuilt from scratch, four products instead of fifty. It was painful. It was necessary. It worked.

The Pattern in Your World

You don't need to be Apple to face destination problems. I see this constantly: Companies implementing systems because "everyone else is" without asking if they solve actual problems. Teams building features competitors have without asking if customers want them. Leaders chasing metrics that look good in board meetings but don't drive real outcomes. Organizations optimizing processes that shouldn't exist in the first place.

The pattern is always the same: good people, working hard, executing well, going nowhere, because the destination itself is wrong. The fix is always the same too: Stop optimizing the journey. Question the destination.

How to Change Destination

First, name what's actually wrong. Not "execution needs improvement" but "we're building the wrong thing." Be honest and specific about the misalignment.

Second, understand why the wrong destination was chosen. Not to blame, but to prevent repeating the error. Was it based on old assumptions? Competitive pressure? Internal politics? Misunderstood customer needs?

Third, define the right destination. Not vague ("be better") but specific ("build four excellent products instead of fifty mediocre ones"). What does success actually look like? What value does it create? For whom?

Fourth, make the hard cuts. Kill what doesn't serve the new destination. Even if it's good work. Even if people invested in it. Steve cut 70% of Apple's products. That's the kind of ruthlessness required.

Fifth, align everything to the new destination. Metrics, incentives, processes, communication. Everything has to point the same direction. You can't change destination while keeping the old map.

When the product is the problem, you don't optimize the engine. You change the destination. Only then, with true north restored, can you ask the next question: Who is driving?

Because the best driver in the world can't save you if you're heading toward the wrong horizon.

Steve's brutal honesty, "The products suck," wasn't an attack. It was a diagnosis. The destination was wrong. The goal itself was flawed. Once he named that, he could fix it. Not by working harder. Not by optimizing better. By choosing a different destination and driving toward it with absolute clarity.

If you're stuck, working hard but going nowhere, ask honestly: Is the destination itself wrong?

Not "could we execute better?" but "are we building the right thing?" Not "are we efficient?" but "are we effective?" Not "are we hitting targets?" but "do the targets matter?"

Be ruthlessly honest. Because if the destination is wrong, every step forward is a step in the wrong direction. And the bravest thing you can do isn't work harder. It's stop, reassess, and choose a destination worth reaching. Then drive toward it without compromise.

That's what Steve did. Not because the teams were failing. Because the destination was wrong. Fix that first. Everything else follows.

The Driver

"If the person at the wheel refuses to ask for directions, it is time for a new driver." — Gov. Jennifer Granholm

When Steve returned to Apple in 1997, the machines still powered on. The lights still came on in Cupertino. But the engine was misfiring badly. Not from a lack of fuel, but from a driver who kept taking their hands off the wheel.

The problem wasn't incompetence. It was diffusion. Accountability had been outsourced to committees. Decisions were deferred, diluted, and delayed until doing nothing felt safer than doing something wrong.

The Exodus

Nowhere was this more visible than in the exodus of talent. Engineers who had shipped the original Mac. Designers who had fought for every pixel. Marketers who knew why people loved Apple, not just used it. Handing in resignations on a conveyor belt.

These people weren't quitting for greener pastures. They were walking away from a promise that had gone stale. There's only so many 'Anniversary Mac' stunts you can pull.

Their stock options, once a symbol of shared destiny, were now underwater and sinking. At thirteen dollars a share, a grant that had felt like a stake in the future now felt like an IOU from a bankrupt friend.

Steve saw it in the exit interviews. In the vacant offices. In the way people spoke. Voices thick with anger, not resignation. "I gave my best years to this. Now I'm supposed to believe again on faith?" they were saying.

The First Test

His fix was surgical: Reprice the options. Now. Not next quarter. Not after a risk assessment. Now. Restore the covenant. Prove the future was still worth betting on.

The board's response was textbook corporate caution: Let's form a committee. Commission a study. Benchmark against industry peers. Two months, bare minimum, lay ahead of being broken down by the side of the road awaiting a tire change.

To Steve, that timeline wasn't prudent. It was surrender. Every day of delay meant another designer packing their desk. Another engineer taking a call from a recruiter. Another thread in the fabric snapping.

So he did what no one expected, but what the moment demanded. He didn't negotiate. He exposed the fault line: "Guys, if you don't want to do this, I'm not coming back on Monday. Because I've got thousands of key decisions that are far more difficult than this, and if you can't throw your support behind this kind of decision, I will fail. So, if you can't do this, I'm out of here."

This wasn't ego. It was mechanics. A car can't steer if the wheel turns in your hands while you're trying to hold the map.

They relented. Options were repriced. But Steve knew: one decision didn't fix the system. It just proved the system could be fixed. The real rot was higher up.

The Board Problem

The board wasn't malicious. They were exhausted, worn down by years of decline, of firefighting, of trying to manage a collapse instead of leading a revival. They asked for data not to obstruct, but because they no longer trusted their own instincts. And in that vacuum, inertia ruled.

So Steve did the hardest thing a leader can do. He didn't just change course. He changed the crew. He called the board together in a conference room where the coming raw, unvarnished truth of the moment would reverberate: "This company is in shambles, and I don't have time to wet-nurse the board. So I need all of you to resign and not come back on Monday."

No soft landings. No phased transitions. Just a clean break that created room for people who believed recovery was possible before the proof arrived and wanted on the road again.

The New Board

The new board wasn't stacked with yes-men. It was built of doers. Larry Ellison, who knew what it meant to bet everything on a vision. Ed Woolard, a DuPont veteran who understood scale and discipline. Millard Drexler, who had rebuilt Gap by putting human experience at the center.

This would be a board that didn't oversee. They were men of vision who enabled. They didn't second-guess the turn. Instead, they cleared the lane.

The Signal

Then came the memo, distributed company-wide, signed not by "Apple Leadership" or "The Office of the Interim CEO," but: Steve and the Executive Team.

That signature was the first honest signal in years. It said: We are together. We are accountable. We are moving and we won't stop to ask permission.

The market felt it instantly. Stock jumped from thirteen dollars to twenty, not on a product launch, not on earnings, on relief. The kind you feel when the brakes release after a long, grinding stop.

They were back on the road. Picking up speed. And as Steve knew from NeXT, from Pixar, from the years in the wilderness, speed often attracts unwanted attention. The analysts who wrote Apple off would now scramble to explain its return. The competitors who celebrated its decline would sharpen their knives. The press that loved a funeral would now demand a coroner's report even as the patient walked out of the hospital.

But none of that mattered. Not yet. Because for the first time in twelve years, the wheel was in the right hands. And the road was finally open.

What This Actually Teaches

This isn't just about Steve replacing Apple's board. It's about recognizing when the driver, not the destination, not the vehicle, is the problem.

The symptoms of a driver problem: leadership that defers decisions instead of making them, committees that study problems instead of solving them, accountability that's diffused across so many people that nobody's actually responsible, talent exodus because people have lost faith in direction, inertia masquerading as prudence.

The hard truth: Sometimes capable people are in roles that require different capabilities. Sometimes authority and accountability are misaligned. Sometimes the person at the wheel is paralyzed by the weight of past failures. And when that's the case, no amount of motivation, coaching, or patience will fix it.

The Two Types of Driver Problems

Type One is wrong person, right structure. The role is clear, the authority exists, the accountability is aligned, but the person in the role can't or won't execute. Maybe they're risk-averse when the moment requires boldness. Maybe they're consensus-driven when decisions need to be made. Maybe they've lost belief in the mission. The fix: Replace the driver.

Type Two is right person, wrong structure. The person is capable, but the structure prevents them from actually driving. Authority is fragmented. Decisions require committee approval. Accountability is unclear. Like Steve facing a board that needed two months to decide on stock options. The fix: Change the structure or replace the people maintaining it.

Steve faced both. He had to replace himself as consultant with himself as CEO (structure). Then he had to replace the board that would block his decisions (people).

How to Diagnose a Driver Problem

Ask these questions.

Question One: Are decisions getting made? Not studied, discussed, or tabled, actually made. With clarity, speed, and commitment. If decisions keep getting deferred, you have a driver problem.

Question Two: Is there accountability? When something fails, is there one person who owns it? Or does accountability diffuse across committees until nobody's responsible? If accountability is unclear, you have a driver problem.

Question Three: Are your best people staying? Not just employed, but engaged. Do they believe in the direction? Do they trust leadership to make it real? If talent is leaving, you likely have a driver problem.

Question Four: Does the wheel turn when you need it to? Can leadership change course when circumstances demand it? Or is the organization locked into inertia? If you can't steer, you have a driver problem.

Question Five: Is speed appropriate to the situation? If you're ninety days from bankruptcy and decisions take two months, that mismatch is a driver problem.

What Fixing It Requires

Replacing the driver is the hardest fix because it's personal. But here's what Steve's example teaches.

Move fast when the situation demands it. Steve didn't give the board months to decide. He gave them one meeting. Because every day of delay was another day losing.

Be direct about what's broken. "I don't have time to wet-nurse the board" isn't diplomatic. But it's honest. And honesty cuts through in a way politeness can't.

Make it about fit, not fault. The old board wasn't evil. They were exhausted, risk-averse, unable to lead a turnaround. That's not a moral failure. It's a mismatch between role and capability.

Replace with people who enable, not just oversee. The new board didn't just approve decisions, they cleared the lane for them. That's the kind of leadership turnarounds require.

Signal the change clearly. "Steve and the Executive Team," two words that said everything. We're aligned. We're accountable. We're moving.

The Pattern in Your World

You don't need to be Apple to face driver problems. I see this constantly: Projects stuck because leadership can't decide between competing priorities. Initiatives dying because accountability is spread across five stakeholders. Talent leaving because they've lost faith that leadership can execute. Organizations paralyzed because committees have replaced decisiveness.

The symptoms are always the same: good people, working hard, but nothing moves, because nobody's actually driving. Or someone's at the wheel, but they're not steering, just holding on while hoping things work out.

If you're stuck, decisions deferred, accountability unclear, talent leaving, motion stopped, ask honestly: Is this a driver problem?

Not "could our leader try harder?" but "is the right person in the role?" Not "does leadership need support?" but "does leadership have the capability and authority to actually lead?" Not "should we give them more time?" but "is time helping or just delaying the inevitable?"

Be ruthlessly honest. Because if the driver is the problem, everything else you fix will fail. The best destination and perfect vehicle don't matter if nobody's steering.

Steve made thousands of hard decisions at Apple. This might have been the hardest: telling the board, including people who'd supported him, who'd believed in him, that they needed to leave. Not because they were bad people. Because they were the wrong people for what came next.

That's the decision most leaders can't make. They hope the driver will improve. They convince themselves more support will help. They give it another quarter, another year, another chance. Meanwhile, the company bleeds talent, loses momentum, and drifts further off course.

Steve didn't wait. He acted. Not because he enjoyed it. Because the alternative was watching Apple die while a paralyzed board studied how to save it.

The Real Lesson

When the driver is the problem, you have two choices: change the driver, or accept that you're not going anywhere. Everything else, strategy, process, tools, motivation, is irrelevant if nobody's steering.

Steve changed the driver. Then the board. Then the executive team. Not as a power grab. As a prerequisite for motion. Because for the first time in twelve years, the wheel was in the right hands. And the road was finally open.

That's the lesson. Not "be ruthless" but "be clear about what the moment requires." Not "fire everyone" but "put the right people in the right roles." Not "consolidate power" but "align authority with accountability." Then drive. Because the best destination in the world doesn't matter if nobody's steering toward it.

Sideswipes

"If they can get you asking the wrong questions, they don't have to worry about answers." — Gravity's Rainbow

"Paranoia seems more reasonable when you've got twelve stitches in your side." — The Midnight Mayor

When you're sitting by the side of the road, listing the hows and whys of your predicament, it's quite possible you'll realize that the real culprit isn't inside your organization at all.

It's not whining to recognize treachery or relationships that hamper your success and then take appropriate action to get yourself back on the road.

Microsoft and Apple began their journeys together. Microsoft wrote the first Apple Basic programming language. Microsoft Excel and Word began on the Mac. Steve had seen both Bill Gates and Microsoft as great supporters and partners of Apple for years.

Then, a little farther down the road, they tried slamming Apple off the road entirely. And they very nearly succeeded.

The Partnership That Became a Weapon

In 1996, Apple was sitting on the side of the road Dented, two flat tires, steam rising. Wounded in finances. Scarred in reputation. Practically everyone declared it ready for the junkyard. Developers and consumers fled the Mac in droves, hitching rides on the Windows 95 hotrod.

The final straw? The critical Microsoft Office for Mac appeared to be abandoned, no updates, no commitment on the horizon.

The rot went back to 1985 during Steve's exile. Microsoft persuaded CEO John Sculley to sign a three-page agreement that effectively surrendered all exclusive rights to the Mac's look and feel. Their leverage was a threat to pull Excel and Word off the Mac entirely unless you sign. Sculley's win? A promise of two more years of Excel on the Mac.

Before that deal, Windows had no visual resemblance to the Mac and barely registered with users. But with Apple's interface now legally fair game, Microsoft built Windows 95 into a near replica of the Mac's menus, icons, drag and drop. Overnight, it became the first Windows version with mass adoption.

Microsoft upheld the letter of the agreement while violating its spirit. Yes, they kept releasing Mac Excel, but always clearly inferior to the Windows version. Incompatibilities abounded. Once Windows 95 shipped, they placed Office for Mac in hibernation. No updates for three years. The last new version came in 1994. Gee, what a coincidence.

Meanwhile, Windows got Office 96, 97, and 8.0. Mac users watched competing alternatives like ClarisWorks and WordPerfect rise in the vacuum.

Apple sued. Sculley later claimed he only licensed Windows 2.0 to 3.0, not the future. But the case still dragged through courts in 1996, when Steve returned.

In his eyes, Apple would likely win, but the three-page agreement made the case wobbly. From his view, it was rough road ahead. The courts moved slowly. Litigation would be expensive. Bloody. And Apple didn't have time to bleed.

So Steve shifted focus and went off-road. He realized what mattered wasn't winning the past. It was about securing the future. Apple needed credibility. It needed to run industry-standard office software.

So he did the unthinkable. He set aside his fury over the look and feel betrayal. He wasn't seeking justice. He was seeking spare tires, even willing to take factory seconds if they'd get Apple moving.

They wouldn't fit perfectly. They weren't built for the long haul. But an expert driver doesn't need perfection, just traction.

The Leverage

His leverage? Open a second front using a new media technology from Apple called QuickTime.

In 1991, Apple launched QuickTime as a groundbreaking digital video architecture. Microsoft's Video for Windows (1992) was slow, limited, broken. Desperate, Microsoft hired the San Francisco Canyon Company, a third party Apple had contracted previously, and gained access to Apple's QuickTime for Windows code. Much of it was reused, verbatim.

By 1996, Microsoft had been caught stealing code multiple times and ended up paying hundreds of millions in settlements. Apple had sued in 1994. Won a restraining order in 1995. And now, with Steve at the helm, they were ready to file for hundreds of millions in damages plus dozens of other patent claims on OS and browser tech.

The Deal

The deal, announced at Macworld 1997: Microsoft invests one hundred fifty million dollars in non-voting Apple stock (held three years minimum). Microsoft commits to Office for Mac for five more years.

In exchange, Apple drops all lawsuits, including the one point two billion dollar IP claim. Apple ends the look and feel case. And, to seal the deal, Apple ships Internet Explorer as default browser for five years.

Steve called Gates minutes before going onstage: "Bill, thank you for your support of this company. I think the world's a better place for it."

Mission accomplished, or so it seemed.

The Second Sideswipe

Microsoft quickly realized Steve wasn't bluffing. Turned out, this sucker could drive! Burnt rubber and smoke filled the air as Steve peeled out and took off. Apple was gaining speed. Closing the gap in the rearview mirror.

So Microsoft slammed the brakes and hoped Apple would spin into the ditch. The DOJ later uncovered Microsoft's internal mantra: "Embrace, extend, and exterminate." Now, the Mac entered the kill zone.

The IE shipped on Macs? Designed to fail. Could not render websites using Microsoft's proprietary ActiveX. Could not play media in Windows Media formats. A thousand cuts designed to bleed fuel and momentum. A slowdown strategy.

Then came the final twist: Microsoft leveraged the agreement forcing Apple to ship IE while refusing to update it. Consumers saw a broken browser on Macs and assumed the Mac was broken. It was dastardly. And it worked.

Steve knew: spare tires are temporary help. To reach the destination, he had to replace the components.

First: the browser. Apple engineers built Safari, not from scratch, but by tuning the open-source KHTML engine (used in Linux browsers). Result: a fast, standards-compliant browser that honored the Mac's strengths. One tire replaced.

Second: Office. The Mac versions were crippled by design. Macros failed in Excel. Data filters, tables, sorting were all missing. Images inserted via drag-and-drop or copy-paste vanished when opened on Windows. No Publisher. No Visio.

Consumers didn't see "Microsoft's fault." They saw "Mac doesn't work with Office." Apple's explanations were dismissed as whining.

So Steve asked: Why don't our users have a quality Office-compatible suite? Answer: Our partner won't provide one. Fix: Send engineers to the garage.

They returned with Pages (word processing and page layout), Numbers (spreadsheets that made sense), Keynote (presentations that moved people). Each opened and edited Office files directly. Limits existed only where Microsoft refused to document its own formats.

Now Apple had traction. Control. Momentum.

What This Actually Teaches

This isn't just about Microsoft sabotaging Apple. It's about recognizing when external forces, partners, vendors, competitors, market shifts, are actively working against you, and what to do about it.

The symptoms of a sideswipe: a partnership that once worked now creates friction, a vendor that once enabled you now constrains you, a dependency that once felt safe now feels like vulnerability, an external shock that reveals your fragility.

The pattern is always the same: You trusted. They betrayed. Or circumstances changed. Now you're stuck relying on something that's working against you.

The Three Types of Sideswipes

Type One is the deliberate betrayal. Your partner actively works against you while maintaining the appearance of cooperation. Microsoft kept shipping Office for Mac, just bad enough to hurt Apple without obviously breaking the agreement.

What this looks like: A vendor that sabotages your success while claiming to support you. A partner that shares your strategy with competitors. A relationship where they benefit from your weakness.

Type Two is the slow abandonment. Your partner didn't betray you maliciously, they just stopped caring about your success.

What this looks like: A vendor that deprioritizes your needs. A partner that shifts focus to bigger opportunities. A relationship where you need them more than they need you.

Type Three is the revealed fragility. An external shock, market shift, regulatory change, key departure, reveals that your foundation was weaker than you thought.

What this looks like: You were dependent on one vendor, one partner, one key person. Your competitive advantage relied on information asymmetry that disappeared. You built on ground you didn't actually own.

First, assess the damage honestly. Apple needed Office. That was reality. Litigation might win eventually, but "eventually" meant death.

Second, secure temporary traction. Make the deal you need to survive, even if it's not the deal you want. The Microsoft agreement bought time.

Third, build independence. Safari and iWork weren't perfect replacements initially. But they removed the dependency. Apple no longer needed Microsoft's cooperation to succeed.

Fourth, move forward. Don't get stuck fighting yesterday's battle. Get back on the road.

What This Looks Like in Your World

You don't need to be Apple to face sideswipes. I see this constantly: companies dependent on a vendor who raises prices, reduces service, or threatens to pull support. Partnerships where one side benefits while the other slowly weakens. Critical systems built on platforms controlled by competitors. Relationships where dependency creates vulnerability.

The pattern is universal: You trusted. Circumstances changed. Now that trust has become a liability.

The Diagnostic Questions You Need

Question One: Are you dependent on something you don't control? One vendor? One partner? One platform? One key person? If losing them would cripple you, you have fragility.

Question Two: Is the relationship still mutual? Do they need your success as much as you need theirs? Or has the balance shifted?

Question Three: Are they actively working against you? Not just deprioritizing, actually sabotaging while maintaining appearances?

Question Four: What would it take to build independence? Can you replace them? Build alternatives? Reduce dependency?

Question Five: What's the cost of staying vs. leaving? Sometimes staying in a bad relationship is still better than the alternatives. Be honest about the tradeoffs.

The Fix for Sideswipes

Immediate: Get temporary traction. Do what you need to survive right now, even if it's uncomfortable. Steve made the Microsoft deal knowing it wasn't ideal.

Short-term: Reduce vulnerability. Build alternatives. Develop backup options. Create redundancy where you're currently dependent.

Long-term: Build independence. Safari and iWork took years to develop. But once they existed, Microsoft couldn't hold Apple hostage.

Always: Stay alert. Paranoia seems more reasonable when you've got twelve stitches in your side. Don't ignore warning signs of dependency or fragility.

Sometimes in the long run, it's good when a partner pisses you off. Not because betrayal feels good. Because it forces you to build independence you should have had all along.

Apple should never have been dependent on Microsoft for Office. The betrayal revealed that fragility and forced them to fix it. The sideswipe hurt. But it made Apple stronger. Because once you have Safari, iWork, and your own ecosystem, nobody can slam you off the road again.

If you've been sideswiped, partner betrayal, vendor abandonment, revealed fragility, here's what matters.

First: Assess honestly. How bad is the damage? What do you actually need to survive?

Second: Secure traction. Make the deals you need to get moving again, even if they're not ideal.

Third: Build independence. What would it take to never be this vulnerable again.

Fourth: Move forward. Don't get stuck litigating the past. Get back on the road.

Always keep moving forward. And it doesn't hurt to pack a sturdy tire iron. Because partnerships can change. Markets can shift. Dependencies can become liabilities.

The question isn't whether you'll get sideswiped. It's whether you'll build the resilience to keep driving when you do.

Steve did. Apple survived. Then thrived. Not because the sideswipe didn't hurt. Because they refused to let it be fatal.

That's the lesson. Not "avoid all risk" but "build resilience so risks don't destroy you." Not "trust no one" but "never be so dependent that betrayal means death." Not "fight every battle" but "win the war by refusing to stay stuck on the side of the road."

Get your traction. Build your independence. Keep moving. The road is long. The sideswipes will come. But only you decide whether they stop you.

Traffic Jams

"Americans will put up with anything, provided it doesn't block traffic." —
Dan Rather

A car can be engineered to perfection. The driver can be fearless. The road
ahead can stretch clear to the horizon. And still, somehow, you come to a
dead stop.

Not because the engine failed. Not because the wheel slipped. But because
the road ahead is packed bumper-to-bumper with vehicles that refuse to
move.

In early 2001, Apple faced this exact gridlock. It was the beautiful platform
nobody would build for.

The new Mac OS X was ready. A radical reimagining of computing built on
the rock-solid NeXT foundation.

It featured protected memory to prevent one crashing app from taking
down the whole system. Preemptive multitasking so music could play
while a video rendered. A dazzling Aqua interface with real-time anima-
tions, drop shadows, and translucency that was years ahead of anything
on Windows. Behind the scenes: Unix stability, Cocoa APIs for developers,
and a graphics system called Quartz that treated the screen like a living
canvas.

This was not an upgrade. It was a new beginning. Steve and his team had
poured five years into it, not just to fix the past, but to define the future.
They knew that if developers embraced OS X, the Mac could leap ahead of
Windows in performance, stability, and creative power.

But if developers held back, OS X would become another Copland. A
promise that died in committee. And hold back they did.

The Trap

The problem was technical and all too human. To avoid a revolt, Apple
had included Classic Mode, a compatibility layer that let old Mac OS 9
programs run inside OS X. It was a lifeline. But it was also a trap.

Programs running in Classic Mode were ghosts, present, but powerless.
They couldn't use Quartz graphics, so windows felt sluggish and flat. They
couldn't access Core Audio, so playback stuttered. They shared memory

with the OS, so one crash could freeze the whole machine. And worst of all, they couldn't talk to native apps. A file opened in a Classic app couldn't be edited in a native one without saving, closing, reopening. Death by a thousand clicks.

Only native apps, rewritten for Cocoa, could unlock OS X's full potential: smooth scrolling, real-time effects, fast launches, and deep system integration. But rewriting takes time. Money. Risk. And developers weren't convinced the risk was worth it.

"Why invest millions to rewrite for 3% market share?" they said. "We'll keep one codebase and only ship features that work on Windows and Mac." Translation: The Mac gets the leftovers and is always hog-tied to the level that Windows offered.

The big players set the tone, and it was cautious, even contemptuous. What Steve saw was Apple would sit and run out of gas before even moving a mile unless he got around these bozos.

Adobe, whose Photoshop was the oxygen of graphic design, shipped a version for OS X that was essentially the old OS 9 app wrapped in a Cocoa shell. It ran in Classic Mode, slow, unstable, prone to freezing when memory ran low. Saving a large file could take two minutes. Undo sometimes didn't work. Designers, the Mac's most loyal users, mostly opened it once, swore like sailors, and went back to their G4s running OS 9.

Adobe's internal logic was coldly rational: If you're a designer, you need Photoshop. You'll tolerate the slowness. You have no choice.

Microsoft followed the same script. Office for Mac (Word, Excel, Power-Point) arrived as minimally updated ports. No native toolbars. No OS X services integration. Menus felt foreign. Spell check lagged. And worse, documents created on Mac often broke when opened on Windows, especially if they contained images or formatted tables.

Microsoft's assumption was even more arrogant: Businesses are locked into Office. They won't walk away over a few glitches.

The signal was unmistakable: We are here, but we are not invested.

The Dominoes Fall

Then came the dominoes. Quark, maker of QuarkXPress, the publishing standard at the time, delayed its native version for two years, shipping a half-baked update that crashed on complex layouts. Intuit released Quicken for OS X with missing features, confusing menus, and data sync failures. Smaller developers watched and froze. If Adobe and Microsoft won't go all in, why should we?

Third-party development slowed to a crawl. Startups shelved Mac plans. Venture capitalists asked: Is this platform still alive? The jam thickened. Momentum stalled. Doubt crept back in.

The Breakthrough

Steve saw it all. Not as betrayal, but as physics. You cannot shout your way out of a traffic jam. You must create movement.

So he did something no one expected and everything the moment demanded. He stopped waiting for permission. He stopped explaining why OS X was better. He proved it by building the apps the world needed, and giving them away. For. Free.

iLife: The Consumer Lane Opens

First came iLife, not as a gimmick, but as a covenant.

iPhoto: Import a thousand pictures. In seconds, group them by face, place, event. Fix red-eye with one click. Create a book in minutes. No training. No fear.

iMovie: Drag home video onto a timeline. Add titles, music, transitions. Render HD in the background while you check email. Burn a DVD. All before your coffee got cold.

GarageBand: Plug in a guitar. Record a track. Layer drums, bass, strings, all from a library of real instruments like you were a pro. Mix it. Share it. Sound like a studio. On a laptop!

iWeb: Type a headline. Drag a photo. Add a video. Hit Publish. Your website was live, beautiful, fast, and mobile-ready.

All free. Bundled with every Mac. Overnight, the Mac wasn't just for pros. It was for teachers making yearbooks. For parents preserving birthdays. For students producing documentaries. For musicians recording demos in dorm rooms.

And it worked, not "good enough," but delightfully, reliably, humanly.

Apple drove down the side of the road, waving as he passed the people who thought they controlled Apple's destiny.

The Pro Apps: Declaration of Sovereignty

But Steve wasn't done. Some assumed Apple was retreating to the "consumer" lane because it was safe, simple, low-margin. Steve's reply was not words. It was products.

He unveiled the pro apps, not as supplements, but as declarations of sovereignty.

Aperture (2005): Not just photo editing. A revolution. Adjust exposure across 10,000 RAW files in real time. Stack similar shots. Geotag by map. Export to print, web, or iPhoto seamlessly. Adobe rushed Lightroom to market a year later, and even then, it couldn't match Aperture's speed or integration.

Final Cut Studio: Not just editing, but broadcast in a box. Edit HD footage on a PowerBook. Output to tape, DVD, or web without rendering. Compose sound in Soundtrack Pro. Color correct in Color, all in one workflow. Avid, the industry standard, cost $30,000 and required a dedicated workstation. Final Cut Studio: $1,300. On a laptop.

Logic Pro: A full recording studio, 1,000+ instruments, real-time effects, surround mixing, notation. Priced at $999. Less than a single high-end microphone.

All Mac exclusive. All deeply native. All proof: This platform is not a compromise. It is a competitive advantage.

The Message That Cut Through

The message cut through the noise: If you won't build for the future, we will. And we'll make it so good, your customers will demand you follow.

The jam began to break. Adobe, watching designers switch to Aperture for photo workflow, scrambled. Photoshop CS2 (2005) was the first mostly native version. CS3 (2007) was fully native, fast, stable, OS X integrated. Illustrator, Dreamweaver, InDesign followed.

Quark, seeing Final Cut dominate indie film, finally shipped a true native QuarkXPress, and lost ground to newcomers like Adobe InDesign, built for OS X from day one.

New developers rushed in: OmniGroup with OmniGraffle and OmniOutliner. Rogue Amoeba with Audio Hijack. Bare Bones with BBEdit. They didn't wait for permission. They built and thrived.

What began as a trickle became a flood. AutoCAD. MATLAB. Mathematica. Pro Tools. Ableton Live. Scientific, medical, engineering, creative tools. All native. All fast. All Mac.

By 2008, the traffic jam was gone. The road was open. And Apple was leading the pack, not by forcing others to move, but by building a road so compelling, no one wanted to stay behind.

This isn't just about OS X and software developers. It's about what to do when progress stops because everyone's waiting for everyone else to move first.

The symptoms of a traffic jam: everyone has good intentions, but nobody's moving. Each party is waiting for another party to act first. The excuse is always rational: "Why should we invest if they won't?" The result is gridlock where nothing moves despite everyone wanting progress.

The pattern is universal: Department A won't commit until Department B does. Department B won't commit until Leadership decides. Leadership won't decide until Department A shows proof of concept. Nobody's being malicious. Everyone's being rational. And nothing moves.

The Three Types of Traffic Jams

Type One is the dependency loop. Everyone's waiting for someone else. "We can't launch until Marketing is ready." "Marketing can't start until the product is finalized." "Product can't finalize until we have customer feedback." "We can't get customer feedback until we launch." The fix: Someone breaks the loop by acting first.

Type Two is the risk-averse standoff. Nobody wants to be the first to commit because being first is risky. "Let's see if it works for them first." The fix: Someone demonstrates it works by doing it.

Type Three is the coordination failure. Everyone would move if everyone else moved, but there's no mechanism to coordinate. Classic game theory problem. The fix: Someone creates obvious momentum that others can follow.

How Steve Broke the Jam

He didn't argue with developers about why they should build for Mac. He didn't threaten them with consequences. He didn't beg them to cooperate. He didn't wait for them to see the light.

He built the apps himself (iLife, Pro Apps). He made them so good that users demanded them. He created proof that the platform could support excellence. He demonstrated that Mac-only didn't mean second-class.

The lesson: You don't break a traffic jam by honking louder. You break it by building a new lane and driving through it.

What This Looks Like in Your World

You don't need to be Apple to face traffic jams. I see this constantly: projects where everyone's waiting for someone else to start. Initiatives where departments blame each other for lack of progress. Strategies that require coordination nobody can achieve. Changes everyone agrees on but nobody will lead.

The pattern is always the same: good people, rational thinking, total grid-lock. Because everyone's waiting for someone else to move first.

The Diagnostic Questions

Question One: Is anyone actually blocked, or is everyone just waiting? Sometimes "we're waiting on X" means X is genuinely blocking progress. More often, it means "we don't want to be the first to commit."

Question Two: What would happen if one party just acted? Often the jam exists because nobody's tested whether the dependency is real. What if you just moved forward?

Question Three: Is the risk of moving first greater than the cost of staying stuck? Usually it's not. But inertia feels safe while action feels risky.

Question Four: Can you build what's missing instead of waiting for someone else to build it? Steve didn't wait for Adobe. He built Aperture. That's the move that breaks jams.

How to Break Traffic Jams

First, identify the actual jam. Who's waiting for whom? What's the stated dependency? Is it real or assumed?

Second, test if you can act anyway. Often you can move forward despite the "dependency." Try it. See what happens.

Third, build what's missing. If progress truly depends on something that doesn't exist, build it yourself. Don't wait for someone else.

Fourth, create obvious momentum. Once you're moving, others will follow. But you have to move first, visibly, successfully, obviously.

Fifth, make it easy for others to follow. Steve didn't just build iLife. He showed what OS X could do. That made it easy for other developers to see the opportunity.

Traffic jams are not broken by louder horns. They are cleared by a new road, already paved, already moving, already full of people who refused to wait.

Steve didn't convince developers to build for Mac. He built for Mac himself, made it so good users demanded it, and created proof that the platform was viable. Once the road was moving, others followed. Not because he asked them to. Because they couldn't afford not to.

If you're stuck in a traffic jam, everyone waiting for everyone else, here's what matters.

First: Stop waiting for coordination. It's not coming. If it was, you wouldn't be stuck.

Second: Act anyway. Build what's missing. Move without permission. Create proof instead of asking for faith.

Third: Make your success visible. Others will follow momentum. But only if they can see it.

Fourth: Make it easy to follow. Once you're moving, clear the path for others. Don't hoard the advantage, share it.

Because the deepest truth about gridlock is this: Nobody breaks it by waiting. Someone has to drive down the side of the road, wave as they pass, and show everyone else there's a way forward.

And once it's moving, you don't ask permission to pass. You just go.

Mechanical

"If the machine produces tranquility, it's right. If it disturbs you, it's wrong until either the machine or your mind is changed." — Zen and the Art of Motorcycle Maintenance

There is a particular kind of frustration that comes not from broken parts, but from a machine that should work but just doesn't.

You check the fuel. Top off the oil. Test the battery. Everything reads green. Yet when you turn the key, the engine coughs, sputters, and dies.

The problem isn't failure. It's misalignment. A piston out of phase, a timing belt one tooth off, or a gear meshing just slightly wrong. The energy is there. The intent is sound. But the system refuses to translate effort into motion.

This was Apple in 1996. A company full of brilliant engineers, passionate designers, loyal customers, and yet, for years, it had produced little more than elegant compromises and near misses. The world saw chaos. Steve saw something more precise: a machine with all the right components, assembled in the wrong order, governed by the wrong rhythm.

The Diagnosis

Standing before hundreds of employees in the Town Hall auditorium, Steve didn't offer platitudes or promises. He offered diagnosis.

"There are a lot of great people at Apple," he began, his voice calm but unwavering, "but they're doing the wrong things because the plan has been wrong."

He paused, letting the weight of those words settle. This wasn't about morale. It wasn't about market share or quarterly losses. It was about purpose, and the quiet erosion that happens when a company forgets why it exists.

"I've found people who can't wait to fall in line behind a good strategy," he continued. "There just hasn't been one."

That sentence, in its simple yet devastating accuracy, named the core wound: not incompetence, but drift. For over a decade, Apple had operated like a ship with a working engine but no rudder, powering in circles while the crew argued over which instrument panel mattered most.

Steve had already reset the destination with the iMac. He had replaced the board. He had installed leaders who believed recovery was possible before the proof arrived. He had navigated around toxic partnerships. But none of that would hold if the machine itself remained broken from within.

And broken it was. Not in its parts, but in its process. For years, Apple had run on an assembly line mindset that had nothing to do with factories and everything to do with culture.

Engineering would build what they believed was technically possible, a faster chip, a denser drive, then hand it off to design with a shrug: "Here. Make it look nice." Design would wrap a shell around the compromise, then pass it to marketing: "Here. Make it sell." Marketing, in turn, would spin a narrative disconnected from the product's actual experience, and when users felt the gap, the blame would circle back to engineering: "You gave us a mess!"

It was a closed loop of diminishing returns, where excellence in one department was canceled out by defensiveness in the next. No single person was failing. The system was.

Nowhere was this more evident than in the Advanced Technology Group, Apple's crown jewel of research, a team capable of reimagining computing itself.

They had built the foundation for RSS feeds via their Meta Content Framework. They had created the technology behind MSN TV, later sold to Microsoft for four hundred twenty-five million dollars. They had sponsored the NCSA Mosaic browser, the direct ancestor of Internet Explorer. They had spun off General Magic, whose work powered Windows CE.

These weren't incremental improvements. These were foundational leaps. And yet, almost none of them had shipped as Apple products. Why? Because the group operated in a vacuum. Rewarded for invention, not integration. Celebrated for prototypes, not shipping. They built beautiful engines and left them on the shop floor, waiting for a car that never came.

Steve understood the tragedy: a company that confuses capability with contribution is not a company. It's a museum of almost-weres.

The turning point came not in a boardroom, but in a raw, unscripted moment at an all-hands meeting. An engineer, passionate, protective, and visibly shaken, stood to defend OpenDoc, Apple's component-based software architecture.

"Mr. Jobs," he began, voice tight, "you're a bright and influential man..."

Steve, seated on the edge of the stage, let out a small laugh. "Uh oh. Here it comes."

The engineer didn't hold back. "You have no idea what you're talking about. OpenDoc is the future."

For those who didn't know the history, OpenDoc was more than code. It was a philosophy, modular, flexible, user-driven. It had taken years to build. It was elegant. And Steve was killing it.

In that moment, the entire room held its breath. Would he shut the man down? Would he defend his authority? Would he retreat into CEO-speak? He did none of those things.

Instead, Steve leaned in, not with anger, but with respect.

"One of the hardest things when you're trying to effect change," he said, slowly, deliberately, "is that people like this gentleman are right in some areas."

He gave the truth space to breathe. "I'm sure OpenDoc does things nothing else can. I'm sure you could build a demo or maybe even a small commercial app that proves it."

Then came the pivot, not a dismissal, but a reframe: "The hardest question is: How does that fit into a larger, cohesive vision that lets us sell eight to ten billion dollars a year?"

He wasn't rejecting OpenDoc's brilliance. He was naming the deeper failure: the habit of starting with technology and hoping a market appears.

"I've made this mistake more than anyone in this room," he admitted, voice dropping. "And I've got the scar tissue to prove it."

There was no defensiveness. No ego. Just hard-won humility. And then, with quiet grace: "I'm sorry your beloved OpenDoc is a casualty of this process."

That apology, specific, personal, and unforced, did more than smooth ruffled feathers. It rebuilt trust. It signaled: This isn't tyranny. It's triage.

The Liberation

But Steve didn't stop at empathy. He followed it with liberation: "Some mistakes will be made. That's good. It means decisions are being made. We'll find them and we'll fix them."

For years, fear of failure had frozen Apple. Committees forming to avoid accountability. Decisions deferred to the next quarter. Innovation smothered by the need for consensus. Steve cut through it with a simple truth: motion is safer than stasis. Perfection is the enemy of progress.

What matters is not avoiding error, but building a system that learns from it, fast.

He rebuilt the workflow from the ground up. No more handoffs. No more "not my job." Design, engineering, and marketing would sit together from day one, debating, prototyping, and revising until the product sang.

If engineering said a feature was impossible, design would ask why, and together, they'd find a third way. If marketing feared a choice was too bold, they'd test it with real users, not focus groups, but creators, teachers, students, and let the response guide the next iteration.

The goal wasn't compromise. It was coherence, where every decision, from circuit board to packaging, served the same human truth.

The Anchor

And that truth was anchored in a single, unshakable vision, not a slogan on a poster, but a living filter for every choice.

"I think you still have to think differently to buy an Apple computer," Steve told the room, his voice rising with quiet conviction. "The people who buy them do think different. They are the creative spirits in this world and they're out to change it. We make tools for those kinds of people."

As he said "we," he cupped his hands together and tapped his fingers gently against his chest. It was a small gesture. But it carried the weight of a vow. Not "I." Not "leadership." We. A physical reminder that vision is not declared, it's embodied.

Critics would later dismiss this as "touchy-feely." Steve knew better: shared vision is the ultimate efficiency tool. When everyone knows the why, they instinctively choose the how that serves it, without memos, without meetings, and usually without permission.

He ended that day not with a plan, but with a promise and a challenge: "We too are going to think different and serve the people who've been buying our products from the beginning. Because a lot of people think they're crazy. But in that craziness we see genius."

He had done more than fix a product line or restructure a team. He had tuned the machine, realigning purpose, process, and people until the friction vanished and the power flowed freely. The result wasn't noise. It was tranquility. The quiet hum of a system working as it should.

What This Actually Teaches

This isn't just about Apple's internal processes. It's about recognizing when the machine itself, the system of how work gets done, is broken.

The symptoms of mechanical problems: good people working hard but producing mediocre results, departments that don't talk to each other, brilliant prototypes that never ship, processes that create more work than they solve, innovation that happens in labs but never reaches customers.

The pattern is always the same: The parts are fine. The assembly is broken.

The Three Types of Mechanical Problems

Type One is handoff failures. Work passes from department to department, losing context and coherence at each transfer. Engineering to Design to Marketing to Sales, with each stage operating independently and often at odds. The fix: Integrate the workflow so teams work together from the start.

Type Two is incentive misalignment. Different departments are measured on different things that conflict with each other. R&D rewarded for patents filed, not products shipped. Sales rewarded for volume, not customer satisfaction. Engineering rewarded for features added, not problems solved. The fix: Align incentives around shared outcomes.

Type Three is process over purpose. The system is optimized for avoiding mistakes rather than creating value. Approval chains so long nothing ships. Committees so large nobody decides. Processes so rigid they prevent adaptation. The fix: Restore purpose as the filter for every process decision.

How Steve Fixed It

He didn't blame individuals for system failures. He didn't add more process to fix broken process. He didn't accept that "this is how it's always been done." He didn't prioritize avoiding mistakes over making progress.

He named the system failure clearly and specifically. He rebuilt workflows to integrate rather than separate. He created safety for both dissent and decision-making. He anchored everything to a shared vision that filtered choices.

The lesson: You can't motivate your way out of mechanical problems. You have to rebuild the machine.

What This Looks Like in Your World

You don't need to be Apple to face mechanical problems. Organizations where every department does good work, but nothing coheres. Systems where information gets lost between handoffs. Processes designed to prevent failures that also prevent successes. The pattern is universal: The problem isn't the people. It's how they're organized to work together.

The Diagnostic Questions

Are departments optimizing for their own success or shared success? If Engineering celebrates on-time delivery while Product mourns missing features, your incentives are misaligned.

Does work flow or does it transfer? Flow means continuous collaboration. Transfer means handoffs where context gets lost.

Is innovation rewarded or just tolerated? If your Advanced Technology Group produces breakthroughs that never ship, you're confusing invention with contribution.

Do processes serve the work or have they become the work? If people spend more time navigating approvals than doing their jobs, process has become purpose.

Can people name the shared vision? Not the mission statement on the wall, but the actual "why" that guides daily decisions. If they can't, your machine lacks an anchor.

How to Fix It

Name what's actually broken. Not "we need better execution" but "our workflow separates teams that should collaborate." Be specific about the mechanical failure.

Simplify the system. Remove handoffs. Eliminate unnecessary approvals. Kill processes that exist to serve other processes.

Integrate the teams. Put people who need to work together in the same room from day one.

Align incentives. Make sure everyone's success metrics point in the same direction.

Anchor to shared vision. Give people a clear "why" that filters decisions without requiring constant approval.

If you have good people producing mediocre results, the question is simple: Is this a mechanical problem? Not "are people trying hard enough?" but "is the system allowing them to succeed?"

Machines don't fail from broken parts. They fail from misaligned intent. Steve didn't replace Apple's engineers, designers, or marketers. He rebuilt how they worked together. He didn't add more process. He removed the friction. He didn't demand perfection. He created safety for motion and learning.

The result was tranquility, not the absence of effort, but the presence of alignment. The quiet hum of a system working as it should.

That's not magic. That's mechanics. And mechanics can be fixed.

CHAPTER 11
STOP ASSESSING.
START ARRANGING.

"There are no big problems. There are just a lot of little problems." — Henry Ford

If you read enough about Steve Jobs, you will eventually encounter a phrase so overused it has lost all meaning: "He activated the reality distortion field."

It appears everywhere: in bestselling biographies, in analyst reports, in TED-style talks, in casual office chatter when someone dares to set an audacious deadline.

The implication is always the same: Steve possessed a supernatural ability to bend perception, to convince others, and perhaps even himself, that the impossible was not only possible, but inevitable. Like a Jedi mind trick for product launches.

But here is the quiet, unglamorous, and infinitely more valuable truth: There was no distortion. Only arrangement.

The Method Behind the "Magic"

Steve did not rewrite physics. He rewrote process. He did not ignore reality. He studied it with such relentless attention that he could see the seams, the hidden joints, the movable pieces, the pressure points where a small, precise force could unlock disproportionate change.

What looked like magic to outsiders was, in fact, the result of a lifetime of disciplined practice: the habit of refusing easy answers, of living inside a problem long enough to hear its true shape, of peeling back layer after layer until the elegant core emerged, not as revelation, but as inevitability.

iTunes: A Case Study in Arrangement

Consider iTunes. The popular myth says Steve simply willed the music industry into submission. The reality is far more human and instructive.

In the late 1990s, digital music was a war zone. On one side, illegal file sharing was fast, free, and so frictionless it made paying for music feel archaic, even foolish. On the other, record labels clung to outdated distribution models, terrified of losing control, demanding draconian DRM that punished paying customers more than pirates.

Consumers were caught in the middle: they wanted access, quality, and ownership, but the legal options were clunky, expensive, and riddled with restrictions. Technology itself was a bottleneck: broadband was slow, storage was limited, and streaming was still science fiction.

Steve didn't choose a side and charge. He didn't negotiate from weakness or bluster from ego. Instead, he arranged the pieces. Not all at once, but in sequence, each move building trust for the next.

He began with the user's deepest frustration: "Why steal? Because buying music is worse than stealing it." From there, he designed a covenant, not a contract: "If you pay a fair price, we'll give you a better product, and you'll stop being pirates."

That promise required three things to hold: a device simple enough to use (the iPod), a store intuitive enough to navigate (iTunes), and a pricing model honest enough to trust (ninety-nine cents per song, no hidden tiers).

He didn't demand the labels surrender. He gave them a lifeline: a legal alternative so compelling, piracy became the harder choice. He didn't wait for perfect tech. He worked within the limits of 2003, local storage, FireWire sync, AAC encoding, and made them feel like abundance.

The result wasn't a miracle. It was a system, tuned, tested, and tightly aligned, so perfectly that every component served the same human truth: Music is good for the soul. Let's make it easy to love.

The Method Described

This was Steve's method. Not magic, but mechanics. And he described it plainly, almost offhandedly, in a 2003 interview: "When you start trying to solve a problem, the first solutions you come up with are very complex. Most people stop there. But if you keep going and live with the problem and peel more layers of the onion off, you can oftentimes arrive at some very elegant and simple solutions."

Read that again. Live with the problem. Not skim it. Not delegate it. Live with it. Let it occupy your thoughts on the drive home, sit with you at dinner, keep you awake at night until its contours become familiar, until its false assumptions crumble under scrutiny.

This is not the language of a man who distorts reality. It is the language of a craftsman who respects it deeply enough to reshape it.

The Three Principles

His approach rested on three principles that weren't abstract ideals, but daily practices any leader, builder, or creator can adopt.

Principle One: Solve the Problem, Not the Equation

Too often, we fall in love with a solution before fully understanding the problem it's meant to serve. We optimize a metric, units sold, time saved, features shipped, while the real need goes unmet. Steve refused this trap.

When Apple was hemorrhaging market share in 1997, the surface problem was "We need more models to compete with Dell." The deeper problem was "People don't feel anything when they buy a computer." The first leads to more beige boxes. The second leads to the iMac. More than just a product. A reclamation of joy, color, and humanity in a sea of sameness.

Steve didn't ask, "How do we win on specs?" He asked, "What would make someone smile when they unbox this?" That shift, from equation to essence, is where real innovation begins.

What this looks like: Not "How do we reduce call time?" but "How do we solve the customer's problem?" Not "How do we increase productivity?" but "What's preventing people from doing their best work?" Not "How do we hit the deadline?" but "What are we actually trying to accomplish?" The equation is a proxy. The problem is the truth.

Principle Two: Refuse the Single Narrative

Every challenge exists in a field of forces: history, habit, inertia, and hope. To see only one thread is to miss the weave.

When developers resisted building native apps for OS X, the obvious story was "They're lazy. They don't believe in Apple." Steve saw more: fear of wasted effort, lack of tools, no proof the platform would survive. So he didn't argue. He adjusted the conditions.

He built iLife and made it free, joyful, and impossibly easy to use, then gave it to every Mac buyer. Suddenly, the platform had momentum. He released Xcode, a powerful, free, Mac-native development environment, that lowered the barrier to entry. He launched Aperture, Logic, and Final Cut Pro, not as competitors, but as beacons proving that serious work could thrive on the Mac.

He didn't change minds. He changed the landscape until staying still felt riskier than moving forward.

What this looks like: Not "They're resisting because they're stubborn" but "What conditions make resistance feel safer than action?" Not "We just need to convince them" but "What would we need to change to make this obviously right?" Not "It's their fault" but "What can we control that shifts the dynamic?" The single narrative is simple. The field of forces is real.

Principle Three: Break the Immovable Into the Movable

When a problem feels insurmountable, like "The labels will never agree!" Steve would ask a quieter question: "What's the smallest piece we can move?"

With iTunes, it wasn't the RIAA. It was Warner Music. It wasn't all artists. It was one band willing to experiment. It wasn't global rollout. It was one country, one store, one sync protocol.

Each micro-win built credibility. Each concession, allowing label-specific DRM, delaying album releases, was a trade, not a surrender. He understood that momentum is not born from grand declarations, but from evidence, tiny, undeniable proofs that a new path is possible. Once you have one door open, the others become easier to find.

What this looks like: Not "We need everyone to agree" but "Who's the first person who might say yes?" Not "This requires a complete overhaul" but "What's the smallest change that proves the concept?" Not "It's all or nothing" but "What's the first domino?" The immovable is intimidating. The movable is right there.

The Real "Reality Distortion Field"

This is the real "reality distortion field": the disciplined refusal to accept the world as it is presented, and the steady, unspectacular work of arranging it as it ought to be.

It is not about charisma. It is about clarity of purpose. It is not about force of will. It is about ensuring every piece serves the whole. It is not about believing the impossible. But building the possible, one aligned action at a time, until the wall falls, not with a crash, but with a sigh, as if it had been waiting, all along, to be dismantled.

Steve wasn't superhuman. That's precisely what makes his work available to us.

What This Looks Like in Practice

When you face an "impossible" problem, most people do one of two things. They assess: study it exhaustively, document all the reasons it can't be done, present a thorough analysis of why the barriers are insurmountable. Or they charge: attack it head-on with willpower and determination, hoping force will break through.

Steve did neither. He arranged. He looked at the field of forces and asked: What can I control? What can I influence? What's the smallest piece I can move? What would make the next piece easier to move? Who needs to see proof before they'll believe? What conditions make "no" feel safer than "yes?"

Then he moved those pieces. One at a time. In sequence. Building momentum.

The next time you face a problem that feels impossible, try this: Stop assessing. Start arranging.

First, live with the problem. Don't delegate it immediately. Don't accept the first solution. Sit with it. Let it occupy your thoughts. Study it until you see beneath the surface.

Second, find the real problem. Are you solving the equation or the problem? The metric or the need? The symptom or the cause?

Third, map the field of forces. What's making this hard? Not just one reason, but all of them. What conditions would need to change?

Fourth, find the smallest movable piece. What's the one thing you could change that would make the next thing easier?

Fifth, build momentum. Move that piece. Then the next. Then the next. Each one builds credibility for what follows.

The Deepest Truth

Big problems do not yield to shouting. They yield to attention. To patience. To the quiet courage of someone willing to live with the problem long enough to hear its true name, and then arrange the world, piece by careful piece, until the solution is no longer a dream, but a fact on the ground.

So when you face a wall, don't assess its height and walk away. Start arranging the pieces at your feet. When you can't break down the front door, climb in through a window. And sometimes there's a spare key hidden under the rug that'll open many doors. You just have to be willing to look.

Steve's "reality distortion field" was never about distorting reality. It was about seeing reality more clearly than everyone else, seeing the movable pieces, the leverage points, the sequence that would work, and then arranging them with discipline and patience until the impossible became inevitable.

That's not magic. That's mechanics. And mechanics can be learned.

Stop assessing. Start arranging. The pieces are already there. You just need to see them clearly enough to move them.

CHAPTER 12
FIND THE COMMON THREAD

"We started out to get a computer in the hands of everyday people, and we succeeded beyond our wildest dreams." — Steve Jobs

If you look at a tapestry from across the room, you see a picture, bold, cohesive, and alive. Step closer, and you begin to see the silk, wool, and gold threads, each dyed, spun, tensioned by hand. Step closer still, and you see the result of hands that wove those threads. They may not have created the fibers, but they gathered them, aligned them, and pulled them tight until the image emerged, not as accident, but as intention.

Steve Jobs was not the dyer. Not the spinner. He was the weaver.

Then and now, his critics often miss this. They point to the engineers, the designers, the programmers, and say: They built it. He just took the credit. As if vision were theft. As if arrangement were nothing. As if holding the loom steady while the threads fly were nothing at all.

But Steve never claimed otherwise. To Business Week in 1998, he was blunt: "You're missing it. This is not a one-man show. What's reinvigorating this company is two things: One, there's a lot of really talented people in this company who listened to the world tell them they were losers for a couple of years... But they're not losers. What they didn't have was a good set of coaches, a good plan, a good senior management team. But they have that now."

He didn't say "I saved them." He said "They were never broken." He simply gave them a loom and showed them how to weave.

Two years later, to Time magazine, he went further: "There are different things in life you can do. You can become a painter; you can become a sculptor. You can make something by yourself. But that's not what I do. I do the other thing, which is, you work at things that one person can't do... I know people like symbols, but it's always unsettling when people write stories about me because they tend to overlook a lot of other people."

This wasn't modesty. It was accuracy. Steve understood the weight of interdependence and the danger of the myth of the lone genius.

Because during his absence, Apple did run on engineers alone. No weaver. No loom. Just threads, brilliant, unbound, and flying in all directions.

The result? Dozens of half-finished projects, hyper-technical, esoteric, and frankly unusable. Machines with FireWire ports (a groundbreaking high-speed connection), but no software to use them. Prototypes that dazzled in demos but baffled in practice.

Engineers weren't lazy. They were unled, free to optimize for elegance, power, novelty, but never held to account for coherence.

Steve summed it up with quiet devastation: "Apple was ninety days away from bankruptcy after having made such poor moves as pioneering Fire-Wire and then forgetting to include it in Macs." Pioneering, but not shipping. Inventing, but not integrating. Threads, but no tapestry.

The iMac: 38 Reasons Not To

The return of the weaver was announced not with a memo, but with a machine: the iMac. Steve and Jony Ive together conceived a candy-colored computer fused with a cathode ray tube, translucent, playful, impossibly bold. It looked less like office equipment and more like a toy from the future.

When they brought it to engineering, the reaction was immediate and hostile. "Sure enough," Steve recalled, "when we took it to the engineers, they said, 'Oh.' Then they came up with thirty-eight reasons it wasn't gonna happen."

Power constraints. Heat dissipation. Manufacturing tolerances. Material flow lines. Optical clarity. Each reason was technically sound. Each was also, in isolation, true.

But Steve didn't argue the physics. He named the purpose: "No, no, we're doing this." "Well, why?" "Because I'm the CEO, and I think it can be done."

That wasn't arrogance. It was accountability. He wasn't dismissing expertise. He was demanding synthesis.

And the synthesis came, not from one department, but from all of them working as one. Electrical engineering designed a fanless power system, unheard of at the time, to keep the machine silent. Manufacturing developed new injection molding techniques to create the translucent shell without streaks, bubbles, or imperfections. This was such a precise process, it required custom robotics. Industrial design ensured every internal component, down to the screws, cables, and circuit boards, looked beautiful through the casing, knowing users would see them when they opened the side panel.

When it shipped, Steve didn't call it a computer. He called it a statement: "The iMac is not just the color or translucence or the shape of the shell. The essence of the iMac is to be the finest possible consumer computer in which each element plays together."

That playing together? That was the weaving in action.

The Logic Flaw Detector

Steve's directness wasn't cruelty. It was care, the kind that refuses to let a product ship broken, even if the break is invisible to most. He called it his Logic Flaw Detector. His uncanny ability to spot the weak thread in any argument, any demo, any design. Not to embarrass, but to strengthen, or break before lives were hanging from it.

Mike Evangelist, director of product marketing for video apps, learned this firsthand. He was demoing an early version of DVD Studio Pro, a complex application with multiple windows, nested menus, interdependent controls. He navigated carefully, hoping to impress Steve with functionality.

Steve didn't wait. "Why do you keep moving those objects around like that? Why are there so many windows?" Mike stammered, became defensively technical and vague: "This is the best anyone could come up with."

Steve didn't raise his voice. He deepened it: "Well, it's brain-dead stupid. We'd better get some engineers on it who know what they're doing. There are plenty of existing applications which deal with similarly complex abstractions in much simpler ways."

He named them. Some were obscure, niche tools Mike had never heard of. Skeptical, he checked them that afternoon. Within minutes, he was stunned. Steve was right. Completely right. The LFD hadn't failed. It had revealed.

That frustrating moment in the room became transformative in hindsight, and that was the heart of Steve's role: He protected the user's experience not as a metric, but as a covenant to be protected.

The Breathing Light

Most companies stop at function. Apple obsessed over feeling. Take the sleep indicator on a MacBook, a tiny LED that pulsed when the machine was in sleep mode.

The industry standard was a sharp, mechanical light that went blink-blink-blink, on, off, on, off. Functional. Cold. Steve and Jony wanted something else: calm.

So they studied human breath, not as data, but as rhythm. Research showed the average adult at rest breathes twelve to twenty times per minute. They chose twelve for the new light pulse rate. Slow, steady, grounding.

But engineering it was far from simple. Standard sleep LEDs were controlled by the main chipset, binary: on or off. To create a smooth, analog pulse while the CPU was powered down, without draining the battery, required a new chip, custom designed, just for this one light.

When it shipped, users didn't notice the change. They felt it. They found themselves pausing, watching the gentle rise and fall that didn't feel like a machine, but like something alive.

Apple patented it in 2002: "Breathing Status LED Indicator." Dell, years later, added a sleep light to its laptops, a rapid blinkblinkblinkblink at forty cycles per minute. Close to the breath rate of someone sprinting uphill. Not calm. Panicked.

Steve didn't call this detail "nice to have." He called it essential. To him, it was the difference between a tool that works and one that welcomes.

What This Actually Teaches

This isn't just about Steve being detail-oriented. It's about understanding the role of the weaver in any organization.

The weaver is not the one who does all the work, has all the ideas, or takes all the credit. The weaver is the one who sees how the threads must connect, holds the tension that keeps them aligned, cuts away what doesn't serve the whole, and protects coherence when departments pull in different directions.

Without the weaver, you have brilliant individual contributions that don't add up to anything coherent.

The Pattern in Your World

You don't need to be Apple to need weavers. I see this constantly: Engineering builds technically impressive solutions that users can't understand. Design creates beautiful interfaces that engineering says are impossible. Marketing promises experiences that operations can't deliver. Each department optimizing for their own excellence while the whole falls apart.

The pattern is universal: Brilliant threads, no tapestry.

There are three types of weaving patterns.

Type One is cross-functional integration. Bringing together people who normally work separately (engineering, design, marketing, support) and keeping them aligned toward a shared outcome. This means not sequential handoffs but simultaneous collaboration. Not "here's what I built, make it pretty" but "let's build it together." Not departmental excellence but holistic coherence.

Type Two is relentless simplification. Cutting away complexity until the essence emerges, not making things simple, but finding the simplicity that was always there. This means saying no to features that dilute focus, removing steps that don't serve the user, and cutting through 38 reasons why not to find the one reason why.

Type Three is protecting the covenant. Ensuring every detail serves the user's experience, not as a metric to hit, but as a promise to keep. This means custom chips for breathing lights, fighting for translucent shells, and refusing to ship until it's right.

How to Be a Weaver

First, see the whole, not just the parts. Most people optimize their piece. Weavers see how all pieces interact. Ask: "How does this engineering decision affect the user experience? How does this design choice constrain operations? How does this marketing promise set expectations?"

Second, hold the tension. Departments will pull in different directions. Your job is to keep them aligned without crushing their individual excellence. This means listening to all 38 reasons why not, then saying "we're doing it anyway, now figure out how."

Third, cut ruthlessly. Good weavers add threads. Great weavers remove them. Ask constantly: "Does this serve the whole? Or does it just serve one department's interests?"

Fourth, protect the covenant. The user's experience is sacred. When someone proposes a compromise that breaks that covenant, even for good reasons, your job is to say no.

Fifth, give credit generously. "This is not a one-man show." The weaver doesn't take credit for the tapestry. The weaver makes the tapestry possible.Steve once described his job as "thinking and working with people, meetings and email." It sounds mundane. It was anything but. Because Apple's product wasn't silicon or plastic. It was intellectual property made tangible. Ideas cut into steel, molded in resin, coded in logic gates. It was the translation of intention into experience.

And that translation requires a weaver. Someone who sees the thread of engineering and the thread of design and the thread of emotion and knows how they must cross. Someone who cuts away the loose ends not out of ego, but out of respect for the whole. Someone who measures tension not in pounds, but in human response.

Steve didn't paint the picture. He didn't spin the thread. He stood at the loom, hour after hour, meeting after meeting, and pulled, and aligned, and tightened until the image emerged.

If you're leading any group of talented people who aren't producing coherent results, ask: Are you weaving or just watching? Are you integrating the threads or just hoping they'll align themselves? Are you protecting coherence or letting departments optimize locally? Are you saying no to the 38 reasons why not and demanding synthesis?

Because brilliant people without a weaver produce brilliant fragments. Brilliant people with a weaver produce brilliance.

CHAPTER 13
DROP THE 'T' OFF -
TURN CAN'T INTO CAN

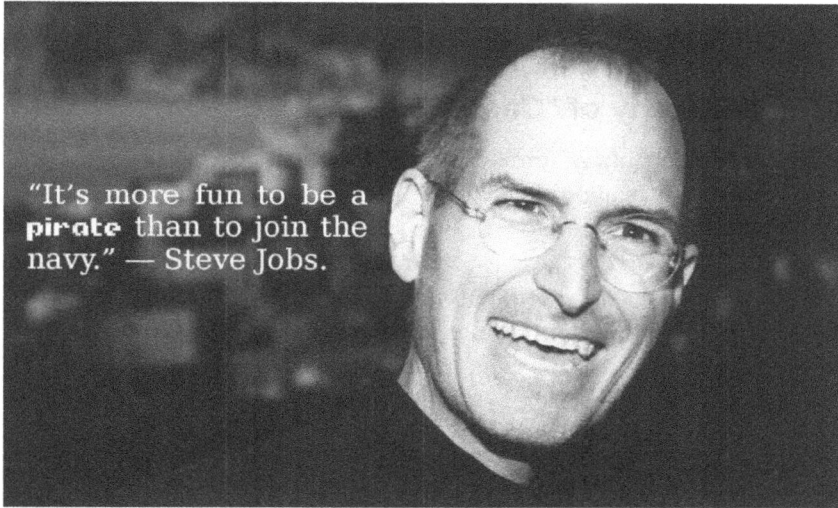

"It's more fun to be a **pirate** than to join the navy." — Steve Jobs.

Photo by Jorge Araya Navarro

"Promise me you'll always remember: you're braver than you believe, and stronger than you seem, and smarter than you think." — Christopher Robin to Pooh

The most dangerous word in business isn't "no." It's "can't." Not because it's untrue. But because it's often untested.

Steve Jobs didn't ignore reality. He interrogated it. Especially when it came wrapped in the authority of experts, tradition, or "how it's always been done."

Because outside manufacturers rarely share your priorities. They've invested in what works, not what could work. Asking them to innovate isn't a request. It's an act of faith. And friction.

Internal teams resist for subtler reasons: office politics, fear of blame, the quiet comfort of known failure over unknown success.

Steve saw both and refused to let "can't" become the final word. Not out of ego. Out of respect for the craft, for the customer, and for the unmet potential in the people around him.

This chapter is about what happens when you drop the T and turn can't into can.

The Anatomy of "Can't"

"Can't" comes in many forms. "We can't because it's never been done" translates to "We're afraid to be first." "We can't because the vendors won't do it" translates to "We haven't asked hard enough or offered the right incentive." "We can't because it would take too long" translates to "We've already decided it's not worth the effort." "We can't because the technology doesn't exist" translates to "The technology doesn't exist yet, or we don't know how to find it." "We can't because management won't approve it" translates to "We're not willing to make the case."

Each "can't" sounds rational. Each protects the status quo. And each dies the moment someone asks: "Says who?"

Steve didn't accept "can't" as final. But he also didn't just override it with force. He did something more surgical: He interrogated the assumption behind it.

Not "we're doing it anyway" but "why, specifically, can't we?" Because sometimes "can't" is real. Physics won't cooperate, economics don't work, time genuinely doesn't allow. But more often, "can't" is untested assumption, risk aversion, lack of creativity, insufficient motivation, or misaligned incentives. And those can be fixed.

When Steve heard "can't," he followed a pattern.

First, get specific. "We can't do that" is vague. Make it concrete. "Why specifically can't we?" "What would need to be true for it to be possible?" "What's the actual barrier, technical, economic, time?" Force precision. Because vague "can't" is often just fear wearing expertise as camouflage.

Second, test the constraint. Once you have specifics, test whether they're real. "Has anyone ever done this?" If yes: It's possible. We just need to figure out how. If no: Is it physically impossible, or just unproven? "What would it take to make this work?" Money? Time? Different materials? Better tools? New partnerships? Often the constraint isn't absolute. It's conditional. And conditions can change.

Third, find the motivation. Sometimes "can't" means "won't," not because it's impossible, but because the person saying it doesn't want to try. Why? Fear of failure? Lack of incentive? Competing priorities? Political risk? If you can change the motivation, "can't" becomes "let's figure out how."

Fourth, remove the obstacle or find another path. Once you understand the real constraint, you have options: remove it (change the condition that makes it impossible), work around it (find a different approach that achieves the same goal), or accept it (sometimes "can't" is real, and you need a different solution). The key is knowing which you're dealing with.

What This Looks Like in Practice

The translucent iMac: "We can't make translucent plastic without streaks and bubbles." Steve: "Why not?" "Standard injection molding can't achieve that level of optical clarity." Steve: "What would it take?" "Custom robotics. New molding techniques. Significant R&D investment." Steve: "Do it." Result: They invented the techniques. The iMac shipped. It defined a generation.

The unibody MacBook: "We can't machine an entire laptop body from a single piece of aluminum." Steve: "Why not?" "The precision required is beyond standard CNC capabilities." Steve: "What would it take?" "Custom milling machines. New tooling. Massive capital investment." Steve: "Do it." Result: They built the machines. The unibody changed laptop manufacturing forever.

The Retina display: "We can't fit that pixel density in a laptop screen at reasonable cost." Steve: "Why not?" "The technology doesn't exist at scale yet." Steve: "When will it?" "Maybe in three years." Steve: "We'll wait." Result: They waited. They partnered with display manufacturers. Retina displays became standard.

You don't need to be building hardware to face "can't." I hear it constantly: "We can't integrate those systems, they're not compatible." "We can't change that process, it's been this way for years." "We can't get leadership to approve that, they'll never go for it." "We can't ship by that date, it's not realistic."

Every single one is untested assumption dressed as fact. When someone tells you "we can't," try this.

Question One: Why specifically can't we? Force specificity. "It's impossible" isn't an answer. "The current API doesn't support that function" is.

Question Two: Has anyone ever done this? If yes: It's proven possible. How did they do it? If no: Is it physically impossible, or just unproven?

Question Three: What would need to be true for it to be possible? Different technology? More time? Different partners? Better tools? More resources? Make the conditions explicit.

Question Four: Can we change those conditions? Sometimes you can. Sometimes you can't. But you won't know until you ask.

Question Five: If we can't do it this way, what other way could work? Sometimes the exact approach is impossible, but the goal is still achievable through different means.

The Three Types of "Can't"

Type One is real constraints. Physics won't cooperate. Economics don't work. Time genuinely doesn't allow. Example: "We can't make this device that violates thermodynamics." Response: Accept it. Find a different solution.

Type Two is conditional constraints. It's impossible given current conditions, but conditions can change. Example: "We can't manufacture this at scale with existing tools." Response: Change the conditions. Build new tools. Find new partners. Invest in R&D.

Type Three is assumed constraints. No one's actually tested whether it's possible. It just seems impossible based on past experience or conventional wisdom. Example: "We can't get customers to pay that much." Response: Test it. You might be wrong.

Most "can'ts" are Type Two or Three. Real constraints are rarer than people think.

What It Takes to Turn Can't into Can

It requires willingness to invest. Sometimes turning "can't" into "can" requires resources: time, money, effort. Are you willing to invest them? Steve was. Custom robotics for translucent plastic. New milling machines for unibody construction. Years of R&D for Retina displays.

It requires willingness to fail. Not every "can't" turns into "can." Sometimes you invest and it doesn't work. Are you okay with that?

It requires willingness to push. People don't like having their "can'ts" interrogated. It feels like criticism. Are you willing to push through that discomfort?

It requires willingness to wait. Sometimes "can't yet" becomes "can eventually." Are you patient enough?

The Danger of Accepting "Can't" Too Easily

When you accept "can't" without interrogating it, you teach your organization: "Don't try hard things." Because if "can't" ends the conversation, why propose ambitious ideas? "Play it safe." Because if constraints can't be challenged, innovation dies. "Protect yourself with 'can't.'" Because "can't" becomes a shield against accountability.

The culture becomes: don't attempt what you're not certain will work. And certainty is the enemy of innovation.

When Steve heard "can't," he didn't accept it automatically, reject it automatically, or override it with authority. He interrogated it: Why specifically? Has anyone done this? What would it take? Can we change those conditions? Is there another way?

Then he decided. Sometimes: "You're right, we can't. Let's find another approach." Sometimes: "We can't yet. Let's invest in making it possible." Sometimes: "We can, you just haven't figured out how yet. Keep trying."

The key was: "can't" started a conversation, not ended one.

The next time someone tells you "we can't," don't accept it. Don't reject it. Interrogate it: Why specifically can't we? What would need to be true for it to be possible? Can we change those conditions? Has anyone ever done this? If not this way, what other way?

You'll find that many "can'ts" are actually "haven't tried yet" or "would require investment" or "seems hard." And those are very different from impossible.

The most dangerous word in business isn't "no." It's "can't." Because "no" is a decision. "Can't" is an assumption. And assumptions, unlike physics, can be challenged.

Steve didn't ignore reality. He interrogated it. He asked: Is this really impossible, or does it just seem that way? Is this physics, or is it convention? Is this a real constraint, or a conditional one we could change?

More often than not, it was conditional. And conditions can change. If you're willing to invest the resources, accept the risk, push through resistance, wait for the technology, or find another path, then "can't" becomes "can, if we're willing to do what it takes."

And that changes everything.

Drop the T. The next time you hear "can't," from your team, from vendors, from yourself, don't let it end the conversation. Start interrogating: Why? What would it take? Has anyone done this? Can we change the conditions? Is there another way?

You'll be surprised how often "can't" turns into "can, here's how." Not always. Sometimes can't is real. But not as often as people think. And the only way to know the difference is to interrogate the assumption.

Drop the T. Turn can't into can. Not through force. Through questions. Not by ignoring reality. By testing whether what we call reality is actually just untested assumption.

That's what Steve did. That's what transformed Apple. That's what you can do too.

Promise me you'll always remember: you're braver than you believe, and stronger than you seem, and smarter than you think. And your team is too. They just need someone to ask: "Says who?"

The Glass Ceiling

"Aim for the sky, and you'll reach the ceiling. Aim for the ceiling, and you'll stay on the floor." — Bill Shankly

In the fall of 2006, deep inside Apple's Cupertino headquarters, two men stood over a prototype unlike any before it.

Steve Jobs and Jony Ive held the early iPhone, not yet named and definitely not yet finished. They knew, with absolute certainty, that its face could not be plastic. It had to be glass. Not just any glass. It had to be thin, thinner than a credit card. Strong, resistant to keys, coins, concrete. Clear, optically pure, with no distortion. And beautiful, warm to the touch and alive with light.

They searched the world. Solicited every major materials supplier. Tested every candidate. Nothing came close.

Then Steve's friend John Brown, a board member at Corning, mentioned a name: Wendall Weeks. Weeks was the CEO of Corning Incorporated, the company that invented Pyrex, fiber optics, and the glass for Hubble's mirror. If anyone had the glass, it would be them.

Steve didn't email. Didn't schedule through channels. He picked up the phone. "Corning switchboard. How may I help you?" "Put me through to Wendall Weeks." "May I ask who's calling?" "Steve Jobs." "I'm sorry, Mr. Jobs. Mr. Weeks is in meetings. May I take a message?" Steve repeated it. Slower, firmer: "No. I'm Steve Jobs. Put me through." Silence. Then: "I still can't connect you."

To Steve, who was used to walking into any room and being the reason it mattered, this was jarring. Not insulting. Just unexpected. He hung up, turned to Brown, and said, half amused, half exasperated: "Typical East Coast BS."

Brown, ever the diplomat, passed the comment along. Weeks didn't take offense. He took interest. A few days later, he picked up his phone and called Apple's main line. "Apple switchboard." "This is Wendall Weeks. I'd like to speak with Steve Jobs." "Certainly, sir. Could you please submit your request in writing? We'll need it faxed to our executive office for processing."

Weeks hung up and laughed out loud. "Typical West Coast BS." He called Brown. "Tell Steve I'd like to meet."

The Meeting

They met in Weeks's office in Corning, New York. A town built on glass, nestled in the Finger Lakes, where furnaces have burned continuously for over a century.

Steve arrived direct, intense, no small talk. Weeks, a materials scientist by training, was equally precise. Steve got straight to the point: "We need glass. For a phone. It has to be strong. Scratch resistant. Thin. Mass producible. In six months."

Weeks listened. Then he leaned back. "We have something you might find interesting." He described a process developed in the 1960s, ion exchange strengthening. Submerge glass in a molten potassium salt bath. Smaller sodium ions on the surface swap with larger potassium ions. The surface compresses. The core stays in tension. The result? Glass five times stronger than untreated. In theory.

"We never made it," Weeks admitted. "It was a lab curiosity. No market. No reason to scale it."

Steve's eyes didn't narrow. They lit. "How much can you make in six months?" Weeks hesitated. "Steve, we don't have a line. No tooling. No yield data. The chemistry is unstable at scale. It's not just hard. It's never been done."

Steve didn't argue the physics. He named the stakes: "This isn't a phone. It's the next step in personal computing. And it needs to be perfect. If we ship plastic, it scratches on day one. Users feel cheated. The whole thing fails."

Then the pivot: "Yes, you can do it." Not a demand. A declaration. "Get your mind around it. You can do it."

Weeks, a man who built his career on data, felt something unfamiliar: not pressure, but possibility. Steve wasn't dismissing the obstacles. He was reframing them, not as walls, but as questions waiting for answers.

Two days later, Weeks called his leadership team. "We're making Gorilla Glass. Full commitment. Six months."

Skepticism rippled through the room. "Wendall, the Kentucky plant is running LCD glass. Retooling would cost millions. Yield could be zero." "We've never run this chemistry outside a beaker." "What if Apple cancels?"

Weeks looked at them. Calm and certain. "Steve Jobs doesn't cancel. He ships. And if he believes we can do this, maybe we should believe it too."

The Kentucky facility was a 500,000 square foot plant built for flat-panel displays, shut down some time ago. Assembly lines were ripped out. Clean rooms reconfigured. Furnace temperatures recalibrated, not for silicon, but for aluminosilicate.

A team of Corning's best materials scientists, process engineers, and chemists was pulled from other projects, not as a task force, but as a mission. For weeks, nothing worked. Glass cracked in the bath. Edges chipped on conveyors. Yield hovered near zero.

Then came a breakthrough. They changed the cooling profile. Made it slower, more controlled. The first full-sized pane came out intact. Then ten. Then a hundred.

By month four, they were shipping samples to Apple. Jony Ive held one up to the light. Perfect. No haze, no green tint, no distortion. He tapped it with a key. No scratch. Dropped it on concrete. No shatter. Steve nodded. "This is it."

No one today talks about what Corning risked then. If the iPhone had failed, if the glass had cracked in testing, if Apple had pivoted to plastic, Corning would have been left with a shuttered plant, a $20 million retooling bill, and a technology with no buyer.

Weeks knew this. Steve knew this. And still they moved. Because the deepest truth about breakthroughs is this: They are not born from safety. They are born from shared conviction, the moment one person's "impossible" becomes two people's responsibility.

The Unveiling

On January 9, 2007, Steve unveiled the iPhone. The world saw a phone. Weeks saw six months of sleepless nights, furnace logs, yield charts, and a team that refused to quit.

Later that day, an email arrived in his inbox. Just three lines: "Wendall, We couldn't have done it without you. Steve"

He printed and framed it. It sits on his desk to this day.

What This Actually Teaches

This is not a story about glass. It is about the moment a CEO stopped defending the possible and started building it.

Weeks didn't lack capability. He lacked permission, not from his board, but from himself, to believe a lab curiosity could become a global standard. Steve didn't provide answers. He provided context: This isn't about glass. It's about trust. It's about the first impression a user has and whether it says 'precious' or 'disposable'.

He didn't say "Figure it out." He said "You already know how. Now go prove it to yourself."

This story contains everything you need to know about breaking through ceilings.

Element One is the vision must be specific. Not "we need better glass" but "thin, strong, clear, scratch-resistant, mass-producible in six months." Vague vision creates vague commitment. Specific vision creates accountability.

Element Two is the stakes must be clear. "This isn't a phone. It's the next step in personal computing." When people understand why it matters, not just to you, but to millions, they find capacity they didn't know they had

Element Three is the confidence must be genuine. "You can do this" only works if you actually believe it. Steve wasn't bluffing. He'd seen Corning's capabilities. He knew about the 1960s research. He understood what they were capable of. His confidence was informed, not blind.

Element Four is the risk must be shared. Steve didn't say "figure it out or we'll find someone else." He made it clear: Apple needed Corning. This was partnership, not procurement. When risk is shared, commitment deepens.

Element Five is the follow-through must be real. "We couldn't have done it without you." Three lines. Printed and framed. Still on the desk. Recognition matters. Not the gesture, the genuineness.

You don't need to be launching the iPhone to apply these lessons. Every time you face a "never been done" moment, you have a choice: accept it as impossible, or reframe it as unexplored.

The pattern is always the same: Someone has capability they don't recognize. Someone else sees it clearly enough to name it. Together, they take the leap.

The Questions That Break Ceilings

When you face an "impossible" ask these questions.

Question One: Who has the capability we need, even if they've never used it this way? Corning had the chemistry. They'd just never scaled it. Steve saw that.

Question Two: What would make this worth the risk to them? Not just money. Purpose. Partnership. Recognition. Being part of something significant.

Question Three: Am I asking them to guess, or giving them clarity? "We need better glass" gets a shrug. "Thin, strong, clear, scratch-resistant, six months" gets action.

Question Four: Do I actually believe they can do this? If you don't, they won't. Confidence has to be genuine.

Question Five: Am I willing to share the risk? If you're not committed, why should they be?

The Real "Reality Distortion Field"

This is what people mean when they talk about Steve's "reality distortion field": the courage to hold a vision so clearly, others begin to see it too, not as fantasy, but as their next assignment.

Not manipulation. Not delusion. Clarity. Steve saw what Gorilla Glass could be before it existed at scale. He saw it clearly enough to describe it. Specifically enough to make it real in Weeks's mind. Then Weeks did the same for his team. And the team did the impossible, because someone they trusted told them it wasn't impossible.

If you're facing a ceiling, technical, organizational, cultural, ask: What would it take to break through? Not "is it possible?" but "what would make it possible?"

Who has the capability we need? Even if they've never used it this way. Even if they don't recognize it themselves.

What would give them the confidence to try? Clarity about the goal. Understanding of the stakes. Belief from someone they respect.

Am I willing to share the risk? Not just ask them to take it. Share it.

Can I hold the vision clearly enough that others can see it too? Not vaguely. Specifically. Compellingly.

That's how ceilings break. Not by force. By shared conviction. One molecule of trust at a time.

Ceilings aren't broken by shouting "it's possible!" They're dissolved by someone who sees clearly enough to say: "Here's exactly what we need. Here's why it matters. Here's why I believe you can do it. And here's the risk I'm willing to share with you."

Then the ceiling isn't a barrier anymore. It's just the next problem waiting to be solved. By people who stopped defending the possible and started building it. Together.

That's the lesson. Not that Steve had magic powers. But that he had clarity, and the courage to share it with someone who had capability but needed permission to use it. Permission not from authority, but from belief.

Weeks had the chemistry. Steve had the vision. Together, they had Gorilla Glass.

What ceiling are you facing? Who has the capability you need? What vision do you need to share with them?

Your version of 'the glass' is already in the lab. It's just waiting for someone to believe it belongs in the world. Be that someone.

The $500 Mouse

"Everything is theoretically impossible until it is done." — Robert A. Heinlein

When Steve Jobs walked into Xerox PARC on December 10, 1979, he wasn't touring a lab. He was stepping into the future, and immediately saw that it was already forming fast.

The demonstration lasted three hours. A researcher named Larry Tesler showed them Smalltalk, a graphical interface where windows overlapped, icons could be dragged, text flowed like ink on paper. A pointing device amusingly being called 'the mouse' moved a cursor with quiet precision.

Steve didn't take notes. He leaned forward, jaw slacked, eyes wide, as if witnessing a miracle. When it ended, he turned to the Xerox team and said, voice thick with disbelief: "You're sitting on a goldmine and you don't even know it."

They did not. To Xerox, this wasn't the future. It was a footnote, a research curiosity in a company built on printing things on paper. And that disconnect between invention and intention would define the next decade of computing.

The Myth of Theft

For years, the story went like this: Apple stole the Mac from Xerox. It's a tidy narrative. Dramatic. Moral. And it's almost entirely false.

Xerox didn't hide its technology. It offered it repeatedly, publicly, but the market refused. In 1981, it launched the Xerox Star, a $16,590 workstation aimed at corporate offices. It had windows. Icons. Ethernet networking. A mouse. It was, in many ways, ahead of the Mac. But it failed spectacularly. Only 30,000 units sold over its entire lifespan.

Why? Because it solved the wrong problem. The Star wasn't built for people. It was built for documents. More specifically, for digitizing paper workflows. Its interface mirrored an office: folders, files, in-baskets. You didn't create. You processed.

Menus had no grayed-out options because the system didn't anticipate error. You could click anything but get an error message: "Command not available." Icons couldn't be dragged. Windows couldn't overlap. Radio buttons? Checkboxes? Absent. It felt less like a tool and more like a bureaucrat in software form.

Xerox tried again in the late 1980s with GlobalView, a version of Star for PCs. By then, the Mac had been on shelves for years and customers knew what good felt like: overlapping windows that responded to a flick of the wrist, menus that knew what you could do and grayed out the rest, a mouse that worked on desks, laps, even jeans.

GlobalView looked like the Mac but it felt like a trap. This wasn't theft. It was evolution. Apple wasn't copying Xerox. It was correcting it.

Even the financials tell the real story: Xerox invested $1 million in Apple for access to PARC. That deal returned $17 million at IPO. Not exploitation. Partnership.

The Mouse Problem

And the mouse? Xerox didn't invent it. It inherited it from Doug Engelbart's 1960s lab at Stanford, and they optimized it for lab conditions, not living rooms.

Their mouse cost over $300 to build, making it prohibitively expensive as a component. It used dozens of precision ball bearings to support a roller bar, elegant in theory, disastrous in practice. Dust clogged the bearings. Friction made it skip. Within weeks, it usually broke.

To Xerox engineers, it was a triumph of miniaturization. To Steve, it was a betrayal of purpose. He wanted a mouse that cost $15. One that worked on formica, wood, and denim. One that lasted years, not weeks. A mouse that moved in any direction, not just the rigid up-down, left-right of Xerox's design.

An Apple engineer heard the specs and laughed: "Impossible." Steve didn't argue. He replaced him. The new engineer walked in the next day, turned to programmer Bill Atkinson, and said: "I can build the mouse." He believed it. He just couldn't do it. So Steve went elsewhere.

The Rooftop Lab

Dean Hovey wasn't a corporate vendor. He was a co-founder of Hovey-Kelley Design, a scrappy firm with one room, one rooftop machine shop, and a big dream.

Their office was the size of a small bedroom. The "machine shop" sat on a roof covered in green outdoor carpeting, shielded by clear corrugated plastic. Tools were borrowed. Parts were scavenged. Budgets were measured in lunch money.

Hovey had come to Apple to pitch new product ideas. Steve let him get two words out, then cut him off: "Build me a mouse." "What's a mouse?" Hovey asked.

Steve explained: "A $300 device that breaks in two weeks. I need one that costs fifteen bucks, lasts years, and works on my blue jeans." Then he leaned in: "This will make computers accessible to ordinary people. This is revolutionary."

That last sentence changed everything. Hovey didn't hear a spec list. He heard a calling.

He left the meeting and went straight to Walgreens. He bought every ball deodorant stick on the shelf, you know, the kind that used a smooth sphere to dispense gel. And a plastic butter dish along with a jar of Ralph's Grocery fruit preserves for the metal lid.

Back on the roof, the real work began. For weeks, the shop looked like a mad inventor's garage: dozens of plastic mouse shells, hand carved from blocks. A spool of guitar wire, bent into tension springs. Tiny wheels from a child's toy train. The Ralph's lid, sanded smooth for bearings.

One morning, Hovey's wife opened the refrigerator and screamed. The compressor was gone. "I needed the motor," Hovey said, not looking up from his bench. "It'll be twenty dollars to fix. No big deal." When you're in the flow of creation, he explained later, "you figure: Either I can stop and wait or I can go forward and wreck the fridge. You just do it."

The Breakthrough

But even with all that ingenuity, the mouse still failed. The ball skipped. The cursor jittered. Xerox's design relied on pushing the ball down with springs and bearings, precise but fragile.

Then came the moment. Hovey set a ball on his worktable, which happened to be slightly tilted. The ball began to roll. Slowly, smoothly, on its own. He froze. Watched it. Touched it. Let it roll again.

"That's exactly what I want it to do," he whispered. "I want it to roll without slipping. It doesn't need to be pushed. It needs to float."

The insight was physics, not engineering. If you support the ball at two points, dead center on opposite sides, there's zero rotational force. It rolls freely. Barely touched, it gives perfect motion data.

The team built a new mechanism based on two polished rollers, perpendicular, capturing the ball at its equator. A light spring allowed it to maintain contact without pressure. A sculptor's idea gave them a plastic cage to hold the wiring, shielded from shocks, tangles, and user error.

Then came the cord, a hidden crisis. Previous mouse cords were either flexible (and fragile) or strong (and stiff). This needed both. The solution? Injection molded channels inside the cage would guide each wire like veins in a leaf. No strain. No fraying.

A removable ring on the bottom let users pop out the ball and clean the rollers, no tools, so no voiding the warranty.

Xerox had spent years perfecting complexity. Hovey-Kelley spent weeks embracing simplicity. When the first $15 mouse shipped, it didn't just work. It delighted. It was smooth, silent, and reliable. A tool that disappeared in the hand, which left only the work.

What This Actually Teaches

This story isn't about genius. It's about conditions.

Xerox PARC was full of brilliant engineers, but their mandate was research, not shipping. Success was measured in papers, patents, and peer approval, not in whether a secretary in Ohio could use the result without training. Apple's mandate was different. Every decision was filtered through a single question: would this make sense to someone who had never used a computer before?

Steve Jobs didn't ignore physics. He rejected false constraints. Ideas like "mice must be expensive" or "people won't understand pointing" weren't laws of nature, they were assumptions. He understood that "impossible" is often just "unattempted," and he had a method for breaking through it. Name the real problem, not the symptom. Computers were intimidating. Find people who hadn't been trained to say no yet. Give them purpose before process. Remove fear of failure not by lowering standards, but by raising the reason for doing the work.

When Hovey's team scavenged a fridge motor, they weren't being reckless. They were unburdened. Free to fail fast, learn quickly, and rebuild without ceremony. That freedom mattered more than polish or pedigree.

You don't need to be building computer mice to recognize this pattern. Every "impossible" problem looks the same. Someone solved part of it, but optimized for the wrong constraints. The solution costs too much, works too narrowly, or serves the wrong audience. Experts declare it can't be improved because they're trapped by their own assumptions.

Breakthroughs come from changing the constraints. Fifteen dollars instead of three hundred. Denim instead of lab benches. Years of use instead of weeks of testing. Different people, often those who haven't been told it can't be done yet. A different purpose, serving ordinary people rather than impressing other experts. And a different kind of freedom, permission to experiment, discard, and try again.

When you face your own version of the $500 mouse, the steps are straightforward. Identify the false constraint. Reframe the real problem beyond the technical spec. Find the unburdened people who aren't locked into industry thinking. Give them purpose before instructions. Then create conditions that reward resourcefulness, not excess. Limited budget, real urgency, and permission to fail often outperform unlimited resources.

Breakthroughs don't happen in boardrooms. They happen where constraints are tight and intent is clear. Xerox had better resources. Apple had better constraints. Xerox optimized for precision. Apple optimized for humanity. They asked different questions and got different results.

So what's your $500 mouse? What "impossible" thing is everyone quietly accepting as necessary? Ask what assumption is being treated as fact. Ask what problem actually needs solving. Ask who might see it fresh. Then build the conditions that let resourcefulness surface.

The $500 mouse became the $15 mouse not through magic, but through method: clear purpose, the right constraints, unburdened people, and permission to fail. You already have access to those ingredients. The only remaining step is to stop treating "impossible" as final, and start treating it as simply never attempted.

Seeing Their Work as Art

"When I say artist, I mean the one who is building things... some with a brush — some with a shovel — some choose a pen." — Jackson Pollock

Steve Jobs did not believe in "creative types" and "technical types." He believed in people, and in the quiet truth that craft is craft, whether it's poured in concrete, coded in C, or carved in marble.

To him, artistry wasn't about medium, but rather about insight: "Putting things together in a way no one else has before and finding a way to express that to others who don't have that insight."

He saw no wall between science and soul. Leonardo da Vinci dissected cadavers and painted the Mona Lisa. Michelangelo studied quarry logistics and sculpted David. The finest computer scientists he knew were musicians, not as hobbyists, but as practitioners of structure, timing, and emotional truth.

"I don't believe the best people in any field see themselves as one branch of a forked tree," he told Time in 1999. "I just don't see that."

This wasn't philosophy. It was operating system. And when he returned to Apple in 1997, he wasn't installing a new CEO. He was reigniting a fire that had nearly gone out, one built to warm the soul with the belief that what you build is an extension of who you are.

The original Macintosh was not born in a boardroom. It was forged in a garage culture where engineers slept under desks, designers sketched on napkins, and deadlines were measured in coffee cups.

Steve didn't manage this team. He sculpted it, by elevating, not by dictating. Take the circuit boards. To engineers, a board was a utilitarian map: traces connecting chips, capacitors, resistors. Function mattered. Aesthetics? Irrelevant. No one would ever see them, sealed inside a beige case, hidden behind plastic.

But Steve did. He would hold a prototype board up to the light and reject it. "The lines aren't straight." Engineers groaned. "It works. No one sees it. Why does it matter?"

Steve didn't argue. He showed them. He laid two boards side by side. One was functional, but messy: traces zigzagged, bent at odd angles, crowded like rush hour traffic. The other was clean and rhythmic: lines flowing in parallel, curves gentle, spacing generous.

"Which one feels like it wants to work?" he asked. Silence.

A board with straight lines wasn't just prettier. It was more reliable. Fewer impedance mismatches meant less signal noise, easier debugging. Perfection wasn't vanity. It was respect, for the machine, for the user, for the craft.

This insistence on the unseen, the uncelebrated, and yes, the sometimes unnecessary was exhausting. Engineers worked days, nights, weekends. Holidays blurred. Families complained. Doubt crept in: Is this worth it?

Then the first Mac shipped. They held it, a presence, not a product. The case smooth as river stone. The screen crisp, scrolling like paper in a breeze. The icons simple, joyful, alive. And when they opened it in the lab, they saw it: The board inside was perfect. Every trace straight. Every joint clean. A silent poem in copper and fiberglass.

They couldn't deny it: Steve's "impossible" standard had delivered not just a computer, but a statement.

The Signatures

Then came the gathering. Twenty engineers. One room. Steve at the front, beaming with not only triumph, but also gratitude.

He held up a sheet of paper and said: "Real artists sign their work." One by one, he called them forward. Burrell Smith, the hardware genius. Andy Hertzfeld, the software wizard. Susan Kare, the icon poet. Each stepped up, pen in hand, and signed.

Steve waited. Let the last signature dry. Then he stepped forward, not with flourish, but humility. He signed his name, jobs, in lowercase. And placed it in the center of the page. Not above. Not apart. Surrounded.

Then he told them: "Every Macintosh that leaves this building will carry your names, inside, where no customer will ever see them." A pause. "But you will know. And that matters."

What This Actually Meant

This wasn't ego. It was covenant. In a world that treats makers as replaceable cogs, Steve declared: You are not labor. You are legacy. You are not assembling. You are composing. You are not coding. You are creating.

The Mac wasn't just a machine. It was a monument, to curiosity, to collaboration, to the quiet courage of people who believed something better was possible. And inside every unit, a single truth, etched in metal: We were here. We cared. We built this not for the applause, but for the art of it.

This wasn't theater. It was the theology of Steve's quiet religion of giving a damn.

He knew: Great products don't come from KPIs. They come from meaning. When a designer knows her icon will be the first thing a child sees on a computer, she doesn't just draw. She listens. When an engineer knows his board will live unseen for decades, he doesn't just route traces. He tends. When a programmer knows her scroll must feel like turning a page in a favorite book, she doesn't just code. She breathes.

That's the artistry Steve nurtured: The conviction that excellence is a form of love. And love, properly channeled, is the most powerful engineering tool of all.

What This Looks Like in Your World

This pattern, treating work as craft rather than mere output, shows up everywhere in great organizations. It's the chef who plates food no one will photograph, the carpenter who finishes the back of the cabinet, the programmer who comments code no user will ever read, the designer who adjusts spacing by a single pixel. They do it not for recognition, but because the work deserves their best, even when no one is watching.

Every organization faces the same choice. Treat people as resources to be optimized, or as craftspeople to be elevated. Measure output alone, or nurture craft. Celebrate what's visible, or honor what's unseen. The difference shows up fast. Labor-first cultures get minimum effort, hollow solutions, high turnover, and products that function without inspiring. Craft-first cultures get people who care, solutions that exceed requirements, lower turnover through ownership, and products people genuinely love. The gap isn't skill. It's meaning.

How to Create This Culture

First, see the artistry. Every role has it: the accountant who makes complexity clear, the support rep who turns anger into trust, the ops leader who creates flow from chaos. As a leader, notice it, name it, and acknowledge it.

Second, honor the unseen. Praise the refactored code, the documentation that prevents confusion, the process that stops fires before they start. What you honor gets repeated.

Third, connect work to concrete meaning. Not slogans, but impact. "Your code helps a student love math." "Your design is the first thing someone sees." "Your process lets us help more people." Meaning unlocks capacity.

Fourth, let people own their work. Give decision rights. Trust judgment. When someone can say "I made that," they treat it differently.

Fifth, model it. Leaders who treat their own work as craft give everyone else permission to do the same.

Yes, this costs time, resources, and emotional energy. But the return compounds. People who believe their work matters don't leave for small raises. Products built with care earn loyalty marketing can't buy. Teams that care solve problems no process can predict.

Treating work as art isn't soft. It's practical. It elevates what people build and who they become while building it. When you honor unseen excellence, give ownership, and connect effort to meaning, people do the impossible.

Real artists sign their work, even when no one will ever see the signature. Especially then.

If It Got Accomplished, It Wasn't 'Impossible'

"It always seems impossible until it's done." — Nelson Mandela

There is a quiet violence in the word impossible. Not because it names a boundary, but because it enforces one. It does not describe reality; it replaces it. It substitutes the weight of past failure for the possibility of future creation and in doing so, it robs people of their most vital resource: hope in their own agency.

For decades, Steve Jobs treated the word not as a verdict, but as a provocation. Hearing it was a signal that someone had stopped asking the right questions and started accepting the wrong answers.

Common sense insists that if something is truly impossible, it remains undone. And yet, how often do we call things "impossible" not because they defy physics, but because they defy patience, funding, or permission?

We say impossible when we mean no one has given us a reason to try. We say impossible when we mean the cost of failure is ours alone to bear. We say impossible when we mean I've been taught to confuse motion with progress, and I am exhausted.

Steve did not banish the word through charisma or willpower. He banished it through recontextualization. Rather than denying difficulty, he was restoring dignity to the struggle. He understood that the greatest barrier to achievement is not computational complexity or engineering constraint. It is disconnection, the gap between the task and its human consequence, between the worker and the world their work serves, between effort and meaning.

This was not mysticism. It was systems design applied with the precision of an engineer and the empathy of a poet.

The Engineer Who Didn't Know It Couldn't Be Done

Consider Bill Atkinson, the software engineer who gave the Macintosh its soul: movable, overlapping windows.

To modern eyes, the feature seems so inevitable it's invisible. Windows floating like sheets of paper, layering, resizing, responding to the cursor with quiet authority. But in 1981, on a machine with 128 kilobytes of RAM and an 8 MHz processor, it was considered computational heresy.

The math alone was daunting, involving calculating region intersections in real time, redrawing only the changed pixels, managing z-order without flicker. It was widely believed to be infeasible. Xerox PARC's engineers had attempted it and given up, settling for fixed, tiled windows they called "efficient." Apple's own engineers warned Atkinson: "Don't waste your time. It can't be done."

Atkinson did it anyway. Not because he was the smartest person in the room, though he was, but because he labored under a liberating illusion: he believed Xerox had already solved it.

He had watched the PARC demo in 1979, saw windows stacking and icons dragging. This made him assume that the foundation was proven and the physics were settled. Only later, after weeks of wrestling with recursive region algebra and pixel-by-pixel redraw logic, did he learn the truth: Xerox's system used non-overlapping windows. Their engineers had deemed true overlap "too slow," "too expensive," "impossible" on available hardware, and so they had built a compromise, not a breakthrough.

Atkinson's naiveté was his greatest asset. "I got a feeling for the empowering aspect of naiveté," he said years later, his voice still carrying the wonder of discovery. "Because I didn't know it couldn't be done, I was enabled to do it."

This was not accidental. It was designed. Steve created an environment where ignorance of limits was not punished. It was protected. He shielded his teams from the noise of conventional wisdom not to foster recklessness, but to preserve possibility. Because sometimes, not knowing the rules is the only way to rewrite them. Sometimes, the most radical act is not to break boundaries, but to forget they were ever drawn.

The Question That Saved a Hundred Lifetimes

Then there was Larry Kenyon. Larry was a firmware engineer whose job was to make the Mac's boot sequence as lean as possible. In late 1982, Steve walked into his office and said: "Ten seconds. I want ten seconds off the startup time."

Kenyon didn't roll his eyes. He didn't sigh. He simply stated the truth, as he saw it: "Shaving ten seconds off isn't worth the effort."

It wasn't defiance. It was calculation. Boot time was already under thirty seconds, quite fast for the era. Optimizing further would require rewriting core ROM routines, reworking memory initialization, squeezing cycles from already tight assembly code. The return on investment? Subjectively negligible. A user wouldn't feel ten seconds. So why endure the pain?

Steve didn't raise his voice. He didn't scold. He leaned forward, not as a CEO but as a teacher, and asked a question that would recalibrate Kenyon's entire frame of reference: "If it would save a person's life, would you shave ten seconds off the startup time?"

Kenyon blinked. "That's a silly question."

"If I could show you a way you could save a person's life," Steve continued, "would you do it?"

Now Kenyon hesitated. He couldn't say no to a question framed in human terms. "I'd probably find a way."

Steve started writing down numbers and said, "Okay, we know around 5 million people will be using this computer every day. We know that 5 million times 10 seconds, every day, is roughly 300 million hours a year. So we know that by cutting 10 seconds off the startup time, you could save the equivalent of at least a hundred lifetimes a year."

The equivalent of a hundred lifetimes saved. Every year. He didn't say "efficiency." He didn't say "competitive advantage." He said "lifetimes."

Kenyon just sat there in shock. He'd never thought of it like that. He suddenly saw the world of computers from Steve's perspective. It wasn't that tiny things didn't matter; it was that tiny things mattered incredibly.

Steve had not demanded optimization. He had revealed obligation.

Two weeks later, Kenyon didn't just cut ten seconds. He cut twenty-six. Nearly double the target. He rewrote the ROM loader. He resequenced hardware initialization. He eliminated redundant checks. He found cycles in the gaps between cycles.

Why? Because he no longer saw a number. He saw a promise.

What All This Actually Teaches

The so-called "reality distortion field" was never about warping physics. It was about realigning priority. Steve did not ignore constraints. He exposed the hidden leverage within them and showed that the space between what is and what matters.

And this was no one-off miracle. It was a pattern repeated across decades, across products, across people. The iPhone's capacitive multi-touch screen, dismissed by engineers in 2005 as "unworkable at scale," shipped in 2007 because Steve asked: What if the phone disappeared, and only the content remained?

The App Store, deemed "too risky" by carriers who feared losing control, launched in 2008 because Steve reframed it not as a distribution channel, but as a covenant: If you build it, we'll ensure they come and pay fairly.

The MacBook Air, ridiculed at launch as "a MacBook without a hard drive, without ports, without sense," became the industry standard for ultra-portables because Steve shifted the question from What can we remove? to What happens if you can fit your laptop in an envelope while keeping all its capabilities?

Each time, the chorus was the same: Impossible. Impractical. Unnecessary. Each time, Steve responded not with defiance, but with enrollment: What if we tried? What if we believed? What if the limit isn't in the machine, but in our imagination of what the machine is for?

He understood that innovation is not a solo act. It is a covenant between leader and team, between engineer and user, between present effort and future impact. And covenants require more than specs. They require the kind of meaning that empowers and drives people to turn overtime into devotion, frustration into focus, and exhaustion into endurance.

This is why Steve's bets succeeded where others failed. He didn't just ask people to do the impossible. He helped them see it as inevitable, not through hype, but through human scale.

Unquestionably, half the time, Accepted Reality won. The other half of the time, Accepted Reality had to pay up to Steve. NeXT failed. The G4 Cube flopped. MobileMe stumbled. He lost often. But he played because he knew the biggest loss is folding before the hand is dealt.

How This Shows Up In Your World

You've heard it a thousand times. In conference rooms, in planning sessions, in the exhausted silence after someone proposes something ambitious: "That's impossible."

Sometimes it's stated plainly. More often, it arrives disguised as prudence: "We don't have the budget for that." "The timeline's too aggressive." "Legal will never approve it." "That's not how we do things here." These aren't assessments. They're artifacts of a system that has learned to protect itself from effort.

I've watched companies strangle themselves with this word. Not because their people lack talent, but because their systems lack permission. The engineer who could solve the problem doesn't try because the last three attempts were killed in committee. The designer who sees the elegant solution keeps quiet because simplicity is always harder to defend than complexity. The frontline employee who interacts with customers daily and knows exactly what's broken never speaks up because "that's above my pay grade."

The pattern is always the same: someone identifies a gap between what is and what could be. Then the organizational immune system activates. Budget committees demand ROI projections for innovations that have never existed. Risk management catalogs every conceivable failure mode. Stakeholders request "more research" until the moment passes. And everyone walks away satisfied that they were "realistic."

But here's what I've learned watching teams that break through versus teams that break down: the difference is never talent. It's rarely resources. It's almost always framing.

The teams that accomplish impossible things don't have special powers. They have special questions. They've learned to treat "impossible" not as a conclusion, but as an invitation to interrogate assumptions. And they've built systems that protect possibility long enough for it to become reality.

CHAPTER 14
PROTECT THE PASSION

"You may have to fight a battle more than once to win it." — Margaret Thatcher

On a sunlit June morning in 2005, Steve Jobs stood before the graduating class of Stanford University not as a titan of industry but as a man who had been fired, bankrupted, and told he had months to live.

He didn't offer any ten-point plan for success. He did not promise them disruption, scale, or exit strategies. No, he offered something rarer and more valuable: truth.

"I'm convinced that about half of what separates the successful entrepreneurs from the unsuccessful ones is pure perseverance," Steve said. "Unless you have a lot of passion about this, you're not going to survive. You're going to give it up."

This was not inspiration. It was forecasting. Because real breakthroughs do not arrive wrapped in ribbon. They arrive bleeding from delayed molds, crashing software, team fractures, budget implosions, and key defections to competitors. Yoga and deep breathing will not save you then. Only the kind of passion that feels less like motivation and more like moral obligation will keep you digging when the hole is deep and the light is gone.

Passion is not enthusiasm. It is staying power. It is the quiet voice that says, "This matters not because it will succeed, but because it should exist." It is what lets you love not just the idea, but the grinding, unglamorous work of making it real. And it is what lets you love what you create not merely as a product, but as a promise you will protect at almost any cost.

Three Stories, One Truth

Steve told three stories that day as proof, not as parables.

The first: Trust the dots. At Reed College, Steve had dropped out of the classes that didn't interest him. He then started dropping into the classes that did. One of those was calligraphy. He began to appreciate examples of the art form in the banners, posters, and signs all across campus. He sat in on calligraphy, studying serif and sans serif, spacing and proportion. No practical use. No career path. Just beauty.

Ten years later, that "useless" knowledge became the foundation of Mac typography, helping to inspire the first computer with multiple fonts, true typography, and on-screen WYSIWYG layout.

"You can't connect the dots looking forward," he told them. "You can only connect them looking backward." The lesson? Follow your curiosity even when it seems irrational. The world will catch up.

The second: Don't settle. The second story was about not settling in work or in love. He explained that he considered himself lucky for having discovered what he loved early in life and how that love enabled him to overcome many life losses. He was in his early twenties when he started Apple because he loved computers.

Only a few years later, he was forced from the company he had co-founded, publicly and incredibly painfully. But he didn't retreat. "I still loved what I did. The turn of events at Apple had not changed that one bit. I had been rejected, but I was still in love. And so I decided to start over."

NeXT. Pixar. His love fueled the creation of a new company, NeXT. It was at NeXT that he met the love of his life, Laurene. "Sometimes life hits you in the head with a brick. Don't lose faith," Steve said. "I'm convinced that the only thing that kept me going was that I loved what I did. You've got to find what you love."

His advice was that if you haven't found a purpose, or person, that feels absolutely in sync with your heart, you should keep looking. "As with all matters of the heart, you'll know it when you find it. And, like any great relationship, it just gets better and better as the years roll on. Don't settle."

The third: Fear nothing. His third story was about the freedom from fear that can come from being aware of our inevitable end. Explaining that he began thinking this way at 17, Steve said, "Remembering that I'll be dead soon is the most important tool I've ever encountered to help me make the big choices in life."

It was an idle consideration that each day might be his last. Then, in 2004, things got real. A routine scan found a tumor. Pancreatic cancer. The prognosis: three to six months. Told that it was time to get his affairs in order, Steve was face-to-face with the impending finality of his mortal existence.

During Steve's biopsy the next day, the doctor began weeping. Against all odds, it turned out that Steve had a very rare form of pancreatic cancer. It was treatable with surgery. Still, that brush with death had left an undeniable mark on him.

"Your time is limited, so don't waste it living someone else's life," he told the gathered crowd. Death, he said, is "life's change agent." "Don't let others' dogma dictate your actions. Don't let the noise of others' opinions drown out your inner voice. Have the courage to follow your heart and intuition; they somehow already know what you truly want to become."

In other words: Trust and follow your heart. Don't settle. Fear nothing. Protect the passion.

What This Actually Teaches

The Stanford speech has been played millions of times, quoted endlessly, reduced to inspirational posters and LinkedIn posts. But strip away the sentiment and you're left with something harder and more useful: a diagnostic framework for why people quit.

They quit because they can't connect the dots forward. They need certainty, a clear line from effort to outcome, from investment to return. But breakthrough work doesn't offer that. It offers only the faith that if you follow what matters to you, the connections will reveal themselves later. Most people can't tolerate that ambiguity. So they quit before the dots have time to connect.

They quit because they settle. Not in a single dramatic surrender, but in a thousand small compromises. They take the safer job. They shelve the ambitious project for the achievable one. They stop asking "what should exist?" and start asking "what will get approved?" Each compromise feels reasonable in isolation. Cumulatively, they're fatal. Because you can't sustain years of grinding work for something you only kind of care about.

They quit because they're afraid. Afraid of judgment, of failure, of wasting time on the wrong thing. So they wait for permission, for consensus, for proof that it will work before they commit. But proof only comes after commitment. The person who needs certainty before they act will never act on anything that matters.

Steve's three stories weren't about him. They were about the structure of perseverance itself. What it requires. What kills it. What protects it.

And here's what he understood that most leaders miss: passion is not a personality trait. It's a relationship between person and purpose that either gets protected or poisoned by the systems around it.

You can hire passionate people and watch them become hollow in six months if your systems punish curiosity, demand certainty, and reward caution over conviction. Or you can hire capable people and watch them become zealots if your systems protect exploration, tolerate ambiguity, and honor commitment to craft.

The passion isn't in the person. It's in the arrangement.

How This Shows Up In Your World

I've watched talented people drain themselves empty in organizations that claimed to value innovation but actually valued predictability. The pattern is always the same.

Someone joins energized. They have ideas, curiosity, a vision for what could be better. For the first few months, they try. They propose new approaches. They question inherited wisdom. They volunteer for the hard problems.

Then the system teaches them otherwise. Their proposals get lost in approval chains. Their questions get answered with "that's how we've always done it." Their volunteering gets interpreted as overstepping. And slowly, almost imperceptibly, they learn. They learn that curiosity is risky. That ambition is exhausting. That caring too much about craft makes you the person who slows everything down.

So they stop proposing. They stop questioning. They stop volunteering. Not because they've lost their ability, but because they've lost the faith that it matters. The passion doesn't die dramatically. It drains slowly, meeting by meeting, compromise by compromise, until one day they realize they're just going through motions.

And here's the cruel part: the organization looks at this hollowed-out person and says, "They lost their edge. They're not hungry anymore.

Maybe we need to hire some fresh blood." But the problem was never the person. It was the system that drained them.

I've also watched the opposite. People who seemed ordinary, competent but not exceptional, suddenly catch fire when they find work that connects to something they care about deeply. They don't become different people. They become what they always could have been when passion and purpose align.

The difference isn't in the people. It's in whether the organization protects passion or suffocates it.

Apple Was Controlled by Map Readers, Not Explorers

To see far is one thing; going there is another." — Constantin Brancusi

There is a profound difference between knowing the way and making it.

Map readers travel well. They follow contours, obey signs, trust the legend. They arrive on time, with minimal fuss. In stable times, they are indispensable.

But when the terrain shifts, when the old roads end in fog, when the compass spins? Map readers hesitate. They consult outdated charts. They wait for consensus. They polish the legend while the world moves on.

Explorers do not wait. They read the wind. They listen to silence. They step into the unknown not because they are certain of the destination, but because they are certain of the need to move.

Steve Jobs was not a map reader. He was an explorer, and Apple, under his guidance, became a vessel built for uncharted waters. This was method, not temperament.

Entering uncharted technology categories, iPod, iPhone, iPad, required not data, but diagnosis. Not market research, but mental and moral clarity.

Steve did not ask, "What do people say they want?" He asked, "What are they doing despite what they say?" He saw the friction of CDs, the rage at carrier control, the quiet frustration of adults trying to use tablets like laptops, and he knew: the map was wrong.

When everyone shares the wheel as Apple did in the Sculley and Amelio years, accountability dissolves. Decisions blur. Momentum stalls. It becomes impossible to say who steered the car into the ditch because everyone was holding on, hoping someone else would correct the course.

But when paths diverge? When one leader chooses the ridge while the rest cling to the valley? The divergence becomes undeniable. Apple's trajectory proves it.

Between 1985 and 1997, Apple drifted not from lack of talent, but from lack of direction. Sculley, while a brilliant marketer, saw the Mac as a tool for productivity. It was merely a machine to bring work home. He optimized for enterprises, ignored creators, and outsourced vision to committees. The result? Beige boxes, fragmented models, and a culture of incrementalism.

Steve's return was not a correction. It was a reorientation. He did not tweak the map. He burned it and drew a new one.

The Boy Who Asked, "What Can I Do With It?"

The clearest early signal of Steve's explorer mindset came not in a boardroom, but at a birthday party.

In 1985, a Playboy reporter found Steve at a gathering for Sean Lennon's ninth birthday in New York. Steve's gift? A Macintosh that was more than a toy. This was invitation to a new way of life.

He sat with the boy, guiding him through MacPaint. Steve wasn't teaching commands, he was unlocking possibility with each new tool he shared excitedly. As the child sketched freely, two giants of art, Andy Warhol and Keith Haring, drifted in, drawn by the quiet intensity in the room.

Warhol peered over Steve's shoulder. "Hmmm, what is this? Look at this, Keith. This is incredible!" He took the mouse, drew a circle. "My God! I drew a circle!"

Later, the reporter asked why Steve seemed more fulfilled with the boy than with the legends.

Steve's answer was at once quiet yet definitive: "Older people sit down and ask, 'What is it?' But the boy asks, 'What can I do with it?'"

That simple but devastating sentence named the fault line in tech. Sculley saw customers as users. People to be served, controlled, upsold. Steve saw them as creators. People to be empowered, trusted, unleashed.

The boy was not a demographic. He was a signal. The future did not belong to executives in corner offices. It belonged to children with questions and adults who still asked them.

The iPod, iPhone, and iPad: Off-Road Shortcuts

In 2001, Apple launched the iPod and the world scoffed: "A $399 music player? In the age of MP3s and file sharing?" "Apple is abandoning computers." "This is a distraction, a dead end.

Map readers saw abandonment. Explorers saw alignment. Steve understood: the real problem was not storage at this point when it came to music, it was friction. Illegal downloads thrived not because people loved theft but because legal music was broken: confusing stores, variable pricing, crippled files.

The iPod plus iTunes was not a product. It was a covenant: "If you pay fairly, we'll give you a better product and you'll stop being pirates." The result was more than just sales. It was a reputation reboot. PC users bought iPods and for the first time, held an Apple product in their hands. They felt the click wheel. Saw the interface. Experienced coherence.

When it came time to buy a new computer, many chose Mac. This was the halo effect, not marketing but magnetism.

In 2007, Steve unveiled the iPhone and the chorus rose again. "No keyboard? Impossible." "Carriers will never allow it." "It's too expensive. Too fragile. Too Apple."

Every phone maker saw the carrier as the customer. Apple saw the human. Steve refused to let AT&T dictate features. He refused to add physical keyboards just to soothe skeptics. He insisted the phone disappear, leaving only content, connection, life. The industry called it hubris. History called it revolution.

Within five years, the iPhone generated more profit per quarter than Microsoft's entire operation.

By 2010, tablets were a graveyard. Microsoft, HP, Samsung all had tried. All had failed. Conventional wisdom declared the category dead.

Steve ignored the obituaries. He watched people and saw how they held devices, how they read, and envisioned how they wanted to create.

Others built shrunken laptops: clunky desktop OS on glass, USB ports for peripherals no one carried, styluses because "real work requires precision." Apple built a blank canvas: 100% touch, no ports, no compromises, an interface that assumed you were the tool.

Critics howled: "Not a real computer." "No multitasking? Unusable." "Where's the file system?" They were reading the old map while Steve was drawing the new one.

Within months, Apple had not just entered the tablet market, it had invented it. Competitors scrambled to follow because the path was now clear, lit by Apple's torch.

In 1996, after announcing his return, replacing the board, cutting the product line from dozens to four, and declaring war not on competitors but on confusion, Steve walked offstage. He turned to a colleague, and with the faintest smile, said: "Madman at the wheel, eh?"

It wasn't bravado. It was acknowledgment. Because the world confuses direction with destiny. Map readers wait for the path to be proven, for data to confirm, for markets to validate, for others to go first. They mistake caution for wisdom and in doing so, surrender the future to those willing to step into the fog.

Explorers know the truth Brancusi named: To see far is one thing. Going there is another. Seeing is insight. Going is courage.

It is the daily choice to ship the imperfect 1.0. To defend the unseen circuit trace. To bet on the child who asks "What can I do with it?" while the world still asks "What is it?"

In a world that praises arrivals but fears navigation, the most radical act is to fold up the map and find new horizons.

What This Actually Teaches

The distinction between map readers and explorers is not about personality. It's about decision architecture.

Map readers optimize for certainty. They want validated paths, proven models, consensus from stakeholders. This is not cowardice. In stable environments, it's efficiency. Why reinvent what works? Why take unnecessary risk?

But markets are not stable. Technology is not stable. Customer needs are not stable. The map that worked last quarter might be obsolete by next. And organizations that can only follow proven paths find themselves perpetually behind, always optimizing for yesterday's landscape.

Explorers optimize for learning. They move toward uncertainty not because they love risk, but because they understand that the most valuable information lives where the map ends. They know that by the time a path is proven and mapped and validated, the advantage is gone. First-mover advantage is real, but it's not about speed. It's about the willingness to move before you're certain.

The tragedy of Apple in the wilderness years, 1985 to 1997, was not that they hired the wrong people. Sculley was brilliant. The engineers were talented. The designers were capable. The tragedy was that they built a system that required certainty before action. Every product needed committee approval. Every decision needed market validation. Every risk needed mitigation plans.

So they made safe bets. Incremental improvements. Line extensions. Products that looked like what came before, just slightly better. And they wondered why customers stopped caring.

Steve's return was not about replacing people. It was about replacing the decision architecture. He built a system that could move without certainty, that could bet on insight over data, that could choose direction over consensus.

And the results speak for themselves. Three category-defining products in nine years. Not because Steve was magic, but because the system he built could tolerate the uncertainty required to create something genuinely new.

How This Shows Up In Your World

I've watched companies strangle themselves by demanding certainty before action. Not obviously, not dramatically, just quietly through their processes.

Someone proposes entering a new market. The response: "Let's do more research. Let's validate the opportunity. Let's build a business case." Six months later, they've built a beautiful PowerPoint deck proving the market exists. And a competitor who didn't wait for certainty already has 30% market share.

Someone suggests redesigning a core workflow. The response: "Let's survey users. Let's test options. Let's make sure we're solving the right problem." A year later, they've validated that yes, the problem exists. Meanwhile, users have found workarounds or switched to alternatives.

Someone proposes a bold product vision. The response: "Let's phase it. Let's start with MVP. Let's prove demand first." Three years later, they've shipped a compromised version that nobody loves because they optimized for reducing risk instead of creating value.

The pattern is always the same: organizations that require certainty get it, but they get it too late. By the time they're certain, the opportunity has closed.

I've also watched the opposite. Companies that move before they're certain, that bet on diagnosis over data, that choose direction over consensus. They don't win every time. But they learn faster. And in fast-moving markets, learning faster is winning.

The difference is never about having better information. It's about how much certainty you require before you act.

Oh Yes, There Will Be Blood

"It ain't about how hard you hit. It's about how hard you can get hit and keep moving forward." — Rocky Balboa

"It ain't about how hard you hit. It's about how hard you can get hit and keep moving forward." — Rocky Balboa

There is a moment in every leader's journey when the path forks not between success and failure, but between compromise and conviction. It does not typically announce itself with fanfare. No boardroom vote. No press release. It arrives as a quiet request: Just this once. Just a little data. Just to stay competitive.

Steve Jobs faced that moment in 2011. And he said no.

The world remembers the fallout, the Maps fiasco of 2012, the headlines, the apology, but the cause gets forgotten. This was not a technical failure. It was a moral boundary that was drawn, crossed, and defended.

To understand why Apple's stumble mattered and why its recovery was inevitable, we must go deeper than bug reports and press cycles. We must examine the architecture of power in the digital age at the time and the two irreconcilable visions of what technology is for.

When Allies Become Adversaries

In 2006, Apple and Google stood as allies, not competitors, hard as that may be to imagine today.

Eric Schmidt, Google's CEO, joined Apple's board. Steve admired Google's search interface because it was clean, fast, and uncluttered. Google admired Apple's hardware for the same qualities. It was at once beautiful, intuitive, and human-centered.

The iPhone launched in 2007 with Google Maps and Google Search built in. YouTube followed. For a time, it worked: Apple provided the vessel; Google, the content.

But beneath the surface, the foundations were shifting. Google's business model was not search. It was surveillance. Its product was not information. It was attention, harvested, profiled, auctioned for its advertising business.

Every query. Every route. Every video watched. Every app opened. All fed into a machine that answered one question above all: How can we predict and profit from what this person will do next?

Apple's model was different, not because it was naive, but because it was old-fashioned. It believed in transactional trust: You pay for a device. We make it work beautifully. Your data stays yours.

These were not competing strategies. They were incompatible cosmologies.

Steve saw the divergence early. In 2008, Android launched not as an original approach, but as a mirror. Same icons. Same gestures. Same philosophy: If you liked the iPhone, you'll love this free version. Left unsaid was the part about you becoming the product as they harvested information for their advertising partners and laughed at the idea of your privacy.

Steve's response was private, but searing: "They want to kill the iPhone. We won't let them."

This cold war was not declared in press conferences. It was waged in API restrictions, data denials, and withheld features.

Google began limiting iOS access: turn-by-turn navigation (Android only), real-time traffic (Android only), high-resolution satellite imagery (Android only), offline map caching (Android only).

Apple's Maps app was built on Google's data feed and began to feel second-class. A lite experience. A preview of what loyalty to Google would earn any partner, frankly.

Apple had a serious dilemma. How could Apple tout a first-in-class iPhone maps experience with a product that lacked standard turn-by-turn directions?

Consumers were uninterested in the behind-the-scenes machinations and simply blamed Apple for falling behind. Apple had negotiated the original terms for the mapping data before features such as turn-by-turn were commonplace. Now, years later, when Apple wanted to license those additional features, Google demanded that Apple hand over their customers' information before any license would be negotiated. Apple thought different.

There were alternative YouTube clients that didn't feed Google all the advertising data, allowed the downloading of videos, and offered more advanced features. These alternatives didn't force users to create a Google account that intermingled all their emails, searches, private instant messages, and social network.

On tablets and mobiles, official Google apps forced a user who simply wanted to bookmark a video to hand over all their private information and enable tracking of their online activity. Some things never change, at least not as of this book's printing.

Apple removed the YouTube official application as a default on the next iOS update. Now, users could simply search the app store and make their own choice among dozens of free and paid YouTube clients. Apple ensured there was choice.

When Apple asked to license the full maps suite of features, Google's terms were explicit: Give us your users' location histories. Their search habits. Their movement patterns. In return, you may have parity.

Steve refused. This was not stubbornness. It was continuity. From the Mac's straight circuit traces to the iMac's radiant heating, Steve had always believed that great products serve people, not extract from them.

To hand over user data without the user's permission would not just violate policy. It would betray the covenant at Apple's core: We make tools for creators. Not subjects. It would be years before the platforms would build in granular levels of explicit privacy permission granting, so that wasn't an option at the time.

The Choice: Surrender or Build

Apple faced three paths.

Surrender: Accept Google's terms, become a data conduit, join the surveillance economy. Pros: Immediate feature parity. Short-term peace. Cons: Erosion of trust. Loss of differentiation. Moral drift.

Stall: Keep using Google Maps, endure degradation, hope users wouldn't notice. Pros: No engineering lift. No risk. Cons: Slow death by a thousand cuts. Brand erosion. Team disillusionment.

Build: Start from zero. Invest billions. Risk public failure. Pros: Control. Privacy. Long-term sovereignty. Cons: Everything else.

Steve chose Build. Not because he was reckless. Because he understood the deeper truth: in a world of data monopolies, independence is not a feature, it is oxygen.

Apple hired over a thousand cartographers, geospatial engineers, and satellite imaging specialists. It flew planes and Lidar-equipped cars across continents. It negotiated with local governments, transit authorities, and emergency services for ground truth data.

The goal wasn't to match Google. It was to redefine the category from surveillance tool back into service. The fact it would put Google in a pinch was icing on the cake.

Apple Maps would be private by design (no profile, no tracking, no ads disguised as results), human-centered (prioritize not just cars, but walking, transit, and even wheelchair access), aesthetically coherent (intuitive hierarchy with smooth vector rendering and clean typography), and integrated (because maps are not destinations but connections, deep links to Calendar, Messages, and Photos).

This was not a "me too" product. It was a manifesto written in code, launched in public.

The Stumble: When Principle Meets Reality

On September 19, 2012, iOS 6 shipped with Apple Maps as default. The reaction was immediate and brutal.

A search for "Washington, D.C." showed a mall in Maryland. The Brooklyn Bridge spanned a parking lot. In Australia, a desert location was labeled a major city.

Headlines screamed: "Apple Maps flaw could be deadly, warn Australian police." (CNN) "So bad it can kill you." (BGR) "A service that used to work well suddenly became not only ineffective but actually counterproductive, even dangerous." (MIT Technology Review)

Forbes declared: "Google Maps War With Apple Is Over — Google Won." Google ran ads mocking Apple's errors while using a fake Manhattan address that didn't exist.

The narrative was set: Apple failed. Steve's perfectionism had cracked. The emperor had no maps.

But the truth was more complex. Apple had made quantum leaps: replaced raster tiles with vector maps (yielding 10x faster rendering using 70% less data), built real-time turn-by-turn with voice guidance (making it no longer a premium feature), launched 3D flyovers (satellite-derived, tilt-enabled, no Street View cars needed), and integrated public transit in over 30 cities (a feature Google wouldn't match for years).

These were not incremental updates. They were architectural revolutions, and like all revolutions, they bled.

The press did not ask: Why did Apple take this risk? They asked: Why wasn't it perfect?

Because perfection is the enemy of principle. And in a world that confuses polish with integrity, shipping a 1.0 with conviction is the ultimate act of courage.

The Fix: In Public, With Purpose

Apple did not retreat. It responded. Tim Cook's apology was not weakness. It was accountability, rare in an industry built on deflection.

"We fell short of this commitment. We are extremely sorry. We are doing everything we can to make Maps better."

He listed alternatives not as surrender, but as respect: Your time matters. Choose what works now.

Then came the work: 400 fixes in 50 days (2012), Flyover in 27 cities and Transit in 228 (2013), Indoor maps for malls and airports (2014), dedicated map data centers and Lidar mapping (2018), Cycling directions, AR walking, Look Around (2020).

Each update was quieter than the last. The firestorm faded. The product improved. Because Apple understood that trust is not restored by promises. It is rebuilt, query by query, route by route, home by home.

By 2015, Apple Maps usage on iPhones had tripled Google's. Not because it was perfect. Because it was theirs. While over time and with new entries like Waze, Apple Maps has fallen, it remains a still respectable roughly one-third of iPhone users versus Google Maps today.

The Deeper War

This was never about maps. It was about what we owe each other.

Google's model assumes: People are data points. Attention is currency. Privacy is friction.

Apple's model assumes: People are ends, not means. Attention is sacred. Privacy is the foundation of freedom.

These are not business strategies. They are ethical positions, and in the digital age, ethics are infrastructure.

When Google demanded your location to "improve the experience," it was not optimizing for you. It was optimizing for the advertiser paying for your attention. When Apple built offline Maps, it was not sacrificing ad revenue. It was honoring a deeper contract: Your life is not for sale.

Steve knew this in his bones. He had seen what happens when technology serves power, not people, at Xerox, at IBM, and at Microsoft. He would not let Apple become another engine of extraction.

To be fair, Apple did eventually enter the advertising business, with an extremely important caveat: Users had to explicitly agree to each data point for each app or website. Location, contact information, and more were all specifically presented to the users and there could be no penalty for refusing on Apple's platform.

Sure, if you want to ignore the complete fundamental difference in that model, you could try to paint them as hypocrites. You could try, anyway.

CHAPTER 15
CREATION REQUIRES CONVICTION

"You have enemies? Good. That means you've stood up for something, sometime in your life." — Winston Churchill

"I don't care. That's what I want," Steve snapped. It was 1998, and Steve and the director of the iMac's hardware, Paul Rubinstein, were arguing over which CD drive it would have. Steve had caved on the original iMac after a fierce battle waged mere weeks before the product's unveiling. He detested the aesthetics of tray-loading CD drives and demanded that Rubinstein switch to a sleeker-looking slot-loading drive. Steve had already gone to the drive manufacturers and persuaded them to do a slot-loading CD drive for the new iMacs. He wasn't backing down.

Rubinstein insisted that "If you go to slots, you will always be behind in the technology." They might look pretty, he was telling Steve, but soon CD drives would arrive that could write CDs. Those writeable CD drives would come in tray form far sooner than they arrived in slot-loading versions. Still, Steve insisted. "I want you to do the slot-load drive for me as a personal favor," he said.

Rubinstein caved, and the effects were felt on the iMac for years. Apple was several years behind PCs when they finally were able to get record-able slot-loading CD drives in the iMacs.

Steve was violating his own product Golden Rule by demanding an Apple product decision that was pleasing in the short run but damaging in the long run. Rubinstein shouldn't have caved, no matter how loud Steve's tantrum was.

Compromising a product's long-term vision to please others in the short run rarely turns out well, and nobody knew that better than Steve himself. The slot-loading drive demand was a rare departure from the principle he had directed Apple to embrace since its return.

When Conviction Means Saying No to Everyone

Why does Apple rarely cave in to highly vocal product design complaints? The company takes a pounding from tech critics, who describe Apple as 'arrogant' for sticking to its product decisions. However, when you dig into the facts of those decisions, Apple always has a method to its madness.

Steve always pushed Apple to go for what he was convinced was the right choice for the product rather than what outside consensus declared correct. The computer world was apoplectic over the iMac rejecting a floppy drive in 1997. PCs still included the pitiful 1.4-megabyte floppy drive, as a matter of course. 'How dare Steve yank away the industry's security blanket!' went the howls of protest.

In an era where most PCs couldn't boot off of a CD, and installing Windows 95 still required a special floppy boot disk, the protests were almost understandable. The floppy drive was a staple of the industry. It was also basically obsolete.

The original Mac was the first in the industry to completely dump the 5" floppy for the 3.5" floppy. Apple introduced the world to Sony's 3.5" floppy in 1985. Beginning at merely 400 kilobytes, Wozniak had wowed the world with his brilliant improvements that doubled the capacity to 800 kilobytes. In 1988, the floppy was up to a whopping 1.4 megabytes of storage. Ten years later, it was at an astounding 1.4 megabytes. A decade had brought absolutely zero improvements in the floppy drive.

Meanwhile, modems, the early internet, email, CDs, and hard drives had all passed the floppy by. Steve wasn't about to include this dead-end tech in his futuristic iMac just because people thought they needed it. He was right that they didn't.

Creating the Vacuum

The PC industry had basically ignored USB for years. It was on the computer motherboards, but that's about it. Mice and keyboards were still old-style serial connectors. Printers were using even older parallel connectors. There were no real peripherals that were using USB. Then, with the iMac, Steve created a vacuum.

The iMac had one method of connecting virtually every peripheral: USB. It had a USB keyboard and mouse. If a printer manufacturer wanted to sell to the new iMac customer, they'd need to step up and release a USB printer. Thanks to the iMac, many peripheral makers launched their first-ever round of USB-based accessories. It wasn't a coincidence that most of them were made in a translucent Bondi-blue housing to match the iMac.

Steve created the pressure to move forward. That pressure won't get created by coddling your customers.

Apple was telling its customers that if they wanted to move their Word document from work to home, they must get with the times and email it. If they wanted to backup their computer's hard drive? It was time to ditch those floppies that held less than one writeable CD.

Customers often resist changes, regardless of the eventual benefits. Apple succeeds by making extremely well-chosen leaps forward in technologies, then bringing their customers on board.

In 2012, the iMac again broke with the industry and shipped without a CD drive. "These old technologies are holding us back," Phil Schiller, Apple's head of marketing, told Time. "They're anchors on where we want to go. We find the things that have outlived their useful purpose [and we remove them]. Our competitors are afraid to remove them." Apple was the first in the industry to release its computer with its OS restore software on a USB key.

This time, the industry isn't quite so behind Apple's lead. Sony announced in 2012 they were exiting the PC CD and DVD drive business entirely.

Apple's leaps forward aren't limited to its desktop computers.

The Keyboard That Wasn't There

The iPhone would never have become the platform for gaming or internet browsing that it is if Steve had approved keeping a physical keyboard on it. A physical keyboard may have been reassuring to consumers, but it was a terrible handicap to a device meant to completely transform itself to suit any interface or application.

An on-screen keyboard could easily switch layouts to fit each purpose. Browsing the internet? Then a devoted '.com' button was a godsend. Holding that button down popped up the less common domains, such as '.net' and '.edu.' Sending an email? Then the keyboard offering both a direct '@' key, as well as the '.com,' becomes extremely time-saving. Critics claimed that adding these keys to a physical keyboard on the device was an equally effective solution. Oh really? Where would all those keys go when you launched a first-person shooter game or a jigsaw puzzle?

Apple wasn't shy about refusing to include 3G before the technology was mature enough not to drain batteries insanely quickly. Customers may have clamored for the quicker download speeds of 3G, but they weren't yet confronted with the drawbacks of terrible battery life.

The original iPhone could browse the web on cellular data for more than five and a half hours. When Apple released the iPhone 3G, the browsing time on cellular fell to just over three and a half hours. Apple hadn't been lying when they said 3G wasn't ready for prime time.

Phones like the Samsung Blackjack were barely getting an hour and a half of browsing when using 3G. Critics and customers were vocal in complaining about the very 3G technology they had been demanding from Apple. Imagine if Apple had joined its competitors and given in earlier.

Steve answered the Wall Street Journal's complaints about the iPhone lacking 3G by saying, "When we looked at 3G, the chipsets were not quite mature, in the sense that they're not low enough power for what we were looking for. They were not integrated enough, so they took up too much physical space. We cared a lot about battery life, and we cared a lot about physical size. Down the road, I'm sure some of those tradeoffs will become more favorable towards 3G, but as of now, we think we made a pretty doggone good decision."

Not only was the power demand an issue, but Steve was pointing to the physical space those 3G chips took up at the time. The iPhone would have been a massive brick if Apple had gone that route. The 2G chips required for the iPhone were just three small chips. The 3G route would have required finding space for seven separate chips, with one of those chips being as large as the three 2G chips combined.

Compromising your vision by catering to knee-jerk, vocal consumer demands rarely turns out well. Those types of consumers rarely think things through, and they will run head-on into the problems you already foresaw.

By not catering to these customers, you'll avoid being the one they blame for their new problems. Give 'em what they need, not what they want.

What This Actually Teaches

The slot-loading CD drive story is instructive precisely because Steve was wrong. He prioritized aesthetics over functionality and Apple paid the price for years. But notice what happened: Rubinstein knew it was wrong, argued against it, and then caved when Steve insisted.

This reveals the difference between conviction and stubbornness. Conviction is holding to a principle even when pressured. Stubbornness is holding to a preference even when proven wrong. Steve usually operated from conviction. The slot-loader was stubbornness. And stubbornness hurt Apple.

But the other stories—the floppy drive, USB-only, no physical keyboard, delayed 3G—reveal conviction. In each case, Steve faced enormous pressure to conform. Industry consensus said he was wrong. Customers complained. Critics attacked. Partners resisted.

And in each case, he was right. Not because he was smarter, though he often was, but because he was operating from principle rather than reaction. The principle: remove anchors to the past even when customers cling to them. Choose technologies based on where they're going, not where they've been. Accept short-term pain for long-term gain.

This is what conviction enables: the ability to withstand pressure when you know you're right. Most leaders fold. Not because they don't know the right answer, but because the cost of defending it feels too high. Critics attack. Customers complain. Sales might suffer. Partners might resist.

So they compromise. They keep the floppy drive "just in case." They add the physical keyboard "to ease the transition." They include 3G "even though battery life suffers." Each compromise seems reasonable in isolation. Cumulatively, they're fatal. Because you've let others define your product. You've optimized for minimizing criticism rather than maximizing value.

Steve's genius wasn't that he was always right. The slot-loader proves he wasn't. His genius was that he was willing to be criticized for holding positions he believed in. And most of the time, those positions were based on understanding tradeoffs better than critics did.

The Diagnostic Questions

Are you operating from conviction or just avoiding conflict? Track your reversal patterns. When you reverse a decision, what caused the reversal?

If it's new information that proves your position wrong, that's good. Learning and adapting. If it's pressure from vocal critics without new evidence, that's appeasement. You didn't change your mind because you were wrong. You changed it because defending the position was uncomfortable. Count your reversals over the last year. How many were evidence-based versus pressure-based? If most are pressure-based, you're not leading. You're reacting.

Measure time between criticism and capitulation. When someone criticizes a product decision, how long do you hold your position? If you reverse within days or weeks, you didn't have conviction. You had a preference. True conviction withstands months or years of criticism. Steve held the no-floppy position despite a year of complaints. He held the no-3G position through two product cycles. If you fold quickly, you're optimizing for comfort over correctness.

Examine who you're optimizing for. When you make product decisions, whose feedback weighs most heavily? If it's vocal minorities, you're appeasing. If it's quiet majorities, you're serving. The problem: vocal minorities are loud, quiet majorities are silent. So appeasement feels responsive while actually serving a tiny segment. Track your feature additions: what percentage serves vocal requests versus validated broad needs? If vocal requests dominate, you're being reactive.

Count your "just this once" exceptions. How many times have you made an exception to your principles "just for this customer" or "just for this situation"? Each exception sets precedent. The second one is easier than the first. The tenth is automatic. If you're making exceptions regularly, you don't have principles. You have suggestions. Principles withstand pressure. Suggestions fold under it.

Building Conviction That Lasts

Steve's approach provides a framework for developing and maintaining conviction.

First, start with principles, not preferences. The difference between the slot-loader and the floppy decision: one was preference, aesthetics over function. The other was principle: remove anchors to the past. Preferences are negotiable. Principles aren't. Before you make decisions, articulate the principle. "We remove technologies that have outlived usefulness." "We choose battery life over speed when chips aren't mature." "We optimize for the core use case, not edge cases." Then defend the principle, not just the decision.

Second, understand tradeoffs better than critics. Steve didn't exclude 3G on a whim. He understood the physics: seven chips versus three, terrible battery life, physical bulk. Critics didn't know or care about these trade-offs. They just wanted faster speeds. Your job is to understand the full cost of what critics request. Because if you don't, you'll implement their suggestions and discover the problems they ignored. Do the analysis. Map the consequences. Then make informed tradeoffs rather than reactive compromises.

Third, create the vacuum. Don't just remove old technology. Force adoption of the new. USB existed but wasn't adopted until the iMac made it mandatory. If Steve had included both serial ports and USB, manufacturers would have stuck with serial. By creating a vacuum, he forced the ecosystem to move forward. When you remove something, make the replacement so necessary that the ecosystem adapts. Don't give people an escape hatch to the past. Make the future the only viable path.

Fourth, give them what they need, not what they want. Customers wanted floppy drives because they were familiar. They needed modern file transfer via email and CDs. Customers wanted 3G immediately. They needed devices with all-day battery life. The gap between want and need is where leadership happens. Your job is understanding what they actually need, even when they can't articulate it. Then delivering that, even when they complain.

Fifth, admit when you're wrong, quickly. The slot-loader was wrong. Steve should have listened to Rubinstein. The mark of true conviction is knowing the difference between a principle worth defending and a preference you should abandon. When you realize you're wrong, reverse immediately. Don't dig in. Don't defend stubbornness as conviction. Say: "I was wrong, here's why, we're changing course." That builds credibility for the times when you hold firm because you're right.

What To Do Monday

If you lead product, list the decisions you're currently defending against criticism. For each, write down the principle behind the decision, the tradeoffs you understood when making it, the critics' position and what they're missing, and the evidence that would prove you wrong. If you can't clearly articulate these, especially the principle, you don't have conviction. You have a guess. And guesses should fold under evidence, not hold under pressure.

Pick one decision where you're facing pressure to reverse. Before you fold, do two things. First, talk to quiet users. The ones who aren't complaining. Ask: "How would you feel if we changed this?" Often you'll discover the quiet majority likes the current approach. The vocal minority is loud but small. Knowing this gives you strength to hold firm. Second, project the consequences. If you reverse, what happens? Not just "critics stop complaining." What about the product architecture? The precedent you set? The customers who will quietly leave? Map the full cost. Then decide whether the benefit of appeasing critics exceeds that cost. Usually it doesn't.

If you decide to hold firm, do it publicly. Don't just ignore critics. Explain your reasoning. Write the blog post. Send the email. Make the case. Because defended positions are stronger than silent ones. When people understand why you said no, even critics who disagree can respect the reasoning.

The Real Lesson

Creation requires conviction. Not arrogance. Not stubbornness. Conviction.

The difference matters. Arrogance is believing you're always right. Stubbornness is refusing to change when proven wrong. Conviction is holding to principles even under pressure, while remaining open to evidence that challenges them.

Steve got this right most of the time. No floppy drive despite protests. USB-only despite compatibility concerns. No physical keyboard despite customer anxiety. Delayed 3G despite criticism. Each time, he understood tradeoffs critics missed. Each time, he held firm. Each time, he was right.

But the slot-loader proves he wasn't infallible. He prioritized aesthetics over functionality. Rubinstein warned him. He insisted anyway. And Apple paid for years.

The lesson isn't "be like Steve and never compromise." It's "develop conviction based on principles and tradeoffs, defend it against pressure, but abandon it quickly when proven wrong."

Most leaders get this backwards. They compromise under pressure even when they're right. Then dig in when proven wrong because admitting mistakes feels like weakness. This is exactly inverted. Hold firm when you're right. Reverse quickly when you're wrong.

The key is knowing the difference. And knowing requires understanding tradeoffs better than critics do. It requires starting from principles rather than preferences. It requires tracking outcomes rather than reacting to complaints.

Customers often resist changes, regardless of the eventual benefits. They cling to floppy drives because they're familiar, even when modems and email have made them obsolete. They demand 3G because it sounds faster, even when it means carrying a brick with two-hour battery life.

Your job is not to give them what they want. It's to give them what they need. And that requires the conviction to withstand criticism when you know you're right.

You will have enemies. Critics who say you're arrogant for not including what they demand. Partners who resist your vision. Customers who complain about changes. That's not failure. That's proof you've stood up for something.

But standing up isn't enough. You must be standing up for the right things. Principles backed by understanding. Tradeoffs made consciously. Decisions defended publicly. And reversals made quickly when evidence proves you wrong.

That's conviction. Not stubbornness. Not arrogance. Conviction.

And creation, real creation that moves industries forward, requires it. Because if you let critics define your product, you'll build what everyone wants and no one loves. You'll include the floppy drive. You'll add the physical keyboard. You'll ship 3G before it's ready.

And you'll wonder why your product feels like a collection of compromises rather than a coherent vision.

Steve created the pressure to move forward. That pressure won't get created by coddling your customers.

Have the conviction to lead them somewhere better. Even when they resist. Even when they complain. Even when they claim you're wrong.

Most of the time, if you've done your homework, understood the tradeoffs, and operated from principle, you'll be right. And eventually, they'll follow.

That's what conviction enables. Not just the courage to decide. The strength to defend. The wisdom to know when you're right. And the humility to admit when you're wrong.

Creation requires conviction. Build yours. Defend it. And when necessary, abandon it.

But never compromise it out of fear of criticism. Because if you have enemies? Good. That means you've stood up for something.

Make sure it's something worth standing for.

Tough Choices Overcome Obstacles

"We cannot solve our problems with the same thinking we used when we created them." — Albert Einstein

When the iPhone was unveiled, the smartphone industry thought it must be a hoax. According to Apple, the iPhone featured nearly 8 hours of talk time, 6 hours of internet use, 7 hours of video playback, or it could play music for a full 24 hours straight.

The iPhone "couldn't do what [Apple was] demonstrating without an insanely power-hungry processor; it must have terrible battery life," a Shacknews poster heard from his colleagues at Blackberry maker, Research In Motion.

RIM, along with Microsoft and other competitors of the iPhone, was insistent that Apple's claims couldn't be true. When the claims were verified by third-party testing, the narrative shifted overnight.

Suddenly, the new complaint was that Apple had 'only' achieved this incredible battery life by cheating, pausing the applications running while in the background. To the PC and smartphone community of the time, this verged on heresy.

The Multitasking Heresy

Applications running in the background on a mobile device can cause several issues. They compete with the frontmost application, slowing the performance. They eat away at processor cycles, which drain precious power from the battery. They can also occupy valuable memory, further slowing the device's performance.

Pausing the background apps sounds like a reasonable solution to better battery life for a mobile phone with extremely limited resources. So why all the outrage?

At the time, mobile smartphones were trapped in a catch-22. Including standard computing features required significant processor power and large amounts of memory, but making an affordable device with useful battery life allowed neither.

For nearly thirty years, the desktop PC world had defined what could be considered 'real' computers. When smartphones first arrived, the thinking just carried over to the new field. A smartphone should be running every conceivable task that a desktop did, only on a small form factor. If that meant sacrificing battery life, performance, or physical size, then that was just part of the deal.

Apple didn't agree and dared to flip the script. The holistic experience was more important to them than some arbitrary set of outdated expectations.

Steve would later compare the shift in computing to the transition from trucks to cars. As America moved away from being an agrarian nation, people had less use for trucks. Cars now suited their lifestyle and needs far better. What Apple was addressing was that consumers now needed mobile, nimble, long-lasting internet devices far more than they needed large workstation computers.

Apple's daring heresy was attacked by virtually every notable media outlet. Its decision to pause applications in favor of battery life was relentlessly derided as some kind of con being run on consumers. 'It doesn't multitask!' blared the headlines, presenting this as a horrible cheat by Apple rather than a brilliant decision that broke the logjam that had prevented truly impressive mobile devices.

Embracing Constraints as Design Principles

Apple had to create a breakthrough phone-iPod-internet device that was affordable and entirely touchscreen. It had to have impressive battery life, to boot. These parameters created some hard limits in battery size, memory, storage, and processor power. Attempting to meet them all in a device that had 'no compromise' would have been impossible and actually meant a severely compromised device.

While certain companies love to promise consumers 'no compromise,' it's hardly ever an honest statement. It's just a fact that the company pretends the areas that their product is compromising on don't matter. Apple doesn't pretend there aren't tradeoffs. Instead, they embrace the possibilities their choices have allowed.

Critics were sure those strictly enforced limits on multitasking would disrupt consumers in their daily use of the device. They were wrong.

iPhones selectively allowed useful multitasking. For example, playing music while you browsed the internet with the phone or holding a phone conversation while browsing the internet, or composing and reading email, worked seamlessly.

Apple boosted battery life with a litany of creative new technologies, working in tandem. Proximity sensors turned off the screen whenever it was held against a person's ear. Ambient light sensors used intelligent algorithms to adjust the brightness of the screen to match the surrounding lighting. The device went into an extremely low-power mode within seconds of being locked. Apple had made the controversial decision to forbid Adobe's Flash, which relentlessly consumed battery power.

The Intelligent Solution

The PC world had operated for years, refusing to enforce any discipline on background programs. Each generation of new processor simply demanded more power and provided more cycles to hide all the inefficiencies. A PC user could easily be losing 45%, or more, of their potential processor power to badly behaved programs they couldn't even see running. Windows Mobile and Android expected users to constantly police their phone's running tasks manually or pay the price in lousy battery life and poor performance.

Apple vehemently rejected that thinking.

In the 4.0 version of iOS, Apple brought a new approach to the table. They methodically broke down the different scenarios where applications might legitimately work better if allowed some leeway. Music programs? OK. Programs that just need an additional few minutes to finish up a task? Permission granted. Applications that use location services to direct a user or inform them about their surroundings? iOS was happy to oblige.

Here was Apple's fine-grained solution, which still stands today, in stark contrast to the competing mobile platforms. Those platforms are still allowing any and all applications to run wild, placing the burden on users to constantly patrol the running processes on their phones.

In 2013, Apple announced iOS 7's version of multitasking. iOS would now monitor how a person used applications and intelligently allow frequently used apps to fetch new data, or updates, in the background. For example, it is even wise enough to notice what time of the day you check Facebook and already have your newsfeed up-to-date with fresh posts and messages.

Almost as an afterthought, Apple casually mentioned that the new multitasking also adapts to your phone's network conditions and battery life. It doesn't waste effort trying to update apps when conditions are poor or your battery isn't sufficiently charged.

That is how it's done, Apple was saying. It's not about compromise; it's about composing the solution offering the best overall experience.

Real breakthroughs require identifying and embracing the tough choices required to make them possible.

What This Actually Teaches

The multitasking story reveals something fundamental about innovation under constraints. Most organizations see constraints as problems to overcome. Apple saw them as design principles to embrace.

The constraint was real: limited battery, limited memory, limited processor power. Competitors looked at this constraint and said: "We need to work around it. Let's add a bigger battery, more RAM, a faster processor." This made devices heavier, hotter, more expensive, and barely extended battery life because inefficient software consumed the gains.

Apple looked at the same constraint and said: "We need to work within it. What if we fundamentally rethink what background tasks actually need to do?" This led to selective multitasking, intelligent task management, and a suite of power-saving technologies that made the constraint work for them rather than against them.

This is the difference between solving symptoms and solving systems. Symptom solving addresses immediate pain without changing underlying dynamics. "Battery life is short? Add a bigger battery." System solving changes the dynamics to eliminate the pain. "Battery life is short? Eliminate wasteful background processing."

Symptom solving is easier in the short term. You can point to the bigger battery and say "problem solved." But it's more expensive, creates new problems like heat and weight, and doesn't actually solve the root cause. System solving is harder. It requires rethinking assumptions, challenging conventions, and enduring criticism from people who don't understand why you're not taking the "obvious" solution.

But system solving creates sustainable advantages. Because once you've solved the system problem, every future product benefits. Apple's intelligent task management wasn't just for iPhone 1. It was the foundation for every iOS device that followed. Competitors who added bigger batteries had to keep adding bigger batteries. Apple's advantage compounded.

The Diagnostic Questions

Are you solving symptoms or systems? Track solution durability. When you solve a problem, how long does it stay solved? If the same issue recurs every few months, you solved a symptom. If it stays solved permanently, you solved a system. Review your last ten problem-solving efforts. How many resulted in permanent fixes versus recurring issues? If most recur, you're not solving systems. You're managing symptoms on a treadmill.

Measure resource accumulation. Are you continuously adding resources to maintain the same performance? More servers to keep speeds acceptable, more staff to maintain quality, more process to ensure consistency. Resource accumulation signals symptom solving. You're compensating for systemic inefficiency with added capacity. System solving reduces resource requirements over time because you've eliminated waste rather than accommodated it.

Examine your "just add more" patterns. How often do your solutions involve adding something versus changing something? "Just add more servers," "just hire more people," "just add more oversight," "just buy a bigger battery." Addition is symptom solving. Change is system solving. If most of your solutions involve adding rather than changing, you're avoiding the hard work of systemic improvement.

Count your workarounds. How many workarounds exist in your organization? Manual processes that compensate for system failures, extra steps that catch errors the system should prevent, special cases that require custom handling. Each workaround is a symptom of an unsolved system problem. If workarounds are proliferating, you're creating symptom solutions faster than you're solving system problems.

Embracing Constraints as Design

Apple's approach to the multitasking problem provides a framework for system solving.

First, make constraints visible and specific. Apple didn't say "we have limited resources." They said "we have X milliamp-hours of battery, Y megabytes of RAM, Z processor cycles per second." Specific constraints enable specific solutions. Vague constraints enable vague, ineffective responses. Map your constraints precisely. Not "we don't have enough budget" but "we have exactly this much and these are the fixed costs." Specificity forces clarity about what must change to work within reality.

Second, challenge the inherited assumptions. The smartphone industry assumed mobile devices should work like desktop computers. This assumption created the catch-22 between features and battery life. Apple asked: "What if mobile devices should work differently?" This question opened solution space. What assumptions are you inheriting from adjacent domains, from past solutions, from industry norms? Write them down. Then ask: "What if this assumption is wrong for our context?" Often the constraint isn't real. It's an inherited belief.

Third, distinguish between user needs and technical implementation. Users don't need background multitasking. They need music to keep playing while they browse. They need location services to keep tracking while they run. These are different things. The PC world conflated the need with one specific implementation: unconstrained background tasks. Apple separated them. What do users actually need versus how has it traditionally been implemented? Often you can meet the need with a different implementation that respects your constraints.

Fourth, build intelligence into the system, not burden onto the user. Android and Windows Mobile made users responsible for task management. Apple made the system responsible. This shift determined everything. Because users won't manage tasks consistently. They'll forget, get confused, make mistakes. Systems can be consistent. The question isn't "how do we help users manage this complexity?" It's "how do we eliminate the need for them to manage it?" Every time you're tempted to solve a problem with user education, ask whether you can solve it with system intelligence instead.

Fifth, optimize for the whole, not the parts. Apple could have optimized battery life alone by removing features. Or optimized features alone by accepting terrible battery life. Instead they optimized the experience: long battery life AND useful functionality. This required innovations across the stack—proximity sensors, ambient light, intelligent task management,

Flash removal, sleep modes. None sufficient alone. Transformative together. Stop optimizing individual components. Optimize the system as a whole. This usually requires multiple coordinated changes rather than one big fix.

What To Do Monday

If you lead product or operations, identify your most persistent problem. The issue that keeps recurring despite repeated "solutions." Write down every attempted solution over the past year.

For each solution, ask: "Did this add something or change something?" If most added resources, capacity, process, oversight without changing how work flows, you've been symptom solving.

Now ask a different question: "What would have to change about how we work to make this problem impossible?" Not unlikely. Impossible. This forces system thinking.

For the iPhone multitasking problem, the system question was: "What would have to change to make background tasks irrelevant to battery life?" The answer: "Tasks would have to either not run, or run so efficiently they're negligible." This led to selective task management.

For your problem, follow the same logic. If the problem is performance, don't ask "how do we make this faster?" Ask "what would have to change to make speed irrelevant or automatic?" If the problem is quality, don't ask "how do we catch more errors?" Ask "what would have to change to make errors impossible?"

These questions are harder. They don't have quick answers. But they force you toward system solutions rather than symptom management.

The Real Lesson

Tough choices overcome obstacles. But only if they're the right tough choices.

Competitors faced the same constraints as Apple: limited battery, memory, and processor power. They made tough choices too. They chose bigger batteries, more powerful processors, and accepted the tradeoffs: weight, heat, cost, and mediocre battery life despite the hardware investments.

These were tough choices. They were also symptom solutions. They addressed battery life without addressing the root cause: inefficient software consuming resources wastefully.

Apple made different tough choices. They challenged the assumption that mobile devices should multitask like desktops. They paused background apps. They built intelligence into task management. They optimized across the entire system rather than throwing hardware at symptoms.

These choices were harder. They required rethinking fundamentals. They invited fierce criticism. They demanded innovations across multiple domains rather than one simple fix.

But they were system solutions. And system solutions compound. Each innovation—proximity sensors, ambient light adjustment, intelligent task management, sleep modes—built on the others. Together they created sustainable advantage that competitors couldn't match by throwing hardware at the problem.

This is what Einstein meant: you cannot solve problems with the thinking that created them. The thinking that created the smartphone battery life problem was "mobile devices should work like desktop computers." More of that thinking—bigger batteries, more powerful processors—just created heavier, hotter devices that still had mediocre battery life.

The solution required different thinking: "mobile devices should work optimally for mobile contexts." This thinking led to different choices, which led to different results.

The lesson extends beyond technology. Every persistent problem in your organization exists because the thinking that created it is still active. More of that thinking will manage the symptom. Different thinking will solve the system.

Real breakthroughs require identifying and embracing the tough choices required to make them possible. But the toughest choice is often the first one: the choice to challenge the thinking that created the problem rather than doubling down on it.

Apple didn't promise 'no compromise.' They promised better compromise. They acknowledged the tradeoffs, made conscious choices about which ones to accept, and built systems that turned constraints into advantages.

That's how it's done. It's not about compromise in the sense of settling for less. It's about composing the solution that offers the best overall experience by making the tough systemic choices rather than the easy symptomatic ones.

Choose systems over symptoms. Change over addition. Intelligence over burden. The whole over the parts.

Make the tough choices. The ones that address root causes rather than just managing their effects. Because that's how obstacles get overcome. Not by throwing resources at symptoms. But by changing the system that creates them.

Decisions

"You will only be remembered for two things: the problems you solve or the ones you create." — Mike Murdock

Apple said no to removable batteries, micro-USB charging cables, and removable SD memory cards. They made the decision to say no to mobile Flash.

Apple offers just one OS for both home and professional markets, compared to PC competitors, who offer a dizzying array of versions with different combinations of features that require a matrix to decode.

Steve explained that, "People think focus means saying yes to the thing you've got to focus on. But that's not what it means at all. It means saying no to the hundred other good ideas that there are. You have to pick carefully. I'm actually as proud of the things we haven't done as the things we have done. Innovation is saying 'no' to 1,000 things."

Say what you will about Apple's choices, but they are never indecisive. Steve said, "We're trying to make great products for people. We at least have the courage of our convictions to say, 'We don't think this is part of what makes a great product. We're going to leave it out.' Some people are going to not like that. They're going to call us names. It's not going to be in a certain company's vested interests, but we're going to take the heat because we want to make the best product in the world for customers."

Making the best of anything, by its very nature, won't make any company popular among its competition. Praise comes easily for competitors that don't really threaten the bottom line. Creating something better than the average requires the courage to make the decisions that others avoided.

The Battery Nobody Could Remove

Why doesn't Apple utilize removable batteries in their mobile products? After all, the aftermarket battery suppliers must be pretty annoyed by being cut off. For years, Apple was the only smartphone maker that wouldn't get with the program, according to the tech media critics. For years, Apple was slammed over their battery decision at every opportunity as 'greedy,' 'planning to obsolesce' and being 'controlling.'

Then, in 2012, the Motorola Droid Razr Maxx and Nokia Lumia 900 joined the party, and the tech media suddenly recognized what Apple had realized almost half a decade earlier: non-removable batteries are better. When the Razr Maxx embraced a non-removable battery, it actually doubled the battery life over its previous generation Razr with the removable battery.

They are better because you have far more options when you don't have to design a product around removing its battery. Batteries can be whatever shape, size, and configuration that best gets the job done. Apple actually designed very precise circuits that tuned exactly the right charge to each individual cell to optimize every recharge while maintaining maximum battery life. By not wasting internal space with the shell around those battery cells, they could use larger cells. The lack of an extra casing allows the battery to stay cooler, boosting its life exponentially.

Apple didn't make that decision lightly. The easy choice would have been to join the smartphone industry in bilking consumers out of millions of dollars a year in replacement batteries. The poor recharging technique, combined with the technology in a removable battery, meant frequent replacement was practically a guaranteed revenue stream. Apple could have been profiting handsomely instead of being slammed for the nonexistent 'greed' of an extremely rare in-store battery replacement.

Making a decision to buck the industry, and forgo aftermarket profits from the frequently replaced batteries, was done for one reason: it was right for the product.

The Lightning That Struck Critics

Apple took another beating in the tech press over the decision not to use a standard micro-USB connector in its new mobile devices. Apple had designed the original iPod's connector and subsequently used it in virtually every mobile device for the next decade. Then, Apple decided it was time to move to a new generation connector, and the tech world lost its mind over it. Apple called the connector lightning, and it took seconds for the thunder to follow its announcement.

CNET writer Molly Wood trumped up the accusations with her article 'Apple's Dock Connector Change Is Awful, Don't Kid Yourselves.' Saying that "Apple calls the new connector Lightning, but giving it a clever name doesn't mean it adds anything but dollars in Apple's bank account." The article tossed mud with abandon.

Pocketnow joined in with 'The Lightning Connector Represents Every-thing Wrong With Apple.' Not bothering with actual facts, that article slapped aside the idea that Lightning offered significant advantages over USB, claiming that there 'just isn't any evidence for that at the moment.' Oh, really?

Gizmodo piped up by claiming, 'Here's the Chip Apple Is Using to Stop You From Buying Cheap Cables.' Readers were treated to the conspiracy theory that multi-billion-dollar-earning Apple was somehow threatened by consumers buying cheap lightning cables from the third world that rarely held up under actual use.

Let's examine the basic facts. Claims that consumers would be over-whelmed by a web of connector cables were seriously overblown. If a consumer owned existing peripherals using the old connector, they could buy an adapter. If a consumer was just entering the iOS ecosystem, it wasn't even an issue. Apple quickly introduced the iPad Mini with the same connector and moved the full-size iPad to it. All of them used the same connector.

The critics were demanding that Apple instead choose MicroUSB as its new connector. "It's a standard" and "It's what everyone uses" were the common justifications. The simple truth is that there is no way Apple could have gone with micro USB. The voltage isn't sufficient. MicroUSB tops out at 1.8A with 5Volts. 1.8A at 5V is 9Watts, whereas most tablet chargers today are 10Watts. The iPad 4 charger is 12 watts. It's not rocket science.

Anyone observant would notice that even companies using micro USB on their phones aren't using it on their tablets. Tablets charge at rates that microUSB isn't designed for. While those same critics were already complaining about the lengthy time the iPad 3 was taking to charge, they expected Apple to switch to a technology that would have limited it to 75% of what the Lightning system supplies to recharge the iPad 4.

The Lightning connector also has other advantages, such as being reversible. This makes it easier to plug in, allows accessories more flexi-bility in design, and improves connector durability. Bottom line? It was the smart decision

One Product, Period

Why doesn't Apple offer multiple versions of its OS, each tuned for some specific market and priced to maximize profit? Because that would be bad for consumers and for the product, and that's not how they do things.

In Insanely Simple, Ken Segall shares a behind-the-scenes example of how Apple really operates and makes these decisions.

Apple offers a professional video editing software application named Final Cut Studio. Years ago, when Final Cut Studio 2.0 was about to be released, the team behind it had acquired a 'color grading' tool used in Hollywood for sophisticated color work. A debate raged about how to package the add-on tool.

Two things were in consideration. The pricing—keep in mind, before Apple bought it, this 'color grading' tool was sold for years at $25,000 per copy—and what to call the different versions. Final Cut Studio's main competitor was Adobe's Premiere. Premiere came in different editions, priced accordingly.

Steve arrived for the meeting to decide between different packaging and naming designs for the product. The presented plan was to have two editions of Final Cut Studio, regular and premium. The premium package would include the new 'color grading' feature and be called Final Cut with 'Color.' It was the first Steve heard of the plan. He wasn't on board.

"Put the software in the box," Steve said. The group was clueless about what that meant.

"Put Color in the Final Cut Studio box. We sell one product, period," he said, plain as day. He didn't care that some companies had gouged customers for $25,000 for that 'color grading.' One product, period, he declared.

The project head tried to bring Steve on board. She told him that she'd promised the CFO that the software group would create a special edition, so it could track and justify the cost of acquiring the new tool. "Looks like you made a big mistake," Steve told her. "What's next?"

It was a done deal. Final Cut Studio 2.0 remained a single product. There wouldn't be any complexity or gouging. That is how Apple operates.

Operating under the discipline required to be successful, without gouging or tricks, tends to enrage your competitors who embrace those shortcuts.

Ignore your competitor's complaints. Create great products that make your customers love you.

People upset by you flipping the script will call you names. Take the heat. Smile, and make the best product in the world for your customers. It's what Steve did.

What This Actually Teaches

The battery, Lightning connector, and Final Cut stories reveal something fundamental about decision-making: most companies optimize for avoiding criticism. Apple optimized for product excellence even when it guaranteed criticism.

This is the central tension in every product decision. You can choose paths that minimize complaints or paths that maximize quality. Usually, these point in opposite directions.

Removable batteries minimize complaints from the minority who swap batteries and maximize profits from replacement sales. But they compromise battery life, thermal performance, and internal space utilization for everyone else.

Micro-USB minimizes complaints from people who want universal chargers and avoids criticism about proprietary connectors. But it compromises charging speed, durability, and user experience with non-reversible insertion.

Multiple OS editions minimize complaints from people who don't want to pay for features they won't use. But they create confusion, support nightmares, and fragment the user base.

In each case, the "safe" choice minimizes immediate criticism while compromising long-term product quality. Apple consistently chose the opposite: accept immediate criticism to preserve long-term quality.

This isn't recklessness. It's clarity about what matters. Critics will attack regardless. The question is whether they attack you for compromising quality or for refusing to compromise it. One type of attack damages your brand. The other validates it.

Most organizations don't see this distinction. They conflate all criticism as equally threatening. So they optimize for minimizing total criticism volume. This leads to products designed by committee, shaped by the loudest complaints rather than the deepest insights.

Apple's approach was different: identify the small decisions that determine long-term quality, then defend those decisions against all criticism until outcomes prove you right. This requires two capabilities most organizations lack: the ability to distinguish signal from noise in criticism, and the courage to stand firm when the noise is deafening.

The Diagnostic Questions

Are you making decisions based on vision or just responding to criticism? Count your criticism-driven reversals. How often do you change course because of criticism versus because of evidence? Review your last year of product decisions. How many were "we're adding this because people complained" versus "we're adding this because data shows it solves a real problem"? If criticism-driven decisions dominate, you're not leading. You're reacting. And reactive organizations don't build great products. They build Frankenstein's monsters assembled from appeased complaints.

Measure the lag between decision and reversal. When you make a decision and face criticism, how long do you hold before reversing? If you reverse within days or weeks, you never had conviction. You had a guess you were willing to abandon at first resistance. Steve held the non-removable battery decision for years despite constant criticism. If you can't hold a decision through one product cycle of criticism, you're optimizing for comfort over quality.

Track your complexity accumulation. How many versions, tiers, options, configurations do you offer? Every addition was probably justified by serving some segment. But cumulatively, have they made your product easier or harder to use, easier or harder to support, easier or harder to explain? If complexity is growing despite your intentions to keep things simple, you're caving to pressure for "just one more option" without recognizing that each option makes the whole system worse.

Examine who's making your decisions. When you reverse a product direction, who drove the reversal? If it's usually sales, or support, or vocal customers, rather than product leadership with long-term vision, you've abdicated product decisions to whoever complains loudest. Each constituency has legitimate perspectives. But only product leadership sees the whole system. If you let parts optimize for their local concerns without considering global impact, you end up with local optimization that degrades the whole.

Deciding With Conviction

Steve's approach to decisions provides a framework for maintaining vision under pressure.

First, distinguish between legitimate and illegitimate criticism. Not all criticism is equal. Legitimate criticism reveals a real problem you missed. Illegitimate criticism reveals the critic's preference for a different product. When Lightning was criticized for not being micro-USB, that was illegitimate. The critics wanted Lightning to be something it wasn't designed to be. The technical constraints—charging power, reversibility—were real. The criticism ignored them. Learn to separate "you built the wrong thing" from "I wish you'd built something different." The former deserves response. The latter deserves explanation but not capitulation.

Second, explain, don't reverse. When facing illegitimate criticism, your job isn't to change the product. It's to explain the reasoning. Steve didn't add removable batteries when criticized. He explained why non-removable was better. He didn't adopt micro-USB. He explained Lightning's advantages. Explanation serves two purposes: it educates critics who might reconsider if they understood the tradeoffs, and it demonstrates conviction to customers who care more about vision than universal approval. Most companies reverse when they should explain. This trains critics that complaining works, ensuring future criticism is even louder.

Third, simplify aggressively, defend ruthlessly. The Final Cut story reveals Steve's principle: one product, maximum quality, minimum complexity. This wasn't about being nice to customers. It was about product integrity. Multiple editions create complexity, confusion, and support costs. They also tempt you to hold back features to justify premium tiers. Steve rejected this temptation. One product meant no artificial feature gates, no version confusion, no complexity tax. When your team proposes adding tiers, versions, or options, ask: "Does this make the product better or just appear to serve more markets?" If the latter, reject it.

Fourth, let outcomes validate decisions. Apple held the non-removable battery decision through years of criticism. Eventually, competitors adopted the same approach. Critics went silent. This is the pattern: early criticism, sustained conviction, eventual validation. You can't rush this.

Outcomes take time to manifest. Your job is holding conviction through the criticism period, not because you're stubborn but because you've done the analysis and know you're right.

Fifth, operate from principle, not preference. Preferences are negotiable. Principles aren't. Before making decisions, articulate the principle. "We don't artificially gate features behind pricing tiers." "We optimize for the 95% use case, not the 5% edge case." "We choose technical superiority over compatibility when they conflict." Principle-based decisions can be defended. Preference-based decisions just reveal taste. One creates conviction. The other invites endless debate.

What To Do Monday

If you lead product, list every criticism you're currently facing. For each, write down: Is this criticism revealing a real problem we missed, or a preference for a different product? What would we have to compromise to address this criticism? How many customers does this criticism represent versus how many it would affect? What principle would we violate or uphold by addressing it?

This exercise forces clarity. Most criticism you're facing is probably illegitimate—people wanting you to build something you're not building. Recognizing this gives you permission to explain rather than reverse.

Pick one criticism you've been considering addressing. Before you make any product changes, write the explanation. Why did you make the decision you made? What tradeoffs did you consider? What evidence supports your approach? Then share that explanation publicly—blog post, customer email, press statement. See what happens.

Often, you'll find that explanation reduces criticism volume. Some critics reconsider when they understand your reasoning. Others reveal themselves as wanting a different product entirely. Either way, you've defended your decision without compromising it.

The Real Lesson

You will only be remembered for two things: the problems you solve or the ones you create

Every decision creates some kind of memory. The question is what kind.

Apple's decision to use non-removable batteries solved the problem of limited battery life and thermal efficiency. It created the "problem" that users can't swap batteries. But which problem mattered more? The one affecting 100% of users daily or the one affecting 2% of users occasionally?

Apple's decision to create Lightning solved the problem of charging speed, reversibility, and durability. It created the "problem" of incompatibility with micro-USB. But which problem mattered more? The one affecting user experience every time they plugged in or the one affecting wallet thickness for people who carry multiple devices?

Apple's decision to ship one version of Final Cut solved the problem of complexity and artificial feature gating. It created the "problem" that some customers paid for features they didn't need. But which problem mattered more? The one creating confusion and support costs or the one affecting people who wanted to pay less for less?

The pattern is clear: Apple chose to solve problems that affected everyone by creating "problems" that bothered some. This is decision-making. Real decision-making. Not trying to make everyone happy. But choosing which problems matter most and accepting the criticism from those who wish you'd prioritized differently.

Most companies do the opposite. They try to solve everyone's complaints, which means creating products that attempt everything, delight no one, and collapse under complexity. They end up being remembered for the problems they created—sprawling product lines, confusing tiers, compromised quality—while failing to solve the problems that actually mattered.

Innovation is saying no to 1,000 things. Not because those things are bad. But because saying yes to them would dilute focus, compromise quality, and create complexity that serves margins over customers.

People think focus means saying yes to the thing you've got to focus on. But that's not what it means at all. It means saying no to the hundred other good ideas. And no to the thousand complaints. And no to the pressure to be like competitors. And no to the easy money from gouging and artificial complexity.

Then taking the heat. The names. The criticism. The attacks on your motives. While you smile and keep making the best product in the world for customers who value the problems you chose to solve over the ones you chose to create.

That's how you get remembered. Not for making everyone happy. But for making the decisions others avoided, solving the problems others ignored, and accepting the criticism others feared.

Be decisive. Know which problems matter. Solve those ruthlessly. Accept the criticism from those who wish you'd solved different ones.

Operating under the discipline required to be successful, without gouging or tricks, tends to enrage your competitors who embrace those shortcuts.

Let them be enraged. Create great products that make your customers love you.

You will only be remembered for two things: the problems you solve or the ones you create.

Choose carefully which is which.

Sometimes You Will Be Wrong.

Get over it.

There is a moment every leader eventually faces, though many spend their careers trying to avoid it.

Reality disagrees with you.

Not quietly. Not politely. Publicly. Measurably. In a way that cannot be spun, reframed, or delayed without consequences. The data comes in. The market responds differently than expected. The team struggles where you were confident. The system breaks in a place you were sure was sound.

And suddenly the question is no longer whether you were right.

It's whether you're willing to notice that you were wrong.

This is where many leaders fail, not because they lack intelligence or vision, but because they confuse conviction with infallibility. They mistake decisiveness for correctness. They assume that changing course is the same as admitting weakness.

It isn't.

The most dangerous leaders are not the ones who are occasionally wrong. They are the ones who refuse to update their beliefs when the world gives them new information. They keep pushing forward, not because the direction still makes sense, but because admitting error would bruise their identity.

Steve Jobs was famously opinionated. He held strong views. He argued relentlessly. But what gets lost in the mythology is how often he changed his mind when reality proved him wrong.

Not instantly. Not gracefully every time. But decisively.

He reversed course on products. He killed projects he once championed. He abandoned ideas that no longer served the whole. He didn't cling to past decisions out of pride. He treated them as provisional, subject to revision if they failed the larger test of coherence.

Being wrong was not a moral failing to him. Staying wrong was.

This is an important distinction.

Good leaders make decisions with the best information available at the time. Great leaders recognize that information changes, contexts evolve, and assumptions age. They don't tie their ego to past choices. They tie it to outcomes.

The moment you realize something isn't working, you have two options: defend the decision that led you there, or fix the problem. Spend your energy explaining why the original plan made sense, or redirect that energy toward making the system better now. One path protects your pride. The other protects the people depending on you.

Only one of those is leadership.

Organizations don't collapse because leaders are wrong. They collapse because leaders refuse to let go of being right. They double down on flawed strategies. They blame execution instead of assumptions. They punish messengers instead of listening to signals.

Over time, this creates a culture where truth becomes dangerous and honesty is filtered. Problems are hidden. Feedback is softened. Reality arrives late and hits harder than it needed to.

All because someone couldn't say, "We got this part wrong."

There is no loss of authority in course correction. There is loss of authority in denial.

Teams trust leaders who adapt. Customers respect companies that improve. Markets reward organizations that learn faster than their competitors. None of that requires perfection. It requires responsiveness.

The irony is that leaders who cling to being right end up looking weaker, not stronger. Everyone can see the disconnect between what's being said and what's happening. Pretending otherwise doesn't preserve credibility. It erodes it.

The most confident leaders are the ones who don't need to pretend they were right all along. They are clear about what they're trying to achieve. They are honest about what's working and what isn't. And when something fails, they treat it as information, not an indictment.

Sometimes you will be wrong. Not because you're careless. Not because you're unqualified. But because you're operating in complex systems with imperfect information and moving targets.

Get over it.

Learn. Adjust. Improve the system. Move forward with better understanding than you had before.

That is not weakness.

That is competence maturing into wisdom.

And it's one of the quiet disciplines that separates leaders who merely make decisions from those who actually build things that last.

CHAPTER 16

SOLUTIONS - INNOVATION VS INVENTION

Patents of Steve Jobs on display. Photo by Rex Hammock

"The guy who invented the first wheel was an idiot. The guy who invented the other three, he was a genius." — Sid Caesar

Sometimes when you enter a market with an improved product, your originality and your right to be there will both be questioned. This is not a sign you're wrong. It is a sign you're changing the game.

Two attacks recur, reliably and predictably.

The first says you didn't invent the category, so your work is derivative. I like to refer to this as N.I.T. Picking.

The second says your product looks too much like what exists, so your improvements are trivial. "Disregarded Details" sums it up.

You can't win for losing, it seems.

N.I.T. Picking, Not Invented There, mistakes origin for value.

Edison did not invent light. Torches and candles predated the bulb by millennia. Yet entire industries rose not around flame, but around electric light, because it was safer, brighter, and scalable. Innovation is not invention. It is making the possible practical.

Disregarded Details is subtler and more dangerous. It assumes surface resemblance equals functional equivalence. But small differences in integration, ergonomics, or human response often create outsized advantages. A slight curve in a handle. A pause in an interface. A magnet in a power cord. These are not tweaks. They are decisions that can magnify utility or remove barriers to adoption.

Steve Jobs saw this plainly. At Apple's Worldwide Developer Conference in 1997, he said: "I don't think that it's good that Apple's perceived as different. I think it's important that Apple's perceived as 'much better.' If being different is essential to doing that, then we have to do that, but if we can be much better without being different, that'd be fine with me. I want to be much better."

That sentence, delivered quietly and without apology, became Apple's operating system for the next sixteen years.

Much better. Not first. Not loudest. Not purest.

Apple delivered not by chasing novelty, but by mastering evolution.

The Categories Apple Didn't Invent

Apple's greatest hits were not inventions. They were integrations.

Personal computers existed before the Apple II. The Altair 8800 shipped in 1975, two years earlier. Hobbyists had already built primitive machines in garages across California. But those machines were puzzles, not products. You needed to solder components, toggle switches in binary, and interpret blinking lights as output.

The Apple II, launched in 1977, came fully assembled in a beige case with a keyboard and color graphics. You plugged it in. It worked. Not because it was first, but because it was finished. The innovation was not the circuit board. It was the recognition that computers should serve people who don't want to build computers.

Graphical user interfaces existed before the Mac. Xerox PARC had windows, icons, and a mouse in 1973. Steve visited in 1979 and saw the future. But PARC's interface was an experiment locked in a lab. The Alto cost $40,000. It was slow and complex, meant for researchers.

The Mac, launched in 1984, brought those same concepts to a $2,500 machine that fit on a desk. Faster rendering. Tighter integration. Friendlier errors. The innovation was not the metaphor. It was making the metaphor fast enough, cheap enough, and coherent enough that normal people could use it daily without a manual.

Digital music players existed before the iPod. Creative's Nomad, Diamond's Rio, and dozens of generic MP3 players cluttered store shelves by 2001. They all held music. They all had buttons and screens.

The iPod, launched in 2001, held 1,000 songs, synced seamlessly with iTunes, navigated with a scroll wheel you could operate without looking, and fit in your pocket. The innovation was not portable music. It was removing friction: confusing interfaces, manual file management, incompatible formats, hostile syncing.

Smartphones existed before the iPhone. BlackBerry dominated email. Palm had touchscreens. Windows Mobile had apps. Nokia had market share.

The iPhone, launched in 2007, removed the keyboard, replaced styluses with fingers, made the screen the interface, and integrated phone, iPod, and internet into one coherent experience. The innovation was not the smartphone. It was the insight that prior smartphones were compromise devices. Phones with features added. The iPhone was a computer that happened to make calls.

Tablets existed before the iPad. Microsoft had TabletPC. HP had prototypes. Windows slates with styluses and desktop operating systems launched and died.

The iPad, launched in 2010, started from zero. Not a shrunk laptop, but a new category. Touch-first. App-native. No stylus. No file system. The innovation was not the tablet. It was the willingness to forget what tablets had been and ask what they could be.

Each time, the critique was identical: "Apple didn't invent this." True. And irrelevant. Because the question was never "Who was first?" The question was "Who made it matter?"

Not Invented There - N.I.T. Picking

Innovation: (noun) In technology, an improvement to something already existing. — Merriam Webster

"Those who do not want to imitate anything produce nothing." — Salvador Dali

The charge is familiar, predictable, and almost always deployed in bad faith: "Apple didn't invent that."

As if invention alone conferred value and qualities such as refinement, integration, and humanization were mere afterthoughts.

This is not critique. It is erasure of the labor, the insight, the stubborn persistence required to turn a prototype into a product people trust.

Tony Fadell, the architect of the iPod and early iPhone, named the shift: "The product now is the iTunes Music Store and iTunes and the iPod and the software that goes on the iPod. We're really about a system."

Jony Ive echoed: "The historical way of developing products just doesn't work when you're as ambitious as we are. When the challenges are that complex, you have to develop a product in a more collaborative, integrated way."

This integration confuses critics who demand rigid credit: Who invented the touchscreen? The chip? The gesture? But real progress doesn't obey those boundaries. It flows across teams, companies, decades.

The Telephone Didn't Have a Single Inventor Either

When the iPhone launched, the refrain began: "Not the first smartphone!" Fine. Let's go further: Apple didn't invent the telephone, either.

Alexander Graham Bell conceived his electromagnetic telephone in July 1874. Three years earlier, Antonio Meucci had filed a statement of intention for a "Sound Telegraph," but described no electromagnetic mechanism. Meucci, in turn, had consulted Innocenzo Manzetti, who built a working "speaking telegraph" in 1864 but had never patented it. Before Manzetti, Charles Bourseul published the theory of a make-and-break transmitter in 1854 but never built it. And long before all of them, Robert Hooke demonstrated an acoustic string telephone in 1667.

If we award credit only to the first spark and dismiss all refinement, then no one after Hooke deserves praise for the telephone. No one after Gutenberg for the printing press. No one after Volta for the battery. This is not rigor. It is intellectual laziness.

When Integration Is the Innovation

Consider the iPhone 5: It integrated LTE data and CDMA voice onto a single chip while competitors used two. Result? Smaller size. Longer battery life. Same eight-hour browsing. Should we honor the first to ship dual-chip LTE, which was bulky and power-hungry, or the one who refined it into something people could live with?

Or take talent: Jim Mergard designed award-winning mobile processors at Samsung after sixteen years at AMD. When Apple hired him, who owned the innovation? The answer is both. But only Apple delivered the A-series: power-efficient, performance-leading, privacy-hardened.

And sometimes, Apple did invent because the world offered no path. MagSafe (2006), US Patent 7,311,526: A magnetic power connector that releases on tension. In-Cell Touch (2012), US Patent 8,388,852: Integrating sensors into the display, yielding a 30% thinner screen. Laser Processing, US Patent 8,482,713: Inventing the machinery to cut display glass because existing tools couldn't.

Apple adds value to both its inventions and others'. It takes "first mover" ideas and builds "second mover solutions" by removing flaws, large and small. When critics dismiss Apple for "not inventing components," they're like those who'd dismiss War and Peace because Tolstoy didn't invent paper. The sum is never just the parts.

The Admission and the Precision

Steve admitted this openly at the Smithsonian: "[Xerox PARC] didn't have it totally right, but they had the germ of the idea: graphical user interfaces, object-oriented computing, and networking."

Apple's own boilerplate is precise: "Apple ignited the personal computer revolution and reinvented the personal computer." And "Apple has reinvented the mobile phone." Note the word: reinvented. Not invented. There is a world of difference.

As Steve said: "My observation is that the doers are the major thinkers. The people that really create the things that change this industry are both the thinkers and doers, in one person."

Apple didn't invent the floppy drive, but it doubled its capacity. Didn't invent power supplies, but it created the switching supply that made laptops light. Didn't invent ones and zeros, but it made them matter in ways never before seen. The genius is not in the spark. It is in the stewardship of the flame.

What This Actually Teaches

The N.I.T. Picking attack reveals a fundamental misunderstanding: it assumes primacy equals importance. That the first demonstration matters more than the first deployment at scale. That the laboratory prototype deserves more credit than the product people trust their lives with.

This is backwards. The hard work is not having the idea. The hard work is making the idea work millions of times, in chaotic reality, for people who don't read manuals.

Xerox PARC invented the graphical user interface. Their Alto cost $40,000, required constant maintenance, and was never intended for sale. They had the idea. Apple made it matter.

Diamond Multimedia invented the portable MP3 player in 1998. It held 32 megabytes, about eight songs. Transfer was clunky. Battery life was terrible. They had the category. Apple made it useful.

The pattern repeats: someone demonstrates technical possibility in limited conditions with massive compromises. Then someone else makes it practically useful by solving the hundred small problems that separate "it works in the lab" from "it works in your life." That second act is where most of the value lives. And it's almost always harder.

How This Shows Up In Your World

I've watched organizations paralyze themselves with invention anxiety. They refuse to build anything unless they can claim they invented it from scratch. They leave obvious problems unsolved because "someone else already has a solution, so we'd just be copying."

This is madness. If a problem exists and current solutions are inadequate, you have permission to solve it better.

I've also seen the opposite. Dyson didn't invent the vacuum cleaner but made one that actually worked consistently. Tesla didn't invent the electric car but made one that could replace gas cars. Airbnb didn't invent short-term rentals but removed the friction. None of these companies can claim invention. All of them can claim innovation.

The Diagnostic: Are You Confusing Primacy with Value?

Audit your "won't build" list. For each item, ask why you decided not to build it. If the answer includes "someone else already did it," you're suffering from invention anxiety. The question should be "Does this solve a real problem and can we do it better?"

Listen to how you describe differentiation. Do you lead with "We're the only ones who..." or "We're the best at..."? The former is primacy framing. The latter is quality framing. Primacy is fragile. Quality compounds.

Count your "invented here" requirements. How often do you build from scratch when adequate solutions exist externally? If you're always building rather than integrating because "we need to own it," you're optimizing for authorship, not outcomes.

Examine your reaction to "copycat" accusations. If defensive, explaining differences, you're focused on distinctiveness. If curious, asking "Where do we fall short?" you're focused on utility.

Test your talent attribution. Do you hire for specific techniques or general excellence? Capabilities compound. Techniques get outdated.

The Framework: Building Through Integration

Steve's approach wasn't to avoid invention but to recognize it's one tool among many, and often not the most important one.

Reframe the question from "What can we invent?" to "What can we solve?" Start with a problem, not a patent. The iPod didn't start with "invent a new music format." It started with "solve the friction of carrying your music collection."

Master integration as a core competency. Integration is the ability to take disparate components and make them work together seamlessly. This is harder than invention because it requires understanding multiple domains simultaneously and obsessing about experience rather than components.

Hire for taste, not just technique. Apple hired Jim Mergard not to copy Samsung's chips but because he had taste: the ability to judge what "good" looks like. Taste is transferable. Techniques are specific.

Document your refinement work. Apple documented making the iPhone 5's LTE chip 30% smaller and more power-efficient. If you don't document your refinements, you can't defend them when critics say "you just copied."

Defend the system, not just the components. When critics attack individual components for not being novel, concede the point while defending the whole: "We invented the system that makes 1,000 songs accessible without compromise."

Be precise about what you reinvented, not invented. Apple says "reinvented," not "invented." That word choice is accuracy. And accuracy gives credibility.

If you lead product, run an "invention anxiety" audit. List the top ten problems your users face. For each, ask if you have a solution on your roadmap. If no, ask why. If the answer includes 'someone else already solved it," you have invention anxiety.

Challenge the team: "What if we gave ourselves permission to solve this better? What would 'better' look like?" Often the answer is yes. You just needed permission to stop chasing novelty.

If you're an individual contributor, find one problem that's "solved" but not solved well. Challenge yourself: "How would I make this work the way it should?" Not "How would I make it different?" but "How would I make it right?" That's where innovation lives.

The Real Lesson

The genius is not in the spark. It is in the stewardship of the flame.

Robert Hooke demonstrated the string telephone in 1667. Alexander Graham Bell made it matter in 1876. The gap: 209 years of contributions from Bourseul, Manzetti, Meucci, and Bell. Who invented the telephone? All of them. None of them. The question is malformed.

What matters is not who had the idea first, but who made it work at scale, made it accessible, made it useful enough that millions adopted it, made it reliable enough to build businesses on.

Apple didn't invent graphical interfaces, portable music players, smart-phones, or tablets. They inherited those sparks and tended them. They refined them. They removed the compromises. They solved the adoption barriers. They made them work.

That's not plagiarism. That's progress.

The N.I.T. Pickers who say "Apple didn't invent that" are technically correct and strategically irrelevant. Because the question was never "Who had the idea?" The question was always "Who made it matter?"

Making things matter requires more than invention. It requires integration, refinement, humanization, scale, reliability, and taste. It requires solving not just the technology problem, but the manufacturing, distribution, support, and adoption problems.

That constellation of solutions is innovation. And it's far more valuable than invention.

Innovation is not invention. It is making the possible, practical. And practical, at scale, for humans? That's the hardest work there is.

Disregarded Details

"Reinventing the wheel is sometimes the right thing, when the result is the radial tire." — Jonathan Gilbert

"Originality is nothing but judicious imitation." — Voltaire

Apple's work is often dismissed as "minor improvement." But this mistake stems from a failure to see the work at human scale.

John Sculley later said of Steve's role in the Macintosh: "He didn't create anything really, but he created everything." That sentence, both paradoxical and profound, names the core truth that innovation is not in the invention. It is in the integration of technology, empathy, and will.

When Making It Work Is Making It Matter

Consider the written word. Ben Franklin did not invent printing. He made it accessible. The printing press did not create ideas. It let them travel.

Steve saw a similar moment arriving in the 1980s and called it desktop publishing. Today, we expect to design a flyer, a newsletter, a book on our laptops. But then? It was radical. Almost absurd.

Few publishers owned computers. Few authors trusted them. Most consumers believed their typewriters were superior because at least the typewriter was honest, reliable, and crash-free. Computers were fragile, cryptic, and punishing.

Programmers lived in a different world. To them, productivity meant keyboard shortcuts, Ctrl Alt Shift Q Z, executed in rapid sequence. They assumed everyone would learn them. Steve fiercely disagreed. Thank God.

"The manual for WordStar, the most popular word processing program, is four hundred pages thick," he said. "To write a novel, you have to read a novel. One that reads like a mystery to most people. They're not going to learn slash q z any more than they're going to learn Morse code."

This was not impatience. It was respect. Because dragging the printing press into the digital age was not a technical challenge. It was a human one. Steve knew he had to battle four hidden horsemen, not in sequence, but all at once: intimidation (computers scare people), frustration (one wrong keystroke, hours of work gone), humiliation (what if I do it wrong in front of everyone?), and fear (what if the computer makes me obsolete?).

His weapon was not specs. It was language. He did not explain "kerning" or "justification." He showed what they did: "We're seeing five-page memos get compressed to one page because we can use a picture to express the key concept. We're seeing less paper flying around and more high-quality communication. And it's more fun."

He reframed the entire effort not as efficiency, but as joy. Not as output, but as expression. This idea, that creation with a machine should feel good, wasn't yet part of our collective consciousness.

The Telegraph That Couldn't Sing

The telegraph had been entrenched for twenty-five years. Experts predicted desks would soon hold telegraphs, not phones. But Steve saw the flaw: "It wouldn't have worked. It required that people learn this whole sequence of strange incantations, Morse code, dots, and dashes. It took about forty hours to learn. The majority of people would never learn how to use it."

The telephone was not a better telegraph. It was a different covenant: No incantations. No training. Just ABCs and the human voice. "The neatest thing about it," Steve said, "was that, besides allowing you to communicate with just words, it allowed you to sing. It allowed you to intone your words with meaning beyond the simple linguistics."

Desktop publishing was the same leap. Not just words on a page, but emotion in print. A headline in bold. A photo that anchors a story. A layout that guides the eye. Subtext, made visible.

This was not engineering. It was emotional intelligence applied at scale, and it worked not because the Mac was faster, but because it turned intent into reality without demanding a tax of incantations.

Details done right make dollars. But more than that, they make dignity. They make inclusion. They make space for people who thought technology wasn't for them.

What This Actually Teaches

The dismissal of "minor improvements" reveals a category error. It assumes that small changes have small effects. But in complex systems, especially systems that interface with humans, small changes often have disproportionate impacts.

The difference between a keyboard shortcut and a mouse click is technically trivial. But that difference determined who could use computers: programmers versus everyone.

The difference between plastic and glass on a phone screen is a material choice. But that difference determined whether people treated their phones as disposable tools or cherished objects.

The difference between resistive and capacitive touch is measured in pressure sensitivity. But that difference determined whether touch felt like work or like magic.

These are not "minor improvements." They are threshold crossings. Below the threshold, the technology serves only the initiated. Above it, it serves everyone. And serving everyone changes everything.

Steve understood that innovation is often found not in the core technology, but in the thousand small decisions that determine whether people can actually use it. The details that seem trivial to engineers because they've already mastered the complexity. But are insurmountable to everyone else.

How This Shows Up In Your World

I've watched organizations optimize metrics while losing users. A B2B software company obsesses over their onboarding flow, tracking completion rates and time-to-value. But they don't notice that their error messages are written in system codes. That their help documentation assumes you already understand the domain. That their success confirmation is a toast notification that disappears in three seconds.

Each seems minor. But cumulatively? They create an experience that feels hostile to anyone who isn't already an expert. The software works. But using it requires courage. And courage is not a sustainable user acquisition strategy.

I've seen consumer products with beautiful industrial design and terrible human interface. The companies defend these choices: "Power users love the granular control." But then they wonder why adoption stalls at early adopters. Why reviews mention "steep learning curve."

The disregarded details, the ones that would make the product accessible to normal humans, get deprioritized because they're "nice to have." But accessibility is the multiplier. A product that only experts can use has a market size of experts. A product that anyone can use has a market size of anyone.

The Diagnostic: Finding Your Disregarded Details

Map the emotional journey, not just the user journey. Standard user journey mapping tracks actions. Emotional journey mapping tracks feelings. Do this for your core workflows. Ask: "Where do users feel stupid? Where do they feel uncertain? Where do they feel disrespected?" Those moments are your disregarded details.

Watch non-experts use your product. Not in a usability lab with tasks. Just watch someone who's never seen it try to accomplish something real. Don't help. Don't explain. Just watch. Where do they hesitate? Where do they click the wrong thing? Where do they succeed but look confused about whether they succeeded? Each hesitation is a detail you've disregarded.

Count the incantations required. Count how many non-obvious actions users must learn to accomplish basic tasks. Keyboard shortcuts. Special click sequences. Configuration settings buried in menus. If your power users have learned twenty incantations to be productive, those are twenty barriers to mainstream adoption.

Audit your language for expert assumptions. Read your interface copy, error messages, help documentation, and onboarding content. Highlight every term that requires domain knowledge. Every acronym. Every jargon word. If more than 10% of your language requires expertise, you're building for experts only.

Measure the gap between "it worked" and "they know it worked." Count how many actions in your product provide ambiguous feedback. Did my save work? Did my message send? Did my payment process? If users have to verify success through secondary means, you have a feedback gap. That gap creates anxiety. Anxiety creates abandonment.

The Framework: Designing for Dignity

Steve's insight about the four horsemen provides a framework for addressing disregarded details. You're not just fixing interface problems. You're removing emotional barriers.

Design against intimidation. Intimidation comes from complexity presented all at once. The solution is progressive revelation. Start with the simplest path. Hide advanced options until they're needed. Provide smart defaults. Use familiar metaphors that let people apply existing mental models. Show people they can succeed before showing them how sophisticated your product is.

Design against frustration. Frustration comes from irreversible mistakes and invisible states. The solution is forgiving systems. Undo everything. Autosave constantly. Show progress for long operations. Provide clear error recovery. Make dangerous actions hard to trigger accidentally. When mistakes are easily undone, people become exploratory.

Design against humiliation. Humiliation comes from failing publicly or feeling incompetent. The solution is private learning and positive framing. Let people practice in sandboxes. Show examples of "how others use this." Use language that assumes the interface might be unclear, not that the user is slow. Never say "You forgot to..." Say "Let's try..." People will tolerate complexity. They won't tolerate feeling stupid.

Design against fear. Fear comes from uncertainty about consequences and irreversibility. The solution is clarity and control. Explain what will happen before it happens. Provide preview modes. Let people back out of commitments. Make data portable. Make changes reversible. When people trust they won't be trapped or lose their work, they commit.

These aren't four separate designs. They're four dimensions of the same thing: respect. Respect for people's time, intelligence, emotions, and agency.

If you lead product, pick your most important user workflow. Map it completely. Every screen. Every click. Every input.

Then experience it as a hostile anthropologist. Assume nothing. Question everything. For each step, ask: "Why would someone know to do this? What happens if they don't? How do they know they succeeded?"

Write down every moment where the answer requires expertise, prior knowledge, or faith. Those are your disregarded details.

Pick three. The three that create the most emotional friction. Then fix them completely. Not with tooltips. With actual design changes that make the obvious action the correct action. Maybe it's adding visible confirmation feedback. Maybe it's replacing jargon with plain language. Maybe it's providing an undo option where currently there's only an "Are you sure?" dialog.

Ship those three fixes. Measure not just completion rates, but emotional outcomes. Support tickets. Return rates. You'll find that small changes have disproportionate impacts.

If you're an individual contributor, pick one thing you've built that you suspect is harder to use than it should be. Bring in someone who's never seen it. Watch them try to use it. Say nothing. Just watch.

You'll be shocked at what they don't understand. Then fix one thing. The thing that created the most confusion. Fix it so completely that the next person doesn't stumble there.

The Real Lesson

The radial tire did not reinvent the wheel. It made it safe at speed. Desktop publishing did not reinvent writing. It made creation accessible. The telephone did not reinvent communication. It removed the incantations.

In each case, the innovation was not in the core technology. It was in the details that determined who could use it. And those details seemed minor until someone recognized they were actually the entire point.

Because technology that only experts can use is not innovative. It's exclusive. And exclusivity limits impact.

John Sculley's paradox captures this perfectly: "He didn't create anything really, but he created everything." Steve didn't invent graphical interfaces, desktop publishing, digital music players, smartphones, or tablets. But he created the versions that everyone could use. And "everyone" changes everything.

The world rarely notices disregarded details until they're gone. But their absence is what makes the impossible feel inevitable. What makes the complex feel simple. What makes the intimidating feel welcoming.

Details done right make dollars. But more than that, they make dignity. They make inclusion. They make space for people who thought technology wasn't for them.

And when you make space for everyone? You don't just improve a product. You expand what's possible.

Been There, Done That

Awarding novelty for mere arrival to market is not just intellectually lazy. It actively punishes the very work that turns technology from curiosity into culture. It confuses first contact with mastery, prototype with product, spark with stewardship.

Apple learned this lesson the hard way in the 1990s, when it poured immense resources into genuinely inventive technologies like HyperCard's hypertext vision, Newton's handwriting recognition, QuickTime VR's immersive imaging, and OpenDoc's component architecture, only to watch them languish in obscurity, admired by engineers but ignored by users, while competitors studied, simplified, and shipped polished versions years later.

This was not a failure of imagination but of alignment: Apple had become so enamored with the act of invention that it forgot the harder work of translation. Taking a technically coherent idea and making it emotionally, cognitively, and practically accessible to people who don't live inside the lab is what separates the thinkers from the doers.

The Discipline of Ruthless Editing

When Steve returned in 1997, he did not arrive with a new gadget. He arrived with a new discipline: ruthless editing, not of features, but of intent. His first executive act was to cancel dozens of projects, not because they lacked technical merit, but because they lacked human resonance.

They solved problems no one felt, or solved them in ways that required too much of the user. He recognized a brutal truth: Apple had rarely been punished for being wrong. It had been punished for being early, for mistaking internal elegance for external utility, for building wells others would draw from while Apple itself went thirsty.

The tablet was not a new idea. FingerWorks' multi-touch technology, now credited as foundational to the iPad, was itself born from a commercially stalled Apple research effort in the 1990s.

Xerox PARC gave the world laser printing, ethernet, and the graphical user interface, yet failed utterly to bring any of them to market as viable consumer products because its GUI remained a fragile, inconsistent prototype, its mouse a $300, dust-clogged, skip-prone contraption, its vision trapped in the mindset of augmentation rather than empowerment.

Apple's contribution was not replication. It was reconstitution: re-engineering the mouse to cost $15 and work on denim, replacing the bulky linear power supply with the compact switching supply that made the Mac portable, transforming the GUI from an expert tool into an intuitive canvas. This was work so fundamental it reshaped the entire category, yet so unflashy it was labeled "mere refinement."

When Generosity Meets Resistance

Even when Apple invents something truly novel and offers it freely, it is met with resistance. The embedded SIM, designed to liberate users from carrier lock-in by making the SIM virtual and reprogrammable, was squashed not by technical limitation but by institutional fear.

Apple's fallback, the nano-SIM which was one-third the size of its predecessor and offered royalty-free to the industry, was dismissed by Nokia as "an attempt to devalue the intellectual property of others," a stunning inversion where giving away a superior solution is framed as theft.

This is not Apple's pathology. It is the industry's. Windows didn't emerge from Microsoft's native genius: MS-DOS was purchased as QDOS; Windows NT was built by engineers recruited from DEC. Google Earth was invented by Keyhole, Inc., acquired and rebranded. Siri began as a third-party app. Apple's OS X began as NeXT, itself a marriage of BSD UNIX and a custom Mach kernel.

No major platform is built from whole cloth. They are all palimpsests, layers of acquisition, adaptation, refinement. The value lies not in the first inscription, but in the final form, the one that sticks.

The Empirical Truth

The bottom line is empirical: Apple tried the pure invention path for a decade, and the market rejected it, not because the ideas were bad, but because they were unresolved.

Steve saw this with clarity: when you operate too far ahead of the mainstream, when your technology is brilliant but brittle, when you prioritize novelty over need, you don't lead. You hemorrhage talent, capital, and credibility. So he shifted the mission from inventing the new to perfecting the possible by finding the flaws that kept promising technology from becoming great products, and fixing them with obsessive care.

That became Apple's profit line, not in the narrow financial sense, but in the deeper, human one: trust.

What This Actually Teaches

The 1990s Apple experience is a case study in the cost of being right too early. HyperCard anticipated the web. Newton anticipated smartphones and tablets. QuickTime VR anticipated virtual reality. OpenDoc anticipated component-based software architecture. Apple saw the future clearly. But seeing isn't enough.

The gap between vision and viability is where most innovation dies. It's the space where technical possibility meets market readiness, where brilliant engineering meets human willingness to change, where prototype performance meets production reliability.

Apple in the 1990s lived in that gap. They built tomorrow's products with today's technology for yesterday's market. The technology wasn't ready: components were too expensive, too power-hungry, too unreliable. The market wasn't ready: people didn't understand why they needed these things. And Apple wasn't ready: they lacked the discipline to bridge that gap through relentless refinement.

When Steve returned, he didn't reject invention. He contextualized it. Invention without execution is research. Invention with execution is product. And product is what companies ship, what customers pay for, what markets reward.

This reframing changed everything. It gave Apple permission to be second, third, tenth to a category, as long as they were first to make it work for humans. It shifted the question from "Did we invent this?" to "Can people actually use this?" And that second question is harder, more important, and more valuable.

How This Shows Up In Your World

A startup builds an AI-powered feature that works 70% of the time. They ship it because "we're first to market." Users try it, it fails 30% of the time, they lose trust, they never come back. Three years later, a competitor ships the same feature at 95% reliability. Users trust it. The competitor wins. Being first meant nothing. Being reliable meant everything.

An enterprise software company builds a revolutionary architecture. It's elegant, technically superior. But it requires customers to rearchitect their entire stack. The learning curve is steep. The migration path is unclear. So customers stay with the inferior but familiar solution. The company burns years on technology that's brilliant but brittle.

The pattern is always the same: confusing technical achievement with market success, believing that invention creates its own demand, underestimating the work required to make complex things feel simple.

I've also watched companies succeed by deliberately being second or third. They let others pioneer, make mistakes, find problems. Then they study those mistakes, solve those problems, and ship a version that actually works. They're not celebrated as inventors. But they're rewarded with adoption, revenue, and market leadership.

The difference is discipline. The discipline to wait until the technology is ready. The discipline to simplify until normal people can use it. The discipline to fix the unglamorous problems that separate prototype from product.

Measure the gap between demo and daily use. How does your product perform in controlled conditions versus chaotic reality? If your demos require specific sequences, ideal conditions, or retries, you're not ready. Ship when the daily use case works, not when the demo case works.

Count the adoption prerequisites. What must change before people can adopt your product? New hardware? New infrastructure? New skills? New workflows? Each prerequisite is a barrier. One barrier, manageable. Three barriers, you're asking too much. Five barriers, you're too early. Either reduce the prerequisites or acknowledge you're doing research, not building a business.

Track expert versus novice success rates. If your product works great for trained people who understand the domain, that's not a product. That's a professional tool. If you need mainstream adoption, measure novice success. Can someone use it successfully the first time without help?

Listen for "you just need to" language. When users struggle, how do you explain it? If your team says "you just need to restart it," "you just need to update the firmware," "you just need to configure the settings," you're shipping problems, not solutions. Each "you just need to" is an admission that your product doesn't work out of the box.

Examine your support volume and patterns. What percentage of users need help to accomplish basic tasks? If support volume is high and questions are about core functionality, not edge cases, your product isn't ready. You're using customers as beta testers. They'll forgive this once. Then they'll leave.

The Framework: From Spark to Flame

Edit intent, not just features. The mistake of 1990s Apple wasn't having too many features. It was having too many intents. HyperCard wanted to revolutionize programming and publishing and databases and multimedia. Pick one. Newton wanted to be a PDA and a communicator and a handwriting recognizer and a connectivity hub. Pick one. When everything is the priority, nothing is. Articulate the single most important problem you're solving. Then edit everything else.

Wait for the technology to be ready, or make it ready. Steve delayed the iPhone until battery technology could deliver all-day use. He delayed the iPad until processors were fast enough for instant response. He didn't ship compromises with promises to fix them later. If your technology isn't ready, either wait for it to mature or invest in maturing it yourself. Shipping immature technology burns trust.

Simplify until it's obvious. The Xerox Alto had a graphical interface. But using it required training. The Mac had a graphical interface you could understand by looking at it. Trash metaphor for deletion. Folders for organization. Drag and drop for movement. The difference wasn't capability. It was clarity. For every complex capability, ask: "How do we make this obvious?" If the answer is "training" or "documentation," keep simplifying.

Bridge the gap with integration, not explanation. Apple didn't tell people "you need a computer to use the iPod." They made iTunes so seamless the computer became invisible. Every time you're tempted to explain how something works, ask: "How do we integrate this so explanation isn't needed?" Explanations are admissions that your product requires mental effort.

Measure by trust, not technology. The true measure of readiness is not "does it work?" but "do people trust it to work?" Apple Maps worked, technically, when it launched. But people didn't trust it after the high-profile failures. That lack of trust was more damaging than the technical issues. Before you ship, ask: "Will this build trust or destroy it?"

Learn from being early, don't defend it. When Apple's early inventions failed, they could have insisted the market was wrong. Instead, they learned: you're solving problems we don't feel yet, in ways that cost too much effort. When you're too early, the temptation is to blame the market. Resist. Listen to why people aren't adopting. That feedback is more valuable than any validation of your vision.

What To Do Monday Morning

If you're leading a product that's technically impressive but struggling to gain adoption, run an honest assessment. Don't ask "Is this good technology?" Ask "Is this ready technology?"

Review your support tickets, user feedback, and adoption metrics. Are people struggling with core functionality or edge cases? Are early adopters succeeding while mainstream users fail?

If the patterns suggest you're too early, you have three options:

Simplify radically. Pick the one use case that works reliably and ship only that. Cut everything else. This is painful. But shipping complexity that doesn't work is worse. Simplify until you have something that absolutely, reliably works. Build from strength, not vision.

Invest in maturity. If the core technology isn't ready, make it ready. This might mean delaying launch. It definitely means unglamorous engineering work: edge case testing, failure mode analysis, performance optimization, reliability hardening. Set clear maturity criteria and don't ship until you meet them.

Reframe as research. If you're genuinely pioneering something the market isn't ready for, acknowledge it. Position the product as early access, beta, research preview. That reframing changes expectations. Users who opt in expect rough edges. But don't pretend it's a production product.

The Real Lesson

The world doesn't need more sparks. It needs more people willing to tend the flame.

Apple's 1990s experience proves that being first means nothing if you can't make it work. HyperCard, Newton, QuickTime VR, OpenDoc, all brilliant ideas. All commercial failures. Not because the vision was wrong, but because the execution was incomplete.

The market doesn't reward vision. It rewards viability. It rewards products that work reliably, that solve real problems, that people can actually use without training or frustration.

Steve's genius was recognizing this truth and restructuring Apple around it. From inventing the new to perfecting the possible. From being first to being right. From shipping vision to shipping trust.

This shift wasn't retreat. It was maturity. The hard work isn't having ideas. The hard work is making ideas work. And making them work requires discipline, patience, and obsessive attention to the unglamorous details that separate brilliance from brittleness.

Been there, done that is not an insult. It's an acknowledgment that someone else saw the future first. Fine. The question is: who made it work? Who solved the problems that kept it from being viable? Who did the grinding work of refinement, integration, and humanization?

Because sparks are easy. Anyone can have an idea. Anyone can build a prototype. Anyone can announce a vision.

But tending the flame, feeding it, shielding it, refining it until it's strong enough to light the way forward, that requires something deeper than genius. It requires discipline. Patience. Humility to learn from failure. Courage to be second if second means being right.

Apple learned this through pain. Through bleeding credibility and capital in the 1990s. But they learned. And that learning became the foundation for everything that followed. The iPod wasn't first. The iPhone wasn't first. The iPad wasn't first. But they were right. They worked. They built trust.

And trust, compounded over decades, is what transforms companies from innovators into institutions. From sparks into flames that never die.

CHAPTER 17
QUALITY PRODUCTS ARE POWER

In 2022: Apple generated $394.3 billion revenue
52% came from iPhone sales

232 million iPhones, 61 million iPads and 26 million Mac and MacBook units were sold

82 million AirPods & 53 million Apple Watches were sold
Apple Music has 88 million subscribers

Photo by Ross Dunn

"That's what makes great products. It's not process. It's content." — Steve Jobs

Before the iPhone, the cellphone industry operated like a closed ecosystem. This was not by accident, but by design. Carriers were not service providers. They were gatekeepers. And their customers weren't the people holding the phones. Their real customers were the phone makers, who existed at the carriers' sufferance.

Consumers were an afterthought. Basically bait to be hooked, locked, and bled. Phones were cheap, disposable tools designed for one purpose: to trap users in two-year contracts while carriers upsold proprietary services at exorbitant markups. Want Tetris? Pay $5/month, forever. Replace your broken phone? Buy the game again.

Walt Mossberg called the carriers "Soviet ministries," bureaucracies that "sit athwart the market, breaking the link between the producers of goods and services and the people who use them."

Then came the iPhone. It was not the first smartphone. It was not the fastest. It did not have the most features. What it had was coherence, a relentless alignment of hardware, software, and human need. And that coherence gave Apple something no other phone maker possessed: leverage.

Because when consumers love your product, not just like it, but love it, the balance of power flips. Carriers no longer dictate terms. They beg for access.

The AT&T Deal: A Masterstroke in Leverage

The AT&T deal was not a surrender. It was a masterstroke. Apple kept control of the product, the software, the customer relationship. AT&T got exclusivity, true, but only in exchange for reinventing its entire backend, launching visual voicemail, and offering unlimited data. And when AT&T stores tried to bundle accessories to inflate commissions? Steve shut it down immediately.

This was not ego. It was ethics: the refusal to let a partner degrade the user's experience for short-term gain.

The result? In its first year, 40% of iPhone buyers switched to AT&T or were new to the market entirely. By 2013, the iPhone accounted for 85% of mobile internet traffic and over half of Verizon's smartphone sales, despite years of Android competition.

The lesson is not subtle: Quality is not a cost center. It is your greatest source of power. It gives you the right to say no. To walk away. To rebuild the rules.

What This Actually Teaches

The iPhone story is taught as product design triumph. It was. But the deeper lesson is about power dynamics and how quality creates negotiating leverage.

Most companies believe they're powerless against larger partners. Carriers are too big. Retailers are too powerful. Platforms set the terms. So companies accept whatever deals they can get. They compromise on pricing, on presentation, on customer relationships, on product integrity.

This is backwards. You have no leverage when your product is replaceable. When you're selling commodity goods to partners who control distribution, they set the terms. But when your product is exceptional, when consumers actively seek it out, when not having it means losing customers to competitors who do, the dynamic inverts. Now the partner needs you more than you need them.

Steve understood this viscerally. The iPhone wasn't just a good phone. It was so much better than alternatives that carriers couldn't afford not to carry it. AT&T accepted unprecedented concessions not because they were generous, but because they knew: if they said no, Verizon would say yes. And whoever got the iPhone would gain millions of high-value customers.

That's leverage. Not from size or market share. From quality so undeniable that partners compete for access rather than you competing for shelf space.

The inverse is equally instructive. Before the iPhone, Apple partnered with Motorola on the ROKR. Apple compromised. They let Motorola design the hardware. They let carriers control the experience. They accepted artificial limitations: 100-song cap, slow syncing, clunky interface. The ROKR failed precisely because Apple had ceded quality for access. And without quality, they had no power.

The lesson: compromise on quality to gain market access, and you gain neither

How This Shows Up In Your World

I've watched companies surrender power they didn't know they had. A software company with a genuinely superior product accepts punitive terms from a distribution platform because "we need to be where the users are." They give up revenue share, customer data, and pricing control.

But here's what they missed: their product was good enough that users would have sought it out directly. They didn't need to be in the platform's app store to be discovered. Users were already recommending it. They had organic demand. They had leverage. But they didn't recognize it, so they traded it away.

The pattern is always the same: companies don't recognize that quality creates power. They think power comes from size, from market position, from being first. So they chase scale before excellence. They expand distribution before perfecting the product. They optimize for visibility before creating something worth seeing.

The companies that build enduring power do the opposite. They obsess over quality first. They say no to distribution that would compromise the product. They accept slower growth to maintain integrity. They bet that if they make something exceptional enough, people will seek it out. And that seeking creates leverage.

The Diagnostic: Do You Have Leverage or Do You Think You Don't?

Test your replaceability. If you disappeared tomorrow, how hard would it be for your partners to replace you? If the answer is "trivial," you have no leverage. If the answer is "difficult" or "they'd lose customers," you have leverage, even if you're not using it. The question is not "Are we big?" The question is "Are we necessary?"

Track partner behavior changes. When you make requests, how do partners respond? If they immediately accommodate, you have more leverage than you think. If they push back on everything, you might have less. But watch for a pattern: partners who seem inflexible on standard issues but flexible on you specifically are signaling that you matter more than they let on.

Count your organic demand. How many customers find you directly versus through partner channels? If most customers discover you through partners, you need those channels. If many customers come to you directly and then ask "where can I buy this?" you have leverage with any channel that wants to serve those customers.

Listen to competitive intelligence. What do competitors say about you? If they dismiss you, you probably don't have much leverage. If they emphasize how they're different from you, they're worried. That worry is evidence of your power.

The Framework: Building Power Through Quality

Optimize for love, not just satisfaction. Satisfied customers are replaceable. They'll switch for a 10% discount. Customers who love your product are loyal. They recommend you. They complain when partners don't carry you. That complaint is your leverage.

Build something partners can't replicate. The iPhone's leverage came from integration. Carriers couldn't build it themselves. Phone makers couldn't match it. That uniqueness created dependency. If your differentiation is superficial, you have no durable leverage.

Make your quality visible to end users, not just partners. Partners evaluate you on margins and terms. End users evaluate you on experience. If your quality only shows up in B2B metrics, you have no consumer pull. But if end users feel the difference and demand you specifically, partners must accommodate.

Use quality to filter partners, not chase them. When you have leverage, you can be selective. Steve didn't try to get the iPhone on every carrier immediately. He picked one, negotiated hard, got unprecedented terms, then expanded from strength.

Build alternatives before you need them. Leverage only works if you can walk away. Apple could demand concessions from AT&T because they had Verizon as an alternative. Always cultivate alternatives: second suppliers, alternative channels, direct-to-consumer options.

What To Do Monday Morning

If you lead product or partnerships, audit your current partner relationships. For each major partner, ask: "If we proposed more favorable terms, what's the worst that happens?" Often it's "they might say no." But "might say no" is not "will definitely say no."

Pick one partnership where you suspect you have unused leverage. Make one request. Not a complete renegotiation, one specific ask that protects quality or improves economics. Present it professionally, with rationale. Don't threaten. Just ask. Then watch what happens.

You'll learn immediately whether you have leverage. If they accommodate easily, you've been leaving value on the table. If they negotiate, you have some leverage. If they refuse flatly, you either don't have leverage or you're asking the wrong partner.

If you're building a product, ask yourself honestly: "If a partner said no to us, how hard would it be for them to replace what we provide?" If the answer is "easy," your first job is not distribution. It's differentiation. Make the product so good that saying no hurts them.

The Real Lesson

Quality is not a cost center. It is your greatest source of power.

This is not philosophical. It's mechanical. Quality that users notice creates demand. Demand creates options. Options create leverage. Leverage creates power.

The iPhone succeeded not just because it was well-designed, but because that design created consumer love strong enough to invert the power structure of an entire industry. Carriers who had dictated terms to every phone maker for decades suddenly found themselves negotiating from weakness.

That leverage let Apple protect quality. No carrier bloatware. No artificial limitations. No bundled accessories. Every protection maintained the quality that created the leverage in the first place. A virtuous cycle.

The companies that fail this test cede quality for access. They compromise to get distribution, then wonder why the distribution doesn't work. Because distribution of mediocrity is just efficient failure.

The companies that pass this test do the opposite. They protect quality even when it limits access. They say no to partnerships that would compromise the product. They accept smaller initial markets to build something exceptional. Then they let quality create demand, demand create leverage, leverage create access on their terms.

Quality, maintained obsessively, creates power that compounds. Every product that exceeds expectations builds reputation. Every customer who loves you becomes an advocate. Every partner who needs you accepts your terms.

Not because you're big. Because you're necessary.

The Danger Zone

"Quality is everyone's responsibility." — W. Edwards Deming

To create products with the power of true consumer demand, you must enforce your standards down the entire creation chain. Not selectively. Not politely. Relentlessly.

Apple is known for its meticulous control: who sells its products, how they're displayed, what sits nearby on the shelf. Critics call this control "overbearing." They mistake coherence for compulsion.

Steve wasn't inventing a new standard. He was honoring an old one. Great brands from Coca-Cola to Disney have always dictated terms to protect experience. Because when you don't, you surrender to chaos. You get over-worked stockers who don't care how your product is stacked. Salespeople who confuse specs and push the wrong model. Retailers trying to please everyone and offend no one.

Steve had been burned before. He knew: an unbroken chain of quality must run from development to delivery. And when Apple outsourced quality once under him, the result wasn't just disappointment. It was humiliation.

The ROKR: A Masterclass in Compromise

In 2005, Apple and Motorola announced a partnership: the ROKR. Pitched as a fusion of the iPod and the RAZR. The promise? Sleek design, seamless music, Apple's magic, Motorola's reach.

The reality? A hodgepodge of concessions. It wasn't sleek like an iPod. Not slim like a RAZR. Consumers couldn't wirelessly buy music. Loading songs via iTunes took minutes. Motorola imposed an arbitrary 100-song limit. The interface was clunky, confusing, genuinely un-Apple.

At the launch event, Steve demoed the phone. He ended a call and tried to resume music. "Well, I'm supposed to be able to resume the music right back to where it was." A beat. "Oops! I must've hit the wrong button." The core feature, switching between phone and music, was broken.

This wasn't bad luck. It was intent misalignment. Motorola's CEO, Ed Zander, had famously scoffed: "Screw the iPod Nano. What the hell does it do? Who listens to 1,000 songs?" He wasn't designing for users. He was protecting carriers who wanted music sold through them, not iTunes.

The ROKR bore the Apple brand but none of its soul. Steve knew better: A brand is not a sticker. It's a covenant. Break it once and trust evaporates.

The Carrier Trap

After ROKR, Steve knew: to build the iPhone, Apple had to own the experience across hardware, software, service, sales.

Carriers said no. Verizon slammed the door. Sprint refused control. T-Mobile gave a tepid maybe. Only Cingular said yes, signing a five-year exclusivity deal without hesitation, without even seeing the phone.

Why? Cingular was far below the big three in cellular market share. At their level, a powerful motivator for consumers to leave a competitor and sign up with Cingular carried massive heft. The iPhone carried the power to double their market share in a year or less.

Need proof? AT&T found out about the iPhone deal and immediately purchased Cingular to gain the exclusive rights.

The iPhone launch exposed the fault line. At an AT&T store on Broadway: Lines of eager customers. No updates on wait times or stock. Staff announcing the store would close at 11 p.m., line or no line. 8GB models sold out, but employees hid it, hoping to upsell 16GB. Activations took hours. Hundreds of people, $699 in hand, treated like beggars.

Minutes away, the Apple Store: Longer lines, faster flow. Wireless checkouts. Smiles. High fives. At home: plug in, pick a plan, done.

And the final insult: AT&T stores refused to sell iPhones unless customers bought $50 in accessories, a practice so egregious, AT&T's regional VP publicly apologized.

Apple took the blame for MMS delays, data caps, FaceTime bans, all AT&T's doing. The public didn't care about backend deals. They saw a phone that "couldn't send pictures" and blamed Apple.

The Leverage of Excellence

But excellence compounds. By 2013: 4.8 of AT&T's 6 million smartphone sales were iPhones. Over half of Verizon's 7 million were iPhones, on a network that once said no.

The lesson is not about carriers. It's about non-negotiables. Your product's power comes not from features but from fidelity: To the user's time. To the team's craft. To the promise in your name.

Outlets will balk. Partners will resist. Let them. Because when consumers love your product, truly love it, you don't beg for access. You set the terms.

What This Actually Teaches

The danger zone is the gap between your quality standards and your partners' incentives. In that gap, your brand dies slowly, one compromised interaction at a time.

The ROKR failed not because Apple built a bad product, but because they didn't build the product at all. Motorola did. And Motorola's incentives, protecting carrier relationships, maximizing hardware margins, shipping fast, were fundamentally incompatible with Apple's standards.

This is the danger: when you let partners control the customer experience, they optimize for their goals, not yours. Retailers optimize for margins and inventory turns. Carriers optimize for lock-in and upsells. None of them optimize for your brand promise.

And customers don't distinguish between you and your partners. When the AT&T store treated iPhone buyers poorly, customers blamed Apple. The backend deals, the technical constraints, the political compromises, none of that mattered. All that mattered was the experience fell short of the promise.

This is why control matters. Not control as ego, but control as brand protection. Your brand is the sum of every interaction a customer has with anything bearing your name. If you can't control those interactions, you can't control your brand.

How This Shows Up In Your World

A software company partners with a large consultancy to implement their product. Six months later, complaints arrive. The implementations are bloated, taking six months when the software company's team does it in six weeks. The consultancy is adding unnecessary customizations. Customers are frustrated. And they blame the software company, not the consultancy.

Why? Because the consultancy's incentives, maximize billable hours, create dependency, conflicted with the software company's promise of simplicity. The software company gained access to enterprise customers. They lost the ability to deliver value to them.

A consumer brand partners with a big-box retailer. The retailer demands packaging changes, price concessions, promotional support. The brand complies. Six months later, their product looks like every other product on the shelf. The differentiation is gone. Sales are okay but not great. Margins are terrible.

The pattern is always the same: you trade control for access, then discover the access is worthless because you can't deliver your value without control.

The Diagnostic: Are You in the Danger Zone?

Map the customer journey end-to-end. For each step, ask: "Who controls this interaction? Us or a partner?" If partners control more than half the journey, you're in the danger zone. Partners define your brand more than you do.

Audit for incentive misalignment. For each major partner, write down their key metrics. Then write down yours. Look for conflicts. Where their incentives push them to behave in ways that hurt your brand promise. Every conflict is a danger point.

Track blame attribution. When something goes wrong, who do customers blame? If customers blame you for partner failures, you're in the danger zone. You're absorbing reputation damage for things you didn't control.

Measure quality variation across channels. How consistent is the customer experience across different partners? If variation is significant, you have a control problem. Customers don't care which channel they bought from. They care whether you kept your promise.

Test your ability to course-correct. When you identify a partner quality problem, how quickly can you fix it? If you can mandate changes and they happen immediately, you have control. If you have to negotiate, escalate, threaten, you have suggestions. And suggestions don't protect brands.

The Framework: Protecting Quality Across the Chain

Own the critical touchpoints. You can't control everything. But you must control the moments that define your brand. For Apple, that was product design, the retail experience, and the unboxing moment. Identify your critical touchpoints. Those you must own or control completely.

Choose partners for alignment, not reach. Cingular wasn't the biggest carrier. They were the most willing to align with Apple's standards. Choosing reach over alignment is choosing volume over quality. Filter partners by how willing they are to subordinate their preferences to your standards.

Build standards, not guidelines. Guidelines are suggestions. Standards are requirements. Apple didn't give AT&T guidelines for in-store experience. They audited stores, measured metrics, and pulled product from locations that didn't comply.

Create alternatives to create leverage. Steve couldn't force AT&T to improve if AT&T was his only option. But once Verizon wanted the iPhone, suddenly AT&T had competition. Always cultivate backup partners, alternative channels, direct-to-consumer options.

Measure brand health, not just sales. Revenue through partners looks good until you realize it's destroying brand equity. Survey customers who bought through partners versus direct. If partner channels consistently score lower, you're trading long-term brand value for short-term volume.

What To Do Monday Morning

If you work with partners to reach customers, run a brand protection audit. List every partner that touches your customers. For each, write down what they control, what their incentives are, where their incentives conflict with your brand promise.

Pick your worst-performing partner relationship. You have three options:

Fix it. Go to the partner with specific standards and enforcement mechanisms. Not "please do better" but "here are the metrics, here's how we'll measure, here's what happens if you don't comply."

Filter it. Remove your product from that partner. Yes, you'll lose revenue. But you'll stop the brand damage. Better to be in fewer places with quality than everywhere with mediocrity.

Replace it. If you can't fix or filter, you need alternatives. Start building direct channels, different partner types, new distribution models.

The Real Lesson

A brand is not a sticker. It's a covenant.

The ROKR taught Steve that slapping an Apple logo on a Motorola product didn't make it an Apple product. It made it a broken promise with an Apple logo. And broken promises destroy brands faster than any competition.

The danger zone is real. It's the space between your quality standards and your partners' incentives. In that space, your brand dies. Not dramatically. Just slowly, one compromised interaction at a time.

Steve learned to stay out of the danger zone by demanding control. Not as ego, but as necessity. Because he understood that every customer interaction shaped what people believed about Apple. And if he couldn't control those interactions, he couldn't protect what people believed.

This made him difficult. Partners complained. Retailers resisted. Carriers fought. But he didn't care about being liked by partners. He cared about being loved by customers. And that love required quality that extended beyond the product to every touchpoint.

Your product's power comes not from features but from fidelity. To the user's time. To the team's craft. To the promise in your name.

Protect that fidelity. Relentlessly.

Because when you surrender quality to partners who don't share your standards, you enter the danger zone. And in that zone, your brand dies.

Stay out. Or get out. Because the world lines up not for the logo, but for the integrity behind it.

Be In High Demand

"Some things scratch the surface, while others strike at your soul." — Gianna Perada

Sales outlets are kings of piggybacking on the value you create.

Steve understood that Apple created the inherent value in its products. The combination of enhanced function, quality materials, and design, along with their investment in product and brand marketing promotional efforts, is what increases their product's value.

He showed us that we best succeed when we remember that our product is the main attraction, not the sideshow, and act accordingly.

Layering that quality in your product won't happen by coincidence. You must demand that greatness if you expect anyone to ever supply it.

When Distribution Leaches Value

When Steve returned to Apple, Amelio's sales plan was to stick Macs in Sears. Sears stuck them next to the home appliances—dishwashers, refrigerators, and vacuums sat side-by-side with Apple's cutting-edge computers. It was a sad sight.

After returning, Steve had produced amazing computers like the iMac and then saw firsthand how third parties leeched off their value. Best Buy was caught sticking their entire stock of iMacs on the back walls of stores, with none available on the sales floor for customers to explore or experience directly.

A customer that Apple had invested a small fortune in creating was walking in and practically begging to hand Best Buy money for that computer. What did Best Buy contribute to earn their cut of that sale? Other than physically storing and displaying Apple's products and paying a cashier to operate the register, next to nothing.

Stores that stock your product don't fuel your sales. High demand for your product does. Focus on enhancing and promoting demand for your quality product. The outlets will beat your door down to carry it.

For example, carriers may love to publicly pout about Apple being arrogant during negotiations, but the fact is Apple makes them a small fortune by allowing them to carry the iPhone.

Not All Customers Are Created Equal

The first principle is that all customers are not created equal. If customers that prefer your product tend to buy more accessories, add-ons, and higher-profit services, then the outlet is gaining far greater value from those customers. If customers that buy your product tend to buy a few accessories or add-ons and stick to the discount plans, they offer little value beyond that initial sale.

Numbers for 2013 peg Apple's iPhone as accounting for more than 85% of mobile internet use. Customers have to buy higher-priced plans that cover the high volume of monthly cellular data. For example, iPhone usage alone quickly tripled the carrier's volume of data traffic in cities like New York and San Francisco. This resulted in billions of additional dollars for carriers.

What many don't understand about the iPhone's competition is that after the initial sale, the competition's customers only account for a fraction of any given month's cellular data. Premium data plans are unneeded by customers who only sporadically use the internet. Despite occupying a massive slice of the market, the customers buying those smartphones barely utilize them in a way that benefits carriers financially.

Monthly bills are where the real money occurs, and customers who buy a phone with a ton of obscure capabilities but little practical benefits don't increase revenue much. If you don't watch Netflix movies on your phone, your data usage will be a tiny sliver of a Netflix user.

The type of customer you choose to attract is a major factor in your power over your outlets. Steve knew Apple benefited in many hidden ways from attracting demographics that were more social, more interested in the arts, and more financially successful. That combination may be much maligned in the counter-culture, but money speaks volumes at the end of the day.

Study after study has shown that Apple's products attract the cream-of-the-crop customer. 67% of Apple's customers have household incomes over $60K. 68% of them hold a four-year degree or better. They're more likely to be self-employed and aged 18-34 than non-Apple households.

Customers shopping from their iPhones outspent Android or Blackberry shoppers by a large margin, according to IBM's data from retailers. The trend was mirrored in tablets. iPad shoppers accounted for more than 88% of purchases made from tablets during 2012's early holiday shopping. It crushed Amazon's Kindle, which trailed at 2.4%, and Barnes & Noble's Nook, which accounted for 3.1% of purchases from tablets.

Now, let's take into consideration that iPhone and iPad customers have a 90% loyalty rate. Devices that customers love and customers with tremendous buying power demographics—that's a killer combination that brings major negotiating power.

Reaching that level of power requires being relentless in layering quality in your product and ensuring that the most desirable customers share your passion for it. You must demand greatness at multiple steps and from every direction during production if you ever expect to supply it in the market.

What This Actually Teaches

The retail relationship is often misunderstood. Most companies see it as supplicant to sovereign: the retailer controls shelf space, so the manufacturer must compete for access. This framing is backwards when you have genuine demand.

Steve's insight was that retailers don't create demand. They capture it. Apple created demand through product quality, design, marketing, and brand building. Retailers simply stood at the point of capture and collected a percentage. When Best Buy hid iMacs on back walls, they weren't hurting Apple's demand. They were losing their share of it. Customers who couldn't find iMacs at Best Buy found them at Apple Stores or ordered direct.

This inverts the power dynamic. The retailer needs the high-demand product more than the manufacturer needs that specific retailer. Because if the retailer doesn't carry what customers want, customers go elsewhere. And retailers who consistently don't stock what customers seek lose those customers permanently.

But this only works if three conditions are met. First, your product must create genuine demand, not interest or awareness, but demand. People actively seeking it out, willing to pay full price, recommending it to others. If you have to discount to move volume, you don't have demand. You have inventory that needs disposing. Second, that demand must be visible to retailers. If customers come in asking for your product by name, if they're disappointed when it's not available, if they leave to find it elsewhere, retailers notice. That's signal. But if customers are indifferent, if they'll accept an alternative, if they don't know your product exists, retailers have no reason to prioritize you. Third, your customers must be valuable beyond the initial sale. The iPhone's power came not just from device sales but from what iPhone customers did after purchase: bought data plans, downloaded apps, purchased accessories, upgraded regularly. They were high-lifetime-value customers. Retailers and carriers who served them well captured that value. Those who didn't, lost it.

This combination—demand that's genuine, visible, and valuable—creates leverage. Not from size or scale, but from being necessary to capture the customers retailers want most.

The Diagnostic Questions

Do you have genuine demand or just optimized distribution? Here's how to tell. Measure unprompted requests—how often do customers come to your retailers asking for your product by name? If you're in retail, ask store associates what customers request. If you're in B2B, ask your partners what clients specifically seek. If the number is low, you don't have demand. You have product that gets sold when customers are open to suggestion. That's not leverage. That's substitutability.

Test your discount dependency. What percentage of your volume moves at full price versus on promotion? If most sales require discounting, you don't have demand. You have inventory that needs incentives to clear. Genuine demand commands full price because customers want it enough to pay it.

Track channel performance variation. How does your product perform across different retailers or distribution channels? If performance is consistent, demand is driving sales. Customers find you wherever you are. If performance varies wildly, distribution quality is driving sales. Some retailers sell you well, others don't. That variance signals you're dependent on retail execution, not benefiting from consumer pull.

Examine your customer economics. What's the lifetime value of customers who buy your product versus competitors' products? If your customers are higher LTV, more loyal, more likely to buy adjacent products or services, you're attracting valuable customers. That gives you leverage with distribution partners. If your customers are price-sensitive, one-time buyers, low engagement, you're not creating value beyond the initial sale.

Monitor your waitlist and backorder patterns. When you're out of stock, what happens? Do customers wait, backorder, express frustration? Or do they buy alternatives without concern? Genuine demand creates willingness to wait. If out-of-stocks don't create any customer push-back, you don't have demand. You have availability-based sales.

If these diagnostics reveal weak demand, distribution optimization is premature. You're building shelf space for a product customers aren't seeking. Better to contract distribution, invest in demand creation, then expand from strength.

Building Demand That Creates Leverage

Steve's approach wasn't just "make great products." It was "make products people love enough to seek out, then use that seeking as leverage."

First, invest in product excellence before distribution. Most companies do this backwards. They build an acceptable product then focus on getting it everywhere. Better to build an exceptional product with limited distribution, let demand build, then expand to capture it. The iMac launched in Apple Stores only initially. As demand built, retailers begged to carry it. That sequence—excellence then expansion—creates leverage. The reverse creates dependence.

Second, create customers who evangelize, not just buy. One-time buyers give you revenue. Evangelists give you leverage. Because evangelists don't just repurchase, they recruit. They tell friends. They post reviews. They create organic demand that retailers can't ignore. Optimize your product and experience not just for satisfaction but for love. Ask: "Would our customers recommend us unprompted?" If not, fix that before scaling distribution.

Third, make your customer value visible to partners. Retailers and distributors see your sales but often miss your customer quality. Show them. Share data on customer LTV, repeat purchase rates, cross-category purchasing, premium service adoption. When Best Buy realizes iPhone customers also buy more accessories, apps, and services, Apple becomes more valuable to Best Buy.

Fourth, build brand that creates preference, not just awareness. Awareness without preference is noise. Everyone knows your name but nobody cares. Preference is "I want that one specifically." That's what creates demand retailers can't ignore. Invest in marketing that builds preference: demonstration of superiority, customer testimonials, comparative advantages that matter.

Fifth, design for loyalty, not just acquisition. New customers are expensive. Repeat customers are profitable. And loyal customers create leverage because they're predictable demand. iPhone's 90% loyalty rate meant carriers could count on iPhone customers renewing, upgrading, staying in the ecosystem. That predictability was valuable. Design your product experience to drive loyalty: easy upgrades, ecosystem integration, accumulated value that makes switching painful.

What To Do Monday

If you're responsible for sales or partnerships, audit your current distribution strategy. Map out where you're sold and how you got there. For each channel, ask: "Did they come to us or did we chase them?" If you chased most of your distribution, you're operating from weakness.

Then run the demand diagnostics: unprompted requests, discount dependency, channel performance variation, customer LTV, backorder patterns. If the results reveal weak demand, you have two choices. Contract and strengthen—pull back from low-performing distribution, focus on fewer better channels, redirect saved resources into product improvement and demand creation. Better to be strong in few places than weak everywhere. Or segment and target—identify which customer segments show strong demand and loyalty, focus marketing and product development there, build a passionate core before chasing the indifferent mass.

If you're in product development, ask: "Are we building for customer love or market coverage?" If your roadmap is driven by competitive feature parity, you're building for coverage. If it's driven by delighting your core users, you're building for love. Shift toward the latter.

Start measuring advocacy explicitly. Track Net Promoter Score. Monitor review sentiment. Count social mentions and recommendations. These are leading indicators of demand. If they're strong, lean into distribution expansion. If they're weak, focus on product and experience before scaling.

Steve's genius was recognizing that retailers don't create demand, they capture it, and structuring Apple around this truth. The iMac in Sears next to dishwashers was distribution without demand. Retailers stocked it, but customers didn't seek it. Best Buy hiding iMacs on back walls was distribution betraying demand. Customers wanted them, but retailers didn't facilitate the sale properly.

The solution wasn't better retail relationships. It was stronger demand. Make products so good that customers actively seek them. Build brands so strong that absence is noticed. Create customer value so high that retailers compete to serve them.

That's leverage. Not from size or scale, but from being necessary. From creating demand that retailers can't afford to miss.

All customers are not created equal. iPhone customers used more data, bought more accessories, showed higher loyalty, drove more recurring revenue. That made them valuable beyond the device sale. Carriers who served them well profited. Those who didn't, lost market share.

Your product is the main attraction, not the sideshow. Act accordingly.

Invest in making it exceptional. Build customers who love it enough to seek it out. Create value that extends beyond the initial sale. Make that value visible to distribution partners.

Then watch as the dynamic inverts. Instead of chasing retailers, retailers chase you. Instead of accepting their terms, you set terms. Instead of competing for shelf space, you're allocating access.

That's the power of demand. Not hope that someone might buy. But certainty that they will, and disappointment when they can't.

Layering that quality in your product won't happen by coincidence. You must demand that greatness if you expect anyone to ever supply it. Demand it from your team. Demand it from your process. Demand it from every component and interaction. Because the outlets will beat your door down to carry it, but only if customers are already beating down doors to buy it.

Be in high demand. Everything else follows.

Demand & Supply

"Quality has to be caused, not controlled." — Philip Crosby

Steve was not known for pussy-footing around with his team members. He didn't mince words or send mixed signals. Either something they did was great, or it was shit. This earned him an undeserved reputation for brutality.

He was emphatically brutal about the idea or the work, not the human being. He operated in an environment where praise didn't come for delivering excellence because that was the expectation. During an interview conducted in the 1990s, but only recently recovered, the conversation turned to the tough working conditions around Steve. "I've built a lot of my success off finding these 'A' players and not settling for 'B' and 'C' players," he said. "I found that when you get enough 'A' players, they only want to work with 'A' players. That's what the Mac team was; they were all 'A' players."

Steve often used the sheer force of will to accomplish miracles. That didn't mean he was a tyrant, nor did it reduce the rest of Apple's incredible team to bit players.

Beginning in 1981, the Macintosh team presented an award to the person who did the best job of standing up to Steve. Not only was Steve aware of the award, he liked the very idea of it.

The People Who Stood Up

Joanna Hoffman was the first winner. After she realized Steve had 'adjusted' her marketing projections in ways she didn't agree with, she was on the warpath. Heading into Steve's office, she told his assistant that she was "going to take a knife and stab it into his heart," Hoffman told Steve's biographer. Still, Steve heard her out and backed down on the projected numbers.

Tim Cook has called Steve's ability to change his positions without holding onto the past a 'gift.' Cook astutely realized that 'things change.' Being able, or willing, to swiftly reassess your position and change it if needed is a virtue, not a vice.

Debi Coleman won the award in the third year and also learned that Steve respected people standing up for what they believed in. In fact, he began promoting her after she stood up to him. She ended up becoming the head of manufacturing.

Bill Atkinson trained his engineers in Steve-speak. When Steve confronted them and declared, "This is shit," all they needed to do was defend their decision. Recalling one example, Atkinson first remembered Steve backing down from an engineer's defense but then admitted the engineer eventually found a better solution more in line with Steve's criticism. "He did it better because Steve had challenged him," Atkinson said, "which shows you can push back on him, but you should also listen to him, for [Steve's] usually right." That seems to get said a lot by the very people who worked with Steve directly: '[Steve] was usually right.'

Steve's method may not be 'nice,' but it's an effective way to ensure your team consistently performs at that level.

The fact is that quality is rarely reached on the path of least resistance. It requires a champion willing to argue for quality. Be the guardian of quality.

Overcoming Inertia

Steve returned to an Apple that needed a major overhaul. He was up against legions of entrenched employees who had made a career out of outlasting and virtually ignoring three CEOs while doing whatever they wanted.

Overcoming that type of inertia was essential to his success, and it is essential to yours, as well. Some of your employees will hope by throwing tantrums or turning on the waterworks, they will take your mind off the poor quality of their contribution. Don't fall for it. Stay focused.

Get used to making others uncomfortable when you demand quality. It's the only way you will reliably teach them that striving for excellence is non-negotiable.

Steve explained the reason for his impossible demands: "My job is to not be easy on people. My job is to make them better. My job is to pull things together from different parts of the company and clear the way and get the resources for the key projects. And to take these great people we have and to push them and make them even better, coming up with more aggressive visions of how it could be."

More recently, Apple employee Mike Evangelist wrote: "I was incredibly grateful for the apparently harsh treatment Steve had dished out the first time. He forced me to work harder, and in the end, I did a much better job than I would have otherwise. I believe it is one of the most important aspects of Steve Jobs's impact on Apple: he has little or no patience for anything but excellence from himself or others."

Steve's well-known confrontational style didn't phase Evangelist. He called it Steve's 'logical flaw detector' and described it as Steve's uncanny ability to see through any BS and to instantly zero in on the weak point(s) of any argument. "He grasps the salient points of any situation faster than anyone I've met, and if you can't keep up, that's not his problem," Evangelist said.

The Hero-Shithead Roller Coaster

Nuances can be messy and difficult to grasp. It's much easier to just label someone as erratic, or claim, in Steve's case, that they put people on a 'hero-shithead roller coaster.' Numerous writers present incidences of the same individual being wonderful in Steve's eyes one moment yet considered an idiot by him in another as if that were a contradiction.

It's not that Steve's assessment of the person was wildly flipping; it's that he saw them in terms of their ideas and views. If their position on one thing was clear and brilliant to Steve, they were a 'hero' at that point. When another position was front and center that he vehemently disagreed with, or he was certain they didn't know what they were talking about, they fell into the 'shithead' category.

It's easy to feel sympathy for an individual becoming upset or crying because their idea or work was rejected publicly. When you look at it that way, it's understandable that some people saw Steve as cruel. However, take a step back and consider three things: Steve was completely candid when giving his opinion to friends and foes, he didn't shift with the wind, and he said what he meant and meant what he said, which was invaluable to everyone around him. No energy was wasted trying to uncover his actual position in a discussion. Varnished truth gums up the works. Sparing feelings or trying to avoid wrecking a feel-good meeting means employees don't understand the real issues. Unvarnished truth lets them learn exactly what isn't up to snuff and to fix it. Steve did a hard reset between meetings. A huge clash over an idea one day had no effect on an encounter the next. This hard reset ensured that every situation was handled solely on its merits. Regaining standing was as simple as demonstrating competence.

When you understand those three things, it's simple to recognize the 'roller coaster' wasn't unreasonable or unpredictable at all. Being straight with people, despite discomfort or awkwardness, doesn't mean being heartless, manipulative, or mean. Say what needs to be said. It will deliver a level of quality that you won't find yourself making excuses for later.

It's vital that everyone clearly know where they stand, what needs to be accomplished, and when it's expected. They also need to know the consequences of failing to deliver.

The Price of Admission

Steve didn't consider himself immune from criticism. He didn't inject his ego or position to demand everyone bow down to him. Challenging Steve directly, loudly, even at the top of your lungs, when you felt it necessary, didn't earn you a reprimand.

Steve laid it on the table for his biographer. "I'm brutally honest because the price of admission to being in the room with me is that I get to tell you 'you're full of shit', if you're full of shit. You get to say to me that I'm full of shit, and we have some rip-roaring fights. That keeps the B players and the bozos from larding the organization. Only the A players survive. The people who do survive say, 'Yeah, he was rough.' They say things even worse than 'He cut in line in front of me,' but they say, 'This was the greatest ride I've ever had, and I would not give it up for anything.'"

If you knew your facts, were effective in arguing them, and didn't back down, you won Steve's respect. When it came to debating ideas, Steve's priority was only that the best won out. He naively expected others to also leave their egos at the door

iPod for Windows: When Steve Lost

When the iPod first came out, it was limited to Mac users, both by design and by Apple not writing the software necessary for it to function on Windows. This was a source of massive contention and debate.

The argument had raged for months. Everyone had their positions staked out, but it was still a stalemate.

Steve was against his 'baby' being available on PCs. He fought against it over and over whenever the topic was raised in meetings. The fact of the matter was he didn't want iPods being debased by Windows.

Steve's rejection was emotional and instinctive. The entire executive team disagreed with him.

He didn't run a dictatorship, so expressing his 'feeling' didn't end the debate. No matter how vehemently he expressed that objection, the team raised the issue repeatedly. There was no shutting them up.

Finally, Steve recognized that this wasn't going away. In a last-ditch effort, he dug in his heels and proclaimed, "Until you can prove to me that it will make business sense, I'm not going to do it."

That was his challenge: prove that it made business sense to allow Windows users to buy iPods.

Phil Schiller was the director of worldwide marketing for Apple at the time. Schiller was positive that Steve was being a stubborn ass about expanding the iPod to Windows. He called in experts and developed sales scenarios that all concluded that this would bring more profits. The facts were clear.

"We developed a spreadsheet," said Schiller. "Under all scenarios, there was no amount of cannibalization of Mac sales that would outweigh the sales of iPods." He took it to Steve.

"Screw it," Steve said when they showed him the analysis. "I'm sick of listening to you assholes. Go do whatever the hell you want." Nobody said he enjoyed losing a battle. He was human, after all.

The iMac Name: When Steve Changed His Mind

Naming the iMac seems like a simple thing in hindsight. Try telling that to Ken Segall. It was Segall's job to come up with a name Steve would approve for the new flagship computer.

Naming a product is second only to naming a child in its importance to the creators. Telling someone you don't like their preferred name is pretty close to just saying they have an ugly baby. You can do it, but I recommend being out of spitting distance.

Steve was in love with Phil Schiller's idea, the 'MacMan.' "I think it's sort of reminiscent of Sony," Steve said to Segall, "if MacMan seems like a Sony kind of consumer product, that might be a good thing."

Segall and his team saw so many things wrong with that name that he couldn't begin to list them. Apple was supposed to be about originality, for God's sake. Blatantly echoing another company had to be a joke. The 'man' part of the name was obviously gender bias. Steve said he didn't want people to consider it a toy or portable. Merging Pac-man with Walkman, you basically get MacMan, implying both. The name also just flat out gave him hives, Segall later said.

Segall was about to call Steve's baby 'fugly' to his face. He was a brave man.

A week later, he brought Steve five names. Four were just sacrificial lambs for the name Segall loved: iMac.

Segall made his case to Steve. It referenced the Mac, and the 'i' meant internet. It also meant individual and imaginative. He even pointed to future possibilities. The 'i' prefix could be applied to other internet products. Steve rejected them all, including iMac. "I hate them all. 'MacMan' is better," he said. My baby might be ugly, Steve was saying, but he's got my eyes, and I love him.

Segall went back again with three or four new names but once again included "iMac." Steve said, "I don't hate it this week, but I still don't like it."

Segall didn't hear any more about the name from Steve personally, but friends told him that he was silk-screening the name on prototypes of the new computer. He was testing it out to see if it looked good.

He walked it around the campus, asking what people thought of 'iMac.' Steve found everyone was on the other side of the issue, so the name stuck. "He rejected it twice, but then it just appeared on the machine," Segall says, laughing. "He never formally accepted it."

That's how he worked. He had an opinion that could knock you down and stomp on your chest a few times, but he was still reasonable when confronted with heartfelt and passionate opinions.

The Team Above the Individual

One major aspect of creating quality that's rarely mentioned is the larger commitment demanded by membership in a team. All too often, leaders excuse underperforming individuals on a team in an effort to be 'nice.' That's a huge mistake.

When you excuse poor performance by one team member, you actually inflict damage on the team as a whole. It damages morale, it belittles the sacrifices others have made to deliver the expected quality, and it puts the individual above the team's goal.

Have you found yourself dealing with an employee or fellow team member that used emotional terrorism to make you fear calling out their lousy work? Don't let them force you to tiptoe over eggshells. Grab a broom and get rid of those shells for the good of the team.

Some people think that pitching a fit or making you feel sorry for them with a flood of tears will excuse their unacceptable work quality.

The next time you find yourself presented with low-quality work, take note if you feel a gut hesitation to call it out. If your first thought is dreading an impending tsunami of hostility from the responsible individual, there is a problem. If you immediately register a desire to minimize your critique to only the most glaring issues to avoid a confrontation, there is definitely a problem.

This must be addressed. It's not just for your mental health; it's for the team, too. Amazing products thrive in an environment that refuses to tolerate that kind of hostility.

Steve was well aware of his attitude. He once called Fortune's editor to complain about an article about him, only to say, "Wait a minute, you've discovered that I'm an asshole? Why is that news?"

It wasn't news to Jony Ive, who said in the tribute ceremony that Apple held two weeks after Steve's death, "It cost him most. He cared the most. He worried the most deeply. He constantly questioned: Is this good enough? Is this right? And despite all his successes, all his achievements, he never presumed, he never assumed that we would get there in the end. And when the prototypes failed, it was with great intent, with faith he decided to believe we would eventually make something great. So his, I think, was a victory for beauty, for purity, and as he would say, for giving a damn."

What This Actually Teaches

The "demand" part of this chapter is obvious: Steve demanded excellence relentlessly. The "supply" part is less obvious but more important: he created an environment where excellent people could supply excellence.

This is the paradox most leaders miss. They think demanding quality is enough. It's not. You must also build systems that make quality possible and protect people who deliver it.

Steve's approach worked not because he was mean, but because he was consistent. Three principles structured everything: ideas separate from identity, process through conflict, and reset between interactions.

When Steve called work "shit," he was evaluating output, not worth. The person who delivered poor work today could deliver brilliant work tomorrow. There was no permanent judgment, only assessment of current performance. This separation let people hear harsh feedback without internalizing it as personal failure. The work failed. The person didn't.

Steve didn't seek consensus. He sought truth. And truth emerged through debate, through people defending positions, through conflict that tested ideas against reality. The Mac team award for standing up to Steve wasn't rebellion. It was recognition that quality required people willing to fight for what they believed. Unanimous agreement meant nobody was thinking critically.

The "hero-shithead roller coaster" wasn't erratic. It was deliberate. Each meeting started fresh. Your status from yesterday meant nothing. This forced continuous performance and prevented both complacency from past wins and paralysis from past failures. You couldn't rest on laurels. You couldn't be crushed by mistakes. Every day was a new chance to be brilliant.

These three principles created an environment where excellence was both demanded and possible. Most organizations get this wrong in one of two ways. They demand excellence but punish failure, which creates fear. People hide problems, avoid risks, and optimize for safety over quality. Or they tolerate mediocrity to preserve comfort, which creates complacency. People coast, underperform, and drag down high performers.

Steve's system was different. He demanded excellence and made failure survivable. As long as you learned, adapted, and brought better work next time, you survived. But if you made excuses, blamed others, or stopped trying, you didn't.

The Diagnostic Questions

Are you demanding without supplying? Here's how to tell. Measure the feedback loop speed—how quickly do people learn whether their work meets standards? If feedback is immediate, direct, and specific, people can adapt quickly. If it's delayed, filtered through layers, or vague, people can't improve because they don't know what's wrong. Fast feedback loops accelerate learning. Slow ones create confusion and frustration.

Track the failure recovery rate. When someone delivers poor work, how often do they deliver excellent work shortly after? If recovery is common, you're challenging people effectively. They fail, learn, adapt, succeed. If people who fail once continue failing or leave, you're not challenging them. You're crushing them. The goal is to make failure a step toward excellence, not a death sentence.

Audit your protection of truth-tellers. Who gets promoted? People who tell you what you want to hear, or people who tell you what you need to know? If your promotions favor agreeableness over accuracy, you're incentivizing conformity. The best organizations reward people who bring hard truths, who challenge bad ideas, who fight for quality even when it's uncomfortable.

Count how many people argue with you. Not complain. Argue. About ideas, about direction, about quality. If nobody argues, you have a problem. Either you're infallible, which you're not, or people have learned that disagreeing with you is dangerous. Healthy organizations have constant debate about the right path. Unhealthy ones have silent compliance followed by passive resistance.

Examine your reset pattern. When someone delivers poor work in one area, does that affect how you treat their work in another area? If you carry negative judgments across contexts, you're punishing people, not evaluating work. True reset means each interaction stands alone. Past failures don't doom current attempts. Past successes don't excuse current mediocrity.

If these diagnostics reveal you're demanding without supplying, you're creating pressure without support. That produces burnout, not excellence.

Building the System

Steve's approach provides a framework for creating environments where excellence emerges.

First, separate work from worth. Make it explicit that critique of output is not critique of character. When you say "this work isn't good enough," clarify that you're evaluating the product, not the person. This sounds obvious but requires discipline. Because humans conflate work and worth automatically. You must actively separate them, repeatedly, until people internalize the distinction. The way to do this: follow criticism of work with confidence in the person. "This isn't good enough" followed by "I know you can do better" sends a clear message: the work failed, but you haven't.

Second, create permission to argue. Don't just tolerate disagreement. Reward it. The Mac team award for standing up to Steve wasn't a joke. It was a signal: challenging authority in service of quality is valued here. Build explicit mechanisms that encourage dissent. Reserve time in meetings for "what's wrong with this?" Ask people to poke holes. Promote people who disagree productively. Make it clear that consensus is not the goal. Quality is.

Third, demand evidence, not opinions. Steve's "prove it makes business sense" challenge to Phil Schiller was brilliant. It moved the debate from emotion to evidence. When you disagree with someone's position, don't just override them. Ask them to prove it. If they can, you should change your mind. If they can't, they should. This makes debates about data, not power. And data-driven debates reach better conclusions.

Fourth, reset deliberately and visibly. Don't just reset internally. Show people you're resetting. Start meetings with "clean slate." After a harsh critique, explicitly note that it's about that work, not overall competence. After a brilliant success, remind people that tomorrow starts fresh. This prevents people from camping on past wins or being paralyzed by past failures. Each day is a new chance to be excellent.

Fifth, protect A-players from B-player drag. When B-players bring drama, excuses, or mediocrity, they drain A-players. Your job is to protect A-players by removing B-players. Not because B-players are bad people, but because they're wrong for this environment. Some people thrive in low-accountability cultures. That's fine. But if you're building for excellence, those people need to work elsewhere.

What To Do Monday

If you lead a team, audit your last ten critical feedback conversations. For each, ask yourself: Did you critique the work or the person? If you said "you did this wrong" instead of "this approach didn't work," you conflated work with worth. Rephrase mentally: "I said X, I should have said Y." Practice until the distinction becomes automatic.

Did the person argue back? If nobody ever defends their work, you've created a culture where disagreement is dangerous. In your next feedback conversation, explicitly invite pushback: "Tell me why you think this approach is right." If they can't or won't, you have a safety problem, not a performance problem.

Did you provide resources to improve? If you identified problems but didn't offer paths to solutions, tools, time, or support, you're demanding without supplying. After every critique, ask: "What do you need to fix this?" Then provide it.

Look at who's leaving. Are they B-players who couldn't keep up, or A-players who got tired of carrying B-players? If you're losing your best people, you're not demanding enough. You're tolerating mediocrity, and excellence is leaving in frustration.

Run this simple test: Think of your lowest performer. Now imagine telling them their work isn't acceptable and they need to improve significantly or leave. How do you feel? If you feel relieved, you should have had that conversation months ago. If you feel guilty, ask why. Are you guilty because you haven't given them resources to succeed? Fix that. Or are you guilty because you've been too nice to be clear? That's not kindness. That's harm to them and the team.

The Real Lesson

Quality has to be caused, not controlled.

You can't inspect quality into products. You can't mandate it through process. You can't achieve it through fear or niceness or slogans.

Quality emerges from environments where it's both demanded and possible. Where excellence is expected but failure is survivable. Where critique is harsh but separated from identity. Where debate is encouraged and evidence prevails. Where A-players are protected from B-player drag.

Steve's method created that environment. Not through niceness, through clarity. Not through consensus, through conflict. Not through stability, through constant reset that prevented complacency.

Was it harsh? Yes. Was it effective? Undeniably. The Mac team, the iPod team, the iPhone team—these weren't normal groups. They were collections of people who chose to work at levels they didn't know they could reach. Because Steve demanded it. And because he created conditions where reaching it was possible.

You don't need Steve's personality to create similar conditions. You need his structure: separate work from worth, invite conflict, demand evidence, reset deliberately, protect A-players, resource appropriately.

The demand is necessary. Without it, standards drift downward. Mediocrity becomes acceptable. Excellence becomes optional.

But demand alone is insufficient. Without supply, without creating conditions where excellence is achievable, demand becomes abuse. People burn out. Talent leaves. Quality remains elusive.

Demand and supply. Standards and support. Challenge and resource.

That's how quality gets caused.

Be the guardian of quality. Don't apologize for demanding it. But build systems that supply it. Give people clarity, resources, protection, and permission to be excellent.

Then watch what they create.

Corner Cutting Leads You Off a Cliff

"One of the reasons I think Microsoft took ten years to copy the Mac is 'cause they didn't really get it at its core." — Steve Jobs

Knocking the iPad off its pedestal seemed like a simple task to the competition. That's what happens when you rush in with only a 'surface' understanding.

The competition cackled with glee as they assembled their complaints about the iPad. It had no USB ports for connecting extra peripherals. It didn't have a physical keyboard. There wasn't a command line for typing

PC-style commands. The processor wasn't compatible with PC or Mac desktop applications, and it ran a very optimized OS.

They drew up a long list of obscure or techie-sounding specs and then assembled a device with everything thrown in but the kitchen sink. The competition was oh-so-sure they knew best. Nothing could have been further from the truth.

Adding USB ports made their tablet devices bulky and unattractive. Giving it a physical keyboard just made developers lazy about creating truly useful and touch-oriented interfaces.

Programs being so dependent on a physical keyboard also meant the device needed to sit on a table to be useful. Using powerful Intel processors sounded great until the cruel reality of pathetic battery life and a device too hot to comfortably hold set in. Powering the beast required a heavy battery, making comfortable one-handed use nearly impossible.

Choosing a so-called 'full power' desktop OS also seemed like a step up, as long as the reality of its laggy performance and storage space demands were ignored. The marketed device actually left barely half the advertised storage space available for the consumer.

Application developers saw little reason to make any concession to a new touch interface since they were doused in a disdain for the very concept.

They declared their creation the 'ultimate and innovative tablet.' The reality was that it was ultimately just a pile of junk assembled from the iPad's discard pile.

When Features Become Failures

How can major companies fail so miserably to compete with Apple's products? Hint: it's not innovation to take shortcuts and avoid real design discipline.

Take the original iPhone, for example. It lacked 3G connectivity. Why didn't Apple include it? Because 3G chipsets of the time had terrible battery life.

One of the major advances of the time touted by Apple was the device's major leap forward in battery life. Apple understood that including the faster connection chip would have cut battery life nearly in half. The competition released a swarm of 3G phones.

A few early consumers believed the competition's marketing hype, that Apple was behind the times or purposely withholding the better technology to force upgrades later. What those consumers learned was that the alternative 3G smartphones they bought gave them lousy battery life, just as Apple had said all along.

Wisely, Apple waited until the next generation of 3G chipsets arrived. They combined that with improved battery technology and released the iPhone 3G. Battery life was only slightly worse than the original iPhone. The tradeoffs were acceptable, so they released a 3G iPhone.

Did the competition learn anything? Nope.

Hot on the iPhone 3G's heels, the competition fired a volley of phones with the emerging LTE standard. The battery life was pathetic, but they touted the speed. Apple ignored the hype.

Once again, Apple took its time, eventually building a single, custom networking chip that covered all the main standard network types, including LTE, while drawing as little power as 3G had. The iPhone LTE arrived. Boom!

It's a pattern that keeps repeating. They dismiss Apple's decisions, declare that they can offer a product 'with no compromise,' and then deliver the epitome of compromise.

The Touchscreen That Actually Worked

On even the most basic element of a touchscreen smartphone, the touchscreen itself, the competition dissed Apple's choice to include a higher quality capacitive touch technology. They piled on with a ton of cheap knockoffs, telling consumers they were every bit as good. Then a company named Moto Labs actually put it to the test. Their conclusion? "All touchscreens are not created equal."

The iPhone passed, touches registered straight, unbroken lines, with only a loss in sensitivity at the extreme screen edges. The Droid Eris, Nexus One, and Droid all experienced stair-stepping accuracy problems. "On inferior touchscreens, it's basically impossible to draw straight lines," MOTO reported. "Instead, the lines look jagged or zig-zag, no matter how slowly you go, because the sensor size is too big, the touch-sampling rate is too low, and/or the algorithms that convert gestures into images are too non-linear, to faithfully represent user inputs."

Apple clearly wasn't being nit-picky about the screen technology they chose. They respected the investment required to ensure quality. The competition arrogantly declared Steve had made the wrong product decisions. It didn't end well for them.

It also didn't end well for the iPod killers, the iTunes killers, the iPhone killers, or the iPad killers.

Rather than matching the challenges that Apple's products pose, competitors tend to instead belittle Apple's discipline, leading them to lower their quality threshold and deliver lousy products to market. The sad part is they often convince themselves that their shortcuts give them some sort of edge over Apple's offerings.

The Flash Fiasco

Apple didn't lightly make the decision to refuse to support Adobe's Flash on its mobile devices. The competition bleated at every turn that they, unlike Apple, supported Flash on their tablets and smartphones.

Oh, they piled on with condemnation of Apple. Apple was painted as a warden trying desperately to lock everyone away from the wondrous Flash websites.

Apple was repeatedly declared to be acting 'proprietary' in the media. Every nasty motive under the sun was postulated, including Steve being bitter over some minor tiff about Adobe's Creative Suite a decade before.

The competition fully supported Adobe Flash. What did they get for it? Websites were buggy and erratic since the mobile Flash performed so poorly. Watching a Flash video drained battery life like nobody's business. Trying to maneuver around a Flash-based website was an exercise in futility and aggravation.

Why?

From a purely technical standpoint, the problem was that almost all Flash website videos required an older generation decoder that wasn't implemented on mobile processors and was run in software.

The difference was striking: on an iPhone, non-flash videos played for up to 10 hours. Flash videos, decoded in software, drained a battery completely in less than 5 hours. Flash videos effectively robbed a consumer of half their potential battery life.

Steve gave an insightful explanation for his decision to reject Flash. Flash interfaces were mouse-based. They required what is known as a 'mouseover' state. Mouseover refers to the way Flash knew when a user moved their mouse cursor into a certain area. Flash got quickly confused and often crashed on mobile devices since touch interfaces don't support the idea of a 'mouseover.'

Steve pointed out that, without that information, most Flash website interfaces broke. Users would be presented with a confusing mess of sites with no consistent function. They would encounter more frustration than content.

It was shockingly obvious.

He also listed Flash's other two strikes. It is 100% proprietary, being only available from Adobe, and they have sole authority over its future enhancements and cost. Apple preferred an open standard. Flash also had one of the worst security records and was the leading cause of crashes on the Mac platform. Apple didn't want to reduce the reliability and security of iPhones, iPods, and iPads by adding insecure and crash-prone Flash.

Within a short while, even Adobe announced they were killing Flash on mobile. It simply performed too poorly, despite their best efforts. Silently, all the Apple mobile competition lined up with Steve's original position, ending their support for mobile Flash. Apparently, their consumers were suddenly no longer losing 'the full web' without Flash.

They had wasted so much time and energy supporting something obviously deeply flawed just to spite Apple's decision to take a stand. They gained nothing in the end, while Apple is remembered for standing up for quality.

"I get asked a lot why Apple's customers are so loyal. It's not because they belong to the Church of Mac! That's ridiculous," Steve told Businessweek.

Loyal customers come from not cutting corners. Creating outstanding products requires not cutting corners. Having the courage to do so, and stay the course, requires a deep conviction.

What This Actually Teaches

The pattern is consistent: competitors mistake Apple's omissions for oversights. They assume Apple couldn't include USB ports, or 3G, or Flash, or physical keyboards. So they rush to market with "complete" products that have everything Apple "forgot."

Then reality hits. The USB ports add bulk. The 3G chips drain batteries. Flash crashes constantly. Physical keyboards make touch interfaces lazy. And the "complete" product becomes a compromise machine that does everything poorly.

This reveals a fundamental misunderstanding of product design. Most companies treat features as additions. More features equal better product. If competitor A has ten features and competitor B has twelve, obviously B is superior.

But great products aren't built through addition. They're built through subtraction and integration. The question isn't "What can we add?" It's "What can we remove without losing the essential experience?"

Apple's approach was systematic: identify the core experience you're trying to create, then ruthlessly cut everything that compromises that experience, even if it looks like a feature.

The iPad's core experience was "content consumption that feels natural in your hands." USB ports compromise that by adding bulk. Physical keyboards compromise it by forcing the device onto tables. Desktop processors compromise it through heat and weight. Desktop OS compromises it through complexity and lag.

Competitors looked at these omissions and saw opportunity. "We'll add what Apple left out!" But they didn't ask why Apple left them out. They assumed incompetence or strategy tax, when the real answer was physics and human factors.

This is the danger of corner cutting: it looks like taking the easy path, the path Apple was "too stubborn" to take. But that "easy" path leads off a cliff. Because shortcuts in product design aren't shortcuts to success. They're shortcuts past the hard problems. And the hard problems don't disappear just because you ignored them. They resurface as user frustration, poor reviews, and market failure.

The Diagnostic Questions

Are you corner cutting or making disciplined tradeoffs? Test your omissions reasoning. For everything your product doesn't do or doesn't include that competitors do, write down why. If the answer is "we haven't gotten to it yet" or "it would cost too much," that's a corner cut. You're planning to add it when you can. If the answer is "it would compromise the core experience," that's discipline. You're protecting something more important.

Measure compromise accumulation. Track how often you make tradeoff decisions. For each, ask: "Did we choose the option that's better for users or easier for us?" If most tradeoffs favor your convenience, development speed, cost structure, or technical preferences, you're corner cutting. If most favor user experience even when it costs you more, you're being disciplined.

Examine your competitive response pattern. When competitors add features you don't have, what's your reaction? If it's defensive, "We need to match that or we'll lose," you're in reactive mode. You're letting competitors define the feature set. If it's analytical, "Does that feature serve the core experience or dilute it?" you're in principled mode. You're evaluating against your vision, not against competitors' moves.

Count your "just in case" features. How many capabilities exist in your product primarily because "users might want it" or "it's easy to add" or "competitors have it"? These are often corner cuts disguised as customer service. You didn't validate that users need them. You included them to avoid hard decisions about what not to build. Every "just in case" feature adds complexity, divides focus, and dilutes your core. If more than 20% of your product is "just in case," you've lost discipline.

Audit your quality inconsistency. Where does your product have obvious quality gaps? Rough edges, confusing workflows, features that feel bolted on rather than integrated. These often mark where you cut corners. You added something fast to match competitors or check a box, but didn't invest in making it great. Quality inconsistency signals misaligned priorities: you're optimizing for feature count over feature excellence.

Building Through Discipline

Steve's approach to product design provides a framework for avoiding corner cuts.

First, start with the core experience, not the feature list. Before you build anything, articulate the single most important thing your product should do for people. Not three things. One. For the iPad: "consume content naturally." For the iPhone: "access the internet in your pocket." For the iPod: "carry your music collection everywhere." Everything else is evaluated against that core. Does it serve the core or compromise it? If it compromises, cut it, no matter how appealing the feature seems in isolation.

Second, understand the physics of tradeoffs. Every choice has consequences. Faster processors mean more heat and battery drain. More features mean more complexity. Cheaper components mean lower reliability. You can't escape these tradeoffs through cleverness or wishful thinking. Apple didn't exclude 3G because they couldn't include it. They excluded it because including it would violate a more important promise: all-day battery life. Map the physics of your domain. Understand what tradeoffs are real versus imagined. Then make choices that protect what matters most.

Third, wait for technology to mature. This is the hardest discipline. When new technology emerges, the temptation is to include it immediately to appear innovative. But immature technology often creates more problems than it solves. 3G existed, but early chips were power-hungry. LTE existed, but early implementations were terrible. Flash existed, but it wasn't designed for touch. Apple's discipline was waiting until technology matured enough to meet their quality standards. This made them look "late" to features. But it made their implementations work properly when they arrived.

Fourth, say no to spite-driven development. Competitors will add features specifically to make you look deficient. "We support Flash and Apple doesn't!" The pressure to respond is enormous. Don't. If the feature compromises your core experience, stay the course. Let competitors waste energy supporting things that don't work well. Eventually, reality catches up.

Fifth, make omissions intentional and visible. Don't quietly leave things out hoping no one notices. Explain your reasoning. Steve wrote a public letter about why Flash wasn't on iOS. He explained the technical problems, the user experience issues, the philosophical conflicts. This turned an apparent weakness into a position of strength. Because when you articulate why you've chosen not to do something, you're defending a vision, not hiding a gap.

What To Do Monday

If you lead product, audit your roadmap. List every feature planned for the next release. For each, ask: "If we shipped without this, would it compromise the core experience or just make the feature list shorter?" Be honest. Most features fall in the latter category. They're nice-to-haves that you've convinced yourself are must-haves.

Now make a painful choice: cut half the roadmap. Not delay, cut. Pick the half that serves the core experience most directly. Remove the rest. This creates two benefits: the team can make the remaining features truly excellent instead of adequately functional, and you force clarity about what actually matters.

Then, write down why you cut each feature. Not for users initially, for yourselves. "We cut USB ports because they add bulk and weight, compromising the core experience of comfortable handheld use." If you can't articulate a principle-based reason, you didn't cut for the right reasons. You cut arbitrarily. Find the principle.

For features competitors have that you don't, run the Flash test: Is the competitor's feature actually working well for users, or are they suffering problems they don't yet realize? Sometimes competitors add features that look good but work poorly. Don't match those. Wait and watch.

The Real Lesson

Corner cutting doesn't lead to shortcuts. It leads off cliffs.

When competitors "improved" the iPad by adding USB ports, keyboards, desktop processors, and full operating systems, they thought they were taking the easy path to superiority. Just add what Apple left out. Simple.

But Apple didn't leave those things out because they couldn't include them. They left them out because including them would compromise the core experience they were protecting: natural content consumption in your hands.

The competitors didn't understand this. They saw limitations where Apple saw discipline. They saw features to add where Apple saw experiences to protect. So they built "complete" tablets that were heavy, hot, clunky, and uncomfortable. They did everything the iPad didn't do. And they failed at everything the iPad succeeded at.

This pattern repeats across industries and categories. The disciplined player makes hard choices about what not to include, protecting a core experience. The challenger mistakes those omissions for opportunities, adds everything the leader left out, and creates a compromised product that satisfies no one fully.

Loyal customers come from not cutting corners. They come from having the courage to say no to features that would compromise the core experience. They come from waiting for technology to mature rather than rushing to market with immature implementations. They come from making tradeoffs that favor user experience over feature count.

Creating outstanding products requires not cutting corners. It requires deep conviction that your core experience matters more than your feature list. That quality in the essential beats adequacy in the comprehensive. That saying no to the wrong things is how you say yes to the right things.

The competition declared their creations the 'ultimate and innovative tablets.' The reality was that they were ultimately just piles of junk assembled from the iPad's discard pile.

Because when you cut corners, you don't take shortcuts to success. You take shortcuts past the hard problems. And the hard problems don't disappear. They resurface as user frustration, market rejection, and brand damage.

Have the courage to do less, better. To protect the core experience even when it means omitting popular features. To wait for technology to mature even when it makes you look late. To explain your reasoning even when critics attack.

That courage, that discipline, that refusal to cut corners even when the easy path beckons—that's what creates products people love. Products people trust. Products people stay loyal to.

Not because they belong to some church. But because the products keep their promises. Every time. Without compromise.

Corner cutting leads you off a cliff. Discipline leads you to loyalty. Choose discipline.

CHAPTER 18
BOZOS AREN'T BRILLIANT

Bozos are just a fact of life in business. If you want to be successful, the faster you can identify them, and the more nimble you become in neutralizing them, the more momentum you'll build.

Steve knew how to quickly assess a person and realize when he was dealing with one of the 'bozo' brothers. He knew when to neutralize bozos, when to engage them, and when to ignore them.

Steve conveyed his passion for a product or service in simple, potent, and visceral language. His words were never vague, choosing instead to paint vivid images with phrases such as, 'insanely great, phenomenal, awesome, revolutionary, amazing,' and, of course, 'magical.'

His word choice matched his passion for minimalism in design and the simple elegance of his presentation. Uncomplicated. Straightforward. Direct. Powerful and simple words were packages of complex judgments and assessments that were chosen with care and delivered with passion. They told a story.

When Steve called someone, or their idea, a bozo, it meant that they just didn't get it.

Bozos were more interested in bureaucracy than innovation. Bozos were those that were ineffective and lacked authenticity. Bozos focused on everything except what was important. Not surprisingly, Steve pissed off a lot of bozos over the years.

Once you know how to spot the 'Three Bozos' and gain the skills to ignore or neutralize them when they block your path, you'll be laughing all the way to the bank.

What This Actually Teaches

The "bozo" label is harsh. It's also precise. Steve wasn't calling people stupid. He was identifying a specific pattern: people who optimize for appearance over substance, process over results, politics over progress.

This matters because bozos don't announce themselves. They often sound smart. They use impressive vocabulary. They reference frameworks and methodologies. They participate actively in meetings. On the surface, they look like contributors.

But beneath the surface, they're obstacles. Not because they lack intelligence, but because they lack the ability or willingness to focus on what matters. They get lost in secondary concerns: how decisions look, who gets credit, whether process was followed, what the org chart says, how to avoid risk.

Steve's directness about this served a purpose. By naming the pattern clearly and consistently, he created a shared language for identifying when work was drifting away from substance toward theater. When someone was "being a bozo," the team knew exactly what that meant: stop focusing on what doesn't matter and return to what does.

The challenge for most organizations is that bozos are often rewarded. They're good at managing up, creating impressive presentations, and navigating politics. They look productive because they produce a lot: documents, processes, initiatives. What they don't produce is actual value.

And because they're good at looking productive, they often rise into positions where they can do real damage. Not through malice, but through their fundamental orientation toward appearances rather than reality.

The Three Types of Bozos

While Steve used "bozo" as a catch-all, the pattern actually manifests in three distinct forms. Learning to recognize each type helps you respond appropriately.

The Process Bozo believes that following the right process guarantees the right outcome. They confuse activity with progress. Give them a project and they'll create a project plan, schedule meetings, establish working groups, define governance structures, and build documentation systems. What they won't do is solve the actual problem.

Process Bozos aren't lazy. They're often quite busy. But they're busy with meta-work: work about work. They optimize for looking organized rather than being effective. When you ask about progress, they'll show you Gantt charts, not results.

The danger with Process Bozos is that in large organizations, their behavior looks like leadership. They appear to be "bringing discipline" to chaos. Boards and executives see structured processes and assume competence. Only the people actually doing the work recognize that all this process is slowing everything down without improving anything.

The Politics Bozo believes that managing relationships and perceptions is more important than doing great work. They spend enormous energy on who gets credit, who sits where in meetings, what titles people have, and how decisions affect political standing.

Politics Bozos are often socially skilled. They read rooms well. They know how to align with power. They're adept at framing their positions to appeal to whoever they're talking to. But they're fundamentally disconnected from the actual work.

When you're in a meeting with a Politics Bozo, you'll notice they rarely take positions on substance. Instead, they read the room, see where consensus is forming, and align themselves with it. Then they take credit for the outcome regardless of whether they contributed.

The danger with Politics Bozos is that they're often successful in the short term. They rise quickly because they're good at being liked and managing perceptions. But organizations full of them become paralyzed because nobody is willing to make hard calls or champion unpopular but necessary positions.

The Complexity Bozo believes that sophisticated problems require sophisticated solutions. They're allergic to simplicity. Give them a straightforward problem and they'll complicate it: add frameworks, create dependencies, introduce edge cases that need handling, and design elaborate systems.

Complexity Bozos often are intelligent. That's part of the problem. They can see many dimensions of an issue. But they can't prioritize. They treat every edge case as equally important as the core case. They build systems that handle everything adequately rather than the main thing brilliantly.

When you ask a Complexity Bozo for a solution, they'll give you a 47-slide deck explaining their intricate system. What they won't give you is something you can actually implement this month. Because their solutions require rewiring the entire organization to work.

The danger with Complexity Bozos is that they often get mistaken for deep thinkers. In technical organizations especially, complexity is often confused with sophistication. Simple solutions get dismissed as "naive" while complex ones get praised as "thorough," even when the simple solution would work better.

The Diagnostic Questions

How do you spot bozos before they derail you? Watch the ratio of talk to action. Track what people produce relative to what they say they'll produce. Process Bozos produce lots of documentation but few results. Politics Bozos produce lots of meetings and "alignment" but few decisions. Complexity Bozos produce lots of analysis but few implementations. If someone consistently talks a good game but fails to deliver tangible outcomes, you've found a bozo. The ratio matters more than absolute output.

Listen for substance versus style. When someone presents an idea or solution, listen to how much time they spend on what versus how. Do they clearly articulate the problem they're solving and why their approach works? Or do they spend most of their time on frameworks, methodologies, and process? Substance-focused people can explain their thinking simply. Bozos hide behind complexity and jargon because they don't actually have clear thinking to explain.

Count the dependencies they create. Bozos love dependencies because dependencies create importance for themselves. "Before we can do X, we need to complete Y. But Y requires input from Z. And Z needs approval from A." Each dependency makes them seem necessary. Effective people minimize dependencies. They find ways to make progress independently. If someone's plans consistently require enormous coordination and multiple dependencies, they're either a bozo or they're protecting their territory, which is just another form of bozo behavior.

Measure their failure recovery. Everyone fails sometimes. The question is how people respond. When effective people fail, they acknowledge it quickly, learn from it, and adjust. When bozos fail, they blame process, politics, or complexity: "If we'd had better stakeholder alignment," "If we'd followed the framework more closely," "If we'd had more time to handle the edge cases." They never acknowledge that their approach was wrong.

They always blame context. This prevents learning and ensures they'll keep failing in the same ways.

Test their reaction to "just ship it." Tell a bozo to ship something simple and imperfect. Watch what happens. Process Bozos will insist on completing all the documentation and approvals first. Politics Bozos will want to ensure all stakeholders are comfortable. Complexity Bozos will list all the edge cases that need handling. None of them will ship. They'll have "good reasons" why shipping isn't possible yet. But the underlying pattern is the same: they can't tolerate imperfection, so they never ship anything.

Neutralizing Bozos

Steve's approach to bozos was direct: identify them, then either convert them or remove them.

First, name the pattern clearly. Don't let bozo behavior hide behind professionalism. When someone is optimizing for process over results, call it out: "We're spending more time on the project plan than on the actual project. Let's shift our focus." When someone is playing politics instead of solving problems, name it: "I'm not interested in who gets credit. I'm interested in what's right." When someone is adding unnecessary complexity, simplify: "This solution is too complicated. What's the simplest version that could work?" Clear naming creates accountability. Bozos thrive in ambiguity where their behavior can be interpreted as diligence or thoroughness. Clarity eliminates that cover.

Second, demand outcomes, not activity. Bozos will show you how busy they are. Don't care. Care about results. "I don't need to see your project plan. I need to see the working prototype." "I don't need another stakeholder meeting. I need a decision." "I don't need a comprehensive analysis. I need the top three options and a recommendation." Focusing on outcomes forces bozos to either produce value or reveal that they can't. Either way, you win.

Third, cut their oxygen by removing dependencies. Bozos create dependencies to make themselves essential. Break the dependencies. "We're not waiting for that approval. We're proceeding with what we can control." "We're not coordinating with six teams. We're solving our piece independently." "We're not handling every edge case. We're shipping for the 90% case." This is scary for organizations trained to seek alignment. But alignment often means waiting for bozos to feel comfortable. Moving independently removes their blocking power.

Fourth, create forcing functions. Bozos hate deadlines and constraints because these force prioritization and action. Use this. "We're shipping in two weeks. Whatever's ready ships. Whatever's not gets cut." "We're spending $X and no more. Design within that constraint." "We're using off-the-shelf tools. No custom development." Constraints force focus on what matters. Bozos can't hide behind "we need more time/budget/resources" when the constraint is non-negotiable.

Fifth, promote their opposites. Organizational culture is shaped by who gets promoted. If bozos rise, you'll get more bozo behavior because people learn that's what's rewarded. Instead, promote the people who ship, who simplify, who make decisions, who drive results. Make it clear through promotions that substance matters more than style.

What To Do Monday

If you lead a team, audit your recent projects. For each project that's moving slowly or producing weak results, identify the people involved. Then apply the diagnostic tests: Are they producing talk or results? Are they focused on substance or style? Are they creating dependencies or removing them? When they fail, do they learn or blame? Can they ship imperfect work?

You'll likely identify a few people who fail most of these tests. These are your bozos. Now make a plan for each.

First, try the direct conversation. "I've noticed you spend a lot of time on process/politics/complexity. I need you to focus on outcomes. Here's what that looks like." Be specific. Give them a chance to change. Some will. They were just following patterns they'd learned elsewhere.

Second, create constraints that force results. Give them a project with a tight deadline, limited budget, and clear success criteria. No room for process theater or political maneuvering. Either they deliver or they don't. This reveals whether they can produce when forced to focus.

Third, if they can't or won't change, move them. Either to a role where their pattern is less harmful, like process documentation if they're Process

Bozos, or out of the organization if no such role exists. This sounds harsh. But keeping them means they'll slow down everyone around them.

If you're an individual contributor, you can't fire bozos. But you can protect yourself. Don't wait for them. If a bozo is blocking your progress with demands for process, approvals, or complexity, find ways to proceed without them. Document their obstruction. When a bozo blocks progress, document it. Eventually, patterns become visible. Build relationships with non-bozos. Find the people in your organization who focus on results, who simplify, who make things happen. Work with them whenever possible.

Bozos aren't brilliant. This seems obvious. But organizations often forget it because bozos are good at appearing smart.

They use sophisticated language. They reference methodologies and frameworks. They create impressive documentation. They participate actively in meetings. On the surface, they contribute.

But strip away the surface and you find people optimizing for everything except results. Process over outcomes. Politics over substance. Complexity over simplicity.

Steve's directness about this served Apple well. By naming the pattern clearly and consistently, he created a culture where bozo behavior was visible and unacceptable. You couldn't hide behind process. You couldn't play politics instead of solving problems. You couldn't add complexity to seem smart.

This wasn't about being mean. It was about being clear. Because unclear organizations reward the wrong behaviors. They promote people who look productive over people who are productive. They celebrate activity over results. They confuse sophistication with intelligence.

Clear organizations do the opposite. They name bozo behavior when they see it. They demand outcomes, not activity. They remove dependencies instead of creating them. They promote substance over style.

Most organizations won't be as direct as Steve was. You probably can't call people bozos in meetings. But you can adopt the same orientation: focus ruthlessly on what matters, call out behavior that distracts from it, and structure work to make bozo behavior impossible or at least visible.

The faster you can identify bozos, and the more nimble you become in neutralizing them, the more momentum you'll build.

Not because you're being cruel. But because you're protecting your organization's ability to focus on what matters. And focus is what separates companies that ship from companies that talk about shipping.

Bozos aren't brilliant. Don't let them pretend to be. Don't let them slow you down. Don't let them consume resources that should go to people who actually produce value.

Identify them. Name the pattern. Demand results. Remove dependencies. Promote their opposites. And when they won't or can't change, move them out of the way.

Because organizations that tolerate bozos become organizations of bozos. And organizations of bozos don't build insanely great products. They build adequately documented processes for building theoretically great products someday, if all the stakeholders align and all the edge cases are handled and all the governance frameworks are in place.

Which is to say, they build nothing.

Don't build nothing. Build something great. And to do that, you need to recognize that bozos aren't brilliant, no matter how smart they sound.

They just don't get it. And people who don't get it shouldn't be making decisions about what you build.

Meet the Bozos

"The difference between genius and stupidity is that genius has its limits."
— Albert Einstein

Bozos are invariably soul-crushing fools who perform three main tasks in the world: slowing you down, giving you the wrong directions, and tripping you up with proclamations about how you'll fail in whatever revolutionary actions you attempt.

Nothing kills momentum quicker than allowing the rapid proliferation of bozos in your environment. Weed bozos out if you mistakenly hire them, and God help any company that allows a bozo to become its CEO.

What Makes a Bozo a Bozo

What is a bozo? Nailing down a precise definition of a bozo is like defining pornography—you'll know it when you see it. However, let's discuss the red flags you should be on the lookout for.

Generally speaking, a bozo overestimates their own abilities while underestimating risks and threats to the business. They aren't actively evaluating information, preferring to instead pick and choose data that confirms their already held bias.

Bozos avoid dealing with the details any chance they get. They operate on the expectation that other people should clean up the messes they create and often push everyone to ignore their recorded mistakes in judgment.

Bozos lack keen judgment when making strategic decisions. They stink at hiring top talent. They lack the self-confidence to hire the smartest applicants, who would probably outshine or challenge them directly. Bozos prefer to hire suck-ups that reinforce their world vision and can be counted on to toe the line.

Steve's list of famous bozos included John Sculley and Gil Amelio. Sculley couldn't learn things quickly, and he preferred promoting other bozos to control Steve's projects. Gil Amelio acted extremely pompous while being out of touch with the actual effects of his decisions.

The Courage to Call It Out

It's certainly a challenge to decorum to confront a bozo. Avoiding calling them out and being part of the get-along-go-along culture is a more comfortable option. It's also a deadly decision in the long run.

Bozos don't go away when you ignore their existence. Steve wasn't shy about addressing the bozos. He knew that they just gum up the works until you neutralize them.

In 1996, Steve was asked by an Apple director his opinion of then CEO Gil Amelio. "I thought to myself, I either tell him the truth, that Gil is a bozo, or I lie by omission. He's on the board of Apple; I have a duty to tell him what I think; on the other hand, if I tell him, he will tell Gil, in which case Gil will never listen to me again, and he'll fuck the people I brought into Apple. All of this took place in my head in less than thirty seconds," Steve said.

"I finally decided that I owed this guy the truth. I cared deeply about Apple. So I just let him have it. I said, '[Amelio] is the worst CEO I've ever seen; I think if you needed a license to be a CEO, he wouldn't get one.' When I hung up the phone, I thought, I probably just did a really stupid thing."

Instead, he had just set in motion the events that led to him replacing Amelio as CEO and setting Apple right.

Steve wasn't saying anything that the Apple director didn't already internally recognize. It wasn't some crafty maneuver, or a power grab. He was calling out the emperor for having no clothes, and the entire Apple enterprise had been suffering under that emperor.

He was also protecting the hardworking and talented people who had come to Apple with the purchase of NeXT. "I wanted to make sure the really good people who came in from NeXT didn't get knifed in the back by the less competent people, who were then in senior jobs at Apple," Steve explained.

The Three External Bozos

If you're running a small business or leading a large one, the bozos you encounter aren't likely to be part of your company since you have the power to remove them. Since you can't fire them, the bozos you'll be stuck dealing with are predominantly outside critics, commentators, and analysts. These bozos aren't any more credible, and it's vital to share Steve's skill in sizing them up quickly. There are three main bozos to watch out for: Commodity Bozo, Narrow-Minded Bozo, and Cheapskate Bozo.

Commodity Bozo is convinced that commodity business, which caters to the lowest common denominator, is the only viable route. If your product is actually innovative and offers unique value, Commodity Bozos will fail to grasp its worth. Don't allow them to dissuade you from offering a quality product at a reasonable and profitable price point.

Narrow-Minded Bozo jams square pegs into round holes and declares the pegs defective. For example, ignoring details, the iPad is just a tablet. In fact, tablets never sold well. Ergo, iPad isn't going to sell well, and Apple is making yet another mistake. Details don't matter to the Narrow-Minded Bozo; they're just dismissed as noise and hype. Don't listen to bozo. Details do matter when you're adding up the facts.

Cheapskate Bozo declares that no matter how much you optimize what you create, there will be those voices advising cutting corners even further to lower the price. Ignore them. That race to the bottom only ends in a chasm of shattered quality that will erase the hard-earned respect your customer has for you. Cheapskate Bozos have zero personal or product loyalty, and they actually rejoice when your customers distrust you. If you follow their foolish advice, you'll deeply wound your product's integrity, break the trust of your most valuable customers and end up chasing after customers who squeeze your profit stream to a trickle. Once Cheapskate Bozo moves into the neighborhood, your company quickly loses the resources required to be a nimble innovator.

What This Actually Teaches

The Amelio story reveals something crucial about organizational dysfunction: everyone usually knows there's a problem, but nobody wants to say it. Not because they're cowards, but because saying it creates personal risk with no guarantee of resolution.

The Apple board knew Amelio was failing. The employees knew it. The press knew it. But within the organization, there was collective silence. Because calling out a CEO is career suicide if the board doesn't act. And boards often don't act because each member assumes someone else will take the risk.

This creates a perverse equilibrium where bad leadership persists not because nobody sees it, but because everyone assumes speaking up will harm them more than staying silent. Steve broke this equilibrium by accepting the personal risk. He told the truth knowing it might cost him influence and harm people he cared about.

This is the fundamental choice with bozos: accept the risk of calling them out, or accept the certainty of their continued damage. Most people choose the latter because risk is immediate and personal while damage is diffuse and collective.

But here's what Steve understood: the damage compounds. Every day a bozo stays in power, they make more bad decisions, hire more bozos, and create systems that protect bozo behavior. The organization gets progressively worse. The cost of tolerating them isn't static. It grows exponentially.

So the "safe" choice to stay silent is actually the riskiest choice long-term. Because eventually the damage becomes catastrophic. The company fails. Everyone loses. The silence that felt protective actually guaranteed the worst outcome.

The External Bozo Pattern

The three external bozo types—Commodity, Narrow-Minded, and Cheapskate—represent three ways critics misunderstand innovation. Learning to recognize each helps you filter signal from noise in external feedback.

Commodity Bozos fundamentally don't believe in differentiation. They think all markets naturally commoditize, so attempting to maintain premium pricing is futile. This viewpoint comes from seeing commodity markets and extrapolating universally. They've watched VCRs, hard drives, and memory chips become commodities, so they assume everything will.

What they miss is that commodity markets are usually component markets or mature categories. When you're building integrated experiences or creating new categories, the dynamics are different. The iPhone didn't commoditize because it wasn't selling chips. It was selling an integrated experience. But Commodity Bozos can't see this distinction. To them, a phone is a phone, differentiation is marketing hype, and prices will eventually converge.

Narrow-Minded Bozos suffer from surface-level analysis. They identify superficial similarity and conclude identical outcomes. "The iPad is a tablet. Microsoft had tablets. They failed. Therefore iPad will fail." The logic seems sound. But it misses everything that matters: execution, integration, user experience, timing.

What they miss is that category names are abstractions. "Tablet" doesn't tell you anything useful. It's like saying "vehicle." A bicycle and a Ferrari are both vehicles. Predicting one's market success based on the other's failure would be absurd. Yet Narrow-Minded Bozos do this constantly with technology categories.

Cheapskate Bozos believe price is the only variable that matters. They see any premium pricing as opportunity for disruption. They constantly predict that lower-priced alternatives will destroy premium products. Sometimes they're right. Often they're not.

What they miss is that different customer segments optimize for different things. Some customers optimize purely on price. Many don't. They optimize for quality, reliability, experience, brand, or ecosystem. These customers will pay premium prices for premium products. The market isn't homogeneous.

The Diagnostic Questions

How do you quickly recognize which type of bozo you're dealing with? Test for Commodity Bozo by asking: "What sustains premium pricing in other markets?" If they say "nothing, all markets commoditize," they're a Commodity Bozo. If they can articulate what makes some categories resist commoditization—differentiation, integration, brand, ecosystems—they might have a legitimate point about your specific situation. The distinction: can they think in categories or only in universal rules?

Test for Narrow-Minded Bozo by asking: "What were the specific reasons that failed?" If they can't articulate the causal factors beyond "it was the same category," they're a Narrow-Minded Bozo. If they can explain the mechanics of why that attempt failed and why those mechanics apply to you, they might have insight. The distinction: are they pattern-matching on surface features or understanding causal mechanisms?

Test for Cheapskate Bozo by asking: "At what price point and for which customer segment does the economics work?" If they just say "lower is always better," they're a Cheapskate Bozo. If they can model the economics —unit costs, customer lifetime value, margin requirements—they might have a legitimate pricing strategy. The distinction: are they optimizing for volume or value?

Test for internal bozos by asking: "Do they learn from failure?" If they repeat the same mistakes, blame externalities, and show no adaptation, they're a bozo. If they acknowledge failures, analyze what went wrong, and adjust their approach, they're learning. The distinction: are they getting better or just getting by?

Neutralizing Each Bozo Type

Steve's approach to bozos was surgical: identify the type, understand their pattern, then neutralize their influence.

For Commodity Bozos, don't argue about whether differentiation is possible. Prove it. Show them examples of sustained premium pricing in your domain or adjacent domains. Apple didn't debate with Commodity Bozos. They shipped products that maintained premium prices for years. When critics said it wouldn't work, outcomes proved them wrong. Your strategy: ignore the abstract argument, demonstrate the concrete reality.

For Narrow-Minded Bozos, don't accept surface-level comparisons. Force specificity. "You're comparing us to Company X. What specifically caused their failure? Does that factor apply to us?" Usually they can't answer because they haven't thought it through. Once you force them to analyze causally rather than categorically, their argument collapses. Your strategy: make them defend the comparison mechanically, not just analogically.

For Cheapskate Bozos, don't debate whether lower prices are good. Make them do the math. "At that price point, with our cost structure, we'd need X volume to maintain current profit. Where is that volume coming from? What's the customer acquisition cost? What's the churn rate?" Usually they haven't modeled it because they're optimizing for a headline price, not business economics. Your strategy: force economic rather than emotional analysis.

For internal bozos, apply Steve's approach: tell the truth to people who can act on it. Don't gossip. Don't complain to peers. Go to decision-makers and clearly articulate the problem, the evidence, and the cost of inaction. Accept that this might create personal risk. But recognize that tolerating the bozo creates organizational risk that's larger and more certain.

What To Do Monday

If you're in leadership, run a bozo audit. List people whose decisions consistently fail to deliver expected results. For each, ask: Do they learn from failures or repeat them? Do they hire people better than themselves or worse? Do they deal with details or avoid them? Do they take responsibility or blame others?

Be honest. You'll likely identify 1-3 people who fail most of these tests. Now ask: "What's the cost of tolerating them for another year?" Lost opportunities, frustrated top performers, accumulated damage. Usually the cost is far higher than the discomfort of acting.

Then make a choice: either convert them through direct feedback and constraints, or remove them. Don't wait. Don't hope they'll improve without intervention. They won't.

For external bozos, create filters. When you receive advice, ask: What's the evidence for this claim? What's the causal mechanism? What's the economic model? What examples support or contradict this? Most bozo advice collapses under scrutiny. Once you develop the habit of demanding substance behind claims, bozos lose influence because their claims don't survive examination.

If you're not in leadership, you can't fire internal bozos. But you can protect yourself and your work. Document their bad decisions. Not maliciously, but factually. Work around them when possible. Build relationships with non-bozos. Find the people who deliver results, who simplify, who face reality.

The Real Lesson

The difference between genius and stupidity is that genius has its limits.

Bozos are unlimited in their capacity for bad judgment because they lack the self-awareness to recognize it. They overestimate their abilities. They cherry-pick data. They avoid details. They don't learn. And they hire people who reinforce rather than challenge their views.

This creates a self-reinforcing system where bozo behavior proliferates. One bozo hires more bozos. Those bozos protect each other. They create processes that favor bozo behavior. Eventually, the organization becomes a bozo ecosystem where competence is threatening and mediocrity is rewarded.

Steve's genius wasn't just avoiding bozos. It was building systems that were hostile to them. He demanded results, not activity. He valued simplicity over complexity. He promoted people who could be told they were wrong. He fired those who couldn't.

This wasn't cruelty. It was organizational hygiene. Because organizations that tolerate bozos become organizations of bozos. And organizations of bozos don't build revolutionary products. They build documented processes for theoretically building products if conditions align and all stakeholders approve and all frameworks are followed.

Which is to say, they build nothing.

Nothing kills momentum quicker than allowing the rapid proliferation of bozos in your environment.

So don't allow it. Identify them quickly. Call them out directly. Neutralize their influence ruthlessly. Remove them when necessary.

Yes, this creates conflict. Yes, it feels harsh. Yes, people might think you're difficult.

Better to be difficult and right than agreeable and failing.

Because bozos will slow you down, give you wrong directions, and predict your failure. If you listen to them, they'll be right about that last part.

Don't listen. Build something great instead. And to do that, you need to recognize that bozos, however smart they sound, however experienced they seem, however confidently they speak, are just bozos.

They don't get it. They won't get it. And they definitely shouldn't be making decisions about what you build.

Weed them out. Protect your team from them. Ignore their predictions.

Then prove them wrong by succeeding anyway.

Laughing All the Way to the Bank

"Convince your enemy that he will gain very little by attacking you; this will diminish his enthusiasm." — Sun Tzu

Being right, while everyone else is wrong is invaluable in business. Waiting for an industry consensus is the quickest ticket to last place. Waiting for bozos to agree is a ticket to nowhere.

Before starting Apple, Steve and Wozniak tried to get several other computer companies to build their envisioned system. The duo went to Atari and said, "Hey, we've got this amazing thing, even built with some of your parts, and what do you think about funding us? Or we'll give it to you. We just want to do it. Pay our salary; we'll come work for you," Steve told Fast Company. Atari wasn't interested. Then the two approached Hewlett-Packard. HP's response? "Hey, we don't need you. You haven't gotten through college yet."

The two Steves could have simply deferred to the judgment of those with more experience who couldn't fathom success based on an unfamiliar paradigm. Instead, they took the leap to found Apple themselves and changed the course of computing forever.

Steve's perspective on the lack of vision was that many in the industry hadn't had diverse experiences. They didn't have enough dots to connect, leading them to only perceive very linear solutions. They were missing a broad enough perspective. "The broader one's understanding of the human experience, the better design we will have," Steve explained. He was being kind.

They were operating on the advice of the Bozo Trinity: Commodity, Narrow-Minded, and Cheapskate.

The Bozo Trinity is full of experience, which they vehemently declare qualifies them to predict tomorrow.

The issue with experience is that it is fundamentally a unit of measuring yesterday. Providing insight on today, let alone tomorrow, is rarely the province of experienced counsel. Experts are usually loaded with experience.

When Experts Predict the Past

Guy Kawasaki has shared some of the wisdom on jumping ahead of the curve that he gained working with Steve firsthand at Apple. For example, the experts were adamant that the two biggest weaknesses of the Mac in the mid-1980s were that it lacked a daisy-wheel printer driver and Lotus 1-2-3.

In reality, the big wins require going beyond 'better sameness.' While the best daisy-wheel printer companies were introducing new fonts in more sizes, Apple leaped to the next curve with laser printers.

Experts can only describe their desires in a framework tied to what they are already using. "Around the time of the introduction of Macintosh, all that people said they wanted was a better, faster, and cheaper MS-DOS machine," said Kawasaki. "When you are jumping curves, defying or ignoring the experts, facing off against big challenges, obsessing about design, and focusing on unique value, you will need to convince people to believe in what you are doing in order to see your efforts come to fruition," he continued.

Steve knew that people needed to believe in Macintosh for it to become real. This also applied to the iPod, iPhone, and iPad. The art lies in refining your bozo detection instincts. Deciding which bozos can be enrolled in a vision and which bozos need to be moved aside so they don't impede your progress is crucial to succeeding.

You will need to accept that not everyone will believe or agree with your plan, product, or vision. That's OK. If everyone already agreed, they'd be raking in the coming profits, not you.

The Story of the Stores

Apple's adventures in retail are a prime example of being right when everyone else was wrong paying off. Businessweek's visiting bozos didn't hesitate to let Steve know how insane the planned Apple stores were.

Steve had said that "Unless we could find ways to get our message to customers at the store, we were screwed." Steve knew how difficult leaping into retail could be. Not wanting Apple to go awry, he first reached out to Mickey Drexler. Drexler had been running the Gap, which had smashed records for rapidly becoming profitable. Steve offered Drexler a seat on Apple's board. Drexler accepted.

In January of 2000, Steve recruited Ron Johnson to run the retail operation. Johnson had been the brains behind Target discount stores' highly successful branded makeover. His retail revelation came after witnessing the way Italian company Alessi presented its pots and juicers as works of art. "It was like walking through a museum," Johnson recalled. "They weren't there to make money. They were there to make great products."

Soon, the two men hammered out the conceptual foundation of the planned Apple stores. They would be elegant, spacious, and comfortable places to interact directly with the company's products.

Apple's sales had plummeted 29% the previous year, and the board was in no mood for a pie-in-the-sky idea. Lucky for Steve, when approached with the idea, board member Mickey Drexler told him to go ahead and build a store. Not in a shopping mall, in an empty California warehouse. Steve and Johnson took Drexler's advice and built a full-sized and fully functional prototype store in a vacant rented lot. For six months, they brainstormed and refined the store prototype together, getting it ready to unveil to the world

"Ron and I had a store all designed," said Steve. Then a light bulb went on for Johnson: Computers were evolving into hubs for video, photography, music, and information. The sale was less about the machine than what you could do with it. The prototype store had it all wrong.

Hardware was laid out by product category, not by how a customer would want to buy things. Making movies, creating photo albums, and burning CDs made more sense. "We were like, 'Oh, God, we're screwed!'" Steve said. After Steve settled down from his shock at the proposal of practically starting over, he had to concede that Johnson had a damn good idea, and they proceeded to rework the layout around Johnson's insight.

A little enrollment and taking steps to present a reality instead of merely a concept had brought the board around to supporting Steve's plan. In 2001, they presented the prototype store to the board. They loved it! The stores were a 'go.'

The Bozo Chorus

Macs were having a tough time selling at retail outlets dominated by PC partisan sales forces. They were poorly maintained, with some Best Buy outlets famously leaving them piled up in their cartons on the back wall of the store while keeping the display model turned off. Steve's brilliant solution was to stop leaving Apple's products in the hands of people who didn't really want them to sell. Apple was building its own retail outlets and interacting directly with its customers.

Steve threw down the gauntlet by announcing the new Apple stores. The moment the world heard of Steve's plans, the Bozo Trinity couldn't help but condescendingly explain how ridiculous Steve's plan was. Steve had dared to point out the obvious to a reporter at a Macworld trade show by saying, "Buying a car is no longer the worst purchasing experience. Buying a computer is now No. 1."

In 'Sorry, Steve: Here's Why Apple Stores Won't Work,' they let loose a volley of bozo logic.

Steve should have stopped reading the first sentence, 'CEO Steven P. Jobs.' That telegraphed trouble, like your mother's shrill hollering of your full name, echoing across the neighborhood during childhood.

Cheapskate Bozo, and Apple's former Chief Financial Officer, Joseph Graziano, declared that "Apple's problem is it still believes the way to grow is serving caviar in a world that seems pretty content with cheese and crackers." For the record, Apple had shown Graziano the door in 1995 for attempting a coup against CEO Michael Spindler.

Graziano adamantly told Apple's directors that the only path available to Apple was surrendering completely and being sold off to IBM, Oracle, or even Cannon. Spindler had made clear the company wasn't for sale, and the board agreed to send Graziano packing. Clearly, this was not an impartial source that could be reasonably expected to evaluate an aggressive march into successful growth for Apple.

Commodity Bozo gravely weighed in. David Goldstein, president of Channel Marketing Corp., claimed that "Since PC retailing gross margins are normally 10% or less, Apple would have to sell $12 million a year per store to pay for the space. Gateway does about $8 million annually at each of its Country Stores." After all, he reasoned, Macs are just the same as

Windows PCs. What could possibly be different? His conclusion was to "Give them two years before they're turning out the lights on a very painful and expensive mistake."

Narrow-minded Bozos were invited to advise Steve. They discounted the numerous bottlenecks retailers were placing on the Mac platform's sales. Best Buy had dropped the iMac, refusing to stock the multiple colors it was available in. "We do not carry inventory in color varieties," Best Buy spokesperson Joy Harris snarked, "We're not a fashion retailer."

Apple offered iMacs in five colors. While it was true that blueberry accounted for 50% of all iMac sales, that left the other colors selling over 100,000 units each. Best Buy was basically refusing half the possible iMac sales and rejecting even more when you considered the three available speed pre-configurations. Apple adjusted the packs the iMacs came in, sending retailers packs of eight that contained four blueberry and one each of the other colors: strawberry, tangerine, grape, and lime.

It wasn't the first time Best Buy had killed the golden goose. Only the year before, they rejected Apple's recommended retail pricing of $1,299 for the original iMac. Best Buy was eviscerating Apple's profit margins on their star product and screwing fellow Apple distributors by selling the iMac for just $999. Still, Narrow-Minded Bozo thought Steve was nuts not to submit to the outlet's planned iMac choke-hold and profit-slicing.

If Apple's iMac sales were declining, Best Buy might have had a reasonable position. Instead, Apple's shipments were up 27%, outpacing PC industry growth. According to Apple's then CFO, 32% of iMac sales were to first-time buyers, and 11% were converts from Windows. Apple was growing, and the iMac was the greatest thing since sliced bread.

Still, Narrow-Minded Bozo had the final word, saying that, 'A good step would be to end the 'think secret' approach that shrouds every new product announcement.' This bozo wanted Steve to end Apple's method of simultaneously keeping competitors and customers in the dark. Despite it being a key way of maintaining the element of surprise while generating tremendous interest and speculation before every product launch, Narrow-Minded Bozo declared it was time for things to change.

"They should let the news leak out to convince the world how exciting their stuff is. That's how everyone else does it. Maybe it's time Steve Jobs stopped thinking quite so differently," said the bozo.

'I don't think so,' replied Steve.

When Reality Defeats Bozos

Instead, Steve recruited one of the best names in retail and launched the brilliant Apple Stores. Computing retail was revolutionized. Genius bars dispensed friendly computing guidance. Hands-on product displays invited unlimited interactions. All-glass storefronts were located in architecturally beautiful locations that became works of art in themselves. A highly trained, non-commissioned staff offered one-on-one Mac or iOS workshops for free. Mac computers had a 33% chance of being repaired the same day and a 66% chance of being ready for pickup the next day. It was a service, unlike anything the computing world had seen before.

"People haven't been willing to invest this much time and money or engineering in a store before," Steve told Fortune magazine, his feet propped on Apple's boardroom table in Cupertino. "It's not important if the customer knows that. They just feel it. They feel something's a little different."

The Apple stores became cultural icons. They changed lives. Just ask Isobella Jade. Better yet, buy her book.

Isobella Jade felt like she just couldn't hold on anymore. All she had was her busted high heels and lunches from Wendy's dollar menu. She was living on a dream in New York City. Her daily destination? The Apple store on Prince Street in SoHo. "It was a place to feel alive, a warm place on a cold day, and there was always a store employee to greet me and ask how I was doing," she says.

Only 5'2" tall, Jade had been fighting upstream as a model. She was one of the shortest models in NYC. To even get in the door at agencies, she had to claim to be 5'4".

With few modeling agencies willing to offer her gigs, she struggled to pay her electric bill, let alone buy a computer. She had hustled for years and was sure her experiences were a story worth hearing. Lacking a computer, she started writing her manuscript on the display computers at the Apple store.

While the Apple store's staff was unaware of Jade's writing venture, they certainly had to notice her daily visits. She was standing there with her fifty-cent cup of coffee, patiently awaiting her turn at a display iMac. Sometimes she'd wait a half hour or more. Still, she says, "Once I was on a 17" iMac, I was on a mission and was meant not to be disturbed or interrupted." Jade sometimes stood and wrote for up to four hours straight.

Can you even imagine ever feeling comfortable or welcome enough in a big box store to entertain such a daydream, let alone actually bring it to life? Luckily for Jade, Steve was catering his business to people just like her, people with the audacity to hope.

A tiny reserve was all she had left. After missing rent for two months straight, she had to surrender her apartment. New York isn't known for being forgiving to dreamers. She whittled all her belongings down to a medium-sized suitcase to simplify her migrations from couch to couch, living among her friends. The Apple store became the stage for her personal comeback.

Among the packed store's loud teens and techies, parents pushing baby strollers while screaming at their kids, and the regulars, Jade worked daily on her manuscript. According to her, "The fast pace of the store actually encouraged me to write and get off my chest what was in my heart and on my mind." Before you romanticize Jade's experience as just some artistic indulgence, remember that this manuscript was her ticket to financial survival.

She normally saved it to her Yahoo email. When the internet was abruptly shut off one time, she pounded her fist on the table and startled those around her. No internet access meant she might lose her precious work. As an employee calmly advised her to 'just go buy a CD and burn your document onto that,' she was torn between laughing and crying. "If only he knew I could barely afford my MetroCard each week, he would know that buying a pack of CDs wasn't an option," she thought.

Jade had no illusions about how much she'd sacrificed for this belief in herself and her book. Her desperation was the result of her choices and lifestyle. Still, she thought about the hours, the days, and the months standing in front of those iMacs, writing page after page, between sips of coffee as she prayed for internet access to return. She did eventually save her document that day and continued writing for a few more months at the Apple store.

Jade finished her manuscript. Her book, Almost 5'4", was self-published in 2007 and has sold quite well.

Macworld magazine described the book as "A very readable, very revealing memoir that feels at times like you are peeking at someone's secret diary."

Jade saw the Apple stores as a shelter for her most desperate moments during her mission to share her story. She reflects on how the store not only inspired her to write but that, "Without it, I might not have written my memoir after all. The Apple store became much more than a place to write; it became a part of my story, as well." She went on to launch her own publishing company Gamine Press in 2009.

Steve brought into reality with the Apple stores the fulfillment of a genuine commitment that he'd articulated when he first returned to Apple. "I think you still have to think differently to buy an Apple computer," he said. "The people who buy them do think different. They are the creative spirits in this world, and they're out to change the world. We make tools for those kinds of people."

Far from the Commodity Bozo's predictions of "Turning out the lights on a very painful and expensive mistake" in their first two years, Apple stores quickly turned a profit. In fact, two years and seventy-three store openings later, Apple recorded $3 million in profit per store per quarter and 60,000 visitors quarterly. In 2004, Apple retail brought in $1.2 billion, shattering an industry record for the fastest billion-dollar milestone.

Since the first store opened in 2001, over one billion people have visited more than four hundred Apple stores across fourteen nations. Each quarter, an average of 250,000 people visit those stores. Apple stores perform seventeen times better than the average retailer. While Harvard accepts 7% of those who apply, Apple stores today only hire the top 2% of applicants.

Best Buy stores bring in just $930 per square foot while selling big ticket items such as washers, refrigerators, and large LCD TVs, along with computers. According to Asymco, Apple made $6,050 for every square foot of store space in 2012. That's more than double the square-foot profits of Tiffany's! Apple stores also posted over 70% growth in year-over-year sales in 2012.

'Stop 'thinking different,' Team Bozo had declared. 'I don't think so,' replied Steve as he continued racking up wins.

Thank God Steve didn't wait for industry consensus. He showed us that waiting for bozos to agree is a ticket to nowhere.

What This Actually Teaches

The Apple Store story demonstrates that being right when everyone else is wrong isn't just about having vision. It's about having the conviction to execute despite unanimous opposition, the discipline to prototype before committing, and the wisdom to recognize when your own plan needs changing.

Steve didn't just announce stores and hope. He enlisted experts—Drexler and Johnson. He built a full-scale prototype in a warehouse. He iterated for six months. When Johnson realized the layout was wrong, Steve swallowed his pride and started over. Then when critics attacked after the announcement, he had reality to point to, not just rhetoric.

This is the pattern for defying expert consensus: First, assemble genuine expertise, not just yes-men. Drexler knew retail. Johnson knew store design. They weren't bozos. Second, prototype before committing. The warehouse store let them test and refine without public failure. Third, be willing to pivot even after significant investment. The layout change was expensive and delayed launch, but it was right. Fourth, ignore critics once you've done the work. The bozos hadn't built prototypes, enlisted experts, or tested assumptions. Their opinions were worthless.

The bozos made three predictable errors. Commodity Bozo compared Apple stores to Gateway Country Stores, assuming all computer retail operates the same. But Gateway was selling commodities at commodity margins. Apple was selling differentiated products at premium margins. The economics were entirely different. Cheapskate Bozo insisted Apple should serve "cheese and crackers" to the mass market instead of "caviar" to their actual customers. But Apple's customers wanted and would pay for premium. Chasing customers who wanted cheap would have destroyed what made Apple valuable. Narrow-Minded Bozo thought Apple should copy how everyone else did things—leak products early, stop being secretive, conform to industry norms. But those norms were why computer retail was terrible. Copying them would have made Apple stores equally terrible.

Each bozo applied patterns from adjacent domains without understanding why those patterns existed or whether they were relevant. This is the fundamental bozo failure: pattern-matching without causal analysis.

What To Do Monday

If you're facing unanimous expert opposition to something you believe in, don't assume you're wrong. But don't assume you're right either. Instead, do what Steve did.

First, distinguish between bozos and genuine experts. Bozos have opinions based on surface patterns. Experts have understanding based on causal mechanisms. Ask critics to explain their reasoning. If they can articulate specific mechanisms, why X causes Y in this context, they might be right. If they just cite analogies and patterns, they're probably bozos.

Second, prototype before committing. Steve didn't open stores nationwide and hope. He built one in a warehouse. He tested, refined, discovered problems, fixed them. Then he rolled out. If you can't prototype the full vision, prototype elements of it. Test assumptions before betting the company.

Third, enlist genuine expertise. Steve brought in Drexler and Johnson because they knew retail. He didn't surround himself with yes-men or generalists. He found people who had solved adjacent problems successfully. When facing opposition, ask: "Who has actually succeeded at something relevantly similar?" Then talk to them, not the critics.

Fourth, be willing to restart when you're wrong. When Johnson realized the layout was wrong, Steve could have insisted on his original plan. They'd spent six months on it. But he recognized Johnson was right and started over. This is the difference between conviction and stubbornness. Conviction is holding to vision despite opposition. Stubbornness is holding to specifics despite evidence.

Fifth, measure outcomes, not opinions. The bozos predicted failure. Steve shipped. Within two years, the stores were profitable. Within four years, they'd hit a billion in revenue. Outcomes proved who was right. But outcomes take time. You can't let critics pressure you into abandoning something before outcomes can manifest. Give your vision time to prove itself or fail on its own merits.

The Real Lesson

Being right while everyone else is wrong is invaluable in business. But "everyone" needs qualification. The bozos were wrong. Drexler and Johnson were right. The distinction matters.

Bozos represent conventional wisdom, surface-level pattern-matching, and optimization for what worked yesterday. Experts represent causal understanding, context-specific analysis, and vision for what could work tomorrow.

When you defy consensus, you're not defying all opinions. You're choosing which opinions to trust. Steve trusted Drexler and Johnson over Graziano and Goldstein because the former had relevant expertise and the latter had bozo reasoning.

This is how you laugh all the way to the bank. Not by ignoring everyone. But by learning to distinguish bozos from experts, conventional wisdom from genuine insight, and pattern-matching from causal analysis.

Then having the courage to bet on your analysis even when the bozos attack. Even when the headlines predict failure. Even when critics call you arrogant or delusional.

Because waiting for bozos to agree is a ticket to nowhere. And being right when they're wrong is a ticket to somewhere extraordinary.

Steve proved this repeatedly. Atari and HP rejected the Apple I. The bozos predicted Apple Stores would fail. In each case, Steve was right and they were wrong. Not because he was lucky. But because he did the work—understood causality, enlisted expertise, prototyped reality, and had the conviction to execute despite opposition.

That's the pattern. That's the lesson. That's how you stop waiting for consensus and start building the future.

The bozos will always predict failure. Prove them wrong by succeeding anyway.

CHAPTER 19
HATERS GONNA HATE

"Never retreat. Never explain. Get it done and let them howl." —Benjamin Jowett

In 2007, Steve Ballmer laughed at the iPhone. "$500? Fully subsidized? With a plan?" he scoffed to a reporter. "The most expensive phone in the world, and it doesn't appeal to business customers because it doesn't have a keyboard."

Six years later, Microsoft wrote off $900 million on unsold Surface tablets and took a $7.2 billion charge related to acquiring Nokia's phone business. The iPhone had become the most profitable product in consumer electronics history.

Ballmer's criticism wasn't random noise. It was a precise map of what Microsoft valued—keyboards, business customers, subsidized pricing—and what they fundamentally misunderstood about where the market was heading. Steve Jobs didn't need to respond. He just needed to decode the signal.

Most leaders treat criticism like incoming fire: duck, defend, or fire back. Steve treated it like reconnaissance. Your harshest critics tell you exactly where you're threatening them, what they value that you don't, and which of your strengths they're most afraid of. The question isn't whether to listen to critics. It's whether you know how to translate what they're actually saying.

What This Actually Teaches

Criticism contains three kinds of information, and only one of them matters.

Surface noise sounds like "Your product is too expensive/too simple/wrong for the market." This is what most people hear. It's also the least useful part.

Value clash sounds like "You're prioritizing X when you should prioritize

Y." This tells you what your critic values that you don't. Sometimes they're right. More often, this clash is precisely why your approach might work.

Threat vector sounds like "You can't succeed because..." This tells you what they fear most about your approach. It's a map of where you're actually dangerous to their position.

Steve didn't ignore critics. He sorted them. The question wasn't whether criticism hurt—it was whether it revealed something true about your work or something true about your critic's position. One requires adjustment. The other requires resolve.

The most valuable critics are the ones who attack your strengths. When competitors criticize your simplicity, your focus, your high standards—when they frame your distinctive approach as a liability—they're telling you exactly what they can't replicate and what threatens them most.

How This Shows Up

I've watched this play out dozens of times. A company launches something genuinely different—a new service model, a restructured pricing approach, a radically simplified product. And the attacks come, usually in predictable patterns.

"Your customers are fanatics. That's not sustainable." Translation: You've built something people actually care about, and we haven't.

"You're leaving money on the table. You could serve more segments." Translation: Your focus threatens our everything-to-everyone approach.

"That won't scale. You can't maintain those standards at volume." Translation: We've compromised on quality to grow, and you're making us look bad.

"You're ignoring what enterprise customers really need." Translation: We've built our business on what enterprises say they want, and you're betting on what they actually need.

The pattern is consistent: competitors don't attack your weaknesses. They attack what makes you different, then frame that difference as a flaw. They call your focus "narrow." Your standards "elitist." Your customer enthusiasm "cultish." Your differentiation becomes your disqualification.

Here's what I've learned: if your critics are attacking your compromises, listen carefully. If they're attacking your commitments, you're probably onto something.

The Diagnostic Questions

When criticism hits—especially the loud, public, confident kind—run it through this filter.

What are they actually criticizing? Strip away the loaded language. "Overpriced" might mean "different value equation." "Too simple" might mean "doesn't do what we do." "Niche appeal" might mean "strong with specific customers." Get to the actual claim beneath the rhetoric.

What does this reveal about what they value? Every criticism contains an implicit "should." You should charge less. You should add features. You should serve more segments. That "should" tells you what your critic prizes. Sometimes they're right—you've missed something important. But often, that value difference is your entire strategy.

What would have to be true for this criticism to be valid? If your critic says you can't succeed with high prices, what market conditions would make that true? If they say you're too focused, what would make broad coverage essential? Sometimes the answer is "those conditions exist"—and you need to adjust. Often the answer is "they're describing a different game than the one we're playing."

Is this criticism coming from success or failure? Microsoft's Ballmer criticized the iPhone from a position of dominance—and completely missed where the market was heading. Later critics attacked Apple from positions of decline, which made their criticism more telling about their own trajectory than Apple's. The struggling competitor who attacks your approach is giving you different information than the thriving one who does.

What would change if this criticism were true? If your product really is too expensive, you'll see resistance in your target market. If it's genuinely too simple, your users will be frustrated by limitations. If your focus is actually narrowness, you'll hit a ceiling. The question isn't whether the criticism sounds convincing—it's whether reality confirms it.

What To Do Monday

First, separate signal from noise immediately. Create a simple filter: Does this criticism identify a real problem with your execution, or does it challenge your strategy? Problems with execution might need fixing. Challenges to strategy need evaluating against reality, not rhetoric.

When someone says your product is too expensive, that's execution-level if your target customers agree. It's strategy-level if the critic simply doesn't understand why anyone would pay your price. One requires response. The other requires confidence.

Second, watch for pattern clusters. If multiple critics in the same position —established players, venture-backed competitors, analysts covering traditional players—all make similar criticisms, that cluster tells you something. Not necessarily that they're right, but that your approach threatens a shared assumption or business model.

When the iPhone launched, technology analysts, enterprise IT departments, and established phone makers all said variations of "no keyboard, too simple, not for business." That cluster revealed an entire worldview about what phones needed to be. Steve didn't need to convince them. He needed to show their shared assumptions were outdated.

Third, track which criticisms disappear versus which ones persist. Critics who stop attacking a particular aspect of your approach are telling you something shifted—either you adjusted, or reality proved them wrong. Critics who double down despite evidence are usually defending their own position, not analyzing yours.

Fourth, use criticism to stress-test your thinking, not determine it. The question isn't "Are the critics right?" It's "What would we need to believe for them to be right, and do we believe that?" If you're building for simplicity and critics say you need more features, the question becomes: Is simplicity actually serving our users, or have we confused constraint with quality?

Fifth, watch what your critics do, not just what they say. This is the ultimate filter. If competitors criticize your high prices but then raise theirs, they're telling you the real story. If they mock your focus but then narrow their own offering, pay attention. If they call your standards unsustainable but their customers keep leaving for you, the market is speaking.

After Ballmer laughed at the iPhone's price, Microsoft spent the next several years trying to build their own premium hardware—Surface, Windows Phone, the Nokia acquisition. Their actions revealed that the criticism was never about iPhone's actual viability. It was about trying to defend a position that was already eroding.

The Real Lesson

Here's what most people miss about Steve's relationship with critics: he didn't ignore them, and he didn't fear them. He sorted them.

Some criticism came from people who'd built great things and understood the challenges. When Andy Grove or Bill Campbell pushed back on something, Steve listened. Not because they were friendly—because they had earned the right to critique through their own achievement.

Some criticism came from people protecting their position. When established players attacked Apple's approach, Steve noted what they were really defending—and whether that defensive posture signaled their decline.

Some criticism came from people who simply valued different things. When analysts said Apple should license their OS or build cheap phones or serve enterprise first, Steve recognized a values mismatch, not a strategic imperative.

The skill wasn't in having thick skin. It was in accurate translation.

Your harshest critics are giving you intelligence. They're telling you what threatens them, what they value that you don't, and where they think you're vulnerable. Sometimes they're identifying real weaknesses. More often, they're identifying your actual differentiation and desperately trying to frame it as a flaw.

The question isn't whether to listen to critics. It's whether you can decode what they're actually saying—and whether you have the resolve to stay focused when they attack the very things that make your approach distinctive.

When competitors call your customers "fanatics," they're really saying "You've built something people care about and we haven't figured out how."

When they call your focus "limiting," they're really saying "We've spread ourselves thin and your concentration threatens our diffusion."

When they call your standards "unsustainable," they're really saying "We've compromised to grow faster and you're making us look bad."

The criticism isn't the problem. Mistranslating it is.

Steve didn't need to defend the iPhone against Ballmer's mockery because the product would speak for itself. He didn't need to explain why simplicity mattered because users would discover it. He didn't need to justify premium pricing because customers who valued integration would pay it.

He just needed to let them howl while he got it done.

The question for you isn't whether critics will come. If you're doing anything distinctive, they will. The question is whether you can extract the signal from the noise, sort the genuine insight from the defensive posturing, and maintain your focus on the work that matters.

Your competitors will attack your strengths and frame them as weaknesses. The market will tell you who's right. Your job is to stay coherent enough to find out.

The 'Fanboy Slam'

"Never interrupt your enemy when he is making a mistake."

—Napoleon Bonaparte

The Accusation That Immunizes Nonsense.

In 2010, a tech blogger named Hank Williams wrote an article titled "John Gruber jumps the shark" attacking one of Apple's most prominent analysts. Williams opened with careful inoculation: "Even a fanboy like myself has to agree..." He established his Mac credentials—used them since 1984, programmed on the Lisa at Penn, clearly a true believer. Then he went for the throat.

His target was John Gruber, who ran the influential site Daring Fireball. Williams's complaint? Gruber defended Apple too effectively. Williams admitted he couldn't find anything "obviously problematic" in Gruber's writing. He acknowledged Gruber's arguments were "pretty airtight"— meaning factual. He called Gruber "thoroughly decent" and his work "thoroughly logical and fact-based."

Then Williams declared Gruber had become "a rabid Apple fanboy."

The evidence? Gruber had written that "iPhone critics have seldom let facts get in their way." Williams claimed this meant Gruber was "saying that anyone who has criticized the iPhone, or presumably Apple, is just someone not dealing with the facts."

Except Gruber never said that. He'd written it in response to a specific claim about the iPhone's closed ecosystem, agreeing that Apple should open up while noting that critics often ignored facts that contradicted their narrative. Williams had transformed a narrow observation about specific critics into a blanket dismissal of all criticism—then attacked Gruber for the position Williams had invented.

This wasn't analysis. It was accusation as prophylaxis. By labeling Gruber a fanboy, Williams created a frame where any factual correction Gruber offered could be dismissed as zealotry. The more accurate Gruber was, the more "partisan" he appeared. Facts became evidence of bias.

Here's what made it brilliant: Williams was attacking someone whose own writing contradicted the accusation. Gruber had called Apple's early iPhone app restrictions "insulting" and accused them of trying to "bullshit developers." He'd written nearly 1,000 words slamming Apple's censorship of a dictionary app, saying "If all you have to offer is a shit sandwich, just say it." This wasn't a shill. This was someone who praised and criticized based on evidence.

None of that mattered once the accusation landed. The label did the work.

What This Actually Teaches

The "fanboy slam" is a specific type of credibility attack that works by making enthusiasm or expertise into a disqualifier. It's not about proving someone wrong—it's about making their rightness irrelevant. Once someone is labeled a fanboy, their accuracy becomes suspicious. The more correct they are, the more partisan they must be.

This pattern shows up in three distinct forms. The preemptive inoculation sounds like "Even as a [X] fan myself, I have to say..." This creates permission to spread distortions while appearing reasonable. The self-applied label acts as credibility armor—"I'm one of you, so you can trust me when I criticize." The accusation sounds like "Of course you'd say that, you're a fanboy." This dismisses factual correction as bias. It converts expertise or enthusiasm into a character flaw. The more someone knows, the less credible they become. The witch trial means any attempt to defend against the accusation proves it true. Silence admits guilt. Response confirms zealotry. Like the medieval test for witchcraft—if you drown, you're innocent but dead; if you survive, you're guilty and will be burned—the accusation itself becomes the evidence.

What makes this effective is that it inverts normal credibility signals. Usually, we trust people who know more, care more, or have better track records. The fanboy slam weaponizes those signals. Your knowledge becomes "bias." Your accuracy becomes "partisanship." Your track record becomes "blind loyalty."

The goal isn't to win an argument with facts. It's to make facts irrelevant by attacking the source.

How This Shows Up

I've watched this pattern destroy productive conversations in nearly every industry I've worked in. A consultant presents data showing a proposed strategy has failed everywhere it's been tried. "Well, you've always been skeptical of this approach." The data doesn't change. But now it's reframed as agenda, not evidence.

An employee corrects factual errors in a competitor analysis. "You're too close to our old way of doing things." The corrections are accurate. But accuracy becomes proof of inflexibility.

A customer voices strong support for your product's approach. Competitors dismiss them: "They're in the tank for you." Their enthusiasm gets recast as gullibility or compensation, never genuine experience.

The pattern is consistent: when someone's position is threatened by facts, they attack the credibility of the source rather than addressing the facts themselves. And they do it by turning the source's strengths—knowledge, experience, enthusiasm, accuracy—into supposed weaknesses.

Here's what I've learned: the fanboy slam almost always signals that the attacker can't win on substance. When someone leads with credibility attacks instead of factual rebuttals, they're telling you they don't have factual rebuttals to offer.

The Diagnostic Questions

When someone deploys a fanboy slam—whether against you, your team, or your supporters—run it through this filter.

Is the accusation specific or vague? "You're biased" is vague. "You're ignoring this specific data point" is specific. Vague accusations are usually about dismissing the source. Specific ones might actually identify blind spots worth examining.

What facts are they not addressing? This is the key diagnostic. Look at what was said immediately before the accusation. Usually, someone stated something factual that the accuser couldn't refute. The fanboy slam is the retreat from that factual claim to an attack on character.

Is their criticism falsifiable? Ask yourself: what would it take to disprove their claim that you're biased? If nothing would change their assessment— if your agreement with them proves you're reasonable but your disagreement proves you're partisan—the accusation isn't analysis. It's a trap.

What's their actual track record? Williams attacked Gruber for being too pro-Apple while Gruber's own writing showed him criticizing Apple harshly when warranted. The accusation contradicted the evidence. When someone's track record shows balanced judgment, the fanboy accusation usually tells you more about the accuser than the accused.

Are they attacking accuracy or agenda? Sometimes people do have agendas that distort their analysis. But the fanboy slam typically attacks accuracy itself as evidence of agenda. "You're too often right about this company" becomes "You must be biased." That's backwards. If someone's consistently accurate, that's evidence of good analysis, not hidden loyalty.

What To Do Monday

First, recognize the pattern when you see it. The fanboy slam typically follows this sequence: someone makes a factual claim, someone else can't refute it with facts, so they attack the source's credibility instead. Once you see the pattern, you stop treating it as legitimate criticism and start recognizing it as a retreat from substance.

Second, don't accept the frame. The fanboy slam wants you to defend your objectivity, which puts you in an unwinnable position. Defending makes you look defensive. Not defending lets the accusation stand. Instead, return immediately to substance. When someone says "You're just defending them because you're too close to this," don't defend your objectivity. Say: "Here's the specific data I'm citing. What part of it is inaccurate?" Force them back to substance or make them admit they're not engaging with it.

Third, maintain your track record of balanced judgment. Gruber's defense against Williams wasn't his response—it was his existing body of work showing he praised and criticized Apple based on evidence. Your best defense against credibility attacks is a history of evaluating things fairly, including criticizing what you generally support when it's warranted.

Fourth, watch for preemptive inoculation in your own thinking. Sometimes you catch yourself saying "Even though I usually support this approach..." before expressing doubt. Ask yourself: are you genuinely reconsidering based on new evidence, or are you performing objectivity to avoid seeming biased? Real reconsideration focuses on what changed— new data, new outcomes, new understanding. Performed objectivity focuses on establishing credibility—"I'm one of you, so trust me." The difference matters. One is thinking. The other is positioning.

Fifth, distinguish between legitimate criticism and credibility attacks. Not every accusation of bias is a fanboy slam. Sometimes people do have blind spots. Sometimes enthusiasm does distort judgment. The question is whether the criticism is falsifiable and whether it engages with substance. Legitimate criticism says: "You're missing this data point, this outcome, this perspective." It's specific and it points to substance you can evaluate. Fanboy slams say: "You're too close to this, too positive about that, too enthusiastic about the other thing." It's about you, not about evaluatable claims.

Sixth, protect your supporters from this attack. When competitors or critics dismiss your advocates as fanboys, don't distance yourself from them or apologize for their enthusiasm. The attack isn't really about your supporters—it's about cutting off your source of credible testimony. Point to specifics: "These customers have chosen to use our product for three years. They're making a choice based on their experience. What about their specific feedback do you disagree with?"

The Real Lesson

Here's what the fanboy slam actually reveals: your opposition can't win on merit, so they're trying to win on dismissal. When someone attacks the credibility of accurate sources rather than correcting inaccurate claims, they're waving a white flag disguised as an accusation.

Gruber's response to Williams wasn't a defense of his objectivity. He just kept writing, kept citing facts, kept correcting distortions. His track record spoke. Williams's accusation faded. The substance persisted.

This is the pattern Steve understood intuitively. When critics called Apple users fanboys, it was because those users had genuine enthusiasm based on actual experience. The critics couldn't match that experience, so they tried to disqualify it. Steve didn't apologize for user enthusiasm. He created more of it.

The fanboy slam wants you to doubt your own judgment when you're consistently accurate, distance yourself from supporters who validate your approach, moderate your confidence even when the evidence supports it, and accept that being right too often makes you suspect. All of those responses weaken your position. They make you run away from your strengths because someone convinced you those strengths were liabilities.

Napoleon's advice about not interrupting enemies during mistakes applies perfectly here. When competitors resort to credibility attacks instead of factual rebuttals, they're making a mistake. They're advertising that they've got nothing substantive to offer. They're showing everyone watching that they can't engage with the actual work.

Your job isn't to defend against the accusation. It's to maintain substance while they flail at character. Keep citing facts while they attack sources. Keep building track record while they question motives. Keep creating results while they manufacture suspicion.

The fanboy slam only works if you accept its premise—that accuracy is suspect, enthusiasm is disqualifying, and expertise is bias. Reject the premise. Return to substance. Let your work and your track record speak.

When someone calls you a fanboy for being consistently accurate, they're really saying: "I can't refute what you're saying, so I'm going to attack why you're saying it." That's not a position of strength. It's a retreat dressed up as an offensive.

Don't interrupt them. They're making your case for you.

CRUCIFY THEM

"They have vilified me, they have crucified me; yes, they have even criticized me." —Richard J. Daley

The Cross They Built for You.

In 1997, Wired magazine put Apple's logo in a crown of thorns on its cover. The headline: "Pray." The message was clear—Apple was being crucified, and only divine intervention could save them. Steve Jobs had just returned as CEO.

Seven years later, after the iPod had resurrected Apple's fortunes, the narrative shifted. Now Steve was the one being cast as deity. Books invoked religious metaphors—"defrocked" from "Eden." Forbes titled a piece about the iPad "Are You There God, It's Me, Steve Jobs." The Independent asked "iGod: Could Apple survive without Steve Jobs?" The Economist put Steve in Jesus robes, sun behind his head, holding up an iPad as holy offering.

When Steve died and Tim Cook became CEO, you might think the religious framing would disappear. Cook was soft-spoken, methodical, an operations expert who'd never cultivated mystique or prophetic aura. Yet CNET wrote "Tim Cook preaches the new Apple gospel." The Guardian called Apple stockholders "parishioners" and declared "Cook runs a minor religion." Over 2,000 words invoking "orthodox relics," "evangelize," "scripture," "salvation," "anointed," "benedictions," and "false idols."

Here's what actually happened: Steve Jobs in 1990, asked if he was "out to build a company or change the world," replied humbly: "When we started Apple, we were out to build computers for our friends, that's all." Speaking about the graphical user interface, he credited Xerox PARC: "They didn't have it totally right, but they had the germ of the idea." He regularly acknowledged predecessors and contemporaries.

The deification wasn't coming from Steve. It was coming from critics who needed to elevate him so they could tear him down. They built the pedestal. They placed him on it. Then they attacked him for standing there.

This is the pattern: inflate claims you never made, then criticize you for making them. It's accusation by construction.

What This Actually Teaches

The "crucify them" pattern works in three stages. First, elevation beyond claim. Critics attribute positions, attitudes, or claims you never made. They frame your confidence as messianic, your success as worship-demanding, your standards as god-complex. They don't quote you claiming divinity—they simply assert that your behavior implies it. Second, moral outrage at the elevation. Having constructed an inflated position for you, they express shock at your arrogance. How dare you think you're special? Who do you think you are? The audacity of your self-regard! Except the self-regard they're attacking is the one they invented, not the one you expressed. Third, takedown as correction. Now they get to be the voice of reason, bringing you back down to earth. They're not attacking success—they're restoring humility. They're not diminishing achievement—they're providing needed perspective. The attack gets framed as service.

What makes this effective is that defending yourself confirms the accusation. If you say "I never claimed to be a god," you sound defensive about a claim no one said you explicitly made—they just "observed" it in your behavior. If you stay silent, the framing stands. If you humble yourself, you're admitting to the arrogance they accused you of.

The goal isn't accurate criticism. It's to create a no-win scenario where your success itself becomes evidence of problematic ego, and any response to the framing validates it.

How This Shows Up

I've seen this pattern deployed against anyone who achieves something significant without performing sufficient self-deprecation. A founder builds something successful. Critics don't attack the business—they attack the founder's "reality distortion field," their "cult of personality," their "messiah complex." These phrases do the same work as religious imagery: they take confidence and success and reframe them as delusion and manipulation.

A leader maintains high standards. Critics don't engage with whether the standards produce results—they frame the standards themselves as evidence of viewing yourself as infallible. "Who does she think she is?" becomes the question, not "Are these standards working?"

A team generates genuine enthusiasm from customers. Critics don't examine why customers are enthusiastic—they call it "worship" or "cult-like devotion." The enthusiasm gets pathologized. The company must be manipulating people, because surely rational humans wouldn't be that genuinely excited about a product or service.

The pattern is consistent: take actual achievement, add exaggerated framing, then attack the exaggeration as if it came from the achiever. The achiever becomes responsible for others' inflated descriptions, then gets criticized for narcissism they never exhibited.

The Diagnostic Questions

When someone deploys this pattern—whether against you, your company, or your work—examine these elements.

What did you actually say versus what they claim you implied? This is the critical distinction. Steve said he wanted to build computers for friends. Critics claimed he thought he was Einstein or Gandhi. The gap between statement and attribution tells you whether you're dealing with criticism or construction. Look for the word "implies" or phrases like "seems to think" or "acts as if." These signal attribution, not quotation. They're telling you what the critic decided your words or actions mean, not what you actually said.

Are they quoting you or characterizing you? Characterizations are where the inflation happens. "He thinks he's special" is characterization. "Here's what he said about himself: [quote]" is quotation. The more a critic relies on characterization over quotation, the more likely they're building a position to attack rather than attacking an actual position.

What's the actual evidence for the elevation? When critics call something a "cult" or a "religion," ask: what specific behaviors are they pointing to? Often it's just success, enthusiasm, or high standards. Harley-Davidson sponsors Sturgis—thousands gather to celebrate motorcycles. Is that a Baptist revival or people enjoying shared interests? The framing does the work.

Is the criticism addressing your work or your attitude? Criticism of work points to results, outcomes, decisions. Criticism of attitude points to how you supposedly view yourself. One is about what you're building. The other is about attacking you for building it successfully.

What would satisfy the critic? If nothing short of failure or self-deprecation would satisfy them—if your success itself is the problem—then the criticism isn't about correcting a flaw. It's about resenting achievement.

What To Do Monday

First, recognize when you're being elevated artificially. The moment critics start using religious metaphors, messianic language, or cult framing, you're watching the construction phase. They're not describing your actual position—they're building one they can attack.

Second, refuse the framing without defending against it. You don't need to say "I don't think I'm a god"—that accepts the premise that this is a reasonable thing to need to deny. Instead, return to what you actually said and did. When New York magazine wrote that Steve's "mammoth self-regard" was "maddening" even though "all too often it has been justified," the contradiction was the point. They couldn't attack his judgment—it kept proving correct—so they attacked his confidence in that judgment. Steve didn't defend his self-regard. He just kept being right.

Third, let your actual words and work speak. The most powerful counter to artificial elevation is your actual track record of what you've claimed and what you've built. Steve credited Xerox PARC. He said he wanted to build computers for friends. His actual statements were humble and accurate. No defense needed.

Fourth, distinguish between confidence and arrogance in your own communication. Confidence speaks clearly about what you know and what you've built. Arrogance claims more than you've earned. The crucifixion pattern tries to conflate them, but they're different. State accurately what you know, what you've built, and where you're uncertain. Earned confidence doesn't need inflation or deflation.

Fifth, watch for the pattern's most insidious effect—making you doubt your own judgment. When critics spend enough time claiming you think you're god, you can start second-guessing every confident decision. This is exactly what the pattern wants—to make you run away from your own judgment. The test isn't whether critics think you're too confident. It's whether your confidence is grounded in reality. Are your decisions proving sound? Are your standards producing results? Is your judgment reliable?

Sixth, don't humble yourself reflexively when they inflate you. When someone builds a pedestal for you that you never asked for, the temptation is to immediately disavow it: "Oh no, I'm not special, I'm just like everyone else." That confirms you were on the pedestal—you just needed reminding to get down. Steve didn't grovel when magazines put him in Jesus robes. He didn't apologize for Apple's success when critics called it a cult. He just kept working.

The Real Lesson

Here's what the crucifixion pattern reveals: critics who can't attack your work attack your character instead. When they can't find flaws in your judgment, they attack your confidence in it. When they can't diminish your achievement, they frame your success itself as problematic.

The Economist put Steve in robes holding an iPad. CNET called Cook's investor communications "preaching gospel." The Guardian claimed Cook ran "a minor religion." None of this described what Steve or Cook actually said or did. It described how critics chose to frame their success.

The religious metaphors did specific work: they took earned confidence and reframed it as delusion, took genuine customer enthusiasm and reframed it as manipulation, took high standards and reframed them as infallibility complex. The framing allowed critics to attack success without having to explain why it was actually failing.

This is what you need to understand: the crucifixion isn't about what you claimed. It's about what you achieved. The elevation isn't honor—it's ammunition. They build the cross so they can nail you to it.

Your job isn't to get down off the cross they built. It's to refuse to climb up on it in the first place. Don't accept their framing. Don't defend against their characterizations. Don't perform humility to prove you're not claiming divinity you never claimed.

Just state accurately what you know, what you've built, and what you're trying to do. Keep your confidence grounded in reality. Let your work prove your judgment. Ignore the pedestals critics construct and the crucifixions that follow.

When New York magazine called Steve's self-regard "maddening" because it was "justified," they told the whole story. They couldn't attack his judgment—it kept being correct—so they attacked his awareness of its correctness. That's not criticism. That's resentment dressed as moral concern.

The people trying to crucify you aren't worried about your humility. They're worried about your success. The religious metaphors are just tools to frame achievement as arrogance so they can attack it without having to prove it's wrong.

Don't interrupt them when they're making this mistake. Just keep building. Let them waste energy on metaphors while you focus on results. The work will speak. The framing will fade. And the critics will move on to someone else who's achieved something worth resenting.

You didn't claim to be god. Don't let them crucify you for a claim you never made.

Call 'Em a 'Cult'

"What is of supreme importance in war is to attack the enemy's strategy."
—Sun Tzu

When Your Culture Becomes Your Crime.

In 2011, Time Magazine ran a headline: "Steve Jobs Is Your God Now—No, Really." The story cited a study showing that Apple fans' brains responded to Apple products the same way religious people's brains responded to religious imagery. The implication was clear: Apple customers were brainwashed zealots, not rational consumers making informed choices.

The actual study? One person. A Mac magazine editor who admitted to "thinking about Apple 24 hours a day" put in an MRI scanner. From this sample size of one, media outlets declared that Apple triggered religious feelings in people.

Calmer analysis revealed something different: the same brain response occurred with Harley-Davidson fans, Guinness drinkers, and fans of other strong brands. It wasn't about Apple creating cult-like devotion—it was about how humans respond to brands they genuinely value. But only Apple customers got labeled fanatics "whipped up into some sort of crazy, evangelical frenzy."

Meanwhile, Google never faced such accusations despite having more elaborate employee culture controls. They called their headquarters the "Googleplex," employed people specifically to keep workers happy, referred to HR as "People Operations," and calculated everything from lunch line length (3-4 minutes exactly) to table sizes (optimized for employee interactions) to greeting protocols (specific phrases managers must use increase productivity 15%). They even manipulated food placement to reduce M&M consumption by three million calories over seven weeks.

Apple trained employees to ask permission before touching someone's iPhone and got called a cult. Google calculated optimal waistline maintenance strategies for employees and got praised for innovative culture.

The difference? Apple was winning.

What This Actually Teaches

The "cult" accusation is the most sophisticated attack on a company's culture because it weaponizes your strengths. It takes genuine enthusiasm, strong values, and cultural coherence—assets that drive performance— and reframes them as liabilities that signal manipulation.

This attack works through several mechanisms. It pathologizes enthusiasm. When customers genuinely love your product, critics call it brainwashing. When employees share values, critics call it indoctrination. The more authentic the enthusiasm, the more suspicious it appears. Strong positive response gets reframed as loss of critical thinking.

It creates impossible standards. If your product is unpopular, you've failed. If it's popular but people are ambivalent, you're mediocre. If it's popular and people are enthusiastic, they're brainwashed. The only way to avoid the "cult" label is to inspire neither loyalty nor passion—which guarantees you'll lose to competitors who do.

It inverts causation. The attack assumes manipulation creates enthusiasm rather than quality creating enthusiasm. It denies that people might be genuinely satisfied. Every data point confirming customer satisfaction becomes evidence of how effective the manipulation is, not how good the product is.

It applies selectively. Strong cultures exist everywhere—from Google to Harley-Davidson to Weight Watchers. But the "cult" label gets applied selectively to whoever threatens established players most. It's not about actual cultishness—it's about competitive positioning dressed as psychological concern.

The goal isn't to identify actual manipulation. It's to make you doubt your own culture's value and distance yourself from the very attributes that make you distinctive.

How This Shows Up

I've watched this pattern deploy against any organization that builds something people genuinely care about. A company develops strong internal culture—shared values, clear mission, consistent standards. Competitors or critics call it "drinking the Kool-Aid" or label employees "mindless drones." The implication: only weak-minded people would genuinely believe in what they're building.

Customers express authentic enthusiasm—they recommend products, they line up for releases, they defend the company when criticism seems unfair. Critics call them "fanboys" or "zealots" or claim they're "in the tank." The implication: rational people wouldn't be this satisfied.

A team operates with alignment—everyone understands the mission, the values, the standards. Critics call it "Stepford-like" or say they "all drank the Kool-Aid, same flavor." The implication: coherence is conformity, alignment is absence of independent thought.

The pattern is always the same: take attributes that enable high performance—cultural coherence, genuine enthusiasm, shared values—and reframe them as evidence of manipulation or loss of critical judgment.

Here's what I've learned: the "cult" accusation almost never comes when you're struggling. It comes when your culture is working. When employee alignment produces better results. When customer enthusiasm drives growth. When your values actually differentiate you in the market.

The attack targets success, not dysfunction.

The Diagnostic Questions

When the "cult" accusation appears—whether against your company, your team, or your customers—examine these elements.

What specific behaviors are they actually citing? Strip away the loaded language. "Brainwashed customers" often means "customers who are consistently satisfied." "Indoctrinated employees" often means "employees who understand and execute on company values." "Mindless zealots" often means "people who will correct factual inaccuracies about the company." Get to the actual behaviors being criticized. Often they're just normal expressions of genuine satisfaction or cultural alignment.

Is there actual evidence of manipulation, or just evidence of satisfaction? This is the critical distinction. Manipulation would show up as pressure to express enthusiasm you don't feel, punishment for criticism, concealment of product flaws, forced participation in company rituals. Satisfaction shows up as voluntary enthusiasm based on experience, willingness to correct misinformation while acknowledging real flaws, choosing to engage with company culture without coercion.

Apple's iPhone had nine consecutive years of highest customer satisfaction scores in J.D. Power surveys—855 out of 1,000 points while competitors scored in the 790s. Their laptops scored 9.2 out of 10 for five straight years while the closest PC manufacturer hit 8.8 once. These aren't manipulation metrics. They're satisfaction metrics.

Are competing companies with similar cultures getting the same criticism? This reveals whether the attack is about actual concern or competitive positioning. Google's culture was more controlling by nearly every measure—calculated lunch lines, measured table sizes, scripted greetings, monitored food choices—yet faced no "cult" accusations while winning. Apple faced constant "cult" accusations while threatening Microsoft's and others' market positions. The difference wasn't the culture. It was the threat.

What would it take to disprove the accusation? If no level of customer satisfaction, employee alignment, or cultural coherence would satisfy critics—if any positive response gets reframed as evidence of manipulation —then the accusation isn't analysis. It's positioning.

What To Do Monday

First, understand what genuine culture actually requires. The "cult" attack works by conflating culture with coercion. But real culture isn't about forcing people to pretend enthusiasm—it's about creating conditions where genuine enthusiasm emerges. Apple's store training taught employees to acknowledge customer problems without lying, ask permission before touching devices, and treat people with respect. That's not brainwashing—that's customer service standards.

Second, track actual satisfaction metrics, not sentiment. The "cult" accusation relies on dismissing positive sentiment as manufactured. Counter it with measurable satisfaction data that can't be explained away as manipulation. J.D. Power scores, retention rates, net promoter scores, product return rates, employee tenure—these tell you whether enthusiasm is authentic or performed. Document this. Not defensively, but as honest feedback about whether your work is actually serving people well.

Third, don't apologize for cultural coherence. When everyone on your team understands your mission and values, when they can articulate what you stand for without reading from a script, that's not Stepford-like conformity—that's successful culture transmission. Time Magazine noted that Apple employees all talked about "deep collaboration" and "cross-pollination" in similar ways, then called it cultish. Jony Ive explained: "When the challenges are that complex, you have to develop a product in a more collaborative, integrated way." The reporter dismissed this as Kool-Aid. The alternative to alignment isn't independent thinking—it's confusion.

Fourth, examine whether your culture is actually serving your work. Not all strong cultures are good cultures. Some do coerce conformity, punish dissent, or create unhealthy dynamics. The test isn't whether people outside call you a cult. It's whether your culture enables or inhibits good work. Does it help people do their best work, or does it demand performative loyalty? Does it welcome legitimate criticism, or only praise? Can people disagree with decisions while staying aligned on values?

Fifth, protect customer enthusiasm from being pathologized. When customers express genuine satisfaction with your work, don't distance yourself from them because critics call them zealots. Their enthusiasm is information about whether you're building something valuable. People lined up for iPhones not because they were brainwashed but because the product solved problems better than alternatives. If your customers aren't enthusiastic enough to recommend you, that's the actual problem.

Sixth, recognize when you're being baited into performing humility about your culture. The "cult" accusation wants you to apologize for cultural strength, distance yourself from employee alignment, and downplay customer satisfaction. All of those responses weaken what actually makes you distinctive. The trap is accepting that strong culture equals dangerous culture, that alignment equals conformity, that enthusiasm equals manipulation.

The Real Lesson

Here's what the "cult" accusation reveals about your critics: they can't build cultures people want to be part of or products people genuinely love, so they pathologize yours.

When BusinessInsider called Apple employees "clapping, smiling zealots" for welcoming new hires with applause, they revealed more about their own culture than Apple's. They couldn't imagine people genuinely enjoying welcoming new colleagues, so they framed it as coerced performance.

When CNN called Apple's training methods "fiendish" for teaching employees not to lie to customers and to ask permission before touching devices, they showed they couldn't conceive of customer service standards as genuine values rather than manipulation tactics.

When critics dismissed nine consecutive years of highest customer satisfaction scores as evidence of brainwashing rather than product quality, they revealed they couldn't explain why people would voluntarily choose something that consistently satisfied them better than alternatives.

The "cult" accusation is ultimately a confession: "We can't create what you've created, so we'll call your success dangerous."

Your job isn't to defend your culture by explaining it's not a cult. That accepts their frame. Your job is to maintain the culture that produces results while they waste energy on metaphors.

Apple trained employees consistently. Competitors called it indoctrination. Apple's customers were genuinely satisfied. Competitors called it brainwashing. Apple's team aligned on values. Competitors called it Stepford-like conformity.

Meanwhile, Apple's customer satisfaction scores stayed highest in the industry. Their products kept working better. Their employees kept producing innovative work. The critics kept complaining. The results kept speaking.

When Time ran that headline about Steve Jobs being your god based on a study of one person, they weren't doing science—they were doing competitive positioning dressed as psychology. The response wasn't to prove you're not religious about Apple. It was to keep building products people genuinely valued.

Your competitors will call your culture a cult when they can't build cultures as strong. They'll call your customers brainwashed when they can't generate genuine enthusiasm. They'll call your team mindless drones when they can't achieve the same alignment.

Let them. Just keep building the culture that serves your work, the products that serve your customers, and the team that makes both possible. Track your actual satisfaction metrics. Maintain your actual standards. Produce your actual results.

The "cult" accusation only sticks if you don't have evidence of genuine satisfaction to counter it. If you do have that evidence—if your customers keep choosing you, your employees keep producing, your results keep improving—then the accusation tells everyone more about the accusers than about you.

They're not worried about your customers' psychological well-being. They're worried about your competitive position. The religious metaphors are just weapons to attack cultural strength they can't match.

Don't interrupt them when they're making that mistake. Just keep building.

Hate Is Great

"Culture is the organization's immune system." —Michael Watkins

When Silence Should Scare You.

In early 2007, after Steve Jobs introduced the iPhone, the response from competitors was swift and loud. Steve Ballmer laughed at the $500 price. BlackBerry's co-CEO said "it's kind of one more entrant into an already very busy space with lots of choice." Palm's CEO dismissed it: "We've learned and struggled for a few years here figuring out how to make a decent phone. PC guys are not going to just figure this out."

Every major phone maker either mocked the iPhone or explained why it would fail. The attacks were constant, confident, and comprehensive.

Five years later, BlackBerry's market share had collapsed from 50% to under 5%. Palm had been acquired and shut down. Nokia, the dominant phone maker, was in freefall. Microsoft had written off nearly a billion dollars on unsold tablets. Every company that had dismissed the iPhone was either declining or dead.

The attacks weren't noise. They were signal. Each one revealed exactly what the attacker valued, what they couldn't replicate, and which of Apple's strengths threatened them most. Ballmer's focus on subsidized pricing told you Microsoft didn't understand value equations. BlackBerry's dismissal of simplicity told you they were committed to complexity. Palm's confidence in their experience told you they thought past success predicted future relevance.

Here's what most people miss: competitive hostility isn't a problem to manage. It's intelligence to decode. The louder the attacks, the more accurate your aim. The more confident their dismissals, the more threatened they actually are.

Silence is what should scare you. When competitors aren't attacking, you're not threatening them.

What This Actually Teaches

Competitive attacks contain three types of valuable information, but most people only hear the surface noise.

Threat confirmation comes from the volume and intensity of attacks. Competitors don't waste energy attacking things that don't threaten them. When they're squealing loudly, you've hit something that matters to their position.

Strategic revelation shows up in the specific nature of attacks. They reveal what competitors value that you don't, what they can't replicate that you can, and where their business model is most vulnerable. Every criticism is a map of their constraints.

Misdirection attempts appear when competitors tell you to change course. They're usually telling you to abandon exactly what's working. "You should lower prices" means your value equation threatens their commodity positioning. "You should add features" means your simplicity threatens their complexity justification. "You should serve more segments" means your focus threatens their diffusion.

The pattern Steve understood: competitors will always tell you to become more like them. That advice serves their interests, not yours. When they're loudest about what you should change, they're often pointing directly at your most powerful differentiation.

This doesn't mean all competitive criticism is wrong—sometimes they identify real weaknesses. But the pattern of attacks over time tells you something more valuable than any single criticism: where your approach most fundamentally challenges their position.

How This Shows Up

I've watched this pattern play out across industries. A company launches with a radically simplified product. Competitors attack the "missing features" and predict failure because "customers need more capability." Translation: their entire business model justifies complexity, and your simplicity threatens that justification.

A business focuses intensely on one segment. Competitors criticize the "limited market" and explain why "you need to expand to grow." Translation: they've spread themselves thin across many segments, and your concentrated success makes their diffusion look like lack of focus.

A team maintains unusually high standards and moves deliberately. Competitors attack "slow execution" and "perfectionism" while praising their own speed. Translation: they've compromised quality for velocity, and your standards make those compromises visible.

The pattern is consistent: competitors frame your differentiation as your liability. They tell you to abandon precisely what makes you distinctive and adopt what makes them comfortable—which usually means what makes you less threatening.

The most valuable attacks are the confident ones. When established players dismiss your approach with certainty, they're telling you they've committed to a different path and can't easily reverse course. Their confidence is brittleness disguised as strength.

The Diagnostic Questions

When competitive attacks arrive—and if you're doing anything distinctive, they will—analyze them for intelligence.

What's the volume and intensity? This tells you how much threat you pose. Occasional dismissals mean you're a curiosity. Sustained attacks mean you're a problem for them. Escalating hostility means you're winning. Track this over time. If attacks are increasing in frequency or intensity, you're likely on the right path.

What specific attributes are they attacking? This reveals what threatens them most. List the actual things they criticize—not the surface rhetoric, but the core attributes. Are they attacking your pricing, your focus, your standards, your simplicity, your speed, your positioning? Each attack points to something they can't easily replicate. If they could match your approach, they'd copy it rather than criticize it.

What do they say you should do instead? This is often the most revealing intelligence. When competitors tell you to change course, they're describing what would make you less threatening to them. The prescription reveals their position. Do the opposite of what they prescribe and you're probably maximizing differentiation.

Who's attacking you? Attacks from declining competitors tell you different things than attacks from ascendant ones. If everyone attacking you is losing market position, their criticism might be projection of their own failing strategy onto yours. If thriving competitors are attacking you, pay more attention—though even then, they might be attacking preemptively because they see the threat coming.

What are they NOT attacking? The things competitors avoid criticizing tell you where they don't see threats—either because those attributes aren't distinctive, or because they're planning to copy them. The silence is data.

What To Do Monday

First, create a competitor attack log. When competitors criticize you publicly—in interviews, analyst calls, marketing materials, social media—document it. Not to get defensive, but to identify patterns. Over time, you'll see clusters. Multiple competitors attacking the same attribute usually means you've hit something structural about the industry that your approach challenges.

Second, use attacks to stress-test your strategy, not determine it. When competitors attack an attribute of your approach, ask: "If this criticism were valid, what would we see in our results?" Then look at actual outcomes. If they say your prices are too high but your market share is growing and customer satisfaction is rising, the market is telling you the criticism is wrong. The test isn't whether the criticism sounds convincing—it's whether reality confirms it.

Third, distinguish between attacks on your strategy versus execution. Criticism of how you're implementing your strategy might be valid. Criticism of the strategy itself is usually revealing their own constraints. "You're not executing your focused strategy well in this segment" is different from "You shouldn't focus on a single segment." The first might identify real problems. The second is usually telling you to abandon differentiation.

Fourth, watch what competitors do, not just what they say. This is the ultimate filter. If competitors attack your pricing but then raise theirs, they're revealing the criticism was positioning, not analysis. If they mock your simplicity but then simplify their own products, they're revealing the attack was defensive. Actions trump rhetoric.

After Ballmer laughed at the iPhone's price, Microsoft spent years trying to build premium hardware—Surface, Windows Phone, the Nokia acquisition. Their actions revealed that the pricing criticism was defensive posturing, not genuine strategic insight. They knew premium positioning could work; they just couldn't execute it themselves.

Fifth, be especially suspicious when competitors tell you to change course right when you're succeeding. When your approach is working—growing market share, improving margins, increasing customer satisfaction—competitors will suddenly become very concerned that you're on the wrong path. "You can't sustain this." "You need to expand to keep growing." "You're leaving money on the table." These warnings almost always come exactly when your focused approach is working, because that's when it most threatens their position.

Sixth, convert competitor intelligence into strategic confidence. When you understand the pattern—that competitors attack your differentiation and prescribe changes that would make you less threatening—their hostility becomes validation. The attacks tell you where you're threatening them. The volume tells you how much. The specific nature tells you what they can't replicate. And the prescriptions tell you exactly what differentiation to maintain.

The Real Lesson

Here's what most people misunderstand about competitive hostility: they treat it as a problem to manage rather than intelligence to decode. They try to quiet the attacks, respond to the criticism, or adjust their approach to reduce competitive hostility.

That's backwards. Competitive hostility is information about whether you're threatening established positions. The goal isn't to eliminate it—it's to understand what it's telling you.

Steve didn't respond to Ballmer's mockery or BlackBerry's dismissals or Palm's confidence. He didn't adjust the iPhone's strategy to address their criticisms. He just kept building what he was building. The competitors' attacks revealed their own constraints, not iPhone's flaws.

Ballmer's focus on subsidies revealed Microsoft didn't understand integrated value. BlackBerry's dismissal of simplicity revealed they were committed to complexity they couldn't abandon. Palm's confidence in their experience revealed they thought past success inoculated them against disruption.

Each attack was a confession of constraint. Each confident dismissal was a revelation of inflexibility. Each prescription to change course was a request to abandon differentiation.

The pattern is universal: competitors will attack your strengths and frame them as weaknesses. They'll tell you to abandon what makes you distinctive and adopt what makes you comfortable for them. They'll express concern for your strategy exactly when it's working best.

Your job isn't to quiet them or respond to them. It's to decode them.

When competitors praise your strategy, worry. When they ignore you, worry. When they attack you loudly and confidently while telling you to change course—especially when your results are strong—you're probably onto something.

The hate isn't a problem. It's a compass. The intensity points toward your most effective differentiation. The specific criticisms reveal their constraints. The prescriptions show you what threatens them most.

Don't try to reduce the hostility. Try to understand what it's telling you about your own position and theirs. The louder they squeal, the more likely you've hit something that matters.

Silence should scare you. Hostility is information. Use it.

When established competitors tell you to change course, when industry analysts echo their concerns, when the chorus behind them chimes in to proclaim you need to adjust—that's often the precise moment to maintain your focus.

They're not worried about your success. They're worried about their decline. The attacks are the sound of threatened positions trying to protect themselves by getting you to abandon what threatens them.

Don't interrupt them. Just decode what they're actually telling you about where you're winning, what they can't match, and what you should maintain.

The hate isn't noise. It's signal. Learn to read it.

Making You Run Away From Yourself

"All war is deception." —Sun Tzu

The Strength They Want You to Surrender.

In the early 1980s, the Apple II dominated home computer gaming. Before PC gaming became an industry, the Apple II had Bubble Bobble, King's Quest, Ultima, Wizardry, The Oregon Trail—the golden age of computer gaming ran on Apple hardware. Steve had worked at Atari. Woz loved games. Gaming was a core strength of the platform.

Then Apple introduced the Macintosh. And Steve made a decision that would cost the company decades of market position: no games on the Mac. He wanted the Mac to be taken seriously by businesses, and businesses didn't take toys seriously. The PC industry was calling Macs "toys for the technically illiterate," and Steve tried to counter the attack by abandoning the strength it targeted.

The result? Apple lost the explosive home computer gaming market while never gaining the business respect they sought. Meanwhile, PC manufacturers had it both ways—they thrived on the gaming community that drove constant hardware upgrades while continuing to call Macs toys. They attacked Apple's strength, Apple abandoned it, and the PC industry claimed the territory Apple vacated.

Decades later, the iPhone faced the same attack. Verizon ran ads placing it on the "Island of Misfit Toys." BlackBerry and Microsoft lined up to call their products "serious" unlike that "tinker toy" iPhone. The pattern was identical: attack the approachability, the visual appeal, the user-friendliness—the very attributes that made the product distinctive.

This time, Steve didn't run away from himself. Apple built powerful gaming frameworks, enabled 3D engines, created Game Center for multiplayer gaming. By 2013, iOS had more games than four generations of gaming consoles combined—NES, Super NES, Nintendo 64, GameCube, Wii, Xbox, Xbox 360, PlayStation, PlayStation 2, PlayStation 3, and more. The platform that critics called a toy became the number one mobile gaming platform, generating more developer revenue than any competitor.

The difference? With the Mac, Apple ran away from their strength. With the iPhone, they ran toward it.

What This Actually Teaches

The most sophisticated competitive attack doesn't target your weaknesses —it targets your strengths and frames them as liabilities. Then it waits for you to reflexively abandon what makes you distinctive in an attempt to gain credibility with critics.

This pattern works through a specific mechanism. First, identify your differentiation. Competitors find the attribute that makes you genuinely different—your simplicity, your focus, your standards, your approachability, your design, your pricing model, whatever actually distinguishes you. Second, frame it as disqualifying. They don't just criticize it—they frame it as the reason you can't be taken seriously. "Too simple" becomes "not professional enough." "Too focused" becomes "too niche." "Too expensive" becomes "not practical." The strength gets recast as a fundamental flaw. Third, trigger defensive response. By framing your strength as a disqualifier, they create pressure to abandon it. You want to be taken seriously, you want broader acceptance, you want to prove you're not what they say you are. The natural response is to move away from the very thing they're attacking. Fourth, claim the vacated territory. Once you've abandoned your strength, they continue doing what you stopped. They attack your approachability while building approachable products. They criticize your focus while benefiting from concentrated positions. They mock your simplicity while simplifying their own offerings.

The deception is complete: they convinced you to surrender your arsenal while keeping theirs intact.

How This Shows Up

I've watched this pattern destroy strategic advantages across every industry I've worked in. A company builds something genuinely simple and approachable. Competitors call it "not enterprise-ready" or "not serious enough." The company adds complexity to prove they're sophisticated. Competitors continue selling simplicity while the company that pioneered it abandons their advantage.

A team maintains unusually high standards and moves deliberately. Competitors attack "slow execution" and "perfectionism." The team speeds up and lowers standards to prove they can move fast. Competitors maintain their own standards while benefiting from the now-lowered bar.

A business focuses intensely on one segment and serves it exceptionally well. Competitors criticize "limited market" and "leaving money on the table." The business expands to prove they can scale. Competitors continue serving focused segments while the expanded business dilutes itself across many.

The pattern is always the same: competitors attack the thing that actually makes you distinctive, frame it as the reason you can't succeed broadly, and wait for you to abandon it. Then they either adopt that approach themselves or benefit from your weakened position.

The most dangerous moment isn't when critics attack your flaws. It's when they attack your differentiation and you believe them.

The Diagnostic Questions

When facing criticism that targets a core attribute of your approach, examine these elements before responding.

Is this actually your strength or actually your weakness? Sometimes critics identify real problems. Sometimes they attack real strengths disguised as problems. The test: Is this attribute producing results? For Apple, gaming on the Apple II was driving sales and user engagement. Abandoning it on the Mac wasn't fixing a weakness—it was surrendering a strength. Look at actual outcomes. If the criticized attribute correlates with your success metrics, it's probably a strength being attacked, not a weakness being identified.

What market are they telling you to compete in? When critics say your product is "just a toy" or "not serious enough," they're usually defining "serious" as their own market position. They want you to compete on their terms, in their territory, by their rules. When critics define the market you should serve or the attributes that matter, ask: whose definition is this? Usually it's theirs, not yours or your customers'.

Who benefits if you abandon this attribute? Follow the incentives. If you stopped being simple, who benefits? If you stopped being focused, who benefits? If you stopped maintaining high standards, who benefits? Usually, the answer is: the people criticizing those attributes. They benefit from you abandoning differentiation and competing on their terms.

What would you become if you "fixed" this? If you addressed the criticism by abandoning the criticized attribute, what would you turn into? More importantly—would you still be distinctive? If fixing the "problem" means becoming more like your competitors, the criticism is probably an attack on differentiation, not an identification of weakness.

Is there evidence this attribute is actually limiting you? Look for concrete data. If you're "too simple" but customers are satisfied and adoption is growing, where's the limitation? If you're "too expensive" but margins are healthy and customers are paying, where's the problem? The absence of actual limiting evidence suggests the criticism is strategic positioning, not honest assessment.

What To Do Monday

First, identify your actual core strengths before critics attack them. Don't wait for criticism to clarify what makes you distinctive. Know it in advance. Document it. Understand which attributes actually drive your results. This clarity is your defense against running away from yourself. When criticism hits, you can evaluate it against what you know actually works rather than reflexively trying to prove critics wrong by abandoning what they attack.

Second, distinguish between criticism of your strength and criticism of your execution of that strength. "Your simplicity isn't serving users well" is different from "You're too simple to be taken seriously." The first might identify poor execution of a good strategy. The second is attacking the strategy itself. Always ask: is this criticism about how I'm executing my approach, or about the approach itself?

Third, watch for the frame shift from "doesn't work' to "not serious." When critics can't prove your approach doesn't work—when results are actually positive—they shift to respectability framing. "Maybe it works, but it's not professional/serious/enterprise-ready/suitable for real work." That frame shift reveals the criticism isn't about effectiveness—it's about category definition. They're trying to define you out of the "serious" category so they can claim that category themselves.

Fourth, examine whether "fixing" the criticism would require becoming your competitors. If addressing the criticism means adopting your competitors' approach, pricing model, feature set, market focus, or values —then the criticism is asking you to abandon differentiation. The Mac gaming decision did exactly this: it tried to make Macs "serious" by adopting PC manufacturers' definition of serious computing.

Fifth, track what happens when you resist the criticism versus when you accommodate it. The market tells you whether the criticism identified a real constraint or attacked a real strength. Trust outcomes over rhetoric.

Sixth, be especially wary when the attack comes from declining competitors. When established players who are losing ground criticize your approach, they're often describing their own failure as your limitation. BlackBerry calling the iPhone a toy wasn't analysis—it was a declining company trying to define away the threat.

Seventh, look for the pattern where they attack what they later adopt. When competitors criticize your simplicity then simplify their products, mock your pricing then raise theirs, dismiss your focus then narrow their own—they're revealing the attack was defensive positioning, not honest assessment. PC manufacturers called Macs toys while building their own business on gaming. That contradiction tells you everything.

The Real Lesson

Here's what the Mac-versus-iPhone comparison teaches: the same attack will keep coming. "Too simple." "Just a toy." "Not serious enough." The framing doesn't change. What changes is whether you abandon your strength or run toward it.

When Apple abandoned Mac gaming to be taken seriously, they lost a massive market while never gaining the respect they sought. PC manufacturers continued building on gaming while calling Macs toys. Apple had disarmed themselves while competitors kept their weapons.

When Apple faced the identical attack with the iPhone—Verizon's toy ads, BlackBerry's "serious device" positioning, Microsoft's enterprise focus— Steve didn't make the same mistake. Instead of abandoning gaming to prove the iPhone was serious, Apple built Game Center, supported major gaming engines, enabled controller support, and became the dominant mobile gaming platform.

The difference wasn't the attack—it was the response. One response was running away from strength. The other was running toward it.

The lesson isn't that all criticism is wrong or that you should never adjust your approach. Sometimes critics identify real weaknesses. Sometimes you do need to change course. But when criticism targets your actual differentiation and frames your strength as disqualifying, that's when you need to question whose interests the criticism serves.

Apple learned this the hard way. The Mac lost decades of gaming market position because Steve believed the "toy" attack and tried to fix it by abandoning gaming. The iPhone dominated mobile gaming because Steve recognized the same attack and refused to abandon approachability.

Your competitors will always attack what makes you genuinely different. They'll frame your simplicity as inadequacy, your focus as limitation, your standards as rigidity, your design as frivolity. They'll tell you that to be taken seriously, to scale successfully, to serve real markets, you need to abandon the very things that make you distinctive.

The question isn't whether the attacks will come. If you're doing anything distinctive, they will. The question is whether you'll recognize them as attempts to get you to surrender your arsenal.

Don't let anyone talk you out of your strengths. Especially when they're framing those strengths as weaknesses while building their own businesses on the territory you'd abandon.

When critics attack what you do well and tell you to be more like them, they're not offering guidance. They're asking you to disarm. The deception is convincing you that your strength is your weakness.

Run toward yourself, not away. Double down on what makes you distinctive, especially when critics say that's precisely what you should abandon. Let them attack your strengths. Just don't surrender them.

The territory you vacate will be claimed by the same people who convinced you to leave it. Learn from the Mac's loss. Remember the iPhone's win. Know the difference between fixing weaknesses and abandoning strengths.

All war is deception. The most effective deception is getting you to defeat yourself.

Tell Your Story, or Your Critics Will

"The great advantage of telling the truth is that nobody ever believes it." — Dorothy L. Sayers

The Vacuum Will Be Filled.

On January 27, 2010, Steve Jobs introduced the iPad. The initial response from technology media was immediate and brutal. "A giant iPhone." "No keyboard." "Who needs this?" "It's just a consumption device, not a creation device." Gizmodo called it "a huge disappointment." TechCrunch said it was "not revolutionary, it's evolutionary." The criticism was so uniform it seemed coordinated.

Apple had created something genuinely new—not a bigger phone, not a smaller laptop, but a different category that required people to understand computing differently. It was intimate like a phone but spacious like a computer. It enabled creation through touch rather than requiring keyboards. It disappeared into activities rather than demanding attention to itself.

But that understanding required explanation. It required showing, not just telling. It required helping people grasp what this new thing was for before they could evaluate whether they wanted it.

Apple didn't leave that vacuum unfilled. They ran ads showing people reading on the couch, kids learning with educational apps, designers sketching with their fingers, musicians composing in coffee shops. They placed iPads in Apple Stores where people could touch them, hold them, experience the weight and responsiveness. They seeded them with developers who built apps that demonstrated new possibilities.

Within three months, Apple had sold three million iPads. Within a year, fifteen million. The critics who'd called it disappointing were now analyzing why it succeeded despite their predictions. The explanation wasn't that critics were wrong—it was that Apple had filled the understanding vacuum before critics' definitions could solidify.

They told their story before critics could tell it for them.

What This Actually Teaches

When you create something genuinely new—not incrementally better but categorically different—you face a specific challenge: people need a framework to understand it before they can evaluate it. Without that framework, they'll default to existing categories that don't fit, or they'll accept critics' frameworks that serve critics' interests rather than accurate understanding.

This isn't about marketing spin or manipulation. It's about the basic challenge of communication: new things require new understanding, and understanding doesn't happen automatically. Someone will provide the framework for understanding your work. The question is whether it's you or your critics.

The dynamic works like this. Innovation creates understanding vacuum. When something doesn't fit existing categories, people need new ways to think about it. "Is this a big phone or a small computer?" isn't the right question about an iPad, but it's the default question when you lack better framework. Vacuum gets filled immediately. Nature abhors a vacuum, and so does public discourse. Within hours of a new product launch, within days of a new strategy announcement, within weeks of a new approach becoming visible, someone will provide explanation. That explanation becomes the default framework for understanding. First coherent explanation wins. Not necessarily the most accurate explanation or the most favorable one—the first one that provides a complete framework for understanding. Once people have a way to think about something, changing that framework requires substantially more effort than establishing it initially. Default frameworks serve their creators. If critics provide the initial framework, that framework will serve their interests— making your innovation seem unnecessary, your approach seem risky, your difference seem like deficit. If you provide the framework, you can help people understand what you actually built and why it matters.

The goal isn't to control the narrative dishonestly. It's to ensure that accurate understanding reaches people before inaccurate understanding solidifies.

How This Shows Up

I've watched this pattern destroy innovative work across every context where I've consulted. A company launches something genuinely different —a new service model, a fundamentally different approach to an old problem, a product that doesn't fit existing categories. They assume the value is self-evident. "When people see what this does, they'll understand why it matters."

Meanwhile, critics rush to define it: "It's just [existing thing] with [superficial change]." "It's missing [features from different category]." "Nobody needs this because [framework from old model]." These definitions spread before the company articulates their own clear explanation.

Six months later, the company is fighting uphill against frameworks they didn't create, explaining why their work isn't what people think it is rather than what it actually is. The battle for understanding was lost before they realized there was a battle.

Here's what I've learned: the window for establishing understanding is smaller than you think. Not weeks or months—often days. The moment something new becomes visible, explanation begins. If you're not providing it, someone else is.

The Diagnostic Questions

Before launching something that requires new understanding, examine whether you're prepared to shape that understanding.

Does your work require people to think differently? If what you've built fits comfortably into existing categories and serves obviously understood needs, explanation may be straightforward. But if it requires reconsidering assumptions, changing mental models, or understanding new value propositions—you need a communication strategy as robust as your product strategy. The iPad required thinking about computing differently —not desktop-or-laptop but intimate-yet-spacious. That wasn't an incremental explanation. Ask: Does understanding our work require unlearning existing frameworks?

What's the most likely misunderstanding? This predicts what critics will say. If you can anticipate the default frameworks people will apply—"it's just a bigger phone," "it's a laptop without a keyboard," "it's a toy for consumption not creation"—you can preempt those frameworks with more accurate ones. Ask people outside your team what they think you're building. Their answers tell you which existing categories they're defaulting to. Those defaults are what critics will amplify if you don't provide better explanation.

Who will fill the vacuum if you don't? Identify who has incentive to define your work inaccurately. Competitors who want to position against you. Analysts who need quick categorization. Critics who resist change. Each will provide frameworks that serve their interests, not accurate understanding. Know who will speak first if you don't, and what they're likely to say.

Can you demonstrate rather than just describe? Apple didn't just describe the iPad—they showed people using it in ways that illuminated what it was for. Demonstration creates understanding more powerfully than description. Ask: Can we show what this enables, not just tell what it is? If you can't demonstrate clearly, your explanation is probably too abstract to compete with critics' concrete frameworks.

Are you prepared for the three-front attack? When you introduce something genuinely new, expect criticism of your supporters and customers who embrace it, your actual innovations and differences, and your team's coherence and conviction. Each front requires different response, but all require you to have established clear understanding of what you actually built and why.

What To Do Monday

First, articulate your own story before launch, not after criticism. Teams build something innovative, launch it, face criticism, then scramble to explain what they actually meant. By then, critics' frameworks have already spread. Write down—before launch—the explanation of what you built and why it matters. Not marketing copy, but clear articulation: What problem does this solve? What does it enable that wasn't possible before? What must people understand differently to grasp its value? If you can't articulate this clearly pre-launch, you're not ready to launch.

Second, identify the most likely misunderstandings and preempt them. Don't wait for critics to define your work inaccurately—predict their definitions and provide better ones first. Before the iPad launch, Apple knew critics would say "it's just a big iPod Touch" or "it's a laptop without a keyboard." They preempted those frameworks by showing what it enabled that neither category did. Make a list of what people will likely misunderstand. Then craft demonstrations or explanations that provide more accurate frameworks before the misunderstandings solidify.

Third, show before telling whenever possible. Abstract explanations compete poorly with concrete criticism. Demonstration beats description. Apple put iPads in people's hands. That demonstration did more to establish understanding than any amount of explanation could have. Find ways to make your innovation tangible, experienceable, demonstrable.

Fourth, accept that coherence will be attacked as groupthink. When your team deeply understands what you're building and can articulate it consistently, critics will call you cultish or claim you're drinking Kool-Aid. Don't let that attack make you muddy your story or introduce artificial disagreement to seem balanced. Coherent understanding isn't groupthink. It's successful communication within a team.

Fifth, prepare for the specific three-front attack pattern. When you launch something innovative with clear story, expect attacks on your supporters—customers called fanboys, advocates called shills, early adopters called naive. Point to actual satisfaction metrics and outcomes. Expect attacks on your innovations—differences framed as deficiencies, new approaches called risky, category creation called niche. Demonstrate what the innovation enables, don't just defend against what critics say it lacks. Expect attacks on your team—coherence called conformity, conviction called arrogance, clarity called rigidity. Show results the coherence produces, don't apologize for understanding your own work clearly.

Sixth, update your story as understanding evolves, but don't abandon it under pressure. As people use your work and discover new value, your explanation should incorporate those discoveries. That's evolution based on learning. But when critics demand you reframe your work to fit their categories—"stop calling it a new category, just admit it's a [existing thing]"—that's not evolution, that's capitulation.

Seventh, document the understanding gap explicitly. When launching something new, create internal documentation of what people need to understand to grasp this, what they'll likely misunderstand initially, what frameworks you're providing to bridge the gap, and what you'll demonstrate to make it tangible. This clarifies your own thinking and provides reference when team members are explaining the work publicly.

The Real Lesson

Here's what the iPad launch teaches: even when you've built something genuinely valuable, critics will fill the understanding vacuum with frameworks that serve their interests, not accurate understanding. Your job is to fill that vacuum first with frameworks that help people understand what you actually built.

The initial iPad criticism—"giant iPhone," "no keyboard," "consumption device"—would have stuck if Apple hadn't provided better frameworks faster. They showed people reading in ways that felt different from phones or computers. They demonstrated creation through touch in ways that didn't require keyboards. They helped people understand intimate computing as a category, not as a compromise between existing categories.

The critics' frameworks didn't disappear—but they didn't define the iPad because better frameworks were already established. People had ways to understand what an iPad was for before they fully absorbed what critics said it wasn't.

This isn't manipulation—it's responsibility. When you create something new, you're obligated to help people understand it. If you don't, you're not just risking your own success—you're letting inaccurate understanding spread and potentially preventing people from benefiting from what you built.

The vacuum will be filled. The only question is by whom and with what accuracy.

Dorothy Sayers was right that nobody believes the truth—but that's often because the truth arrives late, after comfortable lies have already provided explanation. When lies arrive first and offer simple frameworks, truth has to dislodge them, which is exponentially harder than establishing accurate understanding initially.

Your critics will provide simple, concrete, wrong explanations immediately. "It's just [familiar thing] without [expected feature]" is easy to understand even when it's inaccurate. Your job is to provide equally concrete, more accurate explanations first.

Don't assume that building something good is sufficient for people to understand it. Don't wait for critics to define your work and then try to correct their frameworks. Don't let the understanding vacuum persist while you focus on execution and assume communication will take care of itself.

Tell your story before critics tell theirs. Provide frameworks for understanding before default categories fill the gap. Demonstrate what your work enables before critics define it by what it lacks.

The window is smaller than you think. The stakes are higher than they seem. The battle for understanding happens before the battle for market position—and losing the first means fighting uphill in the second.

Fill the vacuum yourself, or critics will fill it for you. Nature abhors a vacuum, and so does the information age. Don't let that vacuum be filled with frameworks that serve critics' interests rather than accurate understanding.

When you create something new, communication isn't an afterthought—it's a central challenge equal to the creation itself. Plan for it. Resource it. Execute it. The innovation only matters if people can understand what it is and why it matters.

Tell your story. Don't wait for critics to tell it for you.

CHAPTER 20
HUMANITY CAN
BE (EN)CODED

"The value of a thing is what that thing will bring." —Larry Niven, Lucifer's Hammer

In the 1990s, Steve Jobs sat in a meeting room at Disney with two NeXT computers. One was black and white, safe and corporate. The other had full color and ran Pixar's impressive graphics software. An hour and a half into his pitch, Steve made a mistake: he got excited about the vision.

He started talking about how millions of ordinary people could create incredible-quality animation in their homes. "Regular folks could express themselves with the artistry of Disney animators!" he said.

Jeffrey Katzenberg, Disney's head of feature films, stood up. He pointed at the black-and-white machine: "This is commerce. Maybe we'll buy a thousand of these." Then he pointed contemptuously at the color machine: "This is art. I own animation and nobody's going to get it." He looked at Steve directly: "If someone tries to take this away, I'll blow his balls off."

Steve's crime? Suggesting that powerful creative tools should be accessible to regular people, not locked behind institutional gates. The idea that you or I could tell animated stories in our homes elicited that kind of fury from someone defending their territory.

This wasn't ancient history—it was the ongoing pattern of Steve's career. "Nobody needs black type on a white screen." "There is absolutely no evidence anyone wants to use this thing called a mouse." "There is no such thing as a home computer market." Every attempt to make technology serve people better rather than demanding people serve technology was met with resistance, mockery, or threats.

When the iPad launched in 2010, Steve received 800 emails in one day. Most were negative. "Fuck you, how can you do that?" one said. The Motley Fool called it "a Margaritaville frozen drink maker—a novelty at first, but then something you just whip out when guests come over." Critics spent hours discussing how its name sounded like a feminine hygiene product. One Apple-friendly site published "16 Reasons the iPad Sucks" before it even went on sale.

Steve sank into depression for weeks after the unveiling. The world had greeted each of his creations with hostility before begrudgingly acknowledging them as the "right direction."

Three years later, the iPad had transformed education, medicine, business, art, and communication. Scientists pinpointed disease origins on hand-held slates. Students across the nation learned through direct interaction with knowledge instead of wading through overly complex technology. The once-maligned device became seamlessly integrated into society.

The critics hadn't changed their minds because they learned something new about the iPad. They changed because the iPad had proven what Steve knew from the beginning: technology that serves people elevates humanity. Technology that demands people serve it becomes a shackle.

What This Actually Teaches

Here's what most people miss about Steve's fights: they weren't about features, specifications, or market positioning. They were about whether technology would serve human needs or whether humans would serve technological complexity.

Every battle he fought—for graphical interfaces, for mice, for typography, for simplicity, for touch interaction, for removing complexity—was fundamentally about the same thing: making tools that let people do what they want to do instead of learning how to operate tools.

This matters because it reveals something crucial about innovation under criticism: you need to know what you're actually fighting for. Not just what you're building, but why it matters beyond your bottom line.

When Katzenberg threatened Steve for suggesting ordinary people should have access to animation tools, Steve wasn't fighting for NeXT computer sales. He was fighting for democratizing creative expression. When critics mocked the iPad for lacking USB ports, Steve wasn't defending a product roadmap. He was defending the principle that computers should fade into the background of activities rather than demanding attention to themselves.

That clarity about purpose does two things. It provides resilience against criticism. When you know you're fighting to elevate people's capabilities rather than just shipping products, criticism of features and specifications lands differently. You can evaluate whether the criticism identifies ways you're falling short of that purpose, or whether it's defending the complexity you're trying to eliminate. It guides decisions when complexity tempts. Every product development faces pressure to add "just one more feature," to preserve "important complexity," to serve "serious users" who need traditional approaches. When you're clear that your purpose is serving people rather than satisfying technical checklists, those decisions become clearer.

The question isn't "what features does the market demand?" It's "what serves people's actual needs versus what serves our industry's assumptions about what they need?"

How This Shows Up

I've watched this pattern play out in every consulting engagement where someone was trying to genuinely simplify or improve how people work. The resistance isn't about whether the improvement works—it's about whose assumptions get challenged.

A company redesigns a workflow to remove steps that frustrate users. Internal experts defend those steps: "Users need to understand this complexity. It's important." Translation: we've built our expertise around managing this complexity, and removing it challenges our value.

A team simplifies a product by removing features that research shows few people use. Long-time users revolt: "You're dumbing it down! Power users need those capabilities!" Translation: we've invested time learning this complexity, and removing it makes our investment feel wasted.

A service eliminates steps that seemed necessary but actually just created busywork. Consultants who advised on those steps attack the simplification: "They're ignoring best practices. This is naive." Translation: we've sold the complexity they're removing, and their success threatens our advice.

The pattern is consistent: whenever you try to make something serve people better by removing unnecessary complexity, those who've built positions around managing that complexity will resist. Not because simplification doesn't work, but because it threatens their relevance.

The Diagnostic Questions

When facing pressure to add complexity, preserve barriers, or restore features that serve technical correctness over human needs, examine these elements.

What is this actually serving? Strip away the justification and ask: does this complexity serve the person using the tool, or does it serve someone else's interest? Does this feature help people do what they want to do, or does it help them manage technical requirements? The mouse didn't serve computer scientists—it served people who wanted to point at things on screen. Each removal of complexity threatened someone's position while serving people better. The test is: whose interest does this serve?

What would people choose if they understood the tradeoff? Sometimes complexity does enable capabilities people value. The question is: if people genuinely understood what they're giving up versus what they're gaining, what would they choose? The iPad's lack of USB ports traded convenient peripheral connections for simpler, more reliable wireless connectivity. Some people genuinely needed those ports—but most people preferred not managing cables once they understood the alternative.

Are you preserving complexity to avoid criticism, or because it serves people? Sometimes you keep features because they genuinely serve important use cases. Sometimes you keep them because removing them will generate loud criticism from a small group, and you don't want the hassle. That's not serving people—that's serving your own desire to avoid criticism.

Can you articulate why this matters beyond your success? Steve could explain why making computers approachable mattered for humanity, not just for Apple's sales. He could articulate why democratizing animation mattered for human expression, not just for NeXT's market position. If you can only explain why something matters for your business, you probably don't have the clarity to resist pressure to compromise.

What are critics actually defending when they attack your simplification? Often critics are defending existing complexity, traditional approaches, or their own expertise in managing what you're trying to eliminate. When Katzenberg threatened Steve over democratizing animation, he was defending Disney's monopoly on animation capabilities. The attacks weren't about what served people—they were about what preserved existing power structures.

What To Do Monday

First, articulate your purpose beyond product success. Before you face criticism, be clear about what you're fighting for that matters beyond your own success. Steve could say "a computer for people who want to use a computer, instead of learning how to use a computer." That clarity let him evaluate every criticism against that purpose. Write down—not for publication, for clarity—what you're fighting for that matters beyond your business.

Second, distinguish between serving people and satisfying checklists. Every feature request, every criticism, every "serious users need this" demand presents the same choice: does this serve what people are actually trying to do, or does it satisfy some abstract requirement? I've worked with teams that knew their simplified approach served users better but added complexity anyway because industry analysts had checklists. That's not innovation—that's capitulation to conventional wisdom.

Third, expect fury from those whose position depends on complexity. When you remove barriers or simplify systems, those who've built expertise around managing complexity will resist. Not necessarily because you're wrong, but because your success threatens their relevance. Katzenberg's threat revealed this perfectly: "I own animation and nobody's going to get it." Don't be surprised when simplification generates outsized anger. That anger usually correlates with how much the simplification threatens existing power structures.

Fourth, track whether criticism comes from people using your work or people defending assumptions. When actual users say "this doesn't serve my needs," listen carefully. When experts say "this violates best practices," ask whether those practices serve users or serve conventional wisdom. The iPad's harshest critics were tech journalists and industry analysts—people defending assumptions about what computers needed to be. Actual users

—students, doctors, artists, seniors—embraced it quickly because it served their needs better than complex alternatives.

Fifth, maintain conviction while staying open to genuine limitations. Some criticism identifies real ways you're not serving people well. Some criticism defends complexity that doesn't serve people but serves someone's interests. The skill is distinguishing between "you've simplified too much and people can't accomplish what they need" versus "you've simplified in ways that challenge our assumptions and we don't like it." The first requires adjustment. The second requires conviction.

Sixth, remember that serving people often means disappointing experts. Tools that serve people well often don't satisfy people who've invested years mastering complex alternatives. Expert photographers resisted iPhone cameras because they "lacked real controls." Expert musicians resisted GarageBand because it "wasn't serious software." Expert designers resisted Canva because it "democratized design in ways that lowered standards." In each case, experts were right that the simplified tool didn't serve expert needs as well as complex alternatives. But they were wrong that this meant the simplified tool didn't serve people.

The Real Lesson

Here's what the Disney meeting and the iPad launch reveal: when you're trying to make technology serve people rather than demanding people serve technology, expect fury from those whose positions depend on maintaining barriers.

Katzenberg didn't threaten Steve because democratizing animation would fail. He threatened Steve because it would succeed—and that success would eliminate Disney's monopoly on animation capability. The fury revealed the threat.

The iPad critics didn't mock it because it didn't serve people well. They mocked it because it served people well in ways that challenged assumptions about what computers needed to be. The mockery revealed the challenge.

Steve spent his entire career fighting versions of the same battle: should technology serve human needs, or should humans adapt to technological complexity? Every time he chose the first option, he faced resistance from those benefiting from the second.

The mouse, graphical interfaces, typography, desktop publishing, intuitive software, touch interaction, removal of file systems—each advance made technology more approachable and faced fierce resistance from those whose expertise was in managing complexity.

The pattern is universal: whenever you try to remove unnecessary complexity that people have built positions around, expect resistance framed as concern for quality, standards, or "serious work." That resistance rarely admits it's defending positions—it frames itself as defending excellence.

Your job is to know the difference between resistance that identifies real limitations versus resistance that defends unnecessary complexity. The test is: does this serve what people are actually trying to do, or does it serve someone's interest in maintaining barriers?

Steve's clarity came from asking: "What elevates humanity?" Not "what sells computers" or "what satisfies analysts" or "what quiets critics." What actually helps people do what they want to do instead of learning how to operate tools?

That question guided every decision, endured every criticism, survived every depression after hostile receptions. Because when you're clear about fighting for people's capabilities rather than just shipping products, criticism of features lands differently. You can evaluate whether it identifies ways to serve people better, or whether it defends complexity that serves someone else's interests.

The iPad initially faced mockery: no USB ports, no file system, "just" a big iPod Touch, a feminine hygiene product, a frozen drink maker. Three years later, it had transformed how people learn, create, heal, and communicate. The critics hadn't discovered something new—people had proven what the iPad was for by using it to do things that mattered to them.

Your critics will defend complexity, preserve barriers, and frame simplification as dumbing down. They'll call your vision naive, your approach unserious, your focus on people a neglect of "real users" who need sophisticated tools.

That criticism tells you you're threatening assumptions that benefit someone other than the people you're trying to serve. Don't let it make you add back complexity that serves critics rather than people.

Know what you're fighting for beyond your own success. Serve people's actual needs rather than abstract requirements. Expect fury from those whose positions depend on maintaining barriers. Distinguish between serving people and satisfying experts.

And remember: "Ultimately it comes down to taste. It comes down to trying to expose yourself to the best things that humans have created and then trying to bring those things into what you create."

Make the world better with what you create. That purpose will sustain you through the criticism that comes from those who benefit from the world staying complicated.

Customers are human beings, and it's a shame to waste the opportunity to contribute something that elevates more than just the bottom line.

CHAPTER 21
NOW GO FIX
WHAT'S BROKEN.

"Our greatest glory is not in never falling, but in rising every time we fall."
—Confucius

Steve Jobs was fired from Apple in 1985. Not eased out, not transitioned—fired from the company he'd founded, publicly humiliated, his life's work taken from him by people who thought they knew better.

He didn't handle it well. He considered leaving Silicon Valley entirely. He bought a mansion and spent months barely leaving it. Friends worried. The press wrote obituaries for his career while he was still alive.

Then he got up and went back to work.

He founded NeXT. He bought Pixar. He spent eleven years building things that didn't immediately succeed while watching Apple decline without him. Every product announcement was met with the same question: "When will Steve Jobs produce something that matters again?"

In 1997, Apple was ninety days from bankruptcy when they brought him back. The company that had fired him needed him to save them. Instead of gloating or extracting revenge, he canceled most products, negotiated investment from Microsoft, and spent the next fourteen years rebuilding Apple into the most valuable company in the world.

The iMac, iPod, iPhone, iPad—every product that defined modern computing came from a man who'd been fired, humiliated, and written off.

The greatest glory wasn't that Steve never fell. It's that he rose every time he did.

You're not building billion-dollar technology companies. You're not launching products to millions of people. You're not fighting Jeffrey Katzenberg or responding to 800 angry emails in a day. So what's the point?

The patterns are the same whether you're running Apple or running a small team, whether you're launching the iPhone or launching a new process. The challenges Steve faced are universal to anyone trying to build something better.

You'll face critics who attack your strengths and frame them as weaknesses. You'll meet defenders of complexity who resist simplification because it threatens their positions. You'll be told to abandon what makes you distinctive to be taken seriously by people who don't take you seriously anyway

The question isn't whether you'll face these challenges. If you're doing anything worth doing, you will. The question is whether you'll recognize the patterns and know how to respond.

The Patterns That Actually Work

Systems over heroes. The trap in studying Steve Jobs is thinking his success came from being Steve Jobs. It came from building systems that produced coherent results. The "reality distortion field" was arrangement, not magic. When you're trying to fix something broken, don't look for the hero. Fix the machine.

Interrogate "can't" until it confesses. Every organization has "impossibilities"—can't launch without all these features, can't simplify without losing serious users, can't maintain those standards. Most are inherited assumptions, not discovered truths. When someone says something can't be done, that's the beginning of investigation: Why can't we? What would have to be true? Who says we can't?

Critics reveal more than they criticize. Attacks aren't noise to ignore—they're intelligence to decode. When competitors attack your simplicity, they're revealing they can't match it. When they criticize your focus, they're revealing their own diffusion. Learn to translate criticism from surface rhetoric to strategic intelligence.

Differentiation gets attacked as disqualification. The most sophisticated attack targets your strengths and frames them as reasons you can't be taken seriously. "Too simple" means your simplicity threatens their complexity justification. "Too focused" means your concentration threatens their diffusion. When criticism targets your differentiation rather than your flaws, that's confirmation you're threatening established positions.

Fill the vacuum or critics will. When you create something new, someone will explain it. The question is whether it's you providing accurate frameworks or critics providing convenient ones. Don't assume value is self-evident. Tell your story first, clearly and demonstrably.

Know what you're fighting for beyond success. When Katzenberg threatened Steve over democratizing animation, Steve wasn't defending NeXT sales—he was defending the principle that powerful tools should serve people, not preserve institutional monopolies. You need clarity about why your work matters beyond your bottom line. That's what lets you distinguish criticism that identifies real problems from criticism that defends threatened positions.

The Method Underneath Everything

Three principles apply universally:

See clearly. Most failure comes from seeing what you want to see instead of what's actually there. Steve's "taste" was clarity about what served people versus what served convention. Your first job: see clearly what's actually broken, what's actually working, what's actually possible. Not optimistically or pessimistically. Accurately.

Stay coherent. Most organizations fail not from lacking good ideas but from lacking coherence between ideas, execution, and outcomes. Steve's breakthrough was aligning everything around a coherent vision. Your second job: maintain coherence. Does everything you're doing serve what you're actually trying to accomplish?

Serve people. Most innovation fails not because it doesn't work technically but because it doesn't serve human needs better than existing alternatives. Your third job: stay focused on serving people. Does this actually help people do what they're trying to do, or does it satisfy some abstract requirement?

That's the method: see clearly, stay coherent, serve people.

What Falling and Rising Look Like

Steve's firing and return is the dramatic version. But most falling in organizational life is quieter and more frequent.

You'll propose something that gets rejected. You'll implement something that doesn't work. You'll advocate for a change that generates more resistance than results. You'll be right about something but unable to prove it before people move on.

These aren't career-ending failures—they're the normal texture of trying to improve things. The question isn't whether you'll fall. It's whether you'll treat each fall as information about what to try next or as evidence you should stop trying.

Improvers treat failure as data, obstacles as information, resistance as signals to decode. They don't take rejection personally or treat setbacks as verdicts.

Steve's eleven years between Apple departures were learning. NeXT's operating system became the foundation for OSX. Pixar's struggle to integrate technology and storytelling informed everything Apple did later. The "failures" were preparations.

Your failures aren't verdicts—they're education.

You're finishing this book with some challenge in front of you. Something broken you want to fix. Something new you want to build. Something better you want to create.

The patterns in this book give you frameworks to recognize what you're facing and respond strategically. But frameworks only matter if you use them.

Pick one thing that's broken that you can affect. Apply the diagnostic questions. See clearly what's actually broken versus what people say is broken.

Identify one "can't" that's actually an inherited assumption. Ask why it can't be done until the answer is either "actually impossible" or "we've just never tried."

Name one criticism that's actually attacking your strength. Stop trying to fix it and start asking who benefits if you abandon it.

Articulate what you're fighting for that matters beyond your success. Write it down. Keep it visible. Use it to evaluate whether criticism identifies real problems or defends threatened positions.

Then do the work. Fix the system. Build the alignment. Serve people. Expect criticism. Decode it. Learn from failures. Get up. Try again.

The glory isn't in never falling. It's in rising every time you fall, with clarity about what matters, conviction about how to pursue it, and coherence in how to organize work around it.

Steve's story isn't exceptional because he never failed. It's exceptional because he kept getting up, kept seeing clearly, kept building coherently, and kept serving people despite every reason to quit or compromise.

You can do the same in your context, at your scale, with your constraints. The patterns work.

Now go fix what's broken.

Make things in your world better. Because you absolutely can.

AFTERWORD

Most executives know what great looks like. Few have the tools to make it happen consistently.

Steve Jobs didn't succeed through genius or tantrums. He succeeded through learnable methods and frameworks. This isn't hagiography. It's a practical toolkit extracted from how Apple actually worked, including the decisions Jobs made, the tradeoffs he understood, and the patterns he recognized that competitors missed.

You'll learn:

- Why "impossible" usually means you're asking the wrong questions—and the five types that reveal what's actually blocking you
- How to distinguish legitimate criticism from bozo noise
- Why Apple optimized for product excellence over avoiding criticism—and how that inverted every negotiation
- When to solve symptoms versus when to change the system
- How to build conviction that survives opposition without becoming stubbornness

The gap between competent and exceptional isn't effort. It's knowing which problems to solve and which to ignore.

Your competitors are reading about innovation theater. You'll be learning why the iPhone paused background apps, how Apple turned Maps failure into privacy advantage, and why saying no created more value than saying yes.

These aren't Steve's secrets. They're your new tools. Now go make things better.